THE ANONYMITY OF A COMMENTATOR

SUNY series in Islam

Seyyed Hossein Nasr, editor

THE ANONYMITY OF A COMMENTATOR

ZAKARIYYĀ AL-ANṢĀRĪ AND THE RHETORIC OF MUSLIM COMMENTARIES

MATTHEW B. INGALLS

SUNY PRESS

Cover image: Frederick Goodall, *Sultan Hassan's School, Cairo*, 1861, oil on canvas. Royal Pavilion & Museums, Brighton & Hove.

Published by State University of New York Press, Albany

Printed in the United States of America

For information, contact State University of New York Press, Albany, NY
www.sunypress.edu

Library of Congress Cataloging-in-Publication Data

Name: Ingalls, Matthew B., 1978– author.
Title: The anonymity of a commentator : Zakariyyā al-Anṣārī and the rhetoric of Muslim commentaries from the Later Islamic / Matthew B. Ingalls.
Description: Albany : State University of New York Press, 2021. | Series: SUNY series in Islam | Includes bibliographical references and index.
Identifiers: LCCN 2020053449 | ISBN 9781438485195 (hardcover : alk. paper) | ISBN 9781438485188 (pbk. : alk. paper) | ISBN 9781438485201 (ebook)
Subjects: LCSH: Anṣārī, Zakarīyā ibn Muḥammad, approximately 1423–approximately 1520. | Sufis—Biography. | Sufism—Doctrines. | Qur'an—Commentaries—History and criticism. | Hadith—Commentaries—History and criticism.
Classification: LCC BP80.A594 I54 2021 | DDC 297.1/2273122—dc23
LC record available at https://lccn.loc.gov/2020053449

10 9 8 7 6 5 4 3 2 1

Thus I rediscovered what writers have always known (and have told us again and again): books always speak of other books, and every story tells a story that has already been told.

—Umberto Eco, *The Name of the Rose*

For my two boys

Contents

List of Figures and Tables		xi
Transliteration Table		xiii
Acknowledgments		xv
Introduction		1
Chapter One	Muslim Commentarial Practices	7
Chapter Two	The Life of Zakariyyā al-Anṣārī	33
Chapter Three	The *Iḥkām* and the Rhetoric of the Sufi Commentary	125
Chapter Four	Fanning the Fire of Islamic Legal Change with the *Mukhtaṣar-Sharḥ* Bellows	155
Chapter Five	The Legacy of al-Anṣārī	197
Conclusion	Commentary, Canonization, and Creativity: A New Case for the "Era of Commentaries and Supercommentaries"	229
Bibliography		243
Index		259

Figures and Tables

Figures

3.1 A sample folio from a manuscript of al-Anṣārī's interwoven commentary *Asnā l-maṭālib: sharḥ Rawḍ al-ṭālib*. Umm al-Qurā University, Mecca, fols. 1v-2r. 149

4.1 A textual genealogy for the *Manhaj al-ṭullāb* and *Fatḥ al-wahhāb*. 160

4.2 A textual genealogy for the *Taḥrīr Tanqīḥ al-Lubāb*, *Tuḥfat al-ṭullāb*, and *Fatḥ al-wahhāb*. 163

4.3 A textual genealogy for the *Asnā l-maṭālib*. 165

4.4 A textual genealogy for *al-Ghurar al-bahiyya*, *Khulāṣat al-fawāʾid*, and *Ḥāshiya*. 167

4.5 A visual representation of the processes of *sharḥ* and *ikhtiṣār*. 192

5.1 The four authorities of the later Shāfiʿī *madhhab*. 203

Tables

2.1 A timeline of Zakariyyā al-Anṣārī's life. 97

2.2 A bibliography of texts attributed to Zakariyyā al-Anṣārī. 100

2.3 A list of teachers and texts that defined Zakariyyā al-Anṣārī's education. 108

Transliteration Table

The following conventions have been adopted for the Arabic transliterations in the study below:

ء	ʾ	ض	ḍ
ا	ā	ط	ṭ
ب	b	ظ	ẓ
ت	t	ع	ʿ
ث	th	غ	gh
ج	j	ف	f
ح	ḥ	ق	q
خ	kh	ك	k
د	d	ل	l
ذ	dh	م	m
ر	r	ن	n
ز	z	ه	h
س	s	و	w, ū
ش	sh	ي	y, ī
ص	ṣ		

Additionally, the Arabic short vowels *ḍamma* [ُ], *fatḥa* [َ], and *kasra* [ِ] have been rendered with "u," "a," and "i," respectively, while the *shadda* [ّ] is represented with a doubled consonant and the *tanwīn* [ٌ ً ٍ] with superscript. Finally, the Arabic definite article is rendered as "al-" (or "l-" if preceded by a long vowel) regardless of whether the following Arabic consonant is *shamsī* or *qamarī*.

Acknowledgments

I wish to express my sincerest gratitude to the following individuals for all of their assistance and encouragement in bringing the present monograph to print: Taha Abdul-Basser, Hussein Abdulsater, Asad Ahmed, Rumee Ahmed, Talal Al-Azem, the late Ather Ali, Omer Bajwa, Michele and Karl Becker, Rocío Amores Bello, Joel Blecher, Simon Bower, Gerhard Böwering, Jonathan Brown, Stephen Burge, Yousef Casewit, Ayesha Chaudhry, Francesco Chiabotti, Stephan Conermann, Bruce Craig, Jackie Crowley, John Curry, Garrett Davidson, Stephen Davis, Khaled El-Rouayheb, Ahmed El Shamsy, Dan Eisenberg, Musa Furber, Tarek Ghanem, Mohammad Gharaibeh, Alan Godlas, Frank Griffel, Josie Hendrickson, Sabrina Joseph, Annabel Keeler, Yasmine Khattab, Cornelis van Lit, James Lockhart, Joseph Lombard, Clark Lombardi, Moez Masoud, Richard McGregor, Matt Melvin-Kushki, Ebrahim Moosa, Elias Muhanna, Seyyed Hossein Nasr, Martin Nguyen, Erik Ohlander, Bilal Orfali, Michael Perez, Judith Pfeiffer, David Powers, Yasir Qadhi, Ella Richards, Omar Sabbagh, Walid Saleh, Kristin Sands, Elham Seyedsayamdost, Ahmad al-Snubar, and Devin Stewart. I also thank the staff at the Annemarie Schimmel Kolleg, the Beinecke Library, the Chester Beatty Library, and the Wabbash Center.

A special word of thanks is due to James Peltz and Jenn Bennett-Genthner at SUNY Press, to my two anonymous reviewers for their invaluable and good-natured feedback on an earlier draft of my manuscript, and to Mohammed Rustom for his persistent encouragement and advice over the past few years.

Several fellowships made the research for this book possible. These include an Annemarie Schimmel Kolleg Junior Fellowship, the H. P. Kraus

Fellowship in Early Books and Manuscripts at the Beinecke Library, a Martin Nelson Summer Research Award, and a Wabash Center Summer Fellowship. I thank the fellowship selection committees for their generous support.

Finally, I wish to thank my family for all of their love and patience.

An earlier version of the first subsection of chapter 3 was originally published in the *Journal of Sufi Studies* in 2013, while the second and third subsections of the chapter were originally published in the journal *Oriens* in the same year.

Introduction

Twentieth-century scholars of Islamic history took it for granted that Muslim scholarship declined after the thirteenth century. Over the past two decades, historians have broken decisively from this decline narrative, and many are excited to rediscover the last five hundred years of Muslim intellectual production, which as an object of historical inquiry still remains largely unexamined. Although the decline narrative is certainly not dead in the field of Islamic studies,[1] it is moribund, at least in its crassest forms. Scholars nonetheless disagree as to whether the legacy of the decline narrative still defines the field in subtler ways,[2] though it would be hard to deny that Islamic studies as a whole has grown to acknowledge the creative merits of Muslim scholarship from more recent centuries.

One stumbling block in appreciating later Muslim scholarship is the outward form that this scholarship often assumes. Here I am referring specifically to the commentarial form that came to dominate the Islamic disciplines beginning in the later Islamic middle period (1250–1500 CE), although similar stumbling blocks have been encountered in the study of premodern Arabic literature in the context of encyclopedias and other compilatory texts.[3]

1. See, for example, the entries "Mukhtaṣar" and "Mawsūʿa" in Brill's *Encyclopaedia of Islam*.

2. Konrad Hirschler, *The Written Word in the Medieval Arabic Lands: A Social and Cultural History of Reading Practices* (Edinburgh: Edinburgh University Press, 2012), 3, 124–25; Thomas Bauer, "Mamluk Literature: Misunderstandings and New Approaches," *Mamluk Studies Review* 9, no. 2 (2005): 105–32.

3. For a pioneering study of an early Mamlūk encyclopedia that confronts many of these stumbling blocks, see Elias Muhanna, *The World in a Book: Al-Nuwayri and the Islamic Encyclopedic Tradition* (Princeton, NJ: Princeton University Press, 2017).

Whereas twentieth-century scholars of Islam viewed commentary texts as a sign of intellectual stagnation in and of themselves, contemporary scholars recognize that these texts are often the repertories of profound thought. Nevertheless, they approach them from scratch, having inherited little insight from the previous generations of researchers who dismissed these texts as derivative.

Contemporary scholars of Islam thus possess the right attitude toward the Muslim commentarial tradition, but they also recognize the Herculean task of analyzing this tradition on its own terms. Even the act of gathering works of commentary is rarely simple. One scholar, by way of example, estimates that only 5 percent of the hundreds of commentaries mentioned in his handlist of philosophical commentaries are currently available to scholars in print.[4] Although he wrote of this problem in 2004 and limited his estimate to commentaries written in philosophy after the twelfth century, the current study of commentaries from across the disciplines of Islamic studies hardly fares much better.

The way forward is for contemporary scholars of Islam to continue their work on the fundamentals of commentary studies—that is, to survey the textual record and analyze it with reference to its own internal values and structures. This work must begin at the level of individual authors, intellectual networks, or textual genealogies before its findings can be extended to assess larger structures like entire intellectual disciplines, which may be the task of the next generation of scholars. As for assessing even larger civilizational trajectories, the horizon remains farther away still, if not forever out of grasp, and it is for this reason that claims of intellectual decline strike many contemporary scholars as especially absurd. Nevertheless, if scholarship from the last century has taught us anything, it is that the burden of proof skews suspiciously in favor of those arguing for Muslim civilizational decline, while even the most basic analysis of the commentarial tradition reveals the hollowness and cynicism inherent in this decline narrative.

In the spirit of continuing the good fight against the decline narrative, the book that follows participates in the ongoing project of Islamic

4. Robert Wisnovsky, "The Nature and Scope of Arabic Philosophical Commentary in Post-Classical (ca. 1100–1900 AD) Islamic Intellectual History: Some Preliminary Observations," in *Philosophy, Science and Exegesis in Greek, Arabic, and Latin Commentaries*, vol. 2, ed. Peter Adamson et al. (London: Institute of Classical Studies, University of London Press, 2004), 160.

commentary studies through an examination of the life, thought, and legacy of the Egyptian scholar Zakariyyā al-Anṣārī (d. 926/1520). It begins at the level of theory and larger historical practices, moves to the biography of al-Anṣārī and the structures of his thought and texts, and concludes with a discussion of the lessons that can be gleaned from this particular case study and extended elsewhere. By the end of the book, I hope that readers will not only know who Zakariyyā al-Anṣārī is but also why they should care about him.

Chapter 1 situates the remainder of the book by providing the reader with a snapshot of Muslim commentarial practices during the Islamic middle period while emphasizing those phenomena that aid in contextualizing al-Anṣārī's commentaries specifically. After examining some pertinent socio-literary trends that shaped the culture of writing during the Islamic middle period, the chapter describes the basic forms of Islamic commentaries, the conventions used by Muslim commentators, and the technical terms needed to appreciate the nature of commentary writing during this period. It then turns its attention to the processes that brought commentary texts into existence while focusing on their connections to Muslim pedagogy. The chapter concludes with a brief analysis of the rhetoric of anonymity that defines commentary writing within most canonical and classical traditions throughout history.

Chapter 2 provides an extensive biography for al-Anṣārī that frames his life through four "acts" that build on all of the primary source data that I could gather. The transitions between these acts correspond with major shifts in al-Anṣārī's life and career, and thus the structure of the chapter exposes the character arc within al-Anṣārī's biography while remaining true to the historical record. In writing this chapter, my goal has been to render al-Anṣārī's life relatable to the broadest readership through a narrative structure that is familiar to all.[5] Because *The Anonymity of a Commentator* may be the only medium in which to tell al-Anṣārī's story in full, this particular chapter is lengthier than the book's other chapters, though when making my decisions about what data to include, exclude, or relegate to the footnotes, my goal has been to maintain a quick narrative pace. At the end of the chapter, I have also included, in the form of three addenda, a timeline of

5. For a further justification of this approach, see Hayden White, *Tropics of Discourse: Essays in Cultural Criticism* (Baltimore, MD: Johns Hopkins Press, 1978), 91.

al-Anṣārī's life, a bibliography of works attributed to him, and a table of the *ijāzas* (licenses) that he received from his many teachers.

Chapters 3 and 4 examine al-Anṣārī's commentaries in the disciplines of Sufism and Islamic law, respectively, as case studies to illustrate the formal mechanics and rhetorical processes that defined Muslim commentary writing. In chapter 3, I focus my analysis on the *Iḥkām al-dalāla*, al-Anṣārī's running commentary on ʿAbd al-Karīm al-Qushayrī's celebrated Sufi handbook the *Risāla* (*Epistle*). Because al-Anṣārī and al-Qushayrī's lives were separated by almost five hundred years and three thousand kilometers, a comparison of the *Iḥkām* and the base text that it is built upon illuminates the various textual and institutional developments that took place in the history of the Sufi commentary. The chapter begins with a rhetorical analysis of the *Iḥkām* to show how al-Anṣārī redirects the substance and tone of al-Qushayrī's *Risāla*. It then shifts to an examination of those instances in the *Iḥkām* in which al-Anṣārī employs a legal hermeneutic and legal language to relieve tensions between his worldview and the worldviews of the Sufis who appear in al-Qushayrī's base text. Finally, the chapter considers commentaries like the *Iḥkām* in their capacity as written artifacts by examining a commentarial form known as the interwoven commentary (*sharḥ mamzūj*), which would endow commentators like al-Anṣārī with new and subtle forms of control over the received tradition.

Chapter 4 next turns its attention to al-Anṣārī's commentaries and abridgments in Islamic law to examine the formal and rhetorical conventions that defined Islamic legal writing during the later Islamic middle period. After a background discussion of al-Anṣārī's stylistics in Islamic substantive law (*furūʿ al-fiqh*) and the texts that he left us in this discipline, the chapter examines three generations of texts from a single textual genealogy to show how the antipodal processes of commentary (*sharḥ*) and abridgment (*ikhtiṣār*) affected legal change within the tradition. The chapter next extends these findings to all eight generations of a textual genealogy through the lens of a single passage from one of al-Anṣārī's commentaries. Finally, with the help of a diagram, a concluding section summarizes the lessons that can be gleaned about the operations of commentary and abridgment within Islamic legal writing in light of the previous two subsections of the chapter.

Chapter 5 shifts its focus to the intellectual tradition that came immediately after al-Anṣārī's life to assess the author's reception and posthumous influence on this tradition. Many Sunni Muslims have viewed al-Anṣārī as the "renewer" (*mujaddid*) of the ninth Islamic century, and this chapter aims to uncover why they saw him as such. To answer this question, the chapter first examines al-Anṣārī's most tangible legacy, namely his later descendants and his most distinguished students within the Shāfiʿī *madhhab* who would secure for their teacher a prominence in that legal school that endures today. The remainder of the chapter then examines al-Anṣārī's more abstract influence on Sunni thought, which took place between the fifteenth and sixteenth centuries. It situates al-Anṣārī's thought within larger trends of formalization in scholarly treatments of Sufism, whereby Sufism would gradually be reconceived as an area of scholarly study akin to other subfields of Islamic scholarship. These formalization trends would parallel other trends of cross-fertilization between Sufism and Islamic law that characterized the period. As this chapter illustrates, al-Anṣārī's influence is found at the epicenter of both sets of trends, and his thought functions as an anchoring point between them.

A concluding chapter examines the nature of canonization and creativity in Muslim commentary texts in light of the preceding chapters. As the starting point for my discussion here, I take a particular passage from one of al-Anṣārī's commentaries in Islamic substantive law that embodies many of the thematic conclusions that are reached in chapters 3, 4, and 5. Through the lens of this passage, I identify some of the idiosyncrasies at play when we attempt to apply the term "canonization"—both canonization *of* commentary and canonization *through* commentary—within the context of Islamic commentary texts. In the chapter's second half, I reference this passage and other examples from the preceding chapters to reflect on the nature of creativity within Islamic commentary texts and the challenges that are posed in assessing it. Though the commentarial form would come to epitomize the antithesis of creativity in the minds of many modern critics, and though al-Anṣārī might have been the first to claim that commentators were merely explaining what the author of a base text had intended all along, it is only when we disregard these earlier assessments and move past the rhetoric of commentarial anonymity that we are able to glimpse the creative potential of commentaries and recognize them as anything but derivative.

Chapter One

Muslim Commentarial Practices

The present chapter situates the remainder of the book by providing a general description of Islamic commentary texts and Muslim commentarial practices during the Islamic middle period. In writing it, I have relied on both the primary- and secondary-source literature, though when compared with the remaining chapters of the book, I have given greater weight here to the secondary literature. In order to filter the data found in this secondary literature, I have chosen to emphasize those phenomena that are most conducive to an analysis of Zakariyyā al-Anṣārī's commentaries specifically, and to understanding the processes that brought them into existence.

The chapter begins with a basic description of important socioliterary trends that defined the Islamic middle period and then turns to examining why Muslim scholars saw the need for commentary texts in the first place. It next describes the form of Islamic commentary texts as we might encounter them in manuscript form today, while using this occasion to introduce readers to some technical terms that are essential to conceptualizing the culture of commentary writing within the context of premodern Islamic scholarship. The chapter then turns to the connections between pedagogy and the writing of commentary texts to illustrate the processes through which Muslim study circles brought new commentaries into existence. Here I paint a picture of these processes for the benefit of those readers who may have little background in Islamic intellectual history. My goal in sketching it has been to provide a digestible description that avoids oversimplification and does justice to the larger tradition without limiting itself to any one intellectual discipline. Finally, the chapter concludes with a brief note on the rhetoric of anonymity that characterizes commentary writing within most canonical and classical traditions throughout history and its connections to the authority projected by, and perceived in, commentary writers.

Textual Trends during the Islamic Middle Period

It could be argued that the need for commentary was written into the DNA of the Islamic tradition. For as long as the Qur'ān and Sunna have existed in the minds of Muslims, they have been conceptually separated more at the level of their textual form than as discrete scriptural essences, and the job of bridging the textual gap between them would fall to Muslim exegetes who reunited them within their works of *tafsīr* (Qur'ānic exegesis).[1] Historians who have studied the development of commentaries within the Islamic tradition often begin their narratives by referencing these early works of *tafsīr* and other rudimentary glosses on pre-Islamic poetry before shifting to nonexegetical commentaries that had emerged by the early fourth/tenth century within the disciplines of Arabic grammar and Islamic law. Commentary works would appear soon thereafter in other intellectual disciplines, thus setting the stage for the Islamic commentary to become the defining medium of scholarly production during the later Islamic middle period (roughly 1258 to 1500 CE), particularly in Syria and Egypt under the Mamlūk sultans.[2]

A few trends in the intellectual culture of the Islamic middle period help to situate this explosion in commentary writing and are worth mentioning here in brief. The first is what Konrad Hirschler has called "textualization" whereby the written word would come to resemble a fetish in many corners of Muslim society and would finally outstrip the oral tradition that had previously held a position of importance that was parallel with, if not superior to, it. During the Islamic middle period, written texts were integrated into public rituals and used in symbolic readings like never before, while their perceived autonomy as storehouses of knowledge increased within

1. Walid A. Saleh, *The Formation of the Classical Tafsīr Tradition: The Qur'ān Commentary of al-Thaʿlabī (d. 427/1035)* (Leiden: Brill, 2004), 193–94.

2. ʿAbdallāh Muḥammad al-Ḥabashī, *Jāmiʿ al-shurūḥ wa-l-ḥawāshī*, 3 vols. (Abu Dhabi: al-Majmaʿ al-Thaqāfī, 2004), 1:7–8.

the public imagination.[3] Another intellectual trend that characterized the period was the popularization of learning activities; it coincided with the proliferation of waqf properties (Islamic endowments)—mosques, madrasas, *khānaqāhs* (Sufi hospices), etc.—in which these activities took place. Formal and informal learning activities now extended to much broader demographics of Muslim society,[4] while study within waqf institutions, particularly madrasas, became more accessible to adolescents from the margins of society. Zakariyyā al-Anṣārī's biography perhaps illustrates this latter phenomenon like no other. Scholarly lessons before large audiences of students and lay readers was another result of this popularization of learning that defined the period, as can be glimpsed, for instance, in the blending of audition certifications (*ijāzat al-samāʿ* and *ijāzat al-qirāʾa*) whereby one's license to transmit a text became equally valid whether a person read the text before a teacher or was merely present in the audience of students as the text was read.[5] Nevertheless, by the close of the Islamic middle period in the tenth/sixteenth century, collation notes would largely displace audition certificates within the manuscript record, as teachers shifted away again from large audiences in favor of smaller groups of students whose notes were collated and scrutinized in a more intimate manner.[6]

Through processes that are examined in more detail below, the proliferation of waqf institutions of learning during the Islamic middle period also allowed manuscripts to be produced (and stored) with more efficiency than before. This streamlining of manuscript production, along with the growing perception of written texts as autonomous storehouses of knowledge, meant that scholars and other intellectuals felt a stronger need for texts that were searchable and able to be mined for specific information. Because of this need, the Islamic middle period witnessed an explosion in new conventions in the layout and design of manuscripts to increase the ease and speed of reading them, as can be glimpsed, for example, in the

3. Hirschler, *Written Word*, 5, 14–15, 20–22, 27, and passim.

4. Hirschler, *Written Word*, 26, 68; Jonathan P. Berkey, *The Transmission of Knowledge in Medieval Cairo: A Social History of Islamic Education* (Princeton, NJ: Princeton University Press, 1992); George Makdisi, *The Rise of Colleges: Institutions of Learning in Islam and the West* (Edinburgh: Edinburgh University Press, 1981), 31–32.

5. Hirschler, *Written Word*, 61.

6. Adam Gacek, *Arabic Manuscripts: A Vademecum for Readers* (Leiden: Brill, 2009), 55.

appearance of overlining, rubrication, indexes, and clearer techniques to mark the end of quoted material.[7] Encyclopedic and anthological works benefitted especially from these new scribal conventions; they were now accessible to readers who wished to search them quickly and on their own time, and would thus become immensely popular during the Mamlūk period.[8] Moreover, writers of commentary works used many of these same scribal conventions, which helped in making commentaries the default medium of Islamic scholarship in Mamlūk lands.

Before examining the *process* of commentary writing by Muslim scholars, it is necessary to understand the reasons why Muslims saw the need for commentary texts in the first place. If commentary is viewed at the most generic level as the interpretation of a canonical tradition, then we can begin with the theories of Jonathan Smith, who lists five situations that are more likely than others to prompt a community to apply their interpretive energies to a canon: for purposes of divination, law, legitimation, classification, and speculation.[9] Of these five situations, Muslim commentary writers from the later Islamic middle period were especially motivated by their need for legal evolution (law), for establishing their intellectual credentials (legitimation), and for refining disciplines that had grown exceedingly complex by this time (classification). Furthermore, to Smith's original list we can add the motive of preservation, as can be glimpsed whenever Muslim authors used their commentaries as repositories for storing information that might otherwise

---

7. Elias Muhanna, "Encyclopaedism in the Mamluk Period: The Composition of Shihāb al-Dīn al-Nuwayrī's (d. 1333) *Nihāyat al-arab fī funūn al-adab*" (PhD diss., Harvard University, 2012), 122–24; Hirschler, *Written Word*, 17–19. According to Franz Rosenthal, "The more scholarly a work was, the greater care was exercised by scholars in the indication and quotation of their sources." Franz Rosenthal, *The Technique and Approach of Muslim Scholarship* (Rome: Pontificium Institutum Biblicum, 1947), 41. Elsewhere in his book, Rosenthal traces the advancing of conventions to mark the end of quoted material to no earlier than the thirteenth century. Rosenthal, *Technique and Approach of Muslim Scholarship*, 39.

8. Muhanna, "Encyclopaedism in the Mamluk Period"; Thomas Bauer, "Literarische Anthologien der Mamlukenzeit," in *Die Mamluken: Studien zu ihrer Geschichte und Kultur: Zum Gedenken an Ulrich Haarmann (1942–1999)*, ed. Stephan Conermann and Anja Pistor-Hatam, 71–122 (Hamburg, Germany: EB-Verlag, 2003).

9. Jonathan Z. Smith, *Imagining Religion: From Babylon to Jonestown* (Chicago: University of Chicago Press, 1982), 50.

be lost to future generations.[10] For their part, the goals of legitimation and classification that motivated Muslim commentators each connected to the growing homogeneity of Muslim religious discourse that prevailed in Mamlūk urban centers. As notions of orthodoxy became standardized within this intellectual context, a scholar's task of differentiating himself from his peers became more challenging, while higher value was placed on activities of knowledge specialization (i.e., within a single discipline) over knowledge brokerage (i.e., across multiple disciplines).[11] Well suited for the purposes of knowledge specialization, commentary texts would function as a productive medium in which a commentator could demonstrate his competence in a subject matter over that of his scholarly peers.

Writing in the eleventh/seventeenth century, Ḥājjī Khalīfa (d. 1068/1657) provides three justifications for writing commentaries on pre-existing texts that we must otherwise assume were intended by their authors to stand alone. The first justification obtains when the author of an original text is so concise and precise that some readers require the aid of a commentary to grasp the subtle meanings that are hidden on the pages before them. The second occurs whenever the author of the original text omits the rationale behind what appears in his text, in which case it becomes the job of the commentator to provide the reader with all necessary background knowledge to appreciate the author's position on a particular matter. The third occurs when an author employs allegorical or metaphorical language that demands commentary to clarify the author's intended meaning in order to prevent misunderstanding.[12]

Although Ḥājjī Khalīfa was writing around a century after the Islamic middle period, his three justifications for commentary writing reflect the essential justifications of earlier generations of Muslim commentators. When discussing the etiquette that a commentator must display toward a base text, however, he advocates for a more conservative and deferential attitude toward the received textual tradition than what we might find

10. Rosenthal, *Technique and Approach of Muslim Scholarship*, 57; Hans Ulricht Gumbrecht, *The Powers of Philology: Dynamics of Textual Scholarship* (Urbana: University of Illinois Press, 2003), 47.

11. I thank Mohammad Gharaibeh for this idea.

12. Ḥājjī Khalīfa (Muṣṭafā b. ʿAbdallāh), *Kashf al-ẓunūn ʿan asāmī l-kutub wa-l-funūn*, 2 vols. (Istanbul: Maarif Matbaası, 1941), 1:36–37.

in commentaries from the middle period. For him, it is essential that a commentator be "a commentator, not a critic nor counter-witness; an interpreter, not an adversary."[13] In contrast, writing only a century earlier, al-Anṣārī's student Badr al-Dīn al-Ghazzī (d. 984/1577) divides all acts of composition into seven categories, or justifications, while at least four of these seven categories exist solely on account of what a later author identifies as clear deficiencies in an earlier piece of scholarship. His second category, for example, encompasses any writing done because of an earlier "defectiveness in composition in order to correct its shortcoming."[14] Al-Ghazzī here assumes that the previous generations of scholars are as susceptible to error as his own generation, and in this regard, he displays a tone that is less reverential toward the past than that of Ḥājjī Khalīfa. But even in Ḥājjī Khalīfa's case, reverence toward the tradition is not meant to suggest that a commentator must approach the tradition without a critical eye or that he must accept it without questioning. In fact, his words imply that a commentator *will* encounter things in the written tradition that he does not agree with, and it is only in the context of addressing such things that his calls for a tone of deference make sense.

Moreover, both al-Ghazzī and Ḥājjī Khalīfa believe that all scholarship, including commentary writing, must be creative—and thus original—in nature. At first glance, Ḥājjī Khalīfa's three justifications for commentary writing might suggest otherwise. But it is only a few pages after listing these justifications that he explains that true knowledge goes beyond mere understanding. Rather, it is synonymous with attaining a scholarly aptitude (*malaka*) to recognize fundamental principles that then enable one to derive new inferences from foundational sources.[15] Similarly, al-Ghazzī insists that, for anybody undertaking written composition (*al-taṣnīf*), there must "not be a written text that makes all of the literary expressions (*asālīb*) in his text superfluous. If [an existing text] makes some of them superfluous, then let him write additional material of a similar nature through which [his text]

13. Ḥājjī Khalīfa, *Kashf al-ẓunūn*, 1:37.

14. Badr al-Dīn al-Ghazzī, *al-Durr al-naḍīd fī adab al-mufīd wa-l-mustafīd*, ed. Abū Yaʿqūb Nashʾat b. Kamāl al-Miṣrī (Giza: Maktabat al-Tawʿiyya al-Islamiyya, 2009), 286. Al-Ghazzī cites an unnamed source when listing his seven categories of composition.

15. Ḥājjī Khalīfa, *Kashf al-ẓunūn*, 1:41. Also see Rosenthal, *Technique and Approach of Muslim Scholarship*, 64.

differentiates itself and which is combined with the other text's expressions that beat him to the punch" (*maʿa ḍammi mā fātahu min al-asālīb*).[16] In other words, if a text has nothing new to offer its readers, it is superfluous and must be infused with some form of creativity to justify its existence. A commentary text that simply rehashes the past tradition would not meet al-Ghazzī's standards, as originality remains the goal of all scholarship regardless of its written form.

The Nature and Form of the Islamic Commentary

To this point I have been using the word "commentary" without a clear reference to its terminological analogue in scholarship from the Islamic middle period. One problem here is that Islamic commentary writing from this period relies on a series of terms that must be taken together when attempting to translate the word "commentary" with any sense of fidelity to the Islamic tradition. In this section I therefore describe the most essential of these terms in order to paint an accurate picture of what Muslim scholars understood by commentary and what their commentary texts look like today when we encounter them in manuscript form.

The most obvious term that maps onto the English word "commentary" is the Arabic *sharḥ*, which I translate below simply as "commentary" unless otherwise specified. When viewed from the perspective of its etymology, *sharḥ* implies disclosure, exposure, and dilation. As a term of art, *sharḥ* denotes the complete explication of the meanings that lie latent within a text.[17] A Muslim commentator would thus do *sharḥ* (*sharaḥa*) to a base text—or *matn*, which is a relative term that theoretically indicates any text that is being commented on even if it be a commentary text itself—and would produce a commentary text in the process that may be referred to as a *sharḥ* but may also carry a number of other synonymous terms in its title (e.g., *taḥrīr*, *nukat*, etc.).

In this light, the term used to designate a commentary on a commentary, namely a *ḥāshiya*—which I translate below as "supercommentary" unless

16. B. al-Ghazzī, *al-Durr al-naḍīd*, 285.

17. Cf. Jaroslav Stetkevych, "Arabic Hermeneutical Terminology: Paradox and the Production of Meaning," *Journal of Near Eastern Studies* 48, no. 2 (1989): 90.

otherwise noted—is also a product of the act of *sharḥ* and could be grouped under that heading as well. *Ḥāshiya* is etymologically connected to the word for the margins of a page and thus suggests marginalia, but in its technical sense, it came to denote something more thorough than marginalia by the very end of the Islamic middle period. Particularly in the subdisciplines of Islamic law, *ḥāshiya*s would proliferate during the Ottoman period, reaching their apex around the seventeenth and eighteenth centuries.[18]

The author of a *ḥāshiya* has taken a preexisting commentary as his base text, though whenever he uses the word *matn* expressly in his text, he is more likely than not referring to the original base text that the previous commentator has built upon (i.e., the text that is two generations removed). Of course, a future commentator may subsequently do *sharḥ* to an existing *ḥāshiya* to generate a supersupercommentary, which is often, though not exclusively, referred to as *taqārīr* (sing. *taqrīr*; literally "determination" or "settling"). Owing to the lack of a fixed nomenclature for each generation of texts that Muslim commentators generated through this process of *sharḥ*, Robert Wisnovsky has proposed a system whereby we refer to the latter text as a third-order commentary, a *ḥāshiya* as a second-order commentary, and so on.[19] Rarely do we need to reference commentaries past the level of the *ḥāshiya* during the Islamic middle period.

In theory, the process of commentating on a commentary could continue indefinitely—Wisnovsky, for example, has located manuscripts of fifth-order commentaries within the discipline of Islamic philosophy. Of course, with each successive generation of commentary, the text that is derived becomes progressively more unwieldy and its mise-en-page more complicated. Two additional factors limit the utility of higher-order commentaries, at least for the reader, though perhaps not for the author, whose text was likely as much an aid to his education as it was a product of his creativity. The first is that the liability increases for a commentary text to shift from a running commentary to a lemmatic commentary with each successive generation of texts that comes between it and the original base text upon which it builds.[20] In other words, a *sharḥ* is more likely to

18. Ahmed El Shamsy, "The *Ḥāshiya* in Islamic Law: A Sketch of the Shāfiʿī Literature," *Oriens* 41 (2013): 303 and appendix.

19. Wisnovsky, "Arabic Philosophical Commentary," 160.

20. For a comparable observation on later commentaries within the Shāfiʿī *madhhab*,

aim for a comprehensive, line-by-line explanation of its base text, while a subsequent *ḥāshiya* might then be forced to pick particular lemmata in the *sharḥ* to comment on, as a line-by-line commentary on it would prove to be too daunting a project. The momentum to move away from comprehensiveness increases as more and more layers of commentary accrete; it would force commentators in later generations of a textual genealogy to become progressively more selective when deciding on which portions of the received text to comment. In turn, this drive toward atomization and a focus on lemmata connects with the second factor that undermines the utility of higher-order commentaries: their tendency to promote digressions that are only tangentially related to the substance of the received text.[21] As soon as it became impractical for later-order commentators to provide comprehensive commentaries on the texts before them, they were forced rely on other methods to demonstrate their intellectual mettle, and the incentive grew for the inclusion of anecdotes and excurses on finer—at times trivial—details. Some would argue that this tendency disrupts the continuity of the commentary text when viewed from the perspective of its antecedent texts, although it certainly makes higher-order commentaries no less interesting as historical artifacts.[22]

True to its etymology, *sharḥ* thus dilates the textual tradition and might expand the latter into infinity were it not for the countervailing process of abridgment, or *ikhtiṣār*. During the Islamic middle period, the ability of a scholar to condense a longer text into a *mukhtaṣar* (abridgment) was as much a sign of his intellectual prowess as was his ability to generate a *sharḥ*,[23] and the proliferation of *mukhtaṣar* works during this time has led at least one historian to refer to this period as the "age of summaries."[24] When compared with any lengthy commentary, supercommentary, or legal

---

see El Shamsy, "*Ḥāshiya* in Islamic Law," 297–98.

21. El Shamsy, "*Ḥāshiya* in Islamic Law," 299.

22. For an assessment of the advantages and disadvantages of *ḥāshiyas* and lemmatic commentaries in general, see El Shamsy, "*Ḥāshiya* in Islamic Law," 301–2; Irene J. F. de Jong, "A Narratological Commentary on the *Odyssey*: Principles and Problems," in *Classical Commentary: Histories, Practices, Theory*, ed. Christina S. Kraus and Roy K. Gibson (Leiden: Brill, 2002), 63.

23. Rosenthal, *Technique and Approach of Muslim Scholarship*, 45.

24. Hirschler, *Written Word*, 20.

compendium (*mabsūṭ*), a concise *mukhtaṣar* work was simpler to copy, cheaper to buy, and—especially when written in didactic verse (*naẓm*)—easier to memorize. A student who had memorized a *mukhtaṣar* had a comprehensive outline of a discipline stored in his or her mind, though the pithiness of *mukhtaṣar* prose or verse meant that *mukhtaṣar*s were never intended to be read without the assistance of a teacher or, at the very least, a *sharḥ*.[25] In fact, the most accurate definition of a *mukhtaṣar* might be any terse work used to teach a discipline that anticipates a subsequent commentary, presented in writing or orally, to expand its dense meanings. This definition encompasses both *mukhtaṣar*s that were abridgments of existing texts and *mukhtaṣar*s that carry the label *mukhtaṣar* but do not claim to be summaries of earlier texts per se. Al-Anṣārī, for example, has this broader definition in mind whenever he uses to the word *mukhtaṣar* in his writings. Abridgment, according to him, is simply "reduction of wording and amplification of meaning."[26]

A dense *mukhtaṣar* would thus require a commentary to fulfill its semantic potential, and a commentator would rely on one of three general forms when deciding how to reproduce or reference the base text within his commentary. The first form is that of a running commentary that reproduces the full base text in segments, each of which follows the phrase "he said" (that is, "The base text author said the following . . ."). The commentator's words then appear after each segment following the phrase "I say," and in this manner, a clear distinction is maintained between the two authors' words. If the base text is copied in a full and unbroken form elsewhere on the page then it is also possible for the commentator to reference only a word or two of the base text after each use of "he said," as readers can locate the full passage with a quick shift of their eyes. This decision to reproduce the base text in segments that are interlaced with commentary or in an unbroken form elsewhere on the page may reflect the preference of a later scribe and not necessarily that of the original commentator. What is more essential to this form of commentary is that it is a running commentary,

25. Al-Ḥabashī, *Jāmiʿ al-shurūḥ wa-l-ḥawāshī*, 1:9. For more on the importance of *mukhtaṣar*s in teaching Islamic law, see Wael B. Hallaq, *Sharīʿa: Theory, Practice, Transformations* (Cambridge: Cambridge University Press, 2009), 138, 181.

26. Zakariyyā al-Anṣārī, *Fatḥ al-wahhāb bi-sharḥ Tanqīḥ al-Lubāb*, Landberg MSS 465, Beinecke Library, Yale University, New Haven, CT, fol. 2v.

that it includes the base text in full in one manner or another, and that the reader can clearly separate the words of the base text from the words of the commentator.

The second form is that of a lemmatic commentary, in which a commentator chooses particular passages of the base text to comment on, while those passages that are referenced typically appear after the phrase "his statement" (*qawluh*, i.e., the statement of the base text's author). With this form of commentary there is less of an imperative to reproduce the base text in full. Of course, if the full base text is not provided, the references to its passages must be clearer and less laconic than what is permissible in the previous form, as readers now require more information should they wish to consult the base text on their own. Later scribes and modern publishers may still opt to reproduce the full base text, either in the center of the page or in the margins, even if the original commentator chose not to do so. What is essential here, however, is that this form of commentary does not depend on a full reproduction of the base text in order to exist.[27]

The third form of commentary demands more creativity from the commentator who adopts it, though it also lends itself to conflating a commentator's words with those of the base text's author. Known as the *sharḥ mamzūj*, or interwoven commentary, this commentarial form embeds the base text within the sentences of a larger commentary such that, for all practical purposes, the two texts can no longer be separated from each other in the mind of a reader.[28] The commentator can choose to cleave the words of the base text as he sees fit and insert commentary of any length to form new sentences that integrate base text and commentary into a new, amalgamated text. The commentator is thus able to control a base text without overtly interrupting it. This operation, however, becomes far more complicated in the case of the *ḥāshiya*, which typically appears separate from the commentary that it is commenting on and is often written in the margins of a manuscript's folios as its etymology implies.[29] In this

27. Al-Ḥabashī groups the first and second commentarial forms together under the heading "*sharḥ bi-l-qawl wa-l-ʿibāra*" (commentary that references "statement" and "expression"). Al-Ḥabashī, *Jāmiʿ al-shurūḥ wa-l-ḥawāshī*, 1:9.

28. Brinkley Messick, *The Calligraphic State: Textual Domination and History in a Muslim Society* (Berkeley: University of California Press, 1993), 31.

29. See Ḥājjī Khalīfa, *Kashf al-ẓunūn*, 1:623, where it is noted that the *ḥāshiya* can be written as an autonomous (*mustaqill*) text, which is sometimes referred to as a

light, a *ḥāshiya* is more likely to conform to the second commentarial form mentioned above. The interwoven commentary, in contrast, fuses base text with commentary within the same area of a folio or page. In the Islamic manuscript tradition, the base text is frequently copied in red ink while the commentary is copied in black ink.[30] Alternatively, the base text may be overlined, though Ḥājjī Khalīfa holds that the overlining style tends to generate confusion and mistakes. For this reason, he advocates for interwoven commentaries in which *sharḥ* and *matn* are differentiated with the Arabic letters ش (*shīn*) and م (*mīm*).[31] None of these scribal conventions differentiate the two composite texts to the degree seen in the first commentarial form noted above. Rather, the interwoven commentary dissolves the line that separates base text from commentary, and the amalgamated text functions as a single unit in the mind of the reader. In fact, it has been argued that when Muslim scholars refer to a specific work of commentary (e.g., al-Anṣārī's commentary on al-Qushayrī's *Risāla*), they are conceptualizing the *sum* of the commentary and the base text that it builds upon.[32] Although we must be careful not to overstate this claim, it is more likely to apply in the case of interwoven commentaries.

---

taʿlīqa. The latter term is treated in more depth below. I can find only two references to "*mamzūja*" *ḥāshiyas* in the *Kashf al-ẓunūn*, where the author is otherwise quick to note (albeit with chagrin) if a commentary is *mamzūj*. Ḥājjī Khalīfa, *Kashf al-ẓunūn*, 2:1147. Both of these *ḥāshiyas* are commentaries on Saʿd al-Dīn al-Taftāzānī's (d. 793/1390) *Sharḥ al-ʿAqāʾid*, which was wont to attract such *ḥāshiyas*, as a manuscript of al-Anṣārī's own *ḥāshiya* on the text attests. Copied in Egypt in 1016/1607, the latter manuscript is *mamzūja*, although it abbreviates the base text of the original *ʿAqāʾid*. Zakariyyā al-Anṣārī, *Fatḥ al-ilāh al-mājid bi-īḍāḥ Sharḥ al-ʿAqāʾid*, MSS Laleli 2188, Istanbul, fols. 1r–65r. Here the original base text is in red ink, while the rest of the text is in black ink with al-Taftāzānī's *sharḥ* overlined in red ink; al-Anṣārī explicitly refers to his work as a *ḥāshiya* at fol. 1v. Ḥājjī Khalīfa traces the first *ḥāshiya* to Majd al-Dīn al-Fīrūzābādī (d. 817/1415). Ḥājjī Khalīfa, *Kashf al-ẓunūn*, 1:624.

30. See Gacek, *Arabic Manuscripts*, 228–29; Devin Stewart, "Notes on Zayn al-Dīn al-ʿĀmilī's *Munyat al-murīd fī ādāb al-mufīd wa-l-mustafīd*," *Journal of Islamic Studies* 21, no. 2 (2010): 241–42; cf. Zayn al-Dīn Shahīd al-Thānī, *al-Fikr al-tarbawī ʿind Zayn al-Dīn b. Aḥmad* (*Munyat al-murīd fī ādāb al-mufīd wa-l-mustafīd*), ed. ʿAbd al-Amīr Shams al-Dīn (Beirut: al-Sharika al-ʿĀlimiyya li-l-Kitāb, 1990), 286. Also see B. al-Ghazzī, *al-Durr al-naḍīd*, 465–66.

31. Ḥājjī Khalīfa, *Kashf al-ẓunūn*, 1:36–37; al-Ḥabashī, *Jāmiʿ al-shurūḥ wa-l-ḥawāshī*, 1:10.

32. Brinkley Messick makes a similar claim. Messick, *Calligraphic State*, 31.

The interwoven commentarial form gained prominence after the eighth/fourteenth century, and while it would quickly become popular in the writing of legal texts,[33] we find manuscripts in a variety of disciplines that make use of it. Al-Anṣārī, in fact, relied heavily on it when composing commentaries in Sufism, jurisprudence, grammar, theology, and other subjects. As is discussed in more detail in the chapters that follow, al-Anṣārī's preference for this particular commentarial form can be explained, at least in part, by examining the substance and structure of his interwoven commentaries in order to appreciate the rhetorical power that this style of writing afforded him.

The Production and Publication of Islamic Commentaries

The previous section has provided a basic description of Islamic commentary texts as we might encounter them in manuscript form today. How then were these commentary texts produced during the later Islamic middle period? The present section aims to answer this question; here I paint a picture of Muslim commentarial writing during the period while filtering the secondary literature through what I have noticed in al-Anṣārī's own commentarial writing process in order to bring my picture into greater focus. Even with this lens in place, it remains challenging to generalize about commentary writing, as the contexts and motives behind individual commentary texts vary widely and are sometimes discipline specific. At the same time, the secondary literature gives disproportionate attention to the writing of legal commentaries, as that discipline is described in clearer detail in the primary sources when compared with commentary writing in other disciplines. Admittedly, my description here has been shaped by the data available to me in both the primary and secondary literature. The data similarly skew in favor of commentary writing done in the presence of others—usually students—and provide less detail on commentaries that were more the products of individual labor. This is all to say that, even though every statement below can be contradicted by counterexamples from the historical record, the present section as a whole describes general processes of commentary writing in the later Islamic middle period and navigates a middle ground between unmanageable detail and vulgarization.

33. Rosenthal, *Technique and Approach of Muslim Scholarship*, 18.

What quickly becomes apparent from a study of commentary writing during the Islamic middle period are the following conclusions: (1) commentary writing cannot be separated from pedagogy and learning; (2) pedagogy and learning cannot be separated from practical application (e.g., the practice of law within courts; the practice of Sufism in ritual and ethics); and (3) practical application cannot be separated from the society in which it operates. Nevertheless, just as an image must be distilled into its constituent shapes and colors when attempting to reproduce it in a painting, so too must we separate pedagogy, practical application, and society in order to paint a digestible picture of commentary writing that helps to contextualize the chapters that follow. In reality, these three levels of social practice operated in tandem and reinforced one another.[34] But if we give ourselves permission to separate them, pedagogy and learning clearly reveal themselves to be the engines of commentarial writing during the later Islamic middle period.

If we then focus our energies on sketching a portrait of Islamic pedagogy and learning during this time, we must take the *ḥalaqa*, or study circle, as our focal point. Contemporary historians often highlight the informal nature of the *ḥalaqa*, and this is certainly a fair assessment in light of modern educational standards. No accrediting bodies set a curriculum to be followed within *ḥalaqa* sessions, individual *ḥalaqa* teachers determined whether or not their students had mastered a subject, and—with the possible exception of madrasa payroll administrators who were on the lookout for absentee teachers—no administrative bodies regulated the quality, frequency, or rigor of a teacher's *ḥalaqas*.[35] Even the location of *ḥalaqa* learning was never fixed. After the predawn prayer, a scholar could conduct a public *ḥalaqa* in a mosque before an audience of several hundred attendees, then in the later morning teach a few dozen students in a madrasa *ḥalaqa* that

34. See Timothy Mitchell, *Colonising Egypt* (Berkeley: University of California Press, 1991), 83–85. A similar act of artificial separation can be seen when Hallaq separates the juristic roles of *qāḍī*, *muftī*, author-jurist (*muṣannif*), and professor. He does so in order to create a more digestible narrative while admitting in the same breath that "these roles rarely stood independently of each other." Wael B. Hallaq, *Authority, Continuity, and Change in Islamic Law* (Cambridge: Cambridge University Press, 2004), 167–68.

35. Hallaq, *Sharīʿa*, 138–41.

provided him with a monthly stipend, and finally in the early afternoon host a handful of his best students at his home for an advanced *ḥalaqa* in which the group collectively drafted a work of commentary that was based on the scholar's teachings.[36]

From another perspective, however, the *ḥalaqa* demanded its participants to adhere to strict protocols and conventions (*ādāb*) that would crystalize during the Islamic middle period and which continue to bind Muslim students and teachers in many parts of the world today. In fact, the social and internalized pressure felt by participants to abide by these conventions made the outward form of the *ḥalaqa* more durable across history than that of many other institutions of modern education. This, of course, is not to suggest that the *ḥalaqa* remained static over the centuries. But it is fair to say that a Mamlūk scholar living six hundred years ago would still recognize most of the dynamics and outward features of a *ḥalaqa* held in contemporary Pakistan, Indonesia, or Yemen.

Students in a *ḥalaqa* would sit on the floor in the form of a major arc, leaving a space open in their circle for latecomers. The shaykh (teacher or professor, depending on the context) sat facing this opening from just outside the arc's circumference in order to glimpse his students collectively. The far side of the *ḥalaqa* opposite the shaykh might comprise multiple rows of students, and beginning learners would sit farthest from the shaykh and would move progressively closer as they advanced in their studies.[37] The shaykh's most advanced students were positioned closest to their teacher in the front row, while the best of them sat to his immediate side at the edge of the *ḥalaqa*'s opening. If the shaykh had a son in attendance, he would often fill this position,[38] though the shaykh's intimacy with all of his

36. Hirschler, *Written Word*, 37.

37. Daphna Ephrat, *A Learned Society in a Period of Transition: The Sunni ʿUlamāʾ of Eleventh-Century Baghdad* (Albany, NY: State University of New York Press, 2000), 77; Johannes Pedersen, *The Arabic Book*, trans. Geoffrey French, ed. Robert Hillenbrand (Princeton, NJ: Princeton University Press, 1984), 26; Hallaq, *Sharīʿa*, 136; Hirschler, *Written Word*, 47; Badr al-Dīn Ibn Jamāʿa al-Kinānī, *Tadhkirat al-sāmiʿ wa-l-mutakallim fī adab al-ʿālim wa-l-mutaʿallim*, ed. Muḥammad Hāshim al-Nadawī (Al-Dammām, Saudi Arabia: Ramādī li-l-Nashr, 1994), 206–8.

38. Hirschler, *Written Word*, 49.

advanced students set a paternal tone to their relationship as well, which would carry beyond the context of the *ḥalaqa*.[39]

Students organized themselves into a similar arrangement when they met to review the shaykh's lessons under the guidance of a *muʿīd*, or teaching assistant—a scholar-in-training who was one of the shaykh's most advanced students and possibly the recipient of a monthly stipend if his activities took place within a well-endowed madrasa. The *muʿīd* served to clarify the shaykh's lessons, add further material to them, and assess the comprehension and memory of less-advanced students before the shaykh's next *ḥalaqa* was held.[40] Another position that advanced students could fill was that of *mustamlī*, the transcriber of the shaykh's lessons during his *ḥalaqa*, whose transcript would aid both students and *muʿīds* and might serve as a template for the shaykh's commentary that was to come.[41] Both the *mustamlī* and the *muʿīd* functioned as intermediaries between students and the shaykh. But, as is symbolized in the *ḥalaqa*'s very seating arrangement, all participants in the *ḥalaqa* fell within a continuum of mastery over the subject material, and it would be a mistake to draw clear dividing lines between beginning learners, advanced students, and the shaykh himself. Moreover, all participants were expected to learn from their equals and superiors among their peers and assist those who were less advanced than they were, while mastery over the subject matter—not age nor social status—determined the teaching-learning dynamics between students.[42] As Timothy Mitchell explains it in a later context, "The process of mastering the art was what gave learning its order."[43] This order that emerged was as formalized in its practice as any dictated from above by school curricula, degree programs, or assessment standards, as we might encounter today.

Of course, only very few *ḥalaqa*s produced commentary texts in the end. What they did produce were seemingly endless notes, which were the material fruit of the shaykh's dictation and extemporaneous exposition, the *muʿīd*'s drilling and supplementary teaching, and the student's questions and private study. The processes that subsequently allowed these notes to

39. Hallaq, *Sharīʿa*, 137.

40. Makdisi, *Rise of Colleges*, 209–10; Hallaq, *Sharīʿa*, 136–38.

41. Pedersen, *Arabic Book*, 26.

42. Ibn Jamāʿa, *Tadhkirat al-sāmiʿ*, 60, 94, 168–69, 178; Hallaq, *Sharīʿa*, 137.

43. Mitchell, *Colonising Egypt*, 84.

distill into commentary proper are easiest to glimpse within the study and practice of Islamic law. From the very beginning of their legal education under a master, students would engage in *taʿlīq*, or note taking. As they progressed in their studies and gained enough mastery to conduct legal research of their own, their notes would grow into a more formal *taʿlīqa*—an expanding notebook in the case of the advanced student, or lecture notes once the former student had been authorized to teach his own *ḥalaqa*s.[44] These sophisticated *taʿlīqa*s did not simply reproduce the lecture materials of a single master jurist. Rather, they also encompassed a host of disputed legal questions that the compiler had researched, the method of answering these questions in light of one or more master jurists' teachings, and other materials taken from legal compendiums (*al-mabsūṭāt*) and appended to the various discussions at hand.[45]

It is at this stage that the *taʿlīqa* might be said to have crossed an imaginary line to form a protocommentary. All that it then needed to constitute a true commentary was editing, reception, and reproduction—activities best performed by one's own students. In fact, some legal commentaries from before the Islamic middle period were recognized as exactly synonymous with the *taʿlīqa*s of their authors,[46] suggesting that the movement from *taʿlīqa* to *sharḥ* may have been simpler in previous centuries. By the middle period, however, starker lines had emerged between the activities of *taʿlīq* and *taṣnīf*, that is, formal writing done by a recognized jurist with a clear readership in mind.[47] *Sharḥ* falls under the category of *taṣnīf* during this period, while *taʿlīq* does not.[48] Leaving aside the variable of authority for the time being, the intention of a writer is also crucial to identifying which

44. Hallaq, *Sharīʿa*, 139; Makdisi, *Rise of Colleges*, 114, 174–75, and passim. For a close analysis of a *taʿlīqa* that illustrates some of the phenomena described by Makdisi, see Bernard Weiss, "Medieval Islamic Legal Education as Reflected in the Works of Sayf al-Dīn al-Āmidī," in *Law and Education in Medieval Islam: Studies in Memory of Professor George Makdisi*, ed. Joseph E. Lowry, Devin J. Stewart, and Shawkat M. Toorawa (Cambridge: E. J. W. Gibb Memorial Trust, 2004).

45. Makdisi, *Rise of Colleges*, 118, 126–27; Ibn Jamāʿa, *Tadhkirat al-sāmiʿ*, 189; B. al-Ghazzī, *al-Durr al-naḍīd*, 270.

46. Makdisi, *Rise of Colleges*, 115, 119.

47. Ibn Jamāʿa, *Tadhkirat al-sāmiʿ*, 192; Hallaq, *Authority, Continuity, and Change*, 167–68. See also Hallaq, *Sharīʿa*, 178–83.

48. Hallaq, *Sharīʿa*, 179–80; Hallaq, *Authority, Continuity, and Change*, 202.

side of the *sharḥ-taʿlīqa* line a particular text falls on. If a jurist intended his *taʿlīqa* to serve as his lecture notes, for example, then we might place it under the Hellenistic category of *hyponēma*, or a private draft text meant to aid in teaching and memorization. If, however, he intended his *taʿlīqa* for publication (*ekdosis*), it would fall under the category of *syngramma*, a book or book draft that anticipates a readership and that is able to function as an autonomous artifact after the life of its author.[49] When a scholar's intentions resonated with the will of an audience to move his *taʿlīqa* into the realm of *syngrammata*, the fruits of his labors were imbued with heuristic permanence and a formal commentary text was born. Without a *taʿlīqa*'s institutionalizing into commentary in this manner, thousands of hours of intellectual toil might be lost to later generations of scholars and students.

To speak in more generic terms that extend the conversation beyond the legal disciplines, a multistep process led to the "publication" of a commentary within the context of a *ḥalaqa*. The first step was the act of dictation (*imlāʾ*), whereby the author of a commentary would read his text aloud to his students, who would copy it individually. For this task, the author relied on his draft manuscript (*musawwada*), which varied in its degree of completeness according to his creative process.[50] In other words, just like the *taʿlīqa*, which was particular to the law, the draft manuscript would fall somewhere on the *hyponēma-syngramma* continuum. Some authors, like al-Anṣārī, sought the assistance of their advanced students in arranging their draft manuscripts and expanding them with additional commentary in response to student questions. They could also include material that students had researched and gathered from external sources at the behest of their teacher.[51] Other authors would come to their *ḥalaqas* with draft manuscripts that were more polished than this, or they might rely on the help of only one or two of their closest students in preparing their drafts.

49. For more on these terms, see Gregor Schoeler, *The Genesis of Literature in Islam: From the Aural to the Read*, trans. Shawkat M. Toorawa (Edinburgh: Edinburgh University Press, 2011), 19–25, and passim.

50. Pedersen, *Arabic Book*, 24–28.

51. For example, al-Anṣārī's students played an essential role in drafting his commentary on al-Bukhārī's *Ṣaḥīḥ* during his later years, as is described in more detail in chapter 2 below. Also see Ḥājjī Khalīfa, *Kashf al-ẓunūn*, 1:161; Hallaq, *Sharīʿa*, 138–39; al-Ḥabashī, *Jāmiʿ al-shurūḥ wa-l-ḥawāshī*, 1:8.

The next step was to collate and edit (*taḥqīq*) the draft manuscripts to generate a fair copy manuscript (*mubayyaḍa*) that the author would attach his name to and approve for transmission.[52] To accomplish this task, an author could choose the best of his students' copies of the text to serve as an exemplar, or his *mustamlī* might read his words back to him multiple times until he was satisfied and a fair copy of the text was thus approved. In either case, the author's words would be presented back to him for review (*ʿarḍ*), and because the review process generally extended over multiple sessions, the author still enjoyed some latitude to edit his words and excise material from his commentary at this stage.[53]

In the context of the Islamic middle period, we can say that the publication of a commentary took place once a fair copy of the text had been generated. All that remained to give the text permanence was its reception and reproduction, which occurred simultaneously. Thus, the third step in the publication process was for the author—perhaps with the help of his *muʿīds*—to hear his students read their copies of the text back to him and confirm that these copies accorded with the fair copy and thereby the will of its author. Once an author was satisfied with the accuracy of his students' copies of his text, with their comprehension of his intended meanings, and with their mastery over the subject matter as he had taught it, he granted an *ijāza* (license) to each of their copies of his text. Within this particular context, the *ijāza* signified both that a student's manuscript represented an accurate reproduction of the author's original copy and that the author had authorized this student to transmit the text to others on his authority.[54]

Upon completion of these three steps, a commentary text was published that carried the approval of its author at a particular point in his life. Nevertheless, premodern commentaries also allowed for later revisions by their authors, just as published books today allow for later editions. In this light,

52. Al-Sakhāwī records, for example, that the *taḥqīq* of al-Anṣārī's *Asnā l-maṭālib* commentary took place in early 892/1487 in front of al-Anṣārī. Muḥammad b. ʿAbd al-Raḥmān al-Sakhāwī, *al-Ḍawʾ al-lāmiʿ li-ahl al-qarn al-tāsiʿ*, 12 vols. (Beirut: Dār al-Jīl, 1992), 2:295.

53. Gacek, *Arabic Manuscripts*, 91–93; Hirschler, *Written Word*, 13–17, 33; Pedersen, *Arabic Book*, 27–28 (see also page 31 for an illustrative description of how an authorized copy of a philological text was produced).

54. Pedersen, *Arabic Book*, 32; Ibn Jamāʿa, *Tadhkirat al-sāmiʿ*, 62; Hallaq, *Sharīʿa*, 139.

a final, elective step in the publication of a commentary occurred whenever an author revised his commentary text after having approved earlier copies of it. Legal commentaries were especially prone to later modifications, as their authors matured and broadened their knowledge through teaching, reading, and practice—particularly practice in issuing fatwas and interacting with court cases.[55] And just as students would publish the fatwas of their shaykh as fatwa collections often after the death of this shaykh,[56] so too can we find examples of students' extracting the marginal notes from their shaykh's copy of a base text and publishing these as his posthumous commentary on the latter.[57] All of these factors contribute to variant readings in the manuscript tradition and demonstrate how this tradition has a complicated relationship with the will of the authors who propelled it. In other words, although the steps that led to the publication of a commentary aimed to maximize an author's control over his text while guaranteeing textual accuracy and fidelity to his objectives, variables that undermined authorial control were always present and—in an ironic twist—might even be a function of an author's later editorial interventions into his own texts.

The Anonymity of a Commentator

Although the descriptions above have emphasized the will and agency of the commentary author, the rhetoric of a commentary text largely functions to efface its author and thereby ground his authority in a veneer of deference to the received textual tradition. Johannes Pedersen has even extended this

---

55. Al-Anṣārī's lifelong revising of his famous commentary on Ibn al-Wardī's *Bahja* provides an illustrative example here; it is described in more detail in chapter 2 below. See also Hallaq, *Sharīʿa*, 139–40, 182. For an example outside of the legal disciplines, see W. Cureton, "An Account of the Autograph MS. of the First Volume of Ibn Khallikān's Biographical Dictionary," *Journal of the Royal Asiatic Society* 6, no. 2 (1841): 223–38. An interesting anecdote in the *Tuḥfat al-aḥbāb* also records how al-Anṣārī would give a dinar to anybody who could find a mistake or an outdated position in one of his texts, which he would then update. Zayn al-ʿĀbidīn al-Anṣārī, *Tuḥfat al-aḥbāb bi-faḍāʾil aḥad al-aqṭāb*, MS Zakiyya Arabic 573/454737, Dār al-Kutub al-Miṣriyya, Cairo, fols. 9r–9v.

56. Hallaq, *Sharīʿa*, 139–40, 180–81.

57. See, for example, Zakariyyā al-Anṣārī, *Asnā l-maṭālib: Sharḥ Rawḍ al-ṭālib*, ed. Maḥmūd Maṭrajī, 6 vols. (Beirut: Dār al-Fikr, 2008), 1:25n1.

observation to the average premodern Muslim book author in general, who "seldom reveals himself as a person," which he illustrates through conventions such as authors' reliance on the third person when offering personal opinions and on narratives grounded in chains of transmitters (*isnāds*).[58] To be sure, Muslim commentators from the Islamic middle period prove themselves to be similar to commentators from a variety of other canonical/classical traditions throughout history; the present section thus expands on some of these similarities.

Just as many critics have observed of historians, commentators consistently project a tone of anonymity through their use of language and the conventions of their craft. That is, both commentators and historians rely on a language that is less self-conscious than that of poets and writers of fiction, while this language allows them to camouflage their personalities behind a rhetoric that purports to be self-evident, free from bias and whim, and—in the case of commentary—a true interpretation of a base text's meanings.[59] In turn, the anonymity afforded by the language and conventions of commentary writing simultaneously buttress the power behind a commentator's interpretation and render it authoritative.

Consider in this context the convention of parallel text citations (parallels) whereby a commentator interjects supplementary, or even digressive, texts written by other authors into the discussion at hand. At first glance, parallels might appear pedantic and superfluous. To some later readers, in fact, a commentator's citing the opinions of earlier authorities was emblematic of unoriginality. It was this very sentiment that fueled narratives of intellectual decline—or, at best, a baroque period—within twentieth-century studies of commentaries from the later Islamic middle period. But, when viewed from the perspective of their rhetorical *impact* and not merely their surface meanings, parallels could inspire entirely new interpretations of a canonical

---

58. Pedersen, *Arabic Book*, 23–24. Of course there are exceptions to this within the Islamic commentary tradition. Consider in this context the fifteenth- and sixteenth-century commentaries cited by El-Rouayheb that "were suffused with the rhetoric of *taḥqīq*, that is, of the need to critically assess received scholarly propositions as opposed to . . . explicating them." Khaled El-Rouayheb, *Islamic Intellectual History in the Seventeenth Century: Scholarly Currents in the Ottoman Empire and the Maghreb* (New York: Cambridge University Press, 2015), 32.

59. White, *Tropics of Discourse*, 127, 130; Roland Barthes, "The Discourse of History," trans. Stephen Bann, *Comparative Criticism* 3 (1981): 3–20.

tradition, undermine alternative interpretations, and facilitate a dialogue between generations by functioning as "the analogies, both metaphorical and metonymical, through which teaching and learning take place."[60] It is for similar reasons that Jaroslav Pelikan, in his study on medieval Christian theology and heresiology, argues that the citation of patristic testimonies within later theological works may serve as a better indicator of an author's thought "than are their own ex professo statements."[61] Within the context of Mamlūk literature, Thomas Bauer has demonstrated how the extensive citation of parallels would birth an entirely new genre of writing, namely the anthology in the form of commentary, which aimed to ward off boredom in its readership by "compiling an anthology of texts of both old and recent origin, both earnest and humorous, in order to give a colorful picture of subjects relevant to any educated person of 'modern' (i.e., Mamluk) times."[62]

Parallels, along with most other commentarial conventions, serve to enhance the authority of the commentator while maintaining the "professional fiction" of this commentator's invisibility.[63] The commentator's invisibility, in fact, endows commentary writing with the flexibility that it needs to adapt canonical base texts to later contexts. If a commentator's voice is too obvious or imperious, it eclipses that of the base text's author and becomes an unequivocal—and thus inadaptable—interpretation of

60. Christina S. Kraus, "Introduction: Reading Commentaries/Commentaries as Reading," in Kraus and Gibson, *Classical Commentary*, 21–22; Francis X. Clooney, "Nammāḻvār's Glorious *Tiruvallavāḻ*: An Exploration in the Methods and Goals of Śrīvaiṣṇava Commentary," *Journal of the American Oriental Society* 111, no. 2 (1991): 266–70, 275. For seven typologies of parallels within classical commentaries on Latin poetry, see Roy Gibson, "'Cf. e.g.': A Typology of 'Parallels' and the Function of Commentary on Latin Poetry," in Kraus and Gibson, *Classical Commentary*, 333–46.

61. Jaroslav Pelikan, *The Christian Tradition: A History of the Development of Doctrine*, vol. 2, *The Spirit of Eastern Christendom, 600–1700* (Chicago: University of Chicago Press, 1977), 9.

62. Bauer, "Mamluk Literature," 113.

63. Kraus, "Introduction," 4–5, 20. In Kraus's words, "The 'I' of the commentator tends towards the mute." Also see Norman Cutler, "Interpreting *Tirukkuṟaḷ*: The Role of Commentary in the Creation of a Text," *Journal of the American Oriental Society* 112, no. 4 (1992): 557. John Vallance has similarly shown how even the simplest of didactic commentaries can function both to spread and explain a doctrine *and* to strengthen the authority of the commentator. John T. Vallance, "Galen, Proclus and the Non-Submissive Commentary," in *Commentaries—Kommentare*, ed. Glenn W. Most (Göttingen, Germany: Vandenhoeck and Ruprecht, 1999), 223.

the tradition.[64] Moreover, we have little reason to doubt the sincerity of commentators, as evidence generally shows them to have internalized their rhetoric of invisibility as they approach the base texts before them. Hoffman, for instance, argues that Greco-Roman commentators of antiquity saw themselves as mere "vector[s] of Truth" who would unravel the canonical texts of authors like Plato and Aristotle through a process of unveiling. These commentators, in other words, considered their interpretations of the canon authoritative by virtue of the fact that they were merely unfolding the doctrines that lie already there within the pages of the base text.[65] This attitude is in no way unique to Greco-Roman commentators of antiquity and in fact finds obvious parallels in the Muslim commentarial tradition. Al-Anṣārī's student ʿAbd al-Wahhāb al-Shaʿrānī (d. 973/1565), for example, argues that all legal interpretations are mere distillations of what was contained in an undifferentiated form (*mā ajmala*) in the words of the preceding generation. In turn, the previous generation distilled their law from what was contained in the words of the generation before them, and so on, until this chain of generations reaches back to the Prophet, who distilled "through his Sharīʿa" what was contained in an undifferentiated form in the Qurʾān. It is the light of the Prophet, which al-Shaʿrānī also refers to as "the substance" (*al-mādda*), that passes from one generation to the next and drives the distillation process forward through time like an unfolding fractal pattern. Moreover, al-Shaʿrānī expressly connects this process to the scholarly production of commentaries and subsequent supercommentaries, whose existence demonstrates that the true scholars of each generation grasp the reality of the undifferentiated meanings that they have inherited from the preceding generation. He quotes in this context his teacher al-Anṣārī, who argues that without the scholarly act of elucidating what was formerly undifferentiated in the received tradition, we would be left without basic knowledge of how to perform correct devotions to God.[66]

64. Gumbrecht, *Powers of Philology*, 48.

65. Philippe Hoffmann, "What Was Commentary in Late Antiquity? The Example of the Neoplatonic Commentators," in *A Companion to Ancient Philosophy*, ed. Mary Louise Gill and Pierre Pellegrin (West Sussex, UK: Wiley-Blackwell, 2009), 599.

66. ʿAbd al-Wahhāb al-Shaʿrānī, *al-Mīzān al-kubrā*, ed. ʿAbd al-Raḥmān ʿUmayra, 3 vols. (Beirut: ʿĀlam al-Kutub, 1989), 1:165–66; Samuela Pagani, "The Meaning of *Ikhtilāf al-Madhāhib* in ʿAbd al-Wahhāb al-Shaʿrānī's *al-Mīzān al-Kubrā*," *Islamic Law and Society* 11, no. 2 (2004): 211–12.

Notwithstanding the attitudes of people like al-Shaʿrānī and al-Anṣārī here, it is clear to contemporary historians who analyze texts with an eye toward their genealogies that commentaries embody varying degrees of subtle innovation—that is, creative revisions that cloak themselves in the received tradition. This subtle innovation stems largely from commentators' idiosyncratic understandings of canonical base texts along with their attempts to reconcile and systematize disparate portions of these same texts. It is owing to variables like these that commentators might generate entirely new doctrines and positions whose novelty was accepted unwittingly by their contemporaries.[67] It would also be a mistake to overstate the veneer of deference that commentators bring to the received tradition, which I have thus far connected to the commentator's rhetoric of invisibility. Commentarial attitudes across the disciplines—and even within a single work of commentary—fall within a spectrum that ranges from complete deference toward a base text to antagonism and subversiveness. In the context of legal commentaries within the Ḥanafī *madhhab*, for example, Brannon Wheeler has convincingly shown how the legitimacy and authority of a Ḥanafī commentator was *not* simply a function of his complete deference to earlier authorities, nor did it owe to his patching over of differences of opinion within the *madhhab* on apologetic grounds. Rather, legitimacy obtained through a commentator's critical engagement with the Ḥanafī canon (here, *Mukhtaṣar al-Qudūrī*) and the commentator's demonstration of familiarity with extracanonical texts and foundational authorities. To be a legitimate Ḥanafī commentator was, in essence, to engage the Ḥanafī canon according to the accepted precepts of the *madhhab* at a given time; it was not a function of the specific legal positions that Ḥanafī commentators outwardly adopted within their commentaries.[68] Similar examples of al-Anṣārī's nondeference

67. Hoffmann, "What Was Commentary?," 602; Carsten Madsen, "The Rhetoric of Commentary," *Glossator: Practice and Theory of Commentary* 3 (2010): 28.

68. Brannon M. Wheeler, "Identity in the Margins: Unpublished Ḥanafī Commentaries on the *Mukhtaṣar* of Aḥmad b. Muḥammad al-Qudūrī," *Islamic Law and Society* 10, no. 2 (2003): 182–209. In a similar vein, albeit in the context of Islamic philosophical commentaries, Asad Ahmed writes that "it is not sufficient to give an argument for the claims of the *matn* that a commentator wishes to prove; rather, a commentator must supply the correct proofs derived from the right kind of scholarly faction." Asad Q. Ahmed, "Post-Classical Philosophical Commentaries/Glosses: Innovation in the Margins," *Oriens* 41 (2013): 336.

to base texts within his commentaries in Sufism and substantive law form a major focus of the analyses of chapters 3 and 4 below.

The rhetoric of invisibility that characterizes commentary writing and the insertion of the statements of past authorities through parallels has led many modern critics of commentary texts to assume that these texts were inherently imitative and thus unoriginal. But as Hussein Ali Agrama has questioned in his anthropological study of contemporary Egyptian fatwas, is it fair to juxtapose creativity with emulation of the tradition? Even if we assume that commentaries blindly emulate the received tradition—a false assumption, to be sure, which derives from a superficial reading of these texts—Agrama remains correct to question the basic dichotomy between creativity and emulation. As he argues, this dichotomy is premised on "the assumption of a fundamental rift between the past and the future, in that the future generally brings on fundamentally new situations and circumstances, not just different from past ones but always potentially containing elements that are irreducibly different."[69] Rather, we might argue that the very raison d'être for the study of history, and arguably the humanities and social sciences writ large, is the humanistic belief that the present is *never* irreducibly different from the past. The past "tradition" that commentary builds upon remains unfixed and is constantly being negotiated and redefined, whereby the phenomena from history that make it up are added and shed according to the inclinations of its interpreters. This negotiation of a tradition occurs within an arena of conventions and power structures that are negotiated over a longer timescale; they imbue the tradition with its inertia and thereby make it as real as any other imagined reality. Commentators, for their part, often employ their rhetoric to make this inertia appear higher than it actually is, while the most skillful among them can cut through the inertia completely to move the tradition in whichever direction they prefer. It is to one such skillful commentator that we now turn our attention.

69. Hussein Ali Agrama, "Ethics, Tradition, Authority: Towards an Anthropology of the Fatwa," *American Ethnologist* 37, no. 1 (2010): 8.

Chapter Two

The Life of Zakariyyā al-Anṣārī

Contemporary historians need only consult eyewitness accounts when reconstructing the biography of Zakariyyā al-Anṣārī, as al-Anṣārī's long life intersected with multiple generations of students and scholarly peers who took the task of documentation seriously. These eyewitness accounts of al-Anṣārī's life can be grouped into four categories of literature: autobiography, hagiography, critical biography, and chronicle. Of these, the autobiographical information that al-Anṣārī has left us is meager, though from it we find a few composition dates for his texts, references to other texts of his, and even a brief rationale for his refusal to accept the chief justiceship at an earlier stage in his career. Additionally, we can place al-Anṣārī's *thabat* (register of collected *ijāzas*) into the category of autobiographical literature. However, while this latter text remains valuable in providing details on al-Anṣārī's teachers and the books that he studied under them, it omits mention of almost all other ingredients needed to write a compelling biography for its author.

The hagiographical accounts of eyewitnesses, in contrast, contain a trove of valuable information on al-Anṣārī's life, albeit information that hews exclusively to a heroic narrative. For example, the two most important hagiographies for al-Anṣārī are found in the biographical dictionaries (*ṭabaqāt*) of his student ʿAbd al-Wahhāb al-Shaʿrānī (d. 973/1565). Each of these records details about al-Anṣārī's mystical life that cannot be found elsewhere. Another source worth mentioning in this context is the unpublished *Tuḥfat al-aḥbāb bi-faḍāʾil aḥad al-aqṭāb* (*The Gift for the Beloved Ones Regarding the Merits of One of God's Axial Saints*). Written about ninety years after al-Anṣārī's death by his great-great-grandson Zayn al-ʿĀbidīn Yūsuf (d. 1068/1657), the text compiles anecdotes about al-Anṣārī by his students and family members that had been preserved as al-Anṣārī family lore and passed down among his descendants.

When reconstructing al-Anṣārī's life, however, critical biographies written by al-Anṣārī's contemporaries prove to be even more valuable than the hagiographical accounts of eyewitnesses, and the present study prioritizes them as a source over the latter whenever possible. Two critical biographies deserve mention here, as they each represent a slightly different form of the genre. The first was written by the talented historian Muḥammad b. ʿAbd al-Raḥmān al-Sakhāwī (d. 902/1497); it appeared originally in his supplement (*dhayl*) to Ibn Ḥajar al-ʿAsqalānī's (d. 852/1449) *Rafʿ al-iṣr ʿan quḍāt miṣr* (*Lifting the Burden Off the Judges of Egypt*) and was later expanded in his biographical dictionary *al-Ḍawʾ al-lāmiʿ li-ahl al-qarn al-tāsiʿ* (*The Shimmering Light of the Ninth-Century Folk*).[1] Al-Sakhāwī was an intellectual peer and lukewarm friend of al-Anṣārī, and his detailed biography furnishes us with a critical assessment of the latter's virtues, weaknesses, and mistakes. Notwithstanding his skills as a critical historian, however, al-Sakhāwī ceased updating his biography for al-Anṣārī no less than twenty-six years before the latter's death.[2] A second example of the critical biographies used below is that of Badr al-Dīn Muḥammad b. Qurqmās al-ʿAlāʾī al-Ḥanafī (d. 942/1535), the son of a high-ranking Mamlūk officer and student of al-Anṣārī.[3] The majority of al-ʿAlāʾī's *Chronicle* (*Taʾrīkh*), which contained his biography for al-Anṣārī, is lost to us today,[4] but fragments of it nonetheless survive in Najm al-Dīn al-Ghazzī's (d. 1061/1651) biographical dictionary *al-Kawākib*

1. On these two works, see Mashhūr b. Ḥasan Āl Sulaymān and Aḥmad al-Shaqayrāt, *Muʾallafāt al-Sakhāwī* (Beirut: Dār Ibn Ḥazm, 1998), 56–57, 106–9.

2. Āl Sulaymān and al-Shaqayrāt, *Muʾallafāt al-Sakhāwī*, 109.

3. For the most accurate information on al-ʿAlāʾī, see Khayr al-Dīn al-Ziriklī, *al-Aʿlām*, 8 vols. (Beirut: Dār al-ʿIlm li-l-Malāyīn, 1992), 7:10; *Fihris makhṭūṭāt Dār al-Kutub al-Ẓāhiriyya*, 17 vols. (Damascus: al-Majmaʿ al-ʿIlmī al-ʿArabī, 1947ff), 1 (1): 100–1. Cf. Najm al-Dīn al-Ghazzī, *al-Kawākib al-sāʾira bi-aʿyān al-miʾa al-ʿāshira*, ed. Jibrāʾīl Sulaymān Jabbūr, 3 vols. (Beirut: Dār al-Āfāq al-Jadīda, 1979), 2:70; Joseph H. Escovitz, "A Lost Arabic Source for the History of Ottoman Egypt," *Journal of the American Oriental Society* 97 (1977): 513–14, and passim.

4. A single manuscript of part five of the text survives in the Damascene Ẓāhiriyya collection (MS *ʿĀmm* no. 4534); this section was completed by al-ʿAlāʾī on 18 Dhū l-Ḥijja 918/24 February 1513 and covers the years 791/1389 through 856/1451–52 and thus was not the fragment (*qiṭʿa*) consulted by al-Ghazzī in compiling al-Anṣārī's biography. N. al-Ghazzī, *Kawākib*, 1:5.

al-sāʾira bi-aʿyān al-miʾa al-ʿāshira (*The Orbiting Planets: On the Notables of the Tenth Century*). Al-Ghazzī includes some of these fragments in his biography for al-Anṣārī, while they appear as his only critical source in what is otherwise a hagiography. Al-ʿAlāʾī's words here remain generally circumspect, but what emerges in the end is the voice of a narrator who harbors a genuine admiration for al-Anṣārī but who is politically powerful enough and uninhibited in his tone to be able to critique his teacher when he feels that it is warranted.

The events recorded in fifteenth- and sixteenth-century Mamlūk chronicles comprise the fourth category of data on al-Anṣārī's life. Here I exclude the necrologies (*wafayāt*) contained in these same chronicles, as necrologies would fall under the category of hagiography or critical biography mentioned above. For example, al-Ghazzī appears to have consulted al-ʿAlāʾī's necrology for al-Anṣārī when writing his biography for the latter, and for this reason, al-ʿAlāʾī's chronicle has been placed in the category of critical biography for the purposes of the present study. Rather, the *events* recorded in Mamlūk chronicles function as a separate category of literature and are a vital supplement to the biographical literature, as the nature of the genre allows chroniclers to record isolated events that biographers might find difficult to accommodate within their narrative structures. However, Mamlūk chronicles focus on the lives and affairs of political elites and tend to record the lives of Muslim scholars mainly where they intersect with the political sphere. Thus, while they preserve unique data at times, Mamlūk chronicles must serve in a supplementary capacity when telling the story of a scholar like al-Anṣārī, and it is the biographical literature that sets the tone for the analysis below.

Finally, a methodological disclaimer is due regarding the supernatural stories that some hagiographers, particularly al-Shaʿrānī, have reported about al-Anṣārī. I have included several of these stories in my biography below and have positioned them side by side with mundane reports about al-Anṣārī's life without differentiating them on the basis of their supernatural nature. To my readers I justify my decision here on four grounds.

First, I believe that my readers are capable of assessing the veracity of supernatural stories without my help. In fact, I invite them to bring a skeptical eye with them as they approach some of the stories that make up al-Anṣārī's biography and weigh them according to their own assumptions about the world.

Second, supernatural stories hold tremendous influence in shaping the popular imagination and thus have a legitimate place in the scholarly record. They help to explain why, for example, many later Muslims considered al-Anṣārī to be the *mujaddid* (renewer) of his time, as is discussed in chapter 5.

Third, because the structure and pacing of my biography for al-Anṣārī is so closely linked to chronology, I have opted to insert all supernatural accounts about him into the same chronological framework. That is to say, I have not corralled such accounts into a separate subsection below because it would disturb the structure of my narrative, which I have prioritized for the sake of clarity and readability.

Fourth, though I frequently weigh competing historical accounts below and identify which of them I believe reflects the more credible telling of history, I am hesitant to wade into epistemological waters when assessing the merits of *uncontested* first-person accounts even if they describe supernatural events. Though I may personally find some of these events more plausible than others, I have not excluded implausible stories if they serve to document how al-Anṣārī's society perceived him. The latter category might include the story reproduced below in which al-Anṣārī is reported to have miraculously cleaved the chain on the sultan's palace door with his notebook. Other stories of al-Anṣārī's visions of his shaykh floating in midair and speaking with seven eyes can be explained through a number of processes—psychological, physiological—without having to rely on the supernatural per se. In any case, I have given my reader a wide berth to decide where he or she sees fit to draw the line between the plausible and the incredible.

Act I: From Hardship to Ease

Egypt was in the beginning of a new period of stability in the year 826/1423. The advent of al-Mu'ayyad Shaykh (r. 815–24/1412–21) and his indirect successor Barsbāy (r. 825–41/1422–38) to the Mamlūk sultanate had ushered in what would be a fifty-year period of relative economic calm, domestic security, and aggressive, albeit expensive, military posturing at the international level.[5] Moreover, Egypt found herself in the middle of a

5. Ira M. Lapidus, *Muslim Cities in the Later Middle Ages* (Cambridge, MA: Harvard University Press, 1967), 32–38.

fourteen-year respite from the bubonic plague, though she would ultimately weather eleven more outbreaks over the century that was to follow.[6]

In this year, in an otherwise inconspicuous village named Sunayka, located within the Sharqiyya Province of the Egyptian delta and lying about fifty kilometers to the northeast of Cairo, a child named Zakariyyā was born to Muḥammad b. Aḥmad b. Zakariyyā al-Anṣārī and his wife.[7] Little is known about al-Anṣārī's parents: his mother's name has not survived in the primary sources, while his father worked as a falconer (or falcon trainer) for the district governor (*ʿāmil al-balad*) and died at some point around the year 841/1437–38. Al-Anṣārī appears to have been his father's only surviving son.

Prior to his father's death, al-Anṣārī would begin his studies under the tutelage of scholars who lived close the village of his birth, and al-Sakhāwī mentions the names of two legists who were associated with al-Anṣārī's early education. The first, Ibrāhīm b. Yūsuf al-Fāqūsī al-Bulbīsī (d. 862/1458), was renowned for his skills in teaching children to memorize the Qurʾān and for his popular shadow puppet shows, which he performed every year at the local Mawlid celebrations.[8] As al-Bulbīsī conducted his lessons for children in the larger town of Bulbīs (Bilbeis), the young al-Anṣārī would have traveled upward of eight kilometers to memorize the Qurʾān with him. It was also under al-Bulbīsī that al-Anṣārī studied two short works in Shāfiʿī substantive law: the *ʿUmdat al-aḥkām ʿan sayyid al-anām* of ʿAbd al-Ghanī al-Jammāʿīlī (d. 600/1203), a legal handbook that is structured around a collection of hadiths agreed upon by al-Bukhārī and Muslim; and Muẓaffar b. Aḥmad al-Tabrīzī's (d. 621/1224–25) *Mukhtaṣar* (*Abridgment*) of Abū Ḥāmid al-Ghazālī's *Wajīz*.[9]

---

6. Eliyahu Ashtor, *A Social and Economic History of the Near East in the Middle Ages* (Berkeley: University of California Press, 1976), 302.

7. For al-Anṣārī's birthdate mentioned here, see Zakariyyā al-Anṣārī, *Tuḥfat nujabāʾ al-ʿaṣr*, ed. Muḥyī Hilāl al-Sarḥān (Baghdad: Baghdad University Press, 1986), 8–9; al-Sakhāwī, *Ḍawʾ*, 3:234. For Sunayka, see Yāqūt al-Ḥamawī, *Muʿjam al-buldān*, 5 vols. (Beirut: Dār Ṣādir, 1977), 3:270.

8. Al-Sakhāwī, *Ḍawʾ*, 1:180–81. On shadow puppet theater, see Hirschler, *Written Word*, 185, 196.

9. On the two texts, see Ḥājjī Khalīfa, *Kashf al-ẓunūn*, 2:1164–65, 1626. For more on children's education during this period, see Hirschler, *Written Word*, 99.

Biographical information about Muḥammad b. Rabīʿ, the second legist mentioned in connection with al-Anṣārī's early education, has not reached us today.[10] However, it is worth noting here that the name of this latter teacher's father, Rabīʿ, is the same name given to a mysterious figure who would play a profound role in shaping al-Anṣārī's formative years. According to a story taken from al-ʿAlāʾī's lost *Chronicle* and preserved in al-Ghazzī's *Kawākib*, a man named Rabīʿ b. ʿAbdallāh was passing through the village of Sunayka when he encountered al-Anṣārī's mother in a distraught state. Explaining that her husband had passed away, she beseeched him to intervene on her behalf before the Christian district governor who had apprehended her son, Zakariyyā, intending thereby to conscript the boy into his late father's falconry post. Rabīʿ intervened and freed the boy but warned his mother that long-term security from the governor's intrigues would be possible only if al-Anṣārī were sent to Cairo to study at al-Azhar seminary. If she agreed to this idea, Rabīʿ promised to cover all of the boy's living expenses. Al-Anṣārī's mother accepted the proposal, thereby freeing her son forever from the peasanthood of his ancestors. This is the last that we read of her.

Al-ʿAlāʾī's anecdote concludes with a note on the lifelong gratitude that al-Anṣārī felt toward Rabīʿ, his wife, and their immediate family members. It would seem that these figures served as a surrogate family to the orphaned student during his years at al-Azhar, and al-ʿAlāʾī mentions that al-Anṣārī would frequently joke with Rabīʿ's wife, who effectively raised him.[11] It is also not unreasonable to speculate, albeit cautiously, that Rabīʿ may have been the father of al-Anṣārī's childhood teacher in Sunayka, as this would account for his unexplained visit to al-Anṣārī's village. Moreover, if al-Sakhāwī's biographical dictionary provides us with any indication of naming practices at the time, the name Rabīʿ was not a common one in Egypt.[12]

A weightier exercise in speculation would further allow us to recon-

10. Al-Sakhāwī, *Ḍawʾ*, 3:234; Muḥammad b. ʿAbd al-Raḥmān al-Sakhāwī, *al-Dhayl ʿalā Rafʿ al-iṣr* (*Bughyat al-ʿulamāʾ wa-l-ruwāh*), ed. Jūda Hilāl and Muḥammad Maḥmūd Ṣubḥ (Cairo: al-Hayʾa al-Miṣriyya al-ʿĀmma li-l-Kitāb, 2000), 140.

11. N. al-Ghazzī, *Kawākib*, 1:196.

12. Al-Sakhāwī lists only two brief biographies under the name Rabīʿ. Al-Sakhāwī, *Ḍawʾ*, 3:223.

cile al-ʿAlāʾī's anecdote with one reported by al-Anṣārī's Sufi adept ʿAbd al-Wahhāb al-Shaʿrānī. In his two biographical entries for al-Anṣārī that appear in both his larger and smaller biographical dictionaries, al-Shaʿrānī records the following story that al-Anṣārī narrated to him:

> I came to al-Azhar from the countryside as a youth, and I didn't busy myself with worldly concerns at all. Whenever I experienced hunger at the seminary and the pangs became unbearable, I would venture out at night to the water faucets and would rinse and eat the watermelon rinds that [I found] nearby. These would suffice me in place of bread. I stayed in this situation for years. Then, God sent to me one of His saints—a man who worked in the mills sifting flour. This person would visit me and would buy for me all the food, drink, clothes, and books that I needed. He would say to me, "Zakariyyā, don't hide any of [your needs] from me." He remained with me in this capacity for years. Then one night, when everyone else was sleeping, he took me by the hand and brought me to the lantern ladder in the mosque courtyard and said, "Climb to the top of this pedestal." I climbed and he kept telling me, "Climb," until I reached the top. At this he said, "Zakariyyā, you will live to see all of your peers die, and your prestige will rise, and for many years you will occupy the highest post of Islam,[13] [B] and your students will become the shaykhs of Islam during your lifetime . . . until you go blind." I asked, "Is my blindness inevitable?" To which he replied, "It is inevitable." Then he withdrew from me and I have not seen him since.[14]

13. Read *mashyakhat al-Islām* for "*manṣab shaykh al-Islām*. The former accords with N. al-Ghazzī, *Kawākib*, 1:196 and the editor's MS "ب" of ʿAbd al-Wahhāb al-Shaʿrānī, *al-Ṭabaqāt al-ṣughrā*, ed. ʿAbd al-Qādir Aḥmad ʿAṭāʾ (Cairo: Maktabat al-Qāhira, 1970), 40–41.

14. Al-Shaʿrānī, *al-Ṭabaqāt al-ṣughrā*, 40–41; ʿAbd al-Wahhāb al-Shaʿrānī, *Lawāqiḥ al-anwār fī ṭabaqāt al-akhyār* (hereafter *al-Ṭabaqāt al-kubrā*), 2 vols. (Cairo: Maktabat al-Ādāb, 1993ff), 2:690; N. al-Ghazzī, *Kawākib*, 1:196–97. The first part of the translated passage is taken from al-Shaʿrānī's *Ṣughrā*, which ostensibly represents the most critical of the three sources. The additional material after "[B]" is common to al-Ghazzī and al-Shaʿrānī's *Kubrā*. Al-Ghazzī records "until you go blind," which I have preferred

When analyzing the information above, it is helpful to consider that al-Sakhāwī reports 841/1437–38 as the year that al-Anṣārī first journeyed to al-Azhar,[15] when he was around the age of fifteen. According to al-Sakhāwī, al-Anṣārī stayed at al-Azhar for a brief period at first, during which time he engaged in the memorization and study of several foundational texts in law, grammar, and hadith. He then returned to his village, after which he journeyed once again to al-Azhar to take up his studies with a renewed diligence.[16] In order to reconcile al-Sakhāwī with al-Shaʿrānī, then, al-Anṣārī's early period of deprivation may in fact coincide with his initial residency at the seminary, as it would not seem reasonable for Rabīʿ to promise al-Anṣārī's mother than he would cover her son's expenses and then leave the boy to subsist on spent watermelon rinds. Al-Anṣārī's return to the village, for lack of a better explanation, may have resulted from either financial hardship or even the death of his father. The latter explanation, in turn, would push Muḥammad al-Anṣārī's death a few months past the date of 841/1437–38 that has been cited above. This reading suggests that al-Anṣārī's fateful meeting with Rabīʿ would have enabled his *return* to al-Azhar, and not his initial journey to the institution, and, accordingly, we can cautiously identify Rabīʿ with the anonymous mill worker in al-Shaʿrānī's narration. However, Konrad Hirschler has noted that the biographies of Muslim scholars from the Islamic Middle Period reveal "a consistent pattern where the entry to an endowed school was indeed linked with the loss of the father and/or poverty,"[17] which certainly holds true in the case of al-Anṣārī and might tie his initial entry into al-Azhar directly to the death of his father.

In any case, it was around this time when he was establishing himself at al-Azhar that al-Anṣārī began a deliberate and methodical study of Egyptian Sufism. He had always been "diligent in attending the *dhikr* gatherings" of the Sufis,[18] and his childhood peers and teachers had recognized Sufism as

---

here. The last sentence of the passage is common to all three versions. For the lantern ladder, see Muḥammad Muḥammad Amīn, *al-Awqāf wa-l-ḥayāh al-ijtimāʿiyya fī Miṣr* (Cairo: Dār al-Nahḍa al-ʿArabiyya, 1980), 194–97.

15. Al-Sakhāwī, *Ḍawʾ*, 3:234.

16. Al-Sakhāwī, *Ḍawʾ*, 3:234; al-Sakhāwī, *Rafʿ*, 140–41.

17. Hirschler, *Written Word*, 104.

18. Al-Shaʿrānī, *al-Ṭabaqāt al-ṣughrā*, 39; N. al-Ghazzī, *Kawākib*, 1:198.

his true passion since the very beginning. In fact, as al-Anṣārī would later recount, "Since I was little, I've always loved the ways of the Sufis. Most of my time was spent reading their books and reflecting on their spiritual states until people would even say [about me], 'No knowledge of the law will come from this guy.' "[19]

But now that he was at al-Azhar, al-Anṣārī's spiritual aspirations were complemented by the highly structured schedule that the seminary provided, and soon his spare time would be consumed by the study and practice of Sufism. The result of this study and practice, according to his own accounts, was that al-Anṣārī would attain a new spiritual station in which his supplications to God were consistently answered. According to a story that he would later tell his student al-Shaʿrānī, al-Anṣārī spent much of his time in isolation on the roof of al-Azhar, and one day, while he was there in retreat (*iʿtikāf*) during the last ten days of Ramaḍān, a man appeared before him who had recently suffered the loss of his vision. Having been referred to al-Anṣārī by the local residents, the unnamed man beseeched the pious student to pray to God on his behalf that his eyesight might return.

As he would explain to al-Shaʿrānī, al-Anṣārī could recognize a heavenly portent that informed him whether his supplications were to be answered or not, and in the case of the blind man, the portent had appeared to him. Placing a dirham in his hand, al-Anṣārī instructed the man to purchase dry zinc from a local apothecary, who apparently knew al-Anṣārī by name. The man returned after some time, however, when the medicine failed to produce an effect, and al-Anṣārī gathered from this that God would not return the man's vision to him in Cairo but only in the village of Qaṭya, on the northern coast of the Sinai, where he was instructed to travel at once.[20] Al-Anṣārī would later explain to al-Shaʿrānī that he had feared that God would expose his spiritual state to the public had he cured the man in Cairo, and for this reason he preemptively drove the man away. In fact, in a later written correspondence with the man, al-Anṣārī warns him never to return to Cairo if he wishes to remain sighted. From what we learn by the end of

19. Al-Shaʿrānī, *al-Ṭabaqāt al-kubrā*, 2:689.

20. For a few scant details on the village of Qaṭya, see Yāqūt al-Ḥamawī, *Muʿjam al-buldān*, 4:378.

the story, the man would reach Jerusalem with his vision restored, and he would reside permanently in this latter city while copying the Qur'ān and other devotional works until the end of his life.[21]

It was most likely in the wake of his meeting with the blind man that al-Anṣārī consulted some unnamed Sufi elders, informing them of his spiritual standing and newfound abilities to heal the sick. Their response would forever alter the course of al-Anṣārī's life as well as that of the later Shāfiʿī *madhhab*: they advised the young student to "conceal his station with Islamic law" (*al-tasattur bi-l-fiqh*), as theirs was not an appropriate time to manifest the states and stations of the Sufis in public. Narrating this event to al-Shaʿrānī toward the end of his life and stipulating that it not be transmitted until after his death, al-Anṣārī explained, "Thus, I have manifested almost nothing of the states of the Sufis (*al-qawm*) until this very day."[22]

The advice of the Sufi elders would mark the beginning of al-Anṣārī's legal preoccupations and eventual career as a jurist. We find evidence of al-Anṣārī's early interest in the law in his extensive *thabat*, which, boasting the names of over one hundred fifty male and female teachers, includes the following oft-repeated names: Ibn Ḥajar al-ʿAsqalānī (d. 852/1449), Muḥammad al-Qāyātī (d. 850/1446), Riḍwān al-ʿAqabī (d. 852/1448), al-Shams al-Shirwānī (d. 873/1468), and al-ʿIzz ʿAbd al-Salām al-Baghdādī (d. 859/1455).[23] However, despite the impressive length of al-Anṣārī's *thabat*, the text provides us with little more than a long list of book titles and teachers' names. In fact, the only information known about al-Anṣārī's talents as a student appears in a critical report of al-ʿAlāʾī, who reports that

21. Al-Shaʿrānī, *al-Ṭabaqāt al-kubrā*, 2:691–92; al-Shaʿrānī, *al-Ṭabaqāt al-ṣughrā*, 43. The account here blends the details of al-Shaʿrānī's two narrations of the event. Also see Ibn Ḥajar al-Haytamī, *al-Fatāwā al-ḥadīthiyya* (Beirut: Dār al-Maʿrifa, n. d.), 51.

22. Al-Shaʿrānī, *al-Ṭabaqāt al-ṣughrā*, 40; al-Shaʿrānī, *al-Ṭabaqāt al-kubrā*, 2:690 (which provides the quoted material above).

23. For the figure of over one hundred fifty teachers, see N. al-Ghazzī, *Kawākib*, 1:198. For biographies of the five teachers named here respectively, see al-Sakhāwī, *Ḍawʾ*, 2:36–40; 8:212–14; 3:226–29; 10:48–49; 4:198–203. In his biography for al-Anṣārī, al-Sakhāwī reproduces the exact wording of Ibn Ḥajar's *ijāza* (license) for him specifically in the sciences of *fiqh* and Qurʾān recitation. Al-Sakhāwī, *Ḍawʾ*, 3:236; al-Sakhāwī, *Rafʿ*, 145.

al-Anṣārī's teacher al-Shirwānī ranked another student ahead of al-Anṣārī when comparing the skills of the two students in comprehending a theological textbook.[24]

As for al-Anṣārī's Sufi teachers, al-Sakhāwī and al-Ghazzī agree on the names of five Shāfiʿīs with whom al-Anṣārī studied *taṣawwuf* and by whom he was initiated into a regimen of routine litanies (*talaqqun al-dhikr*).[25] Beyond these five names, however, the Egyptian Sufi Muḥammad al-Ghamrī (d. 849/1445) appears to have played the most prominent role in the young student's mystical education.[26] According to al-Shaʿrānī, at one point al-Anṣārī traveled to al-Ghamrī's mosque in the Egyptian delta city of al-Maḥalla al-Kubrā, and after al-Ghamrī initiated him into a *dhikr* regimen and vested him with the *khirqa* (initiatory frock), al-Anṣārī remained with him for forty days, reading al-Ghamrī's *Qawāʿid al-ṣūfiyya* (*Rules of the Sufis*) with its author.[27]

According to al-Anṣārī's own account, al-Ghamrī's students were pleased with al-Anṣārī's visit, as he would ask questions of the shaykh that they were too intimidated to ask.[28] As al-Anṣārī was still a relatively young man when al-Ghamrī died, we can glean from this information that either al-Anṣārī was a confident young student or that al-Ghamrī's everyday disciples were especially sheepish. In any case, al-Anṣārī perceived a great mystical puissance in his shaykh. Many years later he would tell his student al-Shaʿrānī about an instance during his stay with al-Ghamrī when he entered upon the shaykh unannounced only to find the latter hovering in the air

---

24. Quoted in N. al-Ghazzī, *Kawākib*, 1:197–98. The text in question was an unnamed commentary on al-Ījī's *al-Mawāqif fī ʿilm al-kalām*.

25. Al-Sakhāwī, *Ḍawʾ*, 3:235; al-Sakhāwī, *Rafʿ*, 143; N. al-Ghazzī, *Kawākib*, 1:198. Al-Ghazzī says that al-Anṣārī took the *dhikr* and was vested in the *khirqa* by all of these shaykhs, while al-Sakhāwī specifies only three of them for his initiation into the *dhikr* and does not mention the vesting of the *khirqa*. For more on this latter term, see *Encyclopaedia of Islam*, s.v. "Khirḳa" (J. L. Michon). Al-Anṣārī's descendant Zayn al-ʿĀbidīn reproduces a daily litany (*ḥizb*) that al-Anṣārī would recite after the evening prayer (*al-ʿishāʾ*). Zayn al-ʿĀbidīn al-Anṣārī, *Tuḥfat al-aḥbāb*, fol. 9r.

26. For his biography, see al-Sakhāwī, *Ḍawʾ*, 8:238–40.

27. Al-Shaʿrānī, *al-Ṭabaqāt al-kubrā*, 2:692; al-Shaʿrānī, *al-Ṭabaqāt al-ṣughrā*, 39; N. al-Ghazzī, *Kawākib*, 1:198.

28. Al-Shaʿrānī, *al-Ṭabaqāt al-kubrā*, 2:692.

close to the ceiling of his private hermitage (*khalwa*). In another instance, he likewise entered upon al-Ghamrī only to find the shaykh looking back at him with seven eyes. Addressing his stupefied disciple, al-Ghamrī explained, "Zakariyyā, when a man becomes spiritually perfected, he comes to possess seven eyes in proportion to the world's [seven] climes."[29]

Lending further credence to the centrality of al-Ghamrī to al-Anṣārī's mystical education and legitimacy is the fact that al-Shaʿrānī cites a single *isnād* for his own *khirqa*-vesting that goes through al-Anṣārī to al-Ghamrī. By his own accounts, al-Shaʿrānī considered al-Anṣārī to be his primary guide in all matters legal, but he did not consider him to be his primary shaykh in Sufism.[30] Nevertheless, al-Anṣārī appears as the only teacher to vest him ritually in the *khirqa* of Sufism—an event that took place in 914/1508 according to al-Shaʿrānī.[31] From the *isnād* behind this ritual, which al-Shaʿrānī provides in his own autobiographical accounts, we discover that al-Anṣārī's mystical lineage traces from al-Ghamrī to the latter's primary

29. Al-Shaʿrānī, *al-Ṭabaqāt al-ṣughrā*, 39; N. al-Ghazzī, *Kawākib*, 1:198. There is some doubt as to whether al-Anṣārī actually narrated these two miraculous events to al-Shaʿrānī, as a very similar narration appears in al-Shaʿrānī's biographical entry for al-Ghamrī, but here the student is a person named Muḥammad b. Shuʿayb al-Ḥabashī, while al-Ghamrī's response is slightly different. Al-Shaʿrānī, *al-Ṭabaqāt al-kubrā*, 2:619. Additionally, al-Munāwī reproduces the second event with the exact response of al-Ghamrī that has been translated above, although here the student's name is reported to be Aḥmad al-Naḥḥāl. ʿAbd al-Raʾūf al-Munāwī, *al-Kawākib al-durriyya fī tarājim al-sāda al-ṣūfiyya*, ed. Muḥammad Adīb al-Jādir, 5 vols. (Beirut: Dār Ṣādir, 1999), 3:256–57. For more on the medieval Islamic understanding of the earth's seven climes, see Wadie Jwaideh, *The Introductory Chapters of Yāqūt's Muʿjam al-Buldān* (Leiden: Brill, 1959), 38ff, esp. note 2.

30. For al-Shaʿrānī's debt to al-Anṣārī in his legal training, see Muḥammad al-Malījī al-Shaʿrānī, *Manāqib al-quṭb al-rabbānī sayyidī ʿAbd al-Wahhāb al-Shaʿrānī* (Cairo: Dār al-Jūdiyya, 2005), 62–63; for his primary shaykhs in Sufism, see al-Malījī al-Shaʿrānī, *Manāqib al-Shaʿrānī*, 63–76; Michael Winter, *Society and Religion in Early Ottoman Egypt: Studies in the Writings of ʿAbd al-Wahhāb al-Shaʿrānī* (New Brunswick, NJ: Transaction Books, 1982), 56–58, and passim.

31. ʿAbd al-Wahhāb al-Shaʿrānī, *al-Anwār al-qudsiyya fī maʿrifat qawāʿid al-ṣūfiyya*, ed. Ṭāhā ʿAbd al-Bāqī Surūr and Muḥammad ʿĪd al-Shāfiʿī, 2 vols. (Cairo: al-Maktaba al-ʿIlmiyya, 1962), 1:49; al-Shaʿrānī, *al-Ṭabaqāt al-ṣughrā*, 45; al-Malījī al-Shaʿrānī, *Manāqib al-Shaʿrānī*, 77. For al-Shaʿrānī's *isnād*s to al-Anṣārī, see ʿAbd al-Ḥayy al-Kattānī, *Fihris al-fahāris wa-l-athbāt wa-muʿjam al-maʿājim wa-l-mashyakhāt wa-l-musalsalāt*, 3 vols. (Beirut: Dār al-Gharb al-Islāmī, 1982ff), 2:971, 1081.

shaykh Aḥmad al-Zāhid (d. 819/1416)[32] to the more obscure Ḥasan al-Tustarī (d 768/1367). Moving higher into the *isnād* we eventually reach the name of ʿUmar al-Suhrawardī (d. 632/1234), who thus would function as the eponym behind al-Anṣārī's otherwise unnamed Sufi order.[33] Nevertheless, for lack of any evidence to the contrary, al-Anṣārī appears uninterested in identifying himself with the name of any particular Sufi order.

By the end of his studies in both the internal and external disciplines, al-Anṣārī could boast in his *thabat* of having studied with the most celebrated Egyptian scholars from the ninth/fifteenth century. Al-Sakhāwī notes, however, that not all of al-Anṣārī's teachers played an equal role in his training, just as his scholarly proficiency and later output was not equal across the Islamic disciplines. Al-Sakhāwī is nevertheless quick to praise al-Anṣārī for his concern for public virtue, intellectual humility, austere self-discipline, and forbearance toward his students and the larger public—all of which he maintained throughout his career as chief justice that was to follow.[34] In fact, al-Sakhāwī presents al-Anṣārī as a genuinely agreeable figure who prayed for all and turned his back on none.[35] This reputation would no doubt smooth his path through the subsequent stage of his career.

Act II: From Obscurity to Prominence

In the year 850/1447, at the age of twenty-four, al-Anṣārī possessed the financial wherewithal to undertake the pilgrimage to Mecca. As was customary for scholars and students who could manage to do so, he remained for at least an additional year in "pious residency" (*mujāwara*) in Mecca

32. For Aḥmad al-Zāhid, who wrote both on law and Sufism like al-Anṣārī and al-Shaʿrānī, see al-Sakhāwī, *Ḍaw'*, 2:111–13; for al-Tustarī, see al-Shaʿrānī, *al-Ṭabaqāt al-kubrā*, 2:571–72.

33. Al-Shaʿrānī, *al-Anwār al-qudsiyya*, 1:49–50; al-Malījī al-Shaʿrānī, *Manāqib al-Shaʿrānī*, 77–78. Using manuscripts of later Sufi lineages, Éric Geoffroy also classifies al-Anṣārī's *isnād* from al-Ghamrī as a Suhrawardī genealogy. Éric Geoffroy, *Le soufisme en Égypte et en Syrie sous les derniers Mamelouks et les premiers Ottomans: Orientations spirituelles et enjeux culturels* (Damascus: Institut français de Damas, 1995), 23, 213, and 517 (Annexe III:2).

34. Al-Sakhāwī, *Ḍaw'*, 3:236; al-Sakhāwī, *Rafʿ*, 144–45.

35. Al-Sakhāwī, *Rafʿ*, 146; al-Sakhāwī, *Ḍaw'*, 3:237.

and Medina, where he met and studied under scholars who hailed from across the lands of Islamdom.[36] The exact source of his money for this trip is not known, but it was also around this same time that his career as a salaried teacher appears to have begun. Al-Sakhāwī, for example, records that al-Anṣārī began to teach while several of his own shaykhs were still living. Furthermore, he was sought out for fatwas, though in a criticism that is mentioned in passing, al-Sakhāwī notes that many of these fatwas were disputed by al-Anṣārī's teachers.[37]

After his return from Mecca, and most likely around the year 852/1448–49, al-Anṣārī was offered the position of imam at the Zayniyya-Ustādāriyya School. The construction of the school had just been completed in Būlāq, and the imam position provided its holder with housing within the building. Despite the attractiveness of the offer, al-Anṣārī wavered in his decision. He consulted his teacher al-Qāyātī, who encouraged him to accept it at once. Before he could do so, however, a friend and colleague named al-Shihāb al-Zawāwī (d. 852/1448),[38] apparently unaware of al-Anṣārī's intentions, approached al-Anṣārī and asked him to intercede with al-Qāyātī in order to secure his own appointment to the post by speaking with the waqf's founder. Rather than inform al-Zawāwī of his own intentions, al-Anṣārī took his friend at once to al-Qāyātī, who in turn agreed to the change but did in fact apprise al-Zawāwī of al-Anṣārī's own appointment to the post. Neither scholar was fated to live in the school, however, as Ibn Ḥajar al-ʿAsqalānī used his influence to appoint a figure named al-Shihāb b. Asad (d. 872/1468) to the position when the other parties failed to make a prompt decision. Nevertheless, al-Sakhāwī's tone and the context of the story suggest that al-Anṣārī's behavior greatly impressed him.[39]

36. Al-Sakhāwī, *Ḍawʾ*, 3:235; al-Sakhāwī, *Rafʿ*, 144. Al-Anṣārī took hadith *ijāza*s from al-Sharaf Abū l-Fatḥ al-Marāghī, al-Taqī b. Fahd, and the two judges Abū l-Yamīn al-Nuwayrī and Abū l-Saʿādāt b. Ẓahīra, among others. Al-Anṣārī also appears to have taken an *ijāza* in the complete works of Ibn ʿArabī from al-Marāghī. Al-Kattānī, *Fihris al-fahāris*, 1:319. ʿAbd al-Raḥmān b. Muḥammad al-Awjāqī (d. 910/1504) says that he and "his friend" al-Anṣārī heard their first hadith from al-Marāghī together in the Grand Mosque of Mecca. N. al-Ghazzī, *Kawākib*, 1:234.

37. Al-Sakhāwī, *Ḍawʾ*, 3:236; al-Sakhāwī, *Rafʿ*, 144–45.

38. Aḥmad b. Sulaymān b. Naṣr Allāh; he was given *ijāza* by al-Qāyātī in 848/1444–45. Al-Sakhāwī, *Ḍawʾ*, 1:310–11.

39. Al-Sakhāwī, *Ḍawʾ*, 3:237. For the date of 852/1448–49, Ibn Taghrībirdī records the opening of the Zayniyya as occurring in 853, however both al-Zawāwī and Ibn Ḥajar

Al-Anṣārī was to suffer other career setbacks soon after the Zayniyya incident. At the end of 852/beginning of 1449, the great Ibn Ḥajar passed away, and al-Anṣārī sought to fill his vacancy as the chief librarian (*khāzin al-kutub*) of the enormous Maḥmūdiyya collection.[40] A sinister figure named al-Naḥḥās (d. 864/1459), however, quickly seized on this post and passed it to his friend al-Turaykī (d. 894/1489).[41] Al-Anṣārī subsequently sought a position as deputy librarian and teaching assistant (*muʿīd*) at the Mosque of al-Ẓāhir,[42] but Burhān al-Dīn al-Biqāʿī (d. 885/1480)—about whom more will be said below—took over the administration of this post, and al-Anṣārī lost interest in it.[43]

It was soon after this event that al-Anṣārī's fortunes began to change. We learn from al-Sakhāwī that al-Anṣārī was appointed to the position of "shaykh of *taṣawwuf*" at the newly constructed Mosque of al-ʿAlam b. al-Jīʿān upon its opening, and he would secure a similar position at the Mosque of al-Ṭawāshī ʿAlam Dār at around the same time.[44] The exact nature of

---

died in the final months of 852. If we accept Ibn Taghrībirdī's dating then we must assume that the appointment process began in the year preceding the actual opening of the school. Shihāb b. Asad's appointment may have also followed al-Zawāwī's death, which came two months before that of Ibn Ḥajar. Yūsuf Ibn Taghrībirdī, *al-Nujūm al-zāhira fī mulūk Miṣr wa-l-Qāhira*, 16 vols. (Cairo: al-Muʾassasa al-Miṣriyya al-ʿĀmma, 1963ff), 15:405. For al-Shihāb b. Asad and Ibn Ḥajar's role in the Zayniyya appointment, see al-Sakhāwī, *Ḍawʾ*, 1:227–31.

40. Rosenthal notes that the Maḥmūdiyya collection held approximately four thousand valuable manuscripts. *Encyclopaedia of Islam*, s.v. "Ibn Ḥadjar" (Franz Rosenthal). For more on the library and its later position as a source of conflict between the Ḥanafī and Shāfiʿī chief justices, see Hirschler, *Written Word*, 132–33, 137, 138, 144, 158n18. For the job of *khāzin al-kutub*, which was often a part-time position that provided only a modest salary, see Hirschler, *Written Word*, 137; Amīn, *al-Awqāf*, 255–59; Carl F. Petry, "Some Observations on the Position of the Librarian in the Scholarly Establishment of Cairo during the Later Middle Ages," *MELA Notes* 2 (1974).

41. Al-Sakhāwī, *Ḍawʾ*, 3:237. For al-Naḥḥās, see 7:63–66. The Maḥmūdiyya incident is briefly repeated in al-Sakhāwī's biography of al-Turaykī at 6:286–87.

42. Both Makdisi and Amīn consider the *muʿīd* little more than an advanced student. Makdisi, *Rise of Colleges*, 193–95; Amīn, *al-Awqāf*, 145–46.

43. Al-Sakhāwī, *Ḍawʾ*, 3:237.

44. Al-Sakhāwī, *Ḍawʾ*, 3:237; al-Sakhāwī, *Rafʿ*, 146–47. None of the primary sources specifies the completion date of Ibn al-Jīʿān's mosque, which is no longer standing. ʿAlī Pāshā Mubārak, *al-Khiṭaṭ al-tawfīqiyya al-jadīda*, 20 vols. (Cairo: Maṭbaʿat Dār al-Kutub, 2005ff), 3:72–73. Al-Sakhāwī notes that al-Anṣārī was replacing the adopted

al-Anṣārī's responsibilities cannot be known without access to the waqf deeds of the two mosques, but in general, such an appointment would demand both external piety and strong managerial skills from its holder, as the shaykh of *taṣawwuf* was responsible for coordinating the devotional activities of professional Sufis, the number of whom might reach upward of several hundred.[45]

Around this time as well, in the year 861/1457, al-Anṣārī's son Muḥammad was born in the Darb Qarājā area near al-Azhar, which we can assume was the neighborhood of his parents' home at that point. Having interacted with Muḥammad extensively during their pilgrimage together in 897/1492,[46] al-Sakhāwī reports that the boy grew up in his parents' household and would ultimately pursue a scholarly career like his father. More will be said about al-Anṣārī's children below, but for now it is worth noting that very little is known about al-Anṣārī's wife or the couple's marriage and its date. Al-Sakhāwī makes several references to persons with the family name "al-Nashīlī" who are in-laws (*aṣhār*) of al-Anṣārī through his wife.[47] In fact, al-Sakhāwī paints one such figure named Aḥmad b. Sulṭān al-Nashīlī as a shameless opportunist who would exploit the connections of his in-law for his own material gains.[48] We further learn that the Nashīlī family is of Kurdish origins and descends from the progeny of Khalīl al-Nashīlī, a companion of the famous Shādhilī master Abū l-ʿAbbās al-Mursī (d. 686/1287). Another Nashīlī is affiliated with the Mosque of al-Ghamrī, while the biographies of a few others suggest scholarly inclinations and connections to al-Azhar.[49]

son (*rabīb*, according to the more credible wording in *Rafʿ*) of his shaykh Abū l-Jūd for the ʿAlam Dār position. This latter figure died in 863/1459, but there is nothing to correlate his death with al-Anṣārī's appointment. For his biography, see al-Sakhāwī, *Ḍawʾ*, 3:211–12. For Ibn al-Jīʿān, who appointed al-Anṣārī to the position at his mosque, see 3:291–92.

45. Amīn, *al-Awqāf*, 207–13.

46. Al-Sakhāwī, *Ḍawʾ*, 7:244–55.

47. For the al-Nashīlī family and the only explicit information on al-Anṣārī's wife, see al-Sakhāwī, *Ḍawʾ*, 11:231. For an unknown reason, al-Sakhāwī refers to her as "the wife of al-Shāfiʿī" (*zawjat al-Shāfiʿī*) and records her father's name as Ibrāhīm.

48. Al-Sakhāwī, *Ḍawʾ*, 1:307.

49. Al-Sakhāwī, *Ḍawʾ*, 11:231; al-Shaʿrānī, *al-Ṭabaqāt al-kubrā*, 2:731–32; N. al-Ghazzī, *Kawākib*, 2:152. For an example of Nashīlīs with scholarly inclinations, see the references to Aḥmad b. ʿUmar b. Muḥammad in al-Sakhāwī, *Ḍawʾ*, 2:57, 4:341, 6:261, 9:177, and

The information available shows how al-Anṣārī's social circles may have overlapped with those of his wife's family, but nothing more definitive about her than this can be said.

It was also during these early years of his scholarly career that al-Anṣārī began to produce texts in a variety of scholarly disciplines, while he would continue to revise and teach many of these texts until the very end of his life. However, as he would reveal to his student al-Shaʿrānī many decades later, not all of his early attempts at scholarly production were well received by his peers. For example, after completing his commentary on *al-Bahja al-Wardiyya* (*The Wardian Splendor*), a didactic poem in Shāfiʿī law by Ibn al-Wardī (d. 749/1349),[50] some of al-Anṣārī's scholarly peers were overcome by jealousy and changed the title of his text to "The Commentary of the Blind Man and the Sighted Man." What they implied through their prank was that al-Anṣārī was incapable of producing a commentary on his own but rather required the assistance of his blind friend ʿAlī al-Nabatītī (d. 917/1512). Al-Anṣārī, for his part, appears to have been emotionally scarred by the event, as is evidenced in his bittersweet tone when telling al-Shaʿrānī about it fifty years later.[51] Nevertheless, he remained undeterred in his work ethic, while his productivity was built upon an austere daily schedule. Al-Anṣārī, for example, would allow himself but one swim in the Nile each year so as "not to lose the taste for it." With his first generation

passim. The figure "Asad al-Basīlī" who is mentioned as another in-law of al-Anṣārī (at 2:279) is most likely a misreading of Asad al-Nashīlī, which would conform with the information at 11:231.

50. The *Bahja* is didactic-verse rendering of al-Qazwīnī's (d. 665/1266) *al-Ḥāwī al-ṣaghīr*. Having completed a draft of the text in the summer of 867/1463, al-Anṣārī would revise his commentary on the *Bahja* (titled *al-Ghurar al-bahiyya*) throughout the remainder of his life. Zakariyyā al-Anṣārī, *al-Ghurar al-bahiyya fī sharḥ al-Bahja al-Wardiyya*, 5 vols. (Cairo: al-Maṭbaʿa al-Maymaniyya, n. d.), 5:334. A holograph manuscript of the text exists in the Chester Beatty Library. Arthur J. Arberry, *The Chester Beatty Library: A Handlist of the Arabic Manuscripts*, 8 vols. (Dublin: Hodges Figgis, 1956), 2:80 (MS 3432), and plate 56.

51. Al-Shaʿrānī, *al-Ṭabaqāt al-kubrā*, 2:689–90; al-Shaʿrānī, *al-Ṭabaqāt al-ṣughrā*, 39–40; N. al-Ghazzī, *Kawākib*, 1:198. For identifying al-Nabatītī with the otherwise anonymous blind man, see al-Munāwī, *al-Kawākib al-durriyya*, 3:423; N. al-Ghazzī, *Kawākib*, 1:281. Al-Shaʿrānī elsewhere records that he would meet al-Nabatītī many times at al-Anṣārī's house. Al-Shaʿrānī, *al-Ṭabaqāt al-kubrā*, 2:693–94. For more on his biography, see al-Sakhāwī, *Ḍawʾ*, 5:268.

of students, however, he would assuage their restlessness by occasionally relocating their lessons to a nearby pond. In this act we catch a glimpse of the paternal qualities that so many of al-Anṣārī's students would later recall fondly in their teacher.[52]

In Ramaḍān 865/July 1461, al-Ẓāhir Khushqadam (r. to 872/1467) ascended to the Mamlūk sultanate, and al-Anṣārī's fortunes were soon to improve. According to al-Shaʿrānī's account, the new sultan attempted to visit a well-known saint in the city. Instead of receiving the sultan, however, this anonymous figure referred him to al-Anṣārī for all of his needs, which were presumably of a spiritual nature. The sultan took the saint's advice, and from that point forward al-Anṣārī's name became synonymous with righteousness and the common folk began to flock to him.[53] Then, in 866/1461, only a few months after this incident, the sultan appointed al-Anṣārī to the head teaching post of his newly opened mausoleum (*turba*) in the nearby desert.[54]

Al-Anṣārī's career would progress rapidly over the subsequent decade, and the sources suggest that the quality of his scholarship improved as well. At the same time, his advancement roused the envy of many colleagues, though al-Sakhāwī does note that al-Anṣārī always possessed an uncanny ability to greet his enemies with civility.[55] Finally in the year 871/1466, Sultan Khushqadam requested that al-Anṣārī assume the chief Shāfiʿī justiceship (*qāḍī l-quḍāt*) after dismissing the previous appointee. As he reports autobiographically in a later hadith commentary, al-Anṣārī refused the sultan's request for nineteen days owing to the enormous responsibility of the post. During this time, Khushqadam would plead with the scholar,

52. Al-Shaʿrānī, *al-Ṭabaqāt al-ṣughrā*, 40.

53. Al-Shaʿrānī, *al-Ṭabaqāt al-ṣughrā*, 41; N. al-Ghazzī, *Kawākib*, 1:200–201. It was also during this same month of Ramaḍān that al-Anṣārī completed his commentary *al-Fatḥa al-unsiyya* in estate division. Zakariyyā al-Anṣārī, *al-Fatḥa al-unsiyya li-ghaliq al-Tuḥfa al-qudsiyya*, MS Laleli 297.4/01304-002, Istanbul, fol. 79r.

54. Al-Sakhāwī, *Ḍawʾ*, 3:237; al-Sakhāwī, *Rafʿ*, 147. Ibn Iyās records the opening date as Rabīʿ I 866/December 1461. Muḥammad b. Aḥmad Ibn Iyās, *Badāʾiʿ al-zuhūr fī waqāʾiʿ al-duhūr*, ed. Muḥammad Muṣṭafā, 7 vols. (Wiesbaden, Germany: F. Steiner Verlag, 1931ff), 2:390.

55. Al-Sakhāwī, *Ḍawʾ*, 3:237; al-Sakhāwī, *Rafʿ*, 147. For an example of the intrigues of jealous colleagues against al-Anṣārī during this time, see al-Sakhāwī, *Ḍawʾ*, 1:62.

even swearing to ride humbly before him all the way to his house.[56] In a corroborating narration reported by al-Shaʿrānī, when al-Anṣārī demurred in front of the sultan, the latter replied with a symbolic gesture of deference, "If you so wish, I'll come down [from the Citadel with you] and lead your mule on foot all the way to your home."[57] According to another source, however, al-Anṣārī chose to flee the scene rather than refuse the sultan's offer directly, and the chief Shāfiʿī justiceship remained unoccupied for twenty-seven days. He and another candidate were eventually brought before the sultan, and when both of them refused to accept the position, Khushqadam was forced to appoint a third party.[58] While it is difficult to uncover a definitive motive in al-Anṣārī's rejection of the offer, the chief justices were responsible for oversight of the city's waqfs, and the burden of this responsibility may have played a role in dissuading him just as it had dissuaded others before him. If this were in fact the case, then al-Anṣārī's fears were reasonable, as waqf difficulties would plague his judicial career in later years.[59]

In spite of his refusal, al-Anṣārī's reputation appears to have emerged unscathed from the incident, and he would soon earn the favor of the next sultan worthy of note: al-Ashraf Qāytbāy (r. 872–901/1468–95).[60] The new sultan appointed him to the primary teaching post at the Sābiqiyya School

56. Zakariyyā al-Anṣārī, *Fatḥ al-ʿallām bi-sharḥ al-Iʿlām bi-aḥādīth al-aḥkām* (Beirut: Dār al-Kutub al-ʿIlmiyya, 1990), 670–71, 689. The text was written in 910/1505, after the author's dismissal from the chief justiceship.

57. Al-Shaʿrānī, *al-Ṭabaqāt al-kubrā*, 2:690; al-Shaʿrānī, *al-Ṭabaqāt al-ṣughrā*, 41–42. The wording quoted here is from the *Kubrā*. The context of al-Shaʿrānī's narration suggests Qāytbāy as the sultan and not Khushqadam.

58. Aḥmad b. ʿAlī al-Maqrīzī, *al-Sulūk li-maʿrifat duwal al-mulūk*, ed. Muḥammad Muṣṭafā Ziyāda, 4 vols. in 12 bound sections (Cairo: Maṭbaʿat Dār al-Kutub wa-l-Wathāʾiq al-Qawmiyya bi-l-Qāhira, 2006–7), 3 (1):197–98. The event is recorded by a fourteenth-century copyist (*nāsikh*) and not al-Maqrīzī himself, who died twenty-four years before the event. For information on the MS that records this information, see page ط, MS "أ." For a less-detailed version of the story, see al-Sakhāwī, *Rafʿ*, 69–70.

59. For an example, see Amīn, *al-Awqāf*, 366. However, al-Anṣārī also records that assuming the post is a virtuous deed for he who is knowledgeable of its demands. Al-Anṣārī, *Fatḥ al-ʿallām*, 670.

60. The year 872/1467–68 would witness the advent of three new sultans after Khushqadam, the third of whom was Qāytbāy.

around Ramaḍān 873/April 1469, thereby giving al-Anṣārī preference over all others who had sought the position.[61] The Sābiqiyya post included an on-site apartment for its holder and his family; it stood as the most prestigious position yet to be held by al-Anṣārī.[62]

It is perhaps around this point in his career that al-Anṣārī, now well into his forties, began to lose sight of his humble origins. Only the critical eye of a friend could remind him of the merits of humility, and ironically it would take the eye of a blind man to do just that. According to what al-Anṣārī would tell al-Shaʿrānī years later, ʿAlī al-Nabatītī would regularly convene with the immortal Khiḍr and would ask the latter about the spiritual standing of various shaykhs and saints. When one day he asked about al-Anṣārī, Khiḍr replied enigmatically, "I have no objection to him, though he has one vanity" (*nufaysa*). When informed of this conversation, al-Anṣārī frantically took to self-scrutiny and begged his friend ʿAlī to ply Khiḍr for more detail. After nine grueling months, word finally came back to al-Anṣārī that his vanity was his insistence on referring to himself as "Shaykh Zakariyyā" in his correspondences with Mamlūk elites. From that day forward, al-Anṣārī insisted that all of his letters to notables be delivered on behalf of "Zakariyyā, the servant of the poor."[63]

In another story from the time of his Sābiqiyya days, al-Anṣārī joined a few other scholars in visiting the home of the famous miracle-worker Ibrāhīm al-Matbūlī (d. 877/1473). When al-Matbūlī split a watermelon and delivered it nonsequentially to the circle of scholars, he was quickly

---

61. Al-Sakhāwī, *Ḍaw'*, 3:237; al-Sakhāwī, *Rafʿ*, 147; ʿAlī b. Dāwūd al-Ṣayrafī, *Inbā' al-haṣr bi-abnā' al-ʿaṣr* (Cairo: Dār al-Fikr al-ʿArabī, 1970), 102–3. According to al-Sakhāwī, al-Anṣārī was hired to teach Shāfiʿī law. Al-Sakhāwī places his appointment after the death of Ibn al-Mulaqqin in 870/1466. Al-Sakhāwī, *Ḍaw'*, 4:101–2; Ibn Iyās, *Badā'iʿ*, 2:439. However, al-Ṣayrafī correctly records that the position was held temporarily by Kamāl al-Dīn al-Nuwayrī until his death at the end of Ramaḍān 873/ April 1469. One of al-Anṣārī's competitors for the post was al-Nuwayrī's friend Mithqāl al-Ẓāhirī Jaqmaq, who sought it for the free housing that it included. This latter figure may have served as the sultan's personal secretary (*al-nāẓir al-khāṣṣ*), though al-Sakhāwī's biography for him does not confirm this. Cf. al-Sakhāwī, *Ḍaw'*, 6:239.

62. On the school and the prestige of this position, see Carl F. Petry, "From Slaves to Benefactors: The Habashis of Mamluk Cairo," *Sudanic Africa* 5 (1994): 65–66; Hirschler, *Written Word*, 102–5; 119–21.

63. Al-Shaʿrānī, *al-Ṭabaqāt al-kubrā*, 2:601; al-Shaʿrānī, *al-Ṭabaqāt al-ṣughrā*, 43; N. al-Ghazzī, *Kawākib*, 1:201, 281–82. The wording here is taken from *al-Ṭabaqāt al-kubrā*. For Khiḍr, see *Encyclopaedia of Islam*, s.v. "al-Khaḍir" (A. J. Wensinck).

criticized for contravening the Sunna. Al-Anṣārī, however, silenced his colleagues for criticizing the saint, and only decades later it would become evident that al-Matbūlī had distributed the watermelon according to the sequence of the recipients' death dates.[64] As this story and the one before it illustrate, al-Anṣārī's scholarly advancement in the external sciences in no way implied his departure from a worldview steeped in the mystical realm. In fact, he frequently faced the disapproval of his scholarly colleagues for his misplaced loyalties to a world that was not fully quantifiable. As he would later tell al-Shaʿrānī when the latter faced disapproval from his own peers, "Even if belief [in the Sufis] holds no benefit, it does no harm."[65] Frustrated by this attitude, al-Sakhāwī writes about al-Anṣārī, "He is even one to glorify Ibn ʿArabī, believing him to be a saint (*walī*) and calling him such! I've rebuked him for this time and again, though he has not stopped but rather the eloquence of his words about this matter merely increased in the end."[66]

Al-Anṣārī's reputation as a Sufi scholar would also play a vital role in resolving the infamous Ibn al-Fāriḍ controversy that erupted in Cairo around the year 874/1469. Following a public reading of a commentary on Ibn al-Fāriḍ's (d. 632/1235) mystical poetry, the scholar Burhān al-Dīn al-Biqāʿī seized on the opportunity to foment a bitter theological split, which saw the poet's scholarly supporters pitted against those who accused him of monist (*al-ittiḥād*) and incarnationist (*al-ḥulūl*) beliefs. In retrospect, the Syrian al-Biqāʿī, who fell into the latter camp, exhibited poor judgment in attacking an Egyptian icon like Ibn al-Fāriḍ, whose poetry enjoyed the favor of many high-ranking Mamlūks, including the sultan himself.[67]

64. Al-Munāwī, *al-Kawākib al-durriyya*, 3:129. For al-Matbūlī, see Winter, *Society and Religion*, 95–97, and passim. For the death date recorded here, see ʿAbd al-Bāsiṭ Ibn Shāhīn, *Nayl al-amal fī dhayl al-Duwal*, ed. ʿUmar ʿAbd al-Salām Tadmurī, 9 vols. (Ṣaydā: al-Maktaba al-ʿAṣriyya, 2002), 7:67.

65. ʿAbd al-Wahhāb al-Shaʿrānī, *al-Anwār al-qudsiyya fī maʿrifat ādāb al-ʿubūdiyya* (hereafter *Maʿrifat ādāb al-ʿubūdiyya*), ed. Ramaḍān Basṭāwīsī Muḥammad (Cairo: al-Hayʾa al-Miṣriyya al-ʿĀmma li-l-Kitāb, 2007), 183.

66. Al-Sakhāwī, *Ḍawʾ*, 3:236; al-Sakhāwī, *Rafʿ*, 145–46. The wording here is taken from *Ḍawʾ*.

67. For more detail on the Ibn al-Fāriḍ controversy, see Th. Emil Homerin, *From Arab Poet to Muslim Saint: Ibn al-Fāriḍ, His Verse, and His Shrine* (Cairo: American University in Cairo Press, 2001), 60–75; Alexander Knysh, *Ibn ʿArabī in the Later Islamic Tradition* (Albany: State University of New York Press, 1999), 209–23.

Al-Anṣārī's role up to this point in the controversy is not clear. Worth noting in this context, however, is an unusual story that al-Anṣārī told to the historian al-Khaṭīb al-Ṣayrafī (d. 900–1/1495) that may have preceded the Biqāʿī incident or even materialized as a result of it. According to al-Anṣārī's account, the sultan's father-in-law, ʿAlī b. Khāṣṣ Bek, was riding toward al-Qarāfa when, in the distance in front of him, he saw a person of noble mien who was soon greeted by another figure of truly striking appearance. As ʿAlī watched, the two men spoke for a moment, after which time the second figure departed. ʿAlī approached and asked the remaining man about his mysterious companion. In astonishment, the man replied, "You don't know him?" and repeated this question three times for each time that ʿAlī confessed his ignorance. Finally, the man explained, "That was ʿUmar Ibn al-Fāriḍ! Every day he rises up from this area, seeking God's protection from those who would malign him."[68]

The story of Ibn al-Fāriḍ's ghost cannot be dated with any degree of precision, however, and in order to explain al-Anṣārī's involvement in the Biqāʿī controversy, we are left with a report that al-Anṣārī narrated to one of his student's toward the end of his life.[69] According to this narration, after the controversy had erupted, two members of the Mamlūk elite (*umarāʾ*) began to quarrel, as one considered Ibn al-Fāriḍ a saint and the other considered him an infidel. The one who considered him an infidel was the first to approach al-Anṣārī for a fatwa, while his written solicitation (*istiftāʾ*) was phrased in a manner that unequivocally condemned the poet. Citing the inherent danger in anathematizing a fellow Muslim, al-Anṣārī excused himself from issuing a fatwa in response to this solicitation. In turn, the other party took this as a sign of al-Anṣārī's support for Ibn al-Fāriḍ and similarly approached him with a solicitation that was phrased to leave little room for anything less than a declaration of the poet's sainthood. To this solicitation as well al-Anṣārī attempted to excuse himself, noting that it is also dangerous to declare someone a saint without perfect knowledge of

68. Al-Ṣayrafī, *Inbāʾ al-haṣr*, 190. Al-Ṣayrafī records the story when discussing events of the first month of 875/1470, though the dating of the story itself is not clear.

69. It was likely narrated in 921/1515–16, as the Syrian narrator Ibn al-Shammāʿ (d. 936/1529) first visited al-Anṣārī in that year, while the narration occurs as part of an introductory exchange between the student and his teacher, al-Anṣārī. ʿUmar b. Aḥmad Ibn al-Shammāʿ, *al-Qabas al-ḥāwī li-ghurar Ḍawʾ al-Sakhāwī*, ed. Ḥasan Ismāʿīl Marwa and Khaldūn Ḥasan Marwa, 2 vols. (Beirut: Dār Ṣādir, 1998), 1:285.

this person's actual standing before God. But this response did not satisfy his questioner, who left his fatwa solicitation with al-Anṣārī for further consideration.[70]

Ibn Iyās's detailed account of the Biqāʿī controversy and al-Anṣārī's role therein informs us that the latter questioner was in fact Sultan Qāytbāy's private secretary (*kātib al-sirr*), who was writing on behalf of the sultan himself.[71] Al-Anṣārī thus found himself in a precarious position indeed. He stalled for time for an unknown number of days. Then, after a Friday prayer at al-Azhar, he sought the counsel of an elder Syrian Sufi named Muḥammad al-Iṣṭanbūlī (d. 878/1474). Based on the little information about this latter figure that has reached us today, al-Iṣṭanbūlī had arrived in Cairo from Damascus ten years prior to the Ibn al-Fāriḍ controversy and took up residency near al-Azhar. Known for his piety, miracle working, and amiable disposition, al-Iṣṭanbūlī was popular in the eyes of both scholars and laypeople, and al-Sakhāwī records only words of praise for him.[72]

According to one narration of their meeting that Friday, before al-Anṣārī could utter a word, al-Iṣṭanbūlī interrupted, "Are we [Sufis] Muslims or not?"

"You are the best of Muslims!" al-Anṣārī replied.

"Then what is stopping you from writing?" he asked.

"I was [simply] waiting for this authorization." With that, al-Anṣārī would later explain, he was inspired with an epiphany (*fatḥ*) that allowed him to pen a mighty defense of Ibn al-Fāriḍ and his poetry.[73] According to al-Shaʿrānī's version of events,[74] al-Iṣṭanbūlī instructed al-Anṣārī with the words "Write it, and aid the Sufis" (*al-qawm*). In a third version of events recorded by al-Munāwī (d. 1031/1621) and presumably based on the words of his shaykh al-Shaʿrānī, al-Iṣṭanbūlī is reported to have chided, "Zakariyyā, we [Sufis] raised you from the dust (*al-arḍ*) to the heavens, and in spite

70. Muḥammad b. Ibrāhīm Ibn al-Ḥanbalī, *Durr al-ḥabab fī taʾrīkh aʿyān Ḥalab*, ed. Maḥmūd Muḥammad al-Fākhūrī and Yaḥyā Zakariyyā ʿIbāra, 2 vols. (Damascus: Wizārat al-Thaqāfa, 1972ff), 1:1015.

71. Ibn Iyās, *Badāʾiʿ*, 3:49. The event in its entirety, including a full reproduction of al-Anṣārī's fatwa, is described at 3:47–51. See also Homerin, *From Arab Poet to Muslim Saint*, 69–71.

72. Al-Sakhāwī, *Ḍawʾ*, 10:117–18; Ibn Shāhīn, *Nayl al-amal*, 7:95.

73. Al-Ḥanbalī, *Durr al-ḥabab*, 1:1016.

74. Al-Shaʿrānī, *al-Ṭabaqāt al-ṣughrā*, 38; N. al-Ghazzī, *Kawākib*, 1:203.

of this you still refrain from writing?!" Al-Anṣārī thus apologized for his behavior and commenced writing his fatwa at once.[75]

Picking up the story from there, Ibn Iyās records that al-Anṣārī soon released his famous fatwa in defense of a metaphorical interpretation of Ibn al-Fāriḍ's verse, thereby exonerating the poet from al-Biqāʿī's charges of incarnationism and monism. Like any of the exoteric disciplines, *taṣawwuf* too possessed a technical terminology (*alfāẓ iṣṭilāḥiyya*) of its own, argued al-Anṣārī, and it would be incorrect to pass judgment on the literal meanings of a Sufi's utterances as long as the arbiter remains outside of the Sufis' semiotic system. Meanwhile, the Sufis, for their part, are responsible for ensuring that their idiosyncratic vocabulary not fall on the ears of the uninitiated.[76]

While al-Anṣārī's fatwa and its later adaptation will be analyzed in more depth in chapter 5, it is worth noting here that the fatwa's censure of Ibn al-Fāriḍ's detractors is far from damning. In fact, Homerin points to the conciliatory tone of al-Anṣārī's words to suggest that al-Anṣārī was aware that his fatwa could lead to severe political consequences if it were not worded carefully.[77] In other words, were he to condemn Ibn al-Fāriḍ's opponents as infidels or heretics, al-Anṣārī might have provided the sultan with effective license to impose whatever punishment he desired on Ibn al-Fāriḍ's opponents, against whom he was already aligned.

Nevertheless, al-Anṣārī's fatwa set off a momentous series of events. For one reason or another, Ibn al-Fāriḍ's most outspoken detractors either fled the city into exile or suffered severe physical ailments, which many interpreted as a form of retribution that emanated from the unseen realm. Moreover, the event marks a clear turning point in al-Anṣārī's relation-

75. Al-Munāwī, *al-Kawākib al-durriyya*, 2:518. Al-Munāwī does not cite his source for the narration, and the context is incorrectly described as a controversy over Ibn ʿArabī and not Ibn al-Fāriḍ. For further analysis of this event, see Matthew B. Ingalls, "Between Center and Periphery: The Development of the Sufi Fatwa in Late-Medieval Egypt," in *Sufism and Society: Arrangements of the Mystical in the Muslim World, 1200–1800*, ed. John J. Curry and Erik S. Ohlander, 145–63 (London: Routledge, 2011), 152–54.

76. Ibn Iyās, *Badāʾiʿ*, 3:50; Homerin, *From Arab Poet to Muslim Saint*, 70–71. Because of the hermeneutical method employed in fatwas like this, al-Shaʿrānī would later cite al-Anṣārī the mufti par excellence in ruling on the affairs of the Sufis. Al-Shaʿrānī, *Maʿrifat ādāb al-ʿubūdiyya*, 203.

77. Homerin, *From Arab Poet to Muslim Saint*, 72.

ship with the sultan. In Ramaḍān 876/February 1472, approximately eighteen months after al-Anṣārī issued his fatwa,[78] the sultan ordered one thousand dinars to be distributed among the scholars, the righteous, and the poor. Al-Anṣārī appears as one of three recipients of the sultan's largess whose names are recorded, while another of the three is known to have similarly issued a fatwa in defense of Ibn al-Fāriḍ during the famous controversy.[79]

We also learn that around this same time al-Anṣārī was overheard speaking with the sultan and insisting that his son Muḥammad be granted certain employment bequests (*waṣāyā*), which would allow him to replace his father in a variety of paid appointments that the latter already held.[80] It is not clear when al-Anṣārī intended to transfer these appointments to Muḥammad, whether after his own death or following a partial retirement. Al-Sakhāwī records, in fact, that starting at some point around this period, Muḥammad would substitute for his father as shaykh of *taṣawwuf* at the mosque of Ibn al-Jīʿān.[81] Nevertheless, the sultan remained silent as al-Anṣārī petitioned him for an official transfer of his appointments to his son, as rumors had reached Qāytbāy that the adolescent Muḥammad remained deficient in knowledge and was certainly not appropriate for the more prestigious posts that his father sought for him.[82] In the end, however, the sultan agreed through a written decree that Muḥammad accede to the majority of his father's appointments at some undisclosed point in the future. Moreover, the sultan's private secretary, Zayn al-Dīn b. Muzhir (d. 893/1488), either on his own initiative or on behalf of the sultan, would

78. Ibn Iyās, *Badāʾiʿ*, 3:47ff. Cf. Homerin, *From Arab Poet to Muslim Saint*, 72 (referencing al-Ṣayrafī, *Inbāʾ al-haṣr*, 186–87).

79. Al-Ṣayrafī, *Inbāʾ al-haṣr*, 407. This latter person is Muḥyī l-Dīn al-Kāfiyājī (d. 879/1474). Ibn Iyās, *Badāʾiʿ*, 3:48. Both al-Ṣayrafī and Ibn Iyās record his name as al-Kāfijī, *pace* al-Sakhāwī at al-Sakhāwī, *Ḍawʾ*, 7:259–61.

80. Al-Ṣayrafī, *Inbāʿ al-haṣr*, 320, 448–49. Al-Ṣayrafī records the son's name as "Maḥmūd," though this is an obvious mistake. Coinciding with the funeral of a chief Ḥanafī justice, the event occurred at the beginning of 876/1471, approximately nine months prior to the distribution of the thousand dinars that has already been mentioned.

81. Al-Sakhāwī, *Ḍawʾ*, 7:244–55.

82. A-Anṣārī is reported to have also requested two teaching posts for his son that he himself did not already hold, namely one at the Mu'ayyidiyya School and another at the Mizdāda School.

bestow costly gifts on Muḥammad every year from that point forward and would later underwrite his first pilgrimage to Mecca in 882/1478.[83]

Al-Anṣārī appears to have maintained the sultan's good favor over the next five years, and toward the beginning of 881/middle of 1476, Qāytbāy appointed him to what was arguably the most prestigious academic position in all of Egypt at the time: the head teaching post (*mashyakhat al-dars*) at the Ṣāliḥiyya School next to the mausoleum of Imām al-Shāfiʿī himself. According to al-Sakhāwī's account of events, al-Anṣārī was offered the position without soliciting it and in spite of the pleading and bribery of so many of his competitors. After accepting the appointment, a large party of scholars, notables, and political elites formed at his home. Al-Anṣārī was then vested in a ceremonial green shawl, and the entire group formed a celebratory procession and marched to the mausoleum of al-Shāfiʿī.[84] Al-Anṣārī's teaching responsibilities began almost immediately after that, while according to al-ʿAlāʾī's estimates, his financial circumstances would improve drastically from this point forward. From the cumulative income of his various administrative posts, teaching positions, and properties, al-Anṣārī accrued approximately three thousand dirhams of income daily—an extravagant amount that, according to al-ʿAlāʾī, had not befallen his like before him.[85]

It was also around this time that the sultan first approached al-Anṣārī to assume oversight (*naẓar*) of his personal waqfs, and immediately after accepting this responsibility, al-Anṣārī instituted a renovation campaign on the most dilapidated and dysfunctional waqfs, while he simultaneously dismissed an untold number of waqf-stipend beneficiaries who had

83. Al-Ṣayrafī, *Inbāʾ al-haṣr*, 320, 448–49. Ibn Muzhir is also reported to have written letters of introduction for al-Anṣārī's son to the local rulers of the Ḥijāz in order to secure his patronage and perhaps employment. For Ibn Muzhir, see al-Sakhāwī, *Ḍawʾ*, 11:88–89.

84. Al-Sakhāwī, *Ḍawʾ*, 3:237; al-Sakhāwī, *Rafʿ*, 147–48; Ibn Iyās, *Badāʾiʿ*, 3:120.

85. N. al-Ghazzī, *Kawākib*, 1:199. Also noteworthy at this time is al-Anṣārī's completion of his commentary on the ascetic poem *al-Munfarija* in Dhū l-Ḥijja 881/March 1477, which he titled *al-Aḍwāʾ al-bahija*. Zakariyyā al-Anṣārī, *al-Aḍwāʾ al-bahija fī ibrāz daqāʾiq al-Munfarija*, MS al-Azhar 315938, Cairo, fol. 14v. Another commentary by al-Anṣārī in Shāfiʿī law titled *Fatḥ al-wahhāb bi-sharḥ Tanqīḥ al-lubāb* was also copied in this year, although it may have been drafted earlier. Arberry, *Handlist*, 7:36 (MS 5111). The text is discussed in more depth in chapter 4 below.

neglected their duties that were stipulated in the waqfs' deeds. Al-Anṣārī's decision here appears to have pleased few people other than the sultan, who subsequently assigned him oversight of the Qarāfa cemetery waqfs in their entirety. Marking this event as a key turning point in al-Anṣārī's rise to celebrity, al-Sakhāwī says that the general public now turned their sights on him whenever they wished to curry favor with the sultan.[86]

The generosity of an autocrat rarely comes without strings, however, and with each new appointment that he extended to the scholar, the sultan increased in his insistence that al-Anṣārī accept the one position that he had thus far managed to avoid: the chief Shāfiʿī justiceship. For his part, al-Anṣārī appears to have been genuinely averse to accepting the chief justiceship, while his son Muḥammad may have contributed to the career pressure that he now felt.[87] At the Ṣāliḥiyya School, Muḥammad would frequently supplement the lessons of his father and conduct classes on behalf of the latter, who was usually seated nearby. At the same time however, al-Anṣārī was growing increasingly anxious over his son's fate, as Muḥammad's wife had birthed several children who subsequently died in infancy.[88] It was in this context that al-Anṣārī attempted to impose an undisclosed list of "stipulations" on the sultan as the inevitability of the chief justiceship appointment grew increasingly apparent to him, and it is reasonable to infer that at least some of these stipulations concerned his son Muḥammad's career, which we know had preoccupied al-Anṣārī for some time already. In the end, the sultan would meet some of al-Anṣārī's stipulations, though we do not learn specifically what these were.[89] Nevertheless, if we accept the reading that I have presented here, then al-Anṣārī would ultimately accept the chief justiceship primarily in the interest of

86. Ibn Shāhīn, *Nayl al-amal*, 7:159; al-Sakhāwī, *Ḍawʾ*, 3:237–38; al-Sakhāwī, *Rafʿ*, 147–48. Read the *Ḍawʾ*'s wording *bi-asrihā* ("in their entirety") in place of *wa-bāsharahā* ("and he attended to them"), which appears in al-Sakhāwī's *Rafʿ*. On the Qarāfa burial grounds, see M. al-Ibrashy, "Cairo's Qarafa as Described in the *Ziyara* Literature," in *Le développement du soufisme en Egypte à l'époque mamelouke*, ed. Richard McGregor and Adam Sabra, 269–79 (Cairo: Institut français d'archéologie orientale, 2006), 269–70, 278–97.

87. Ibn Shāhīn, *Nayl al-amal*, 7:293; al-Sakhāwī, *Rafʿ*, 148–49; al-Sakhāwī, *Ḍawʾ*, 3:238.

88. Al-Sakhāwī, *Ḍawʾ*, 7:244–45.

89. Ibn Iyās, *Badāʾiʿ*, 3:183–84; Ibn Shāhīn, *Nayl al-amal*, 7:293. For a more opaque chronology of events, see al-Sakhāwī, *Ḍawʾ*, 3:238; al-Sakhāwī, *Rafʿ*, 148.

his son's career, or—in the caustic words of al-ʿAlāʾī—"in the interest of his own worldly benefits."[90]

On Tuesday, 3 Rajab 886/28 August 1481, several of the sultan's closest cabinet officials appeared at al-Anṣārī's door and requested his presence before the sultan to accept the chief Shāfiʿī justiceship.[91] According to al-Sakhāwī's wording, al-Anṣārī had no recourse to refuse the appointment, though there is little doubt that the events that day hardly came as a surprise but rather proceeded from multiple negotiation sessions with the sultan. The sixty-year-old al-Anṣārī was placed on a mule and escorted to the Mamlūk Citadel, where at around noontime that day the sultan conferred on him the highest Shāfiʿī judicial authority in the entire Mamlūk Sultanate.[92] A large celebratory procession of Mamlūk notables, judges, scholars, and students left from the Citadel and marched to the Ṣāliḥiyya School and then onto al-Anṣārī's home.[93] Riding in the midst of this fanfare and fleeting moment of exuberance, the new chief justice would thus begin the next chapter of his life.

---

90. N. al-Ghazzī, *Kawākib*, 1:200. Cf. Escovitz, "Lost Arabic Source," 516. Al-Ghazzī cautions, however, that al-Anṣārī had leveled a judgment against al-ʿAlāʾī, and the latter, though a student of al-Anṣārī, remained bitter over the matter.

91. Al-Anṣārī completed his commentary on al-Abharī's *Īsāghūjī* in Aristotelian logic on 25 Ramaḍān 885/28 November 1480, approximately nine months prior to his appointment as chief justice. Yūsuf b. Sālim al-Ḥifnī, *Ḥāshiyat al-shaykh al-Ḥifnī ʿalā Sharḥ Īsāghūjī* (Cairo: al-Maṭbaʿa al-ʿĀmira al-Sharafiyya, 1885), 63 (colophon).

92. Al-Sakhāwī, *Ḍawʾ*, 3:238; al-Sakhāwī, *Rafʿ*, 148–49; cf. Ibn Iyās, *Badāʾiʿ*, 3:183–84. Al-Anṣārī convinced the sultan not to issue an edict of sanction against the outgoing justice Aḥmad al-Asyūṭī (d. 891/1486). Al-Sakhāwī, *Ḍawʾ*, 1:210–13. On the jurisdiction of the chief justices under the Baḥrī Mamlūk sultans, see Joseph H. Escovitz, *The Office of Qāḍī al-Quḍāt in Cairo under the Baḥrī Mamlūks* (Berlin: Klaus Schwarz Verlag, 1984), 1–3, 20–29, and passim.

93. Al-Anṣārī would retain his living quarters at the Sābiqiyya School until at least the end of year 903/1498, though he appears to have continued living there until his death. Aḥmad b. Muḥammad Ibn al-Ḥimṣī, *Ḥawādith al-zamān wa-wafiyyāt al-shuyūkh wa-l-aqrān*, ed. ʿAbd al-ʿAzīz Fayyāḍ Ḥarfūsh (Beirut: Dār al-Nafāʾis, 2000), 278, 332. Later descriptions of landmarks near al-Anṣārī's home correspond to the location of the Sābiqiyya. Al-Shaʿrānī, *al-Ṭabaqāt al-ṣughrā*, 133–34; N. al-Ghazzī, *Kawākib*, 3:221. Al-Anṣārī's funeral procession would also begin from the school. Ibn Iyās, *Badāʾiʿ*, 5:371.

Act III: From Celebrity to Estrangement

According to al-Sakhāwī's appraisal, al-Anṣārī applied himself to the chief justiceship with integrity and impartiality, while he immediately set about appointing his most trustworthy students and colleagues to positions within his judicial cabinet. His student Jamāl al-Dīn al-Ṣānī (d. 931/1525) was assigned the post of *amīn al-ḥukm* (court trustee),[94] and was thus responsible for court documents, waqf records, and property and deposits in escrow. ʿAlāʾ al-Dīn al-Maḥallī al-Ḥanafī (d. 897/1492) was likewise made *naqīb al-ashrāf* (marshal of the affairs of the Prophet's descendants), while a member of al-Anṣārī's entourage (*jamāʿa*) named Shihāb al-Dīn al-Abshīhī (d. 892/1487) was appointed to oversee the activities of the new *amīn* and *naqīb*.[95] Once these high-level appointments were behind him, al-Anṣārī began to visit many of the city's assistant magistrates (*nawwāb*) and reinstated several of those who had been dismissed with the previous justice's cabinet.[96]

But political trouble was not to afford the new chief justice even a year's respite. Already by Rabīʿ II 887/May–June 1482 al-Anṣārī had waded into what would prove to be a protracted and ultimately fruitless clash with a Mamlūk emir. The details of the event are not clear from the sources,[97] but an unspecified waqf stood as the bone of contention between

94. For the biography of al-Jamāl ʿAbd al-Qādir al-Ṣānī, see al-Sakhāwī, *Ḍawʾ*, 4:265–66; al-Shaʿrānī, *al-Ṭabaqāt al-ṣughrā*, 58; N. al-Ghazzī, *Kawākib*, 1:252. Al-ʿAlāʾī describes al-Ṣānī in the latter source as extremely resourceful and competent; he was al-Anṣārī's right-hand man. On the *amīn al-ḥukm*, see Émil Tyan, "Judicial Organization," in *Law in the Middle East*, ed. M. Khadduri and H. Liebesny (Washington, DC: Middle East Institute, 1955), 256–57; Wael B. Hallaq, *The Origins and Evolution of Islamic Law* (Cambridge: Cambridge University Press, 2005), 207; Adam Sabra, *Poverty and Charity in Medieval Islam* (Cambridge: Cambridge University Press, 2000), 62.

95. Al-Sakhāwī, *Ḍawʾ*, 3:238; al-Sakhāwī, *Rafʿ*, 149. For al-Ḥanafī's biography, see al-Sakhāwī, *Ḍawʾ*, 5:301–2; for al-Abshīhī's biography, see 2:143–44; Ibn Iyās, *Badāʾiʿ*, 3:245.

96. Al-Sakhāwī, *Rafʿ*, 149. For al-Anṣārī's theory on magistrates and the degrees of autonomy that they can be given, see al-Anṣārī, *Asnā l-maṭālib*, 6:281.

97. Ibn Iyās, *Badāʾiʿ*, 3:193. For the biography of Dūlāt Bāy al-Ḥasanī, the emir involved in the dispute, see al-Sakhāwī, *Ḍawʾ*, 3:221.

the two men. Ibn Iyās notes that news of the dispute reached the ears of the Egyptian populace, while it was only a few months after this when al-Anṣārī would experience his first taste of true public scorn. In accordance with Mamlūk custom, the four chief justices had assembled at the Citadel to sight the new moon and confirm the advent of the holy month of Dhū l-Ḥijja. Perhaps signaling the beginning of his eyesight troubles that would ultimately leave him blind, al-Anṣārī differed with his colleagues over the sighting of the new moon, and the justices' failure to reach a consensus caused Egypt's Muslims to miss both the supererogatory fast on the Day of ʿArafa and the communal litanies (*takbīrāt*) that precede the next day's ʿĪd prayer. The news quickly spread that al-Anṣārī was responsible for this confusion, and his stubbornness would earn him both the curses of the pious and the outrage of Qāytbāy. Rumors even circulated that the sultan had dismissed him from the justiceship, though nothing of the sort appears to have happened.[98]

Then, only a few months later, another scandal would further tarnish al-Anṣārī's reputation in the sight of the Egyptian public. An unnamed litigant refused to submit to al-Anṣārī's judgment against him in a lawsuit. Al-Anṣārī ordered that he be arrested and, upon deeming him legally insane, committed him to an asylum, where he would die in Shawwāl 888/ November 1483. This tragic turn of events roused the emotions of the deceased's family and supporters to a degree that was extreme by Mamlūk standards, according to al-Sakhāwī, though he does not elaborate further on what he means by this.[99]

It was also within these early years of his chief justiceship that al-Anṣārī's waqf troubles were to begin.[100] Since the time of Sultan Baybars

98. Ibn Iyās, *Badāʾiʿ*, 3:198.

99. Aḥmad b. Muḥammad al-Ḥaṣkafī, *Mutʿat al-adhhān min al-Tamattuʿ bi-l-aqrān*, 2 vols. (Beirut: Dār Ṣādir, 1999), 1:363; al-Sakhāwī, *Rafʿ*, 150. For the latter, read "he punished a person" (*wa-qad ʿazzara shakhṣ^{an}*) for "he deceived a person" (*wa-qad gharrara* [*sic*] *shakhṣ^{an}*). Cf. Carl Brockelmann, *Geschichte der arabischen Litteratur*, 5 vols. (Leiden: Brill, 1932–49), 2:99, where the scandal is mistakenly correlated with al-Anṣārī's dismissal from the justiceship. Al-Ḥaṣkafī similarly correlates the next incident in al-Anṣārī's career with his dismissal, though this too is incorrect. Al-Ḥaṣkafī, *Mutʿat al-adhhān*, 1:363.

100. Also worthy of note is al-Anṣārī's gifting of one thousand dirhams to a person named ʿAlī b. Muḥammad b. Aḥmad toward the end of 890/1485. Al-Sakhāwī reports

(r. 658–75/1260–77), the chief Shāfiʿī justice held exclusive oversight over the waqfs of the two Holy Sanctuaries (*al-ḥaramayn*), while a Mamlūk citizen of particular integrity would be chosen annually to lead a caravan to the Ḥijāz to pay the stipends that were owed to the waqfs' beneficiaries. By the early ninth/fifteenth century, the corruption and ineptitude of earlier justices had bankrupted the balance sheets of the Ḥaramayn waqfs. In order to supplement the income of these waqfs to meet their payroll liabilities, a tax had been levied on the magistrates of each Mamlūk district, though not all districts paid their tax in full, while others made no payments whatsoever.[101] Al-Anṣārī thus inherited a dysfunctional post when he assumed oversight of the Ḥaramayn waqfs. Al-Sakhāwī records that in every year of his justiceship al-Anṣārī forwarded incomplete stipends to the waqfs' beneficiaries. Meanwhile, he attempted a restructuring of the waqfs' balance sheets in order to equalize all stipends that were owed. Not only did it fail to balance the Ḥaramayn accounts, this attempt at reform also alienated many influential beneficiaries who were better off under the old system, and resentment toward al-Anṣārī grew and cut across multiple Mamlūk demographics.[102]

Meanwhile in Egypt, at around this same time, al-Anṣārī similarly initiated a renovation campaign on those waqfs that fell under his jurisdiction that were either in arrears or physically dilapidated. From many waqf payrolls he purged the names of those beneficiaries who had failed to uphold the duties that were stipulated by their waqf's deed or who were absent from their posts for a certain period of time. As might have been anticipated, this move stirred the anger of many Egyptians who now faced either an unexpected loss of income or complete unemployment.[103]

that this latter figure was a Sufi whose relationship with al-Anṣārī was based on their mutual love for Ibn ʿArabī. Al-Sakhāwī, *Ḍaw'*, 5:289.

101. Aḥmad b. ʿAlī al-Maqrīzī, *al-Mawāʿẓ wa-l-iʿtibār bi-dhikr al-khiṭaṭ wa-l-āthār*, 2 vols. (Cairo: Maktabat al-Thaqāfa al-Dīniyya, n. d.), 2:295–96; Amīn, *al-Awqāf*, 113; Ibn Ḥajar al-ʿAsqalānī, *Rafʿ al-iṣr ʿan quḍāt Miṣr*, ed. Ḥāmid ʿAbd al-Majīd et al., 2 vols. (Cairo: al-Maṭbaʿa al-Amīriyya, 1957–61), 2:258–59.

102. Al-Sakhāwī, *Rafʿ*, 149; al-Ḥaṣkafī, *Mutʿat al-adhhān*, 1:363. A chief Shāfiʿī justice prior to al-Anṣārī had faced similar troubles when he attempted to restructure the balance sheets of the Ibn Ṭūlūn Mosque waqf. Hirschler, *Written Word*, 106–8.

103. Ibn al-Shammāʿ, *al-Qabas al-ḥāwī*, 1:284; al-Sakhāwī, *Ḍaw'*, 3:237–38; al-Sakhāwī, *Rafʿ*, 149. Al-Sakhāwī's accounts suggest that al-Anṣārī had initiated similar reforms

More controversial than these purges, however, were al-Anṣārī's physical renovations of dilapidated waqfs. As Amīn explains, the administrator (*mubāshir*) of a waqf property was often not a beneficiary (*mustaḥiqq*) of a waqf stipend, and thus many waqf deeds failed to provide their administrators with any financial incentive to maintain the buildings and agricultural lands that were tied to their waqfs. It is therefore unsurprising that so many waqf properties fell into disrepair in the later Islamic middle period.[104] In response to this situation, al-Anṣārī set about rebuilding many moribund waqf properties that had been neglected by their previous administrators, and al-Sakhāwī admits, in an otherwise negative assessment of this rebuilding initiative, that al-Anṣārī's intentions here were noble.[105]

Nevertheless, it remains clear from the historical record that many aspects of al-Anṣārī's initiative were unprecedented in their time. The chronicler al-Buṣrawī (d. 905/1500), for example, records a fatwa on this matter that Burhān al-Dīn Ibn Abī Sharīf (d. 923/1517) had repeated to him in Damascus in 901/1495.[106] A friend and colleague of al-Anṣārī, Ibn Abī Sharīf had recently been asked in Cairo about al-Anṣārī's decision to renovate a waqf property that was situated among houses that were dilapidated and uninhabitable: Should the waqf be renovated using its own revenues or not when there was no benefit in renovating it, as the entire area in which it existed had been deserted? To the agreement of al-Buṣrawī and an earlier group of supporters in Cairo, Ibn Abī Sharīf responded in his fatwa that the renovation should cease, though al-Buṣrawī is also quick to include in his report that al-Anṣārī paid little heed to the fatwa and continued with his project.[107] Moreover, that Ibn Abī Sharīf's fatwa postdates al-Sakhāwī's account of the renovation initiative by over a decade and yet was still issued in response to current events suggests that al-Anṣārī continued to renovate

while serving as a waqf administrator before his justiceship.

104. Amīn, *al-Awqāf,* 284–85, and passim. Amin also discusses other causes of waqf decay during the Mamlūk period in chapter 7 of his text.

105. Al-Sakhāwī, *Raf*ʿ, 149.

106. For Ibn Abī Sharīf's biography, see al-Munāwī, *al-Kawākib al-durriyya*, 3:308–12; al-Sakhāwī, *Ḍaw'*, 1:134–36.

107. ʿAlī b. Yūsuf al-Buṣrawī, *Ta'rīkh al-Buṣrawī* (Beirut: Dār al-Ma'mūn li-l-Turāth, 1988), 168.

waqfs for many years in spite of public outcry and the sultan's sanctions, which are discussed in more depth below.

It is constructive here to compare al-Sakhāwī's two biographies for al-Anṣārī, as the biography in his *Rafʿ al-iṣr* appears to have been recorded at the onset of al-Anṣārī's waqf difficulties, while the other in *al-Ḍawʾ al-lāmiʿ* records an ex post facto appraisal of the events in a more caustic tone. Both biographies indicate that al-Anṣārī's waqf difficulties sprang from the officers he had delegated and his obliviousness to their activities. Al-Sakhāwī also describes al-Anṣārī's advisor on the renovation project as foolish, and his public spokesman as dishonorable.[108] In addition to renovating waqfs, al-Anṣārī may have attempted to equalize waqf stipend payments as he had done with the Ḥaramayn waqfs, though al-Sakhāwī's wording here is not conclusive.[109] What is clear is that once al-Anṣārī's waqf renovation project began, many waqf beneficiaries stopped receiving their usual stipends, and their resentment toward al-Anṣārī quickly boiled over. In his final analysis of events, al-Sakhāwī ascribes blame equally to the sultan for his imperiousness, al-Anṣārī's officers for their ineptitude, al-Anṣārī himself for his naivety, and the waqf beneficiaries for their agitating.[110]

Matters would deteriorate when news of the controversy reached the ears of al-Anṣārī's jealous peers. In several biographies of his *Ḍawʾ*, al-Sakhāwī describes a scholarly conspiracy that was mounted against al-Anṣārī and his men and was led by a figure named Abū l-Barakāt al-Ṣāliḥī (d. 896/1491), a scholar and gifted bureaucrat who had earlier sought employment in al-Anṣārī's cabinet but was met only with rejection and teasing from other members of that cabinet. Al-Sakhāwī plots this campaign against al-Anṣārī as the event that would precipitate a tragic conclusion to al-Ṣāliḥī's otherwise impressive life.[111] Nevertheless, although it is not clear that al-Ṣāliḥī

108. Al-Sakhāwī, *Ḍawʾ*, 3:238. Also see 1:161–63 for the biography of Burhān al-Dīn al-Maghribī (d. 896/1490), who may be al-Anṣārī's public spokesman, although al-Sakhāwī's language remains inconclusive.

109. Al-Sakhāwī, *Rafʿ*, 149. For a clearer indication that al-Anṣārī attempted to equalize stipend payments in Cairo, see al-Sakhāwī, *Ḍawʾ*, 1:213.

110. Al-Sakhāwī, *Ḍawʾ*, 3:238.

111. Al-Sakhāwī, *Ḍawʾ*, 9:69; Ibn Iyās, *Badāʾiʿ*, 3:282–83. Years later, al-Anṣārī would report to his student al-Shaʿrānī that envy was what motivated the conspiracy against

was its author, a tract titled "Backbiting in the Lessons of the Righteous" (*Al-Ghība fī durūs al-ṣāliḥīn*) was spread within the city, and soon thereafter public opinion in Egypt would shift against al-Anṣārī in favor of his accusers.[112] Appearing as an oblique critique of al-Anṣārī's handling of these events, al-Sakhāwī includes in his account the sentence "It was even said that al-Anṣārī's management was a tribulation for the waqf beneficiaries, and his obliviousness to his own conduct toward these fellow Muslims was an affliction." What was once popular admiration toward him, the author explains, quickly transformed into enmity, and the Egyptian masses began to pray to God that al-Anṣārī be removed from his waqf oversight responsibilities.[113]

In public and private meetings with his critics and the sultan, al-Anṣārī desperately tried to exonerate himself and his men, but al-Sakhāwī explains that his defense was weak because it was based in a misinformed understanding of reality.[114] The crisis persisted for several years. Then, at the dawn of Rajab 892/late June 1487, when the four chief justices had assembled at the sultan's court to welcome in the new Islamic month, Qāytbāy ordered

him. Al-Shaʿrānī, *al-Ṭabaqāt al-kubrā*, 2:691. Al-Sakhāwī provides a few vague details on other figures involved in the conspiracy against al-Anṣārī and his men: a man named ʿAlī al-Sijīnī is cited as the figure who raised a case against al-Anṣārī as he would do against another group of waqf administrators a few years later in 896/1490–91. Al-Sakhāwī, *Ḍaw'*, 11:206, also 156. He is referred to in passing as "ʿAlī the plaintiff" (*al-murāfiʿ*) at 5:103. From al-Anṣārī's side, a man named Jamāl al-Dīn al-Ẓāhirī is mentioned as the leader of the Ḥaramayn caravan who would grow anxious with the sultan's writ against al-Anṣārī's men, as rumors had circulated that he had absconded with the property of orphans. 5:47–48. The name of Ibn al-ʿAkam (d. 893/1488) is recorded as another of al-Anṣārī's men who was included in the sultan's writ (1:325).

112. Al-Sakhāwī, *Rafʿ*, 149. Also see al-Haytamī (*al-Fatāwā al-ḥadīthiyya*, 51) for a reference to a student who may have participated in this conspiracy against al-Anṣārī.

113. Al-Sakhāwī, *Ḍaw'*, 3:238. In his commentary on the text quoted here, Maḥmūd Rizq Salīm objects to al-Sakhāwī's insertion of "Muslims" (or "his fellow Muslims," as I have translated it), as it adds a shrill and unfair tone to the passage. Maḥmūd Rizq Salīm, *ʿAṣr salāṭīn al-mamālīk wa-natājuh al-ʿilmī wa-l-adabī*, 8 vols. (Cairo: Maktabat al-Ādāb, 1947ff), 3:393.

114. Al-Sakhāwī, *Ḍaw'*, 3:238; cf. al-Sakhāwī, *Rafʿ*, 149. In the latter source (line 12), read "*siyyamā al-sulṭān*" (the sultan was especially [angry at him]) for "*siyyamā ibn al-sulṭān*" (the sultan's son), as the latter figure would have only been a toddler at the time of the event.

the arrest of al-Anṣārī's *amīn* Jamāl al-Dīn al-Ṣānī, his *naqīb* 'Alā' al-Dīn al-Ḥanafī, and several of his revenue officers (*jubāt*).[115] Unnamed persons within the group of arrestees were subsequently flogged.[116] Moreover, the entire group was placed under *tarsīm* (a writ of sequestration and sanction),[117] while for his part, al-Anṣārī was relieved of his oversight of the Qarāfa waqfs.[118] A month after this event, a rumor would reach Damascus that al-Anṣārī had been dismissed from his justiceship and placed under *tarsīm* himself. In fact, neither claim was true, and this rumor would appear to stem from al-Anṣārī's refusal at the time to give his customary Friday sermon at the sultan's mosque, as the man who replaced him as sermonizer was the same person in the rumor who supposedly replaced him as chief Shāfiʿī justice.[119] Qāytbāy ordered that the administrators under sanction be given the accounting responsibilities for all waqfs under al-Anṣārī's oversight—perhaps including the now reassigned Qarāfa waqfs as well. The sultan's sentence would last for three long years, during which time he refused even to hear the case of al-Anṣārī's defenders, who themselves were virtually nonexistent according to al-Sakhāwī.[120]

Though we find no mention of an official suspension of the sultan's writ in the sources, a meeting between al-Anṣārī and Qāytbāy in the year 896/1488 suggests that relations between the two had normalized to an

115. Ibn Iyās, *Badāʾiʿ*, 3:241. Al-Shaʿrānī says that al-Ṣānī was arrested and persecuted by the authorities for speaking truth to power, though this is not corroborated by al-Sakhāwī. Al-Shaʿrānī, *al-Ṭabaqāt al-ṣughrā*, 58. Al-Ṣānī's father was asked to fill in for his son but refused owing to his religious scruples. Al-Sakhāwī, *Ḍaw'*, 3:133. A few months prior to the arrest of his men, al-Anṣārī is reported to have finished his commentary on Ibn al-Muqrī's *Rawḍ al-ṭālib* titled *Asnā l-maṭālib*. Al-Sakhāwī, *Ḍaw'*, 2:295. The Chester Beatty Library holds a manuscript of the text that was copied in 900/1495. Arberry, *Handlist*, 7:121 (MS 5406).

116. Al-Ḥaṣkafī, *Mutʿat al-adhhān*, 1:363.

117. For the term, see Reinhart Dozy, *Supplément aux dictionnaires arabes*, 2 vols. (Beirut: Librairie Liban, 1968), 1:528, though the translation here is my own.

118. Al-Sakhāwī, *Ḍaw'*, 3:238.

119. Shams al-Dīn Ibn Ṭūlūn, *Mufākahat al-khillān fī ḥawādith al-zamān*, 2 vols. (Cairo: al-Mu'assasa al-Miṣriyya al-ʿĀmma, 1962ff), 1:77. His replacement was Quṭb al-Dīn al-Khayḍarī (d. 894/1489). For his biography, see al-Sakhāwī, *Ḍaw'*, 9:117–24.

120. Al-Sakhāwī, *Ḍaw'*, 3:238. The length of the sentence is provided in Ibn Iyās, *Badāʾiʿ*, 3:241.

extent, though a lingering grudge would remain. The sultan greeted the four chief justices at a shrine in Cairo at this time with several alarming reports: the Ottomans appeared ready to attack at any moment, the city of Aleppo was in disarray, local traders were unable to bring their goods into Egypt, and the Mamlūk soldiers had not received their pay and were likely to plunder the city if immediate action was not taken. In response to this crisis, the sultan had gathered the four chief justices to obtain their authorization for a temporary one-year tax on waqfs, private lands, and commercial properties in order to meet the budgetary needs of the bankrupt state. After the sultan presented his case, a pall of silence fell over the group, which al-Anṣārī interrupted by saying, "Perhaps God will suffice you in your needs for provision." Within this context, al-Anṣārī's words denoted both opposition to the sultan's proposal and a snubbing of the man who had been so quick to turn against his officers. In fact, his reply reflected a calculated diplomacy that had come only after a decade of close interactions with the Mamlūk executive. The newly appointed chief Mālikī justice, however, would negotiate what he deemed a reasonable middle ground with the sultan and agreed to the tax for a six-month period only. When the Egyptian public learned of the agreement soon thereafter, it would be the Mālikī justice who bore the brunt of their fury.[121]

Al-Anṣārī's relationship with Qāytbāy was nevertheless a complex one. His boycott of the Friday sermon at the sultan's mosque was only a temporary protest, and many years later he would wistfully recount to al-Shaʿrānī a series of particularly harsh sermons that he delivered against Qāytbāy in the latter's presence.[122] These sermons would appear to correspond generally with his waqf difficulties during the early years of his justiceship. With a contrite tone, al-Anṣārī fondly recalled the sultan's remarkable forbearance in the face of this public censure, and his wording to al-Shaʿrānī intimates both a unique connection with Qāytbāy and a retrospective acknowledgment of his own tactlessness. In one particular sermon, al-Anṣārī clearly exceeded the sultan's patience, and after realizing

121. Al-Sakhāwī, *Ḍaw'*, 3:278–79.

122. Al-Shaʿrānī, *al-Ṭabaqāt al-ṣughrā*, 42; al-Shaʿrānī, *al-Ṭabaqāt al-kubrā*, 2:691. For references to al-Anṣārī's delivering the Friday sermon at later junctures in front of various sultans, see Ibn al-Ḥimṣī, *Ḥawādith al-zamān*, 296, 344, 371; N. al-Ghazzī, *Kawākib*, 1:295.

his imprudence, he rushed to kiss the sultan's hand and explain, "Qāytbāy, I swear that I do this only out of compassion for you, and you will thank me on the Day of Judgment (*ʿinda rabbik*). By God, I would truly hate for this body of yours to become a coal for the fire of hell."[123] Qāytbāy is reported to have turned to his entourage and said, "If I were to get rid of him then who would preach to me like this?!"[124]

In spite of his political and administrative preoccupations, al-Anṣārī continued to compose scholarly works throughout the years of his justiceship. In fact, his celebrated commentary on al-Qushayrī's *Risāla* titled *Iḥkām al-dalāla ʿalā taḥrīr al-Risāla*, which forms the focus of chapter 3, was completed in Jumādā I 893/April 1488 during the height of the author's waqf difficulties and only ten months after the arrest of his officers.[125] Similarly, in Rajab 896/May 1491, after three years had passed on the sultan's writ, and administrative matters had begun to normalize once again, al-Anṣārī completed his *Fatḥ al-bāqī*, a commentary on ʿAbd al-Raḥīm al-ʿIrāqī's (d. 806/1404) didactic poem in the science of hadith criticism (*muṣṭalaḥ al-ḥadīth*).[126] The content of the latter commentary helps to explain the criticisms that pop up here and there in al-Sakhāwī's *Ḍawʾ* biography for al-Anṣārī—a tone that is absent in his earlier *Rafʿ al-iṣr* biography. Al-Sakhāwī writes about al-Anṣārī's *Fatḥ al-bāqī*, "I used to believe that his written works were stronger than his speaking skills until the truth of the matter became clear to me when he began to comment on [al-ʿIrāqī's] *Alfiyya* in my absence while relying on my commentary [of the text] to an extent that surprised our distinguished peers. I said to them, 'Whoever claims to know what he does not know has lied about what he knows.' "[127] Nevertheless, al-Sakhāwī may have been unjustly harsh in his appraisal here when he subtly extends his accusation of plagiarism to all of

123. Al-Shaʿrānī, *al-Ṭabaqāt al-kubrā*, 2:691; cf. al-Shaʿrānī, *al-Ṭabaqāt al-ṣughrā*, 42.

124. Al-Shaʿrānī, *al-Ṭabaqāt al-ṣughrā*, 42.

125. Arberry, *Handlist*, 4:27–28 (MS 3843), and plate 114.

126. Zakariyyā al-Anṣārī, *Fatḥ al-bāqī bi-sharḥ Alfiyyat al-ʿIrāqī* (Beirut: Dār Ibn Ḥazm, 1999), 676; *Jāmiʿ al-Zaytūna ʿammarahu Allāh: Barnāmaj al-Maktaba al-Ṣādiqiyya*, 2 vols. (Beirut: Markaz al-Khadamāt wa-l-Abḥāth al-Thaqāfiyya, 1980ff.), 2:230.

127. Al-Sakhāwī, *Ḍawʾ*, 3:236. Al-Sakhāwī's commentary is titled *Fatḥ al-mughīth*. E. M. Sartain notes that al-Sakhāwī accused al-Suyūṭī of plagiarism as well. E. M. Sartain, *Jalāl al-Dīn al-Suyūṭī* (Cambridge: Cambridge University Press, 1975), 74–76.

al-Anṣārī's texts, as we find no additional evidence or complaints of other scholars to support this claim.

It was then in year 897/1492 that tragedy would strike. Plague had once again descended on Cairo, and ten thousand of her residents would perish with each passing day.[128] A son of al-Anṣārī named Muḥyī l-Dīn Yaḥyā would die of the plague in Rajab/May of this year. Very little information about this figure has survived in the sources, although it is reported that he studied under his father at one point.[129] Furthermore, in another biography, al-Sakhāwī makes passing reference to a judge named Abū Bakr ʿAbdallāh who was the grandson of al-Anṣārī through Yaḥyā.[130] The elder al-Anṣārī, as can be expected, was greatly grieved by the passing of his son.[131] In light of subsequent events that are described below, however, we can speculate that his paternal hopes lay disproportionately with his other son, Muḥibb al-Dīn Muḥammad. This latter figure, for his part, made the Ḥajj pilgrimage with his wife in the year of his brother's death; he extended his residency in the holy lands of the Ḥijāz for an additional year as well. Having traveled in a caravan with him between Mecca and Medina during this time, al-Sakhāwī reports nothing but praise for his intelligence and manners and hopes that these qualities might allow him to progress to the point of teaching independently and issuing fatwas.[132] Other sources tell us that it was Muḥammad who would write the introductions (*khuṭab*/*tarājim*) to his father's books.[133]

---

128. Ibn al-Ḥimṣī, *Ḥawādith al-zamān*, 230.

129. Al-Sakhāwī, *Ḍawʾ*, 10:225. Yaḥyā was also known by the sobriquet Abū l-Saʿūd.

130. Al-Sakhāwī, *Ḍawʾ*, 9:203. Beyond serving as a judge, Abū Bakr ʿAbdallāh is recorded to have taught the Islamic sciences, while also attributed to him is a book in estate division titled *Khulāṣat al-bāḥithīn fī ḥaṣr ḥāl al-wārithīn*.

131. Al-Sakhāwī, *Ḍawʾ*, 10:225.

132. Al-Sakhāwī, *Ḍawʾ*, 7:245. Muḥammad would begin teaching at the Sunquriyya School at some point before Shaʾbān 904/March 1499. He was approximately thirty-five years old when al-Sakhāwī met him in the Ḥijāz, and his advancement to teaching independently and issuing fatwas (*al-iqrāʾ wa-l-iftāʾ*) appears to have occurred soon thereafter.

133. Sulaymān al-Bujayrimī, *al-Tajrīd li-nafʿ al-ʿabīd* [*Ḥāshiyat al-Bujayrimī ʿalā Sharḥ Manhaj al-ṭullāb*], 4 vols. (Cairo: Muṣṭafa al-Bābī al-Ḥalabī, 1950), 1:2; Sulaymān al-Jamal, *Ḥāshiyat al-Jamal ʿalā Sharḥ al-Manhaj*, 5 vols. (Beirut: Dār Iḥyāʾ al-Turāth al-ʿArabī, 1970ff.), 1:3. The latter source reports that Muḥammad had no surviving offspring.

Though the death of Yaḥyā left little recorded effect on al-Anṣārī's daily activities,[134] it was the death of the octogenarian Qāytbāy in Dhū l-Qaʿda 901/August 1496 that would open the next chapter in al-Anṣārī's career. After securing the pro forma consent of al-Anṣārī and the other chief justices, al-Nāṣir Muḥammad ascended to the the sultanate following the death of his father Qāytbāy.[135] It was ten months after this event, toward the end of al-Nāṣir's first Ramaḍān in office, that al-Anṣārī faced his first fight with the teenage sultan over the dating of the ʿĪd celebrations. According to Ibn Iyās's account, al-Nāṣir believed it to be a catastrophic omen were ʿĪd to fall on a Friday, and he thus ordered the celebrations to begin on the night of Wednesday 29 Ramaḍān regardless of whether the Shawwāl moon were sighted or not. Upon hearing this, al-Anṣārī rushed to the sultan's court to condemn al-Nāṣir's order in no unclear terms. Al-Anṣārī's confrontational approach almost led to his dismissal, according to some reports, but in the end, the ʿĪd would fall on Friday that year—an outcome that testifies as much to al-Anṣārī's commanding influence as it does to al-Nāṣir's greenness.[136]

From this experience al-Nāṣir quickly learned to defer to al-Anṣārī on matters that demanded a scholar's touch. At the end of the subsequent Ramaḍān, for example, the sultan waited for word from al-Anṣārī before announcing the ʿĪd celebrations.[137] Similarly, two months later, the sultan would send word through his private secretary (*kātib al-sirr*) to request that al-Anṣārī select among four Ḥanafī scholars to fill the position of chief Ḥanafī justice. Al-Anṣārī, however, declined to select a candidate, as they all appeared equally qualified to him, and the sultan chose for

---

134. The chronicler Ibn al-Ḥimṣī would substitute as a judge for his teacher al-Anṣārī at the latter's residence around this time, though there is nothing in the records that ties this to the death of Yaḥyā. Ibn al-Ḥimṣī, *Ḥawādith al-zamān*, 278.

135. Ibn Iyās, *Badāʾiʿ*, 3:324.

136. Ibn Iyās, *Badāʾiʿ*, 3:360. Ibn Ṭūlūn also records a report that reached Damascus only a few days before this altercation in which the sultan was (falsely) rumored to have dismissed all four of his chief justices. Ibn Ṭūlūn, *Mufākahat al-khillān*, 1:175. It was also during this Ramaḍān that al-Anṣārī completed his *Ghāyat al-wuṣūl*, a commentary on his own *Lubb al-uṣūl* in the foundations of law (*uṣūl al-fiqh*). Zakariyyā al-Anṣārī, *Ghāyat al-wuṣūl: Sharḥ Lubb al-uṣūl* (Cairo: Muṣṭāfā al-Bābī al-Ḥalabī, 1941), 167.

137. Ibn al-Ḥimṣī, *Ḥawādith al-zamān*, 327, 329. Al-Anṣārī would deliver the ʿĪd sermon at the sultan's mosque that year.

the position Burhān al-Dīn al-Karakī, a scholar who at one time had defended al-Anṣārī from a group of detractors who had sought to sabotage his teaching circle.[138] One month after this event, the ʿAbbāsid Caliph of Cairo, al-Mutawwakil ʿAbd al-ʿAzīz b. Yaʿqūb, would die, and once again al-Nāṣir sent word through his private secretary to request that al-Anṣārī select between al-Mutawakkil's son and nephew to ascend to the caliphate. Al-Anṣārī responded that in fact the late caliph had chosen his son Yaʿqūb to succeed him, the chief Mālikī justice had notarized this appointment, the chief Ḥanafī justice had executed it, and al-Anṣārī's own magistrates had been apprised of all of these developments. An argument would ensue when the late caliph's nephew Khalīl addressed al-Anṣārī directly to protest his judgment, but in the end, the sultan sided with al-Anṣārī and confirmed Yaʿqūb as the legitimate ʿAbbāsid caliph.[139]

An especially vicious wave of the plague would ravage Cairo that same year. Within Mamlūk lands during a single three-month period, Ibn al-Ḥimṣī records the staggering death toll of 286,016, which included 1,040 of the sultan's personal Mamlūks. In the aftermath of these events, intense social and political unrest swept the streets of Cairo as gangs of criminals and unpaid Mamlūks terrorized the local population.[140] In an attempt to generate new revenue for his moribund state, al-Nāṣir imposed a rigorous tax on the populace and sent large tax invoices to each of his four chief justices that they were to collect from their magistrates and litigants. Al-Anṣārī received an initial bill for twelve thousand dirhams, a substantial fee to be sure, although this was later readjusted to a lower, undisclosed amount.[141] When he next appeared at the sultan's court to usher in the dawn of the new Islamic year in 903/August 1498, al-Anṣārī read pious traditions to

138. Ibn al-Ḥimṣī, *Ḥawādith al-zamān*, 295; al-Sakhāwī, *Ḍaw'*, 1:62.

139. Ibn al-Ḥimṣī, *Ḥawādith al-zamān*, 301. For a biography of al-Mutawakkil (r. 884–903/1479–1497), see al-Sakhāwī, *Ḍaw'*, 4:236–37.

140. Ibn al-Ḥimṣī, *Ḥawādith al-zamān*, 328.

141. Ibn al-Ḥimṣī, *Ḥawādith al-zamān*, 332, 335. To provide a very rough comparison for the sake of perspective, twelve thousand Mamlūk dirhams of account (*dirham fulūs*) could purchase approximately 1.5 metric tons of wheat during the second half of the fifteenth century if we assume the average of this cereal's wildly fluctuating prices. See Stuart J. Borsch, *The Black Death in Egypt and England: A Comparative Study* (Cairo: American University in Cairo Press, 2005), 94–95.

al-Nāṣir in an attempt to petition him to lighten the tax burden that he had imposed on the people. The sultan explained that the taxes, though undesirable, were necessary to pay the salaries of the Mamlūk soldiers who otherwise were wont to pillage the city and dishonor its women, to which al-Anṣārī replied staidly, "Go easy on the people, and the problem will subside."[142] This was not to be the case, however. Less than three months after this meeting, masked assassins would kill Sultan al-Nāṣir Muḥammad along with several influential members of his entourage.[143] The maternal uncle of the deceased ascended immediately to the sultanate, and the next day at the sultan's mosque, al-Anṣārī would read Sultan al-Ẓāhir Qānṣawh's name in the Friday sermon.[144]

Then, in Shaʿbān 904/March 1499, tragedy would strike al-Anṣārī's household again when Muḥammad b. Zakariyyā drowned in the Nile at the age of forty-four after a sudden storm swept through the city and capsized the small boat that he was traveling in near the Nilometer.[145] Muḥammad's body was recovered and transported to his residence at the Sunquriyya School, where it was washed and prepared for burial the next day.[146] An unnamed messenger brought news of Muḥammad's death to al-Anṣārī while the latter was teaching a lesson to his students, and perhaps in an effort to maintain his composure in the face of the tragedy that would ultimately alter the course of his life and career, al-Anṣārī continued to teach his lesson until its end. The next day, a large crowd gathered at al-Azhar to pray over the body of Muḥammad; Ibn al-Ḥimṣī records that a funeral of such a magnitude "had not been seen for the likes of him before." Muḥammad's

142. Ibn al-Ḥimṣī, *Ḥawādith al-zamān*, 337.

143. Ibn Iyās, *Badāʾiʿ*, 3:405.

144. Ibn al-Ḥimṣī, *Ḥawādith al-zamān*, 344. Al-Anṣārī and the other chief justices officiated the coronation of the new sultan. Less than one month after the ascendency of Sultan al-Ẓāhir Qānṣawh, Ibn al-Ḥimṣī would copy al-Anṣārī's *ʿImād al-riḍāʾ bi-bayān Ādāb al-qaḍāʾ*, an abridgment of Sharaf al-Dīn al-Ghazzī's (d. 799/1397) *Ādāb al-qaḍāʾ* on Islamic court procedure. Al-Anṣārī's original text was thus written prior to this date. Arberry, *Handlist*, 2:74–75 (MS 3420-1).

145. Cf. al-Sakhāwī, who records Muḥammad's birth month as Jumādā II 861/May 1457. Al-Sakhāwī, *Ḍawʾ*, 7:244.

146. On the school, located near the *khānaqāh* of Saʿīd al-Suʿadāʾ, see al-Maqrīzī, *Khiṭaṭ*, 2:388.

body was then interred at the burial grounds of the Sufis (*turbat al-ṣūfiyya*) in the outskirts of the city.[147]

Notwithstanding his initial stoicism on learning of his son Muḥammad's death, this tragic event appears to have shaken al-Anṣārī deeply. A few days after Muḥammad's burial, for example, a group of people from the Ḥijāz came to complain to the sultan about the behavior of the Ḥaramayn waqf administrators, who were based in Cairo and still under the oversight of the chief Shāfiʿī justice. When a messenger brought news to al-Anṣārī that a writ had been passed against Jamāl al-Dīn al-Ṣānī's son, who had replaced his father as *amīn al-ḥukm*, al-Anṣārī shut his door at once and refused to meet with anybody until the end of the month.[148] It was also around this time that al-Anṣārī's health would decline, while the sources begin to reference his deteriorating eyesight. When the month of Ramaḍān dawned that year, al-Anṣārī appeared at the sultan's court with the other chief justices and, before anyone else could speak, said, "Sultan, my lord, I am weak and my vision has faded. Relieve me of the justiceship."

The sultan refused, however, saying, "You are our blessing and our pillar!" All those who were present agreed and proceeded to shower al-Anṣārī with words of deference.

The chief Ḥanbalī justice then prayed, "May God debase him who debases you; may He humiliate him who humiliates you." When the sultan was told afterward that this prayer was in fact a prayer against him, he ordered the Ḥanbalī justice to be dismissed immediately.[149]

Al-Anṣārī similarly excused himself from delivering the ʿĪd sermon two months after his son's death owing to an unspecified infirmity (*ḍaʿf*). He also failed to greet the new Islamic month at the sultan's court that

147. Ibn al-Ḥimṣī, *Ḥawādith al-zamān*, 354; Ibn Iyās, *Badāʾiʿ*, 3:410. The latter source provides a brief necrology for Muḥammad and concludes with a vague statement about Muḥammad's poor reputation ("*wa-kān ghayr mashkūr al-sīra*").

148. Ibn al-Ḥimṣī, *Ḥawādith al-zamān*, 355. The elder Jamāl al-Dīn al-Ṣānī continued to serve as an influential Shāfiʿī magistrate until at least 922/1516. Ibn Ṭūlūn, *Mufākahat al-Khillān*, 2:14.

149. Ibn al-Ḥimṣī, *Ḥawādith al-zamān*, 355–66. The Ḥanbalī judge was Shihāb al-Dīn al-Shīshīnī. For his biography, see al-Sakhāwī, *Ḍawʾ*, 2:9–11.

same day,[150] and a few months later, he would excuse himself from a well-attended Mamlūk wedding celebration on similar grounds.[151] At the dawn of Rajab 905/1 February 1500, al-Anṣārī once again excused himself from joining the other chief justices at the sultan's court to greet the new month, though this time he changed his mind and appeared unexpectedly at the Citadel's gate on his mule. In an effort to raise al-Anṣārī's spirits, the sultan ordered that an ornate baldachin be hung above the courtyard, and under it gathered those Mamlūk emirs and notables who were present that day in a show of recognition of al-Anṣārī's stature as a scholar and servant of the state. Afterward, a party of magistrates escorted the septuagenarian al-Anṣārī back to his residence in a celebratory procession. We read that a week later he would deliver the Friday sermon once again at the sultan's mosque, and afterward the sultan vested him in a ceremonial robe of distinction in front of everyone in attendance.[152]

But al-Ẓāhir Qānṣawh's brief reign as sultan would come to an abrupt end in the final month of 905/June 1500, and his successor to the Mamlūk sultanate, al-Ashraf Jān Bulāṭ, would show little patience for al-Anṣārī's conduct at this time.[153] Less than two months after the new sultan's coronation, al-Anṣārī was once again afflicted by infirmity and a further deterioration in his vision. On account of this, he locked his door to visitors, which signaled to those around him that he was tacitly renouncing his post as chief Shāfiʿī justice. The sultan initially remained unfazed by these developments, but after a few weeks, he made al-Anṣārī's retirement official by dismissing him and appointing a dubious figure named Ibn al-Naqīb (d. 922/1516) as his replacement. Ibn al-Naqīb had purportedly paid seven thousand dinars to secure the office, and as there were several other candidates for the position

150. Ibn al-Ḥimṣī, *Ḥawādith al-zamān*, 357. As his replacement for the ʿĪd sermon, al-Anṣārī delegated his *naqīb* at the time Shams al-Dīn al-Ghazzī (d. 918/1512). On the latter figure, see Ibn Iyās, *Badāʾiʿ*, 4:253.

151. Ibn al-Ḥimṣī, *Ḥawādith al-zamān*, 369. Ibn al-Ḥimṣī also records that al-Anṣārī attended a wedding of a Mamlūk notable a few months prior to his son's death at page 321.

152. Ibn al-Ḥimṣī, *Ḥawādith al-zamān*, 371.

153. Ibn Iyās records that al-Anṣārī was present at, and witness to, Jān Bulāṭ's coronation. Ibn Iyās, *Badāʾiʿ*, 4:439.

who were far more qualified than he, many Egyptians protested the sultan's decision to appoint such a corrupt opportunist to a position as powerful as the chief Shāfiʿī justiceship.[154] For his part, the sultan largely ignored these protests and in fact appears to have held a grudge against al-Anṣārī, as he ordered that the latter's name be stricken from a shortlist of candidates for the chief teaching post at the Sunquriyya School—the position that al-Anṣārī's son Muḥammad had held just prior to his death.[155] In the end, however, Jān Bulāṭ's wanton disregard for public opinion may have contributed to his downfall. After a mere six months as sultan, he would die in prison in Rajab 906/February 1501 upon relinquishing the sultanate to his rival, Ṭūmānbāy.[156]

On the very day of his coronation as the new sultan, al-ʿĀdil Ṭūmānbāy ordered the arrest and dismissal of Ibn al-Naqīb, and following this, he sent for al-Anṣārī in order to reinstate him as chief Shāfiʿī justice. Still in self-imposed isolation, al-Anṣārī yielded to the sultan's summons only after a fair amount of cajoling. When he finally appeared before the sultan, the latter lavished praise on him before reinstating him as chief Shāfiʿī justice in the presence of witnesses. The new sultan, the four chief justices, their magistrates, and a host of Mamlūk notables then marched through the streets of Cairo in a celebratory procession.[157]

The remainder of al-ʿĀdil Ṭūmānbāy's one-hundred-day sultanate would intersect unremarkably with al-Anṣārī's life, although the scholar did play a small role in the sultan's offensive against the great polymath Jalāl al-Dīn al-Suyūṭī (d. 911/1505).[158] A month after al-ʿĀdil's coronation, a group of Sufis from the Baybarsiyya Khānaqāh brought a case before the sultan against al-Suyūṭī, who at the time served as chief overseer of the Baybarsiyya. The Sufis accused al-Suyūṭī of mismanagement and also began to question the legitimacy of his appointment. In response, the sultan ordered that al-Suyūṭī be arrested and placed under al-Anṣārī's supervision.

154. Ibn Iyās, *Badāʾiʿ*, 3:448. On Muḥyī l-Dīn ʿAbd al-Qādir Ibn al-Naqīb, see al-Sakhāwī, *Ḍawʾ*, 4:280–81; Ibn Iyās, *Badāʾiʿ*, 5:25.

155. Ibn Iyās, *Badāʾiʿ*, 3:450. For a summary of Jān Bulāṭ's excesses, see 3:463.

156. Ibn al-Ḥimṣī, *Ḥawādith al-zamān*, 385–89, 393.

157. Ibn al-Ḥimṣī, *Ḥawādith al-zamān*, 388; Ibn Iyās, *Badāʾiʿ*, 3:464.

158. Three days before the sultan's altercation with al-Suyūṭī, al-Anṣārī attended a celebration of the sultan's marriage to Qāytbāy's widow at the Citadel, where he was vested with ceremonial robes. Ibn al-Ḥimṣī, *Ḥawādith al-zamān*, 391. For the figure of one hundred days, see page 400.

Al-Anṣārī, however, testified before the Sufi plaintiffs that in fact he had witnessed al-Suyūṭī's appointment to the post by Qāytbāy. Furthermore, he permitted his detainee, in good faith and unescorted, to retrieve additional proof for this appointment from his home. It was then on the way to his house that al-Suyūṭī learned that the sultan had pledged to kill him, and he immediately went into hiding until the end of al-ʿĀdil's brief reign.[159] In the final analysis, this event may have seemed quotidian to al-Anṣārī in his capacity as a Mamlūk chief justice, and it finds no mention in the standard chronicles of the time.

As al-ʿĀdil's sultanate came to an abrupt and violent conclusion toward the end of 906/middle of 1501, we can speculate that al-Anṣārī, then close to eighty years old, may have adopted a cynical outlook toward the deteriorating political order of his time and may have resented the role that he was forced to perform in legitimizing each new despotic sultan. This interpretation helps to explain, for example, why he failed once again to greet the month of Ramaḍān at the sultan's court in the last month of al-ʿĀdil's sultanate,[160] why he arrived late to Sultan al-Ashraf Qānṣawh al-Ghawrī's coronation that followed al-ʿĀdil's demise,[161] and why he would ultimately relinquish his justiceship forever within three months of the new sultan's rise to power. Furthermore, cynicism and resentment may help to explain why al-Anṣārī and Sultan al-Ghawrī quickly developed a mutual distaste for one another from the very outset of their relationship.

Moving away from speculation, however, we can identify two primary impetuses for al-Anṣārī's final resignation—or dismissal, depending on one's interpretation—from the justiceship. The first was his deteriorating vision, which he is reported to have lost entirely by the time of his official departure

159. Sartain, *Jalāl al-Dīn al-Suyūṭī*, 99–100. The author records the story from fols. 32v–33r of an unpublished biography of al-Suyūṭī by a student named al-Shādhilī. For a basic summary of the event with a twist of the miraculous, see al-Shaʿrānī, *al-Ṭabaqāt al-ṣughrā*, 35; al-Kattānī, *Fihris al-fahāris*, 2:969. Al-Suyūṭī himself reports that al-Anṣārī had advised him to appease the sultan after an earlier misunderstanding by sending the latter kind words through a messenger. Al-Suyūṭī, however, refused. Al-Shaʿrānī, *al-Ṭabaqāt al-ṣughrā*, 34. Other interactions between al-Anṣārī and al-Suyūṭī are mentioned in A. H. Harley, "A Manual of Sufism," *Journal of the Asiatic Society of Bengal* 20 (1924): 123; and Leonor Fernandes, "Between Qadis and Muftis: To Whom Does the Mamluk Sultan Listen?," *Mamluk Studies Review* 6 (2002): 106–7.

160. Ibn al-Ḥimṣī, *Ḥawādith al-zamān*, 396. Al-Anṣārī abstained from the customary greeting of the new month citing infirmity once again.

161. Ibn Iyās, *Badāʾiʿ*, 4:4. For a grim assessment of al-ʿĀdil's character, see 3:477.

from office on Thursday, 8 Dhū l-Ḥijja 906/24 June 1501.[162] The second impetus stemmed from Sultan al-Ghawrī's decision to butcher his Mamlūk adversaries and to confiscate the wealth and property of many of his constituents almost immediately after his ascendency to the sultanate. In response, al-Anṣārī took to condemning the sultan publically in his Friday sermons at the Citadel while the latter sat in attendance beneath the *minbar* (pulpit).[163] If we accept this chronology of events, which admittedly is not clear from the sources,[164] then a sensible interpretation would suggest that the sultan in fact dismissed al-Anṣārī from the justiceship.[165] We can also speculate that al-Anṣārī escaped a more violent response from the sultan owing both to the precariousness of al-Ghawrī's legitimacy in these early days of his sultanate and to the potential for political fallout that might stem from the beating of an eighty-year-old blind man and iconic scholar like al-Anṣārī.

With his dismissal in 906/1501, al-Anṣārī would ultimately hold the post of chief Shāfiʿī justice for a span lasting just two months shy of twenty solar years—a feat that had no known precedent among the Shāfiʿīs in Egypt.[166] He nevertheless would end his tenure alienated from the Mamlūk political establishment. As he entered the final decades of his life, however, al-Anṣārī may have hoped for no blessing greater than this.

Act IV: From Suspicion to Redemption

Although he no longer held the chief Shāfiʿī justiceship, al-Anṣārī continued to deliver the Friday sermon at the sultan's mosque over the seven years that

162. Ibn Iyās, *Badāʾiʿ*, 4:12; Ibn al-Ḥimṣī, *Ḥawādith al-zamān*, 396, 401. Al-Anṣārī was replaced once again by Ibn al-Naqīb, whose buying of the office did not save him from being replaced by Burhān al-Dīn Ibn Abī Sharīf after only two weeks. Ibn Ṭūlūn reports that the news of al-Anṣārī's departure from the chief justiceship arrived in Damascus eighteen days after the actual event, which he records incorrectly to have occurred on the ninth of Dhū l-Ḥijja. Ibn Ṭūlūn, *Mufākahat al-khillān*, 1:243. At page 294 the chronicler suggests that al-Anṣārī's dismissal was in fact a result of his blindness.

163. N. al-Ghazzī, *Kawākib*, 1:295.

164. According to Ibn Iyās's chronology of events, for instance, the confiscation of property would begin while al-Anṣārī still held the justiceship, while most of al-Ghawrī's killings would take place after al-Anṣārī's dismissal. See Ibn Iyās, *Badāʾiʿ*, 4:2ff.

165. This interpretation is also supported by al-Ghazzī. N. al-Ghazzī, *Kawākib*, 1:199.

166. Ibn Iyās, *Badāʾiʿ*, 3:448.

were to follow his departure from the post.[167] Residual tensions between him and Sultan al-Ghawrī persisted throughout this period. For his part, the sultan is recorded to have spoken openly of his preference for the sermons of Abū l-Hudā al-Naqshwānī (d. 934/1528), a proxy who al-Anṣārī sent periodically in his stead. Al-Ghawrī's preferences here were purportedly on account of Abū l-Hudā's comparative eloquence and purity of voice, and contrary to what we might believe in light of past and future events, the sultan's assessment here may not be simply a function of his personal dislike for al-Anṣārī.[168] In fact, both al-ʿAlāʾī and al-Sakhāwī report that al-Anṣārī's pen was more eloquent than his tongue.[169] With these facts in mind, there is no compelling reason to doubt the sultan's stated resons for his preference in sermonizers.

In the year 913/1507,[170] however, an event would pit the sultan against a cabal of scholarly notables under the de facto leadership of al-Anṣārī. It fueled an animosity between the sultan and al-Anṣārī that would last until the end of al-Ghawrī's reign. Ibn Iyās records that an Egyptian sermonizer (*khaṭīb*) had made a statement about the Prophet Abraham that was deemed heretical by both his local congregation and the scholarly establishment, although the author leaves the specific details of the man's statement intentionally vague. In response, the congregation attacked the *khaṭīb*, and a group of magistrates would subsequently rule that he was obliged to repent of his beliefs. Soon the matter reached the ears of the sultan, who indignantly vowed to kill the man himself. He thus convened a meeting of his chief justices and the foremost legal authorities of the region, and Ibn Iyās records al-Anṣārī's name first among the latter group. The only legal ruling that Ibn Iyās records from this event is that of al-Anṣārī, who, when questioned about the controversy, replied, "Our *madhhab* holds that if the speaker repents to God and asks for forgiveness, then we accept it from him." Al-Anṣārī's colleague and indirect replacement as chief Shāfiʿī justice,

167. Toward the beginning of this period, in 907/1501, al-Anṣārī's hitherto unpublished *Muqaddima fī l-kalām ʿalā l-basmala wa-l-ḥamdala* was copied by a Muḥammad al-Barmūnī al-Maqdisī in Cairo. Arberry, *Handlist*, 2:75.

168. N. al-Ghazzī, *Kawākib*, 2:97.

169. N. al-Ghazzī, *Kawākib*, 1:200; al-Sakhāwī, *Ḍawʾ*, 3:237; al-Sakhāwī, *Rafʿ*, 146.

170. Two years prior to this event, in Jumādā II 911/November 1505, the news reached Damascus that a chief Shāfiʿī justice had died in Cairo, and rumors circulated that the deceased was either al-Anṣārī or Burhān al-Dīn Ibn Abī Sharīf. After a few weeks, it was Shihāb al-Dīn b. al-Farfūr, Ibn Abī Sharīf's replacement, who was confirmed to have died. Ibn Ṭūlūn, *Mufākahat al-khillān*, 1:294.

Burhān al-Dīn Ibn Abī Sharīf, would similarly agree with the ruling, and after much heated debate, the other scholars present unanimously agreed as well. The blasphemer thus was to be imprisoned until he repented.[171] The sultan, for his part, took no further action at this juncture. Nevertheless, the event would forever tarnish his opinion of al-Anṣārī and Ibn Abī Sharīf, whose calm deliberations on matters of egregious public vice ran contrary to the sultan's own impulses toward zealotry. The tension between the sultan and these two scholars would reach a head six years later, as is seen below.

It was then, near the dawn of year 914/May 1508, that the eighty-five-year-old al-Anṣārī would vest the fifteen-year-old ʿAbd al-Wahhāb al-Shaʿrānī with the Sufi *khirqa* (frock). This ceremony would inaugurate a decade-long relationship between al-Anṣārī and his most important biographer, who also served as his reader and scribe as his eyesight deteriorated to the point of blindness. Writing many years later, al-Shaʿrānī cites this ceremony as the event that conferred on him his shortest chain of spiritual connection to Aḥmad al-Zāhid, as al-Anṣārī was vested in the *khirqa* by Muḥammad al-Ghamrī, who was vested in it by al-Zāhid.[172] In fact, when he first arrived in Cairo in 911/1505, al-Shaʿrānī initially attached himself to the mosque of Muḥammad al-Ghamrī, which was then under the leadership of the latter's son.[173] This connection to al-Ghamrī may account for the unique relationship that was to emerge between al-Shaʿrānī and al-Anṣārī; it may also be explained by the fact that al-Anṣārī had been a classmate and friend of al-Shaʿrānī's grandfather, Nūr al-Dīn ʿAlī al-Anṣārī (d. 891/1486), at al-Azhar.[174]

Soon after the vesting ceremony, al-Shaʿrānī would read and copy al-Anṣārī's commentary on al-Qushayrī's *Risāla* with his new teacher; he also

---

171. Ibn Iyās, *Badāʾiʿ*, 4:120–21.

172. Al-Shaʿrānī, *al-Ṭabaqāt al-ṣughrā*, 45; al-Shaʿrānī, *al-Anwār al-qudsiyya*, 1:49; al-Malījī al-Shaʿrānī, *Manāqib al-Shaʿrānī*, 77. In both the *Anwār* and *Ṭabaqāt al-ṣughrā* accounts, the vesting ritual is coupled with the "lowering of the turban tail" ritual (*irkhāʾ al-ʿadhaba*). On the latter practice, see Muḥammad b. Aḥmad al-Saffārīnī, *Ghidhāʾ al-albāb fī sharḥ Manẓūmat al-Ādāb*, 2 vols. (Beirut: Dār al-Kutub al-ʿIlmiyya, 1996), 2:254; al-Shaʿrānī, *Maʿrifat ādāb al-ʿubūdiyya*, 265; Geoffroy, *Le sufisme en Égypte et en Syrie*, 198.

173. Winter, *Society and Religion*, 46.

174. Al-Malījī al-Shaʿrānī, *Manāqib al-Shaʿrānī*, 21, 23–24, 33–34; al-Munāwī, *al-Kawākib al-durriyya*, 4:458.

received an *ijāza* from the latter to teach the text to others.[175] After this, al-Anṣārī instructed his student to memorize Ibn al-Muqrī's (d. 837/1434) *Rawḍ al-ṭālib*, an abridgment of Yaḥyā b. Sharaf al-Nawawī's (676/1277) *Rawḍat al-ṭālibīn* in Shāfiʿī substantive law. But, having already memorized al-Nawawī's *Minhāj al-ṭālibīn* in the same subject, al-Shaʿrānī objected that the *Rawḍ* was too large to memorize. In response, al-Anṣārī offered his student fatherly words of encouragement, though when al-Shaʿrānī soon began to suffer physical ailments from his intense study routine, al-Anṣārī instructed him to stop.[176] In the years that were to follow, al-Shaʿrānī would read many additional texts with al-Anṣārī in the various Islamic disciplines,[177] while he also read and reread several of al-Anṣārī's works on his own.[178] Al-Shaʿrānī ultimately lists his *isnād* through al-Anṣārī as his shortest (*akhṣar*), and therefore most auspicious, chain of transmission in the disciplines of law, Qur'ānic exegesis, and hadith studies. It stands as the only *isnād* in the external disciplines that he reproduces in full for his readership.[179]

Al-Shaʿrānī, moreover, records many colorful details of his early years with al-Anṣārī, and through these details we glimpse an image of al-Anṣārī as a paternal and empathetic teacher. From al-Shaʿrānī's anecdotes we learn, for example, that al-Anṣārī would correct his student's reading mistakes with a softly muttered "Allah, Allah." He and al-Shaʿrānī would eat lunch together every day, though al-Anṣārī's conscience allowed him to take food only from the *khānaqāh* of Saʿīd al-Suʿadā', as he believed its founder to be a pious ruler who established the waqf after the Prophet

175. Winter, *Society and Religion*, 54; al-Shaʿrānī, *al-Ṭabaqāt al-kubrā*, 2:689. The latter source mistakenly refers to al-Shaʿrānī's serving al-Anṣārī for twenty years, while ten years, as cited elsewhere, is a more accurate assessment in light of al-Shaʿrānī's age, his first appearance in Cairo, and the date of his *khirqa*-vesting ceremony. See, inter alia, al-Shaʿrānī, *al-Ṭabaqāt al-kubrā*, 688; al-Shaʿrānī, *al-Ṭabaqāt al-ṣughrā*, 37; al-Malījī al-Shaʿrānī, *Manāqib al-Shaʿrānī*, 62, and passim.

176. Al-Shaʿrānī, *al-Ṭabaqāt al-kubrā*, 2:689.

177. Al-Shaʿrānī, *al-Ṭabaqāt al-kubrā*, 2:689; al-Shaʿrānī, *al-Ṭabaqāt al-ṣughrā*, 37; al-Shaʿrānī, *Laṭā'if al-minan wa-l-akhlāq fī wujūb al-taḥadduth bi-niʿmat Allāh ʿalā l-iṭlāq*, ed. Aḥmad ʿIzzū ʿInāya (Damascus: Dār al-Taqwā, 2004), 73–74, and passim; al-Malījī al-Shaʿrānī, *Manāqib al-Shaʿrānī*, 54–55.

178. Al-Malījī al-Shaʿrānī, *Manāqib al-Shaʿrānī*, 56–58, 60.

179. Al-Malījī al-Shaʿrānī, *Manāqib al-Shaʿrānī*, 62–63.

told him to do so in a vision.[180] Additionally, we learn that al-Anṣārī would occasionally stop his lesson whenever he noticed something amiss with al-Shaʿrānī and say, "Tell me what's on your mind"—a habit that al-Shaʿrānī cites as evidence of his teacher's capacity for *kashf* (mystical unveiling). In the same vein, whenever al-Shaʿrānī complained of a headache during a lesson, his teacher would instruct him to change his intention and "seek a cure from God through knowledge." Invariably cured of his headache upon following his teacher's instructions, al-Shaʿrānī cites the anecdote as evidence of al-Anṣārī's own sincerity and spiritual blessing.[181] Al-Shaʿrānī explains, "I could not find in others what I found in him," as al-Anṣārī embodied a unique synthesis of both gravitas (*hayba*) and intimacy (*uns*) and "seldom do the two combine within a single person." In fact, according to al-Shaʿrānī, al-Anṣārī's gravitas at this stage in his life outshone that of all of his scholarly peers and the rulers of the day, who carried themselves like children in front of him.[182]

It was during these later years of his life, following his departure from the chief justiceship, that al-Anṣārī would devote himself rigorously to his scholarship. His student and critic al-ʿAlāʾī records that he found great pleasure in the tireless pursuit of knowledge for the entirety of his life, and even after suffering blindness, he managed to author several influential texts in various disciplines.[183] Al-Anṣārī's students were of course instrumental to his research agenda once his eyesight had left him. Al-ʿAlāʾī describes al-Anṣārī's creative process during these later years: his students would cite passages to him from earlier works and lessons that he would then consider in light of what he had already written in the draft manuscript before him, revising it accordingly and without protest. Furthermore, he would submit to any worthy correction even if it came from a person of mean status or

180. Al-Shaʿrānī, *al-Ṭabaqāt al-kubrā*, 2:689; al-Shaʿrānī, *al-Ṭabaqāt al-ṣughrā*, 38. Saladin was the founder of the *khānaqāh*, though al-Shaʿrānī does not record his name. For more on the waqf and its founding, see Yehoshuʾa Frenkel, "Political and Social Aspects of Islamic Religious Endowments (*awqāf*)," *Bulletin of the School of Oriental and African Studies* 62, no. 1 (1999): 4, 7, 10–14.

181. Al-Shaʿrānī, *al-Ṭabaqāt al-ṣughrā*, 37–38; al-Shaʿrānī, *al-Ṭabaqāt al-kubrā*, 2:689. The quotations here and in the following sentence are translated from the narrations found in *al-Ṣughrā*.

182. Al-Shaʿrānī, *al-Ṭabaqāt al-kubrā*, 2:689; al-Shaʿrānī, *al-Ṭabaqāt al-ṣughrā*, 37.

183. N. al-Ghazzī, *Kawākib*, 1:199. Here, al-ʿAlāʾī specifically points to al-Anṣārī's supercommentary on al-Bayḍāwī's Qurʾānic exegesis and his commentary on al-Bukhārī's *Ṣaḥīḥ*, which is discussed below.

from a youth who had studied but little.[184] In fact, several sources note that al-Anṣārī would revise his texts time and time again until the very end of his life, while al-ʿAlāʾī holds that his excellence as a scholar rested on his breadth of knoweldge and his skill at simplifying and condensing the received tradition.[185] Al-Shaʿrānī similarly notes al-Anṣārī's remarkable "taste" for the words of the Sufis, which enabled him to explain their teachings accurately and without vulgarizing them whenever his students experienced confusion.[186] Al-Anṣārī was known to say to his students, "The legist with no knowledge of Sufi terminology is like dry bread with no gravy." After recording this statement, al-Ghazzī provides an illustrative anecdote in which a questioner approached al-Anṣārī with an indecipherable verse of Sufi poetry. After substituting symbolic meanings for various key words in the verse, al-Anṣārī reviewed the verse with his questioner in light of its new reading, after which he arranged the new meanings into a rhymed couplet of his own.[187]

One of al-Anṣārī's more ambitious projects during these later years was the drafting of his celebrated commentary on al-Bukhārī's *Ṣaḥīḥ*, which required that he evaluate and condense the contents of ten existing commentaries.[188] Al-Shaʿrānī appears to have labored assiduously with al-Anṣārī on this project, both reading aloud the earlier commentaries for his teacher and penning the actual manuscript, about half of which he claims to have drafted.[189] Another student named Muḥammad b. Khalīl al-Ḥalabī (d. 966/1559) also assisted in this process; al-Shaʿrānī would work with al-Anṣārī from sunrise until noon, while al-Ḥalabī would continue with him from noon until sunset.[190] Around this time as well, another Egyptian scholar, Aḥmad al-Qasṭallānī (d. 923/1517), had recently completed his own commentary on al-Bukhārī's *Ṣaḥīḥ* when he learned of al-Anṣārī's

184. N. al-Ghazzī, *Kawākib*, 1:199.

185. N. al-Ghazzī, *Kawākib*, 1:200.

186. Al-Shaʿrānī, *al-Ṭabaqāt al-ṣughrā*, 37; N. al-Ghazzī, *Kawākib*, 1:204.

187. N. al-Ghazzī, *Kawākib*, 1:205. Cf. al-Shaʿrānī, *Maʿrifat ādāb al-ʿubūdiyya*, 182–83.

188. Reported by al-ʿAlāʾī in N. al-Ghazzī, *Kawākib*, 1:199. Al-Anṣārī's commentary is titled *Tuḥfat al-bārī* and has been published multiple times, most recently in 2005 by Maktabat al-Rushd (Riyadh) under the title *Minḥat al-bārī*.

189. Al-Shaʿrānī, *al-Ṭabaqāt al-kubrā*, 2:689, 692.

190. N. al-Ghazzī, *Kawākib*, 2:33. Al-Ḥalabī arrived in Cairo in year 911/1505–6 and is known to have written two commentaries on the *Bahja* that draw heavily on al-Anṣārī's writings.

project. Explaining that he had no students of his own to revise his works, al-Qasṭallānī gave a copy of his commentary to al-Shaʿrānī and instructed the young student to mark the passages in which al-Anṣārī's commentary differed from his own.[191]

In addition to writing his commentary on al-Bukhārī's *Ṣaḥīḥ*, al-Anṣārī spent his later years revising his famous commentary on Ibn al-Wardī's *Bahja*, which, according to several sources, would become his most widespread text.[192] It would also be viewed as emblematic of al-Anṣārī's unceasing efforts at revision.[193] Al-Shaʿrānī holds that the text had been read back to its author fifty-seven times by the end of his life, while al-Anṣārī even managed to write a further "elucidation" (*taḥrīr*) of the work when most great authors tended to die soon after completing their magnum opus, according to the experiences of al-Shaʿrānī.[194] Because of the critical role played by the author's students and colleagues in editing this commentary, Shams al-Dīn al-Ramlī (d. 1004/1595) would later say about the text, "This is the commentary of the entire region's men, not the commentary of a single man."[195] Still a bit bitter than al-Anṣārī had plagiarized material from one of his commentaries in hadith criticism, as has been mentioned above, al-Sakhāwī, for his part, specifically vowed to scrutinize the text of

191. N. al-Ghazzī, *Kawākib*, 1:126–27. This story was reported to al-Ghazzī by his father, Badr al-Dīn al-Ghazzī (d. 984/1576), who was also a student of al-Anṣārī. Both the commentaries of al-Anṣārī and al-Qasṭallānī (titled *Irshād al-sārī*) were published in Egypt within a single twelve-volume edition in the early 1900s.

192. See, inter alia, al-Sakhāwī, *Ḍawʾ*, 3:236; al-Sakhāwī, *Rafʿ*, 145. Early draft manuscripts of the text are held by the Chester Beatty Library and were copied in 878/1474, 895/1490, and 901–9/1495–1503. Arberry, *Handlist*, 2:76, 3:3.

193. In his later years, al-Anṣārī also appears to have continued editing and teaching his *Asnā l-maṭālib*, which then comprised four volumes. Al-Sakhāwī, *Rafʿ*, 150; this information appears to be an addition by a later editor, most likely ʿAbd al-ʿAzīz Ibn Fahd (d. 920/1515), who himself is known to have studied with al-Anṣārī around the year 875/1470–71 and would later lavish praise on the latter in his *muʿjam*. See N. al-Ghazzī, *Kawākib*, 1:239; Ibn al-Shammāʿ, *al-Qabas al-ḥāwī*, 1:285; ʿUmar Riḍā al-Kaḥḥāla, *Muʿjam al-muʾallifīn*, 15 vols. (Beirut: Muʾassasat al-Risālat, 1993), 2:165. Al-Anṣārī is noted to have been teaching the text during his chief justiceship. Al-Sakhāwī, *Ḍawʾ*, 2:11. Al-Shaʿrānī also studied the text with the author and alerted the latter to mistakes and misattributions in its passages. Al-Malījī al-Shaʿrānī, *Manāqib al-Shaʿrānī*, 55.

194. N. al-Ghazzī, *Kawākib*, 1:201; al-Shaʿrānī, *al-Ṭabaqāt al-ṣughrā*, 37.

195. Al-Munāwī, *al-Kawākib al-durriyya*, 3:371.

this commentary on the *Bahja* for inaccuracies, as he believed the students of his time to be deficient, while according to him, al-Anṣārī's student assistants were wont to blend the text of the *Bahja* with the text of their commentary on it.[196]

Beyond describing his scholarship and interactions with his students, the historical record sheds additional light on al-Anṣārī's family life during his final decades. From it we learn, for example, that al-Anṣārī fathered a child named Jamāl al-Dīn Yūsuf (d. 987/1579–80) toward the end of his life, perhaps soon after the turn of the tenth Islamic century.[197] Though no explicit mention of the child's mother can be found, Ibn Iyās records in his necrology for al-Anṣārī that the latter had married a black concubine who subsequently birthed him a son,[198] and it seems reasonable to identify Jamāl al-Dīn with this child.

Having kept the company of Jamāl al-Dīn for forty years, al-Shaʿrānī records most of what is known today about this figure. We learn, for example, that he was raised in an extremely sheltered environment—a fact that may reflect his father's anxieties in the wake of his other sons' deaths. In one of their earliest meetings together, the young Jamāl al-Dīn tells al-Shaʿrānī that he had never left his father's house though he longed to experience the sights of Cairo's markets. As the elder al-Anṣārī had not taken a break from his scholarship since the very onset of his blindness, al-Shaʿrānī promised to take the boy with him when his father next needed medicine from the bazaar. Al-Shaʿrānī would thus escort Jamāl al-Dīn through the busy streets of Cairo in the course of his errands, and the boy marveled on various occasions at the boats of the Nile and the *kunāfa* pastries for sale on the street that he had never seen outside of Ramaḍān.[199]

---

196. Al-Sakhāwī, *Ḍaw'*, 3:236.

197. Al-Shaʿrānī, *al-Ṭabaqāt al-ṣughrā*, 133–34; N. al-Ghazzī, *Kawākib*, 3:221. Jamāl al-Dīn's approximate birth date can be deduced from the fact that al-Shaʿrānī delayed interacting with the boy until the latter's beard had begun to grow, and thus Jamāl al-Dīn had yet to enter puberty by the beginning of al-Shaʿrānī's studies under al-Anṣārī in 914/1508. His death date is provided by al-Ghazzī's colleague Muḥammad b. al-Jawkhī, who at one point studied with Jamāl al-Dīn. See Jean-Claude Garcin, "Index des *Ṭabaqāt* de Shaʿrānī," *Annales Islamologique* 6 (1966): 66.

198. Ibn Iyās, *Badā'iʿ*, 5:371.

199. Al-Shaʿrānī, *al-Ṭabaqāt al-ṣughrā*, 133–34; N. al-Ghazzī, *Kawākib*, 3:221. Among other texts, Jamāl al-Dīn studied his father's commentary on al-Qushayrī's *Risāla* with al-Shaʿrānī.

In his final years, al-Anṣārī also enjoyed the company of a grandson named Zakariyyā (d. 959/1552), whom al-Shaʿrānī refers to as al-Anṣārī's son, as the latter raised him from a young age after the death of his true father, whom we can cautiously identify as the late Yaḥyā.[200] The younger Zakariyyā studied with his grandfather and was initiated into Sufism by him; al-Shaʿrānī also notes that the elder al-Anṣārī was particularly fond of his grandson, who for his part displayed great piety and intelligence.[201] More about Zakariyyā's later years is detailed in chapter 5 below.

As can be glimpsed in the anecdotes above, al-Anṣārī would spend almost all of his final years in the company of his family and students, and far away from the political establishment. Nevertheless, his crowning confrontation with Sultan al-Ghawrī would yet come a full ten years after his official retirement from the chief justiceship. In Shawwāl 919/December 1513,[202] al-Ghawrī convened an emergency meeting of his chief justices and Egypt's highest legal authorities, at the forefront of whom stood al-Anṣārī. According to Ibn Iyās's account, a man and woman had admitted to an adulterous relationship but had subsequently withdrawn their confession when presented with the penalty of death. When asked for a fatwa on the

200. Al-Shaʿrānī, *al-Ṭabaqāt al-ṣughrā*, 90; also cf. N. al-Ghazzī, *Kawākib*, 2:145, where the younger Zakariyyā is correctly identified as al-Anṣārī's grandson. I have concluded that Yaḥyā was his father and not Muḥammad, based on a marriage contract, signed in 1011/1602 and currently held in the Egyptian National Archives (no. 1001-000152-0834), between one Aḥmad b. Muḥammad and Āmina b. Zakariyyā b. Yaḥyā b. "ʿAlam al-Dīn" al-Anṣārī. Accessed online at http://nationalarchives.gov.eg/nae/ar/home.jsp on 25 February 2009. This genealogy assumes both that Zakariyyā sired a daughter at a relatively old age and that Āmina married (or remarried) at a relatively old age. Garcin, "Index des *Ṭabaqāt* de Shaʿrānī," 94.

201. Al-Shaʿrānī, *al-Ṭabaqāt al-ṣughrā*, 90; N. al-Ghazzī, *Kawākib*, 2:145.

202. Al-Anṣārī may have written his abridgment of Ibn Ḥajar's *Badhl al-māʿūn fī faḍl al-ṭāʿūn*, on the divine wisdom of plagues, around this time, as the concluding portion of this unpublished text mentions a devastating plague that struck Egypt in the first half of 1513. Zakariyyā al-Anṣārī, *Tuḥfat al-rāghibīn fī bayān amr al-ṭawāʿīn*, MS 56 Taṣawwuf, Ḥalīm ʿArabī/443547, Dār al-Kutub al-Miṣriyya, Cairo. No completion date for the manuscript is otherwise provided. Also see Jalāl al-Dīn al-Suyūṭī, *Mā rawāh al-wāʿūn fī akhbār al-ṭāʿūn* (Damascus: Dār al-Qalam, 1997), 89; Ibn Ḥajar al-ʿAsqalānī, *Badhl al-māʿūn fī faḍl al-ṭāʿūn* (Riyad: Dār al-ʿĀṣima, 1991), 36–37. Also around this time in the year 918/1512, al-Anṣārī is documented to have purchased a plot of land. Muḥammad Muḥammad Amīn, *Fihrist wathāʾiq al-Qāhira ḥattā nihāyat ʿaṣr salāṭīn al-mamālīk* (Cairo: al-Maʿhad al-ʿIlmī al-Faransī li-l-Āthār al-Sharqiyya, 1981), 239.

matter, Burhān al-Dīn Ibn Abī Sharīf ruled that withdrawing their confession in such an instance would free them from a death sentence. The sultan, however, insisted that the *ḥadd* (capital) punishment must stand and, in the heat of the debate, suggested that his authority as sultan outweighed that of the jurists. In response, Ibn Abī Sharīf informed the sultan that executing the two defendants would oblige him to pay the bloodwites of two freemen.[203] Annoyed by the complacency of Ibn Abī Sharīf, the sultan then posed the case before al-Anṣārī, addressing the latter in a disrespectful tone that betrayed a deep-seated animosity between the two that had been festering for well over a decade. The nonagenarian al-Anṣārī corroborated Ibn Abī Sharīf's fatwa and, when pressed by the sultan, responded that this was the position of Imām al-Shāfiʿī himself![204]

It was then, according to a slightly different narration of events reported by al-Munāwī, that the blind al-Anṣārī accidentally poked the sultan in the eye while signaling with his hand, thereby bringing the scholarly meeting to an abrupt and fiery end.[205] Enraged, al-Ghawrī cursed, "You've confused whatever you have left of your intelligence!" The congregation was terrified as the sultan then summarily repudiated his four chief justices, imprecated the chastity of one scholar's wife, and disavowed the long-standing friendship of another scholar in attendance who had waffled in his erstwhile support for the sultan. The brunt of his anger, however, was saved for Burhān al-Dīn Ibn Abī Sharīf, who lost his teaching post because of the confrontation and would soon flee to Jerusalem in fear for his life after finding the corpses of the two adulterers gibbeted outside of his door.[206]

Al-Anṣārī, for his part, appears to have escaped the fate of his colleagues, though the event marks his last recorded interaction with the Mamlūk political elite. In another bizarre and ambiguously dated narration however, al-Ghazzī

203. Cf. al-Munāwī, *al-Kawākib al-durriyya*, 3:311, where Ibn Abī Sharīf is reported to have said to the sultan, "Whoever kills them will be killed on account of them."

204. Ibn Iyās, *Badāʾiʿ*, 4:344–45.

205. Al-Munāwī, *al-Kawākib al-durriyya*, 3:311.

206. Ibn Iyās, *Badāʾiʿ*, 4:344–45; cf. al-Munāwī, *al-Kawākib al-durriyya*, 3:311–12; N. al-Ghazzī, *Kawākib*, 1:103. For a summary of the adultery case, see Carl F. Petry, *Protectors or Praetorians? The Last Mamlūk Sultans and Egypt's Waning as a Great Power* (Albany: State University of New York Press, 1994), 149–51; Yossef Rapoport, "Women and Gender in Mamluk Society: An Overview," *Mamluk Studies Review* 11, no. 2 (2007): 1–2.

reports on the authority of his father that at one point al-Anṣārī rode to the Citadel to confront al-Ghawrī and found that the sultan had chained the palace gate to prevent his intrusion. Miraculously, al-Anṣārī cleaved the chain with his notebook, thereby enabling a crowd of angry claimants to flood into the sultan's court.[207] Regardless of the story's authenticity,[208] al-Ghazzī nevertheless cites al-Ghawrī's abovementioned confrontation with the scholarly establishment and his particularly harsh treatment of Ibn Abī Sharīf as the coup de grâce that would lead to his downfall and eventual death in 922/1516 on the battlefield of Marj Dābiq. In fact, it was al-Ghawrī's failure to heed al-Anṣārī's admonitions during his Friday sermons years earlier that would propel the sultan down a slippery slope of waywardness and tyranny that culminated in his confrontation with the greatest scholars of his age and sealed his inauspicious fate that ensued from it.[209]

Al-Anṣārī's presence at the sultan's court in 919/1513 stands out as an exceptional event during the final years of his life, which he otherwise devoted to scholarship and teaching. In fact, it was his devotion to teaching that allowed his posthumous reputation to transcend any negative stigmas that might have accrued during his twenty-year chief justiceship, which fell during a notorious period of corruption and political decline. If al-Anṣārī's were a story of redemption, as it very well may be, its denouement would hinge on the protagonist's empathy with, and genuine paternal love toward, his untold number of students of all ages and abilities.

The sources agree that al-Anṣārī taught an unusually large number of students. By the end of his remarkably long life, multiple generations of scholars could boast of having attended his study circles.[210] Al-Ghazzī records that he would live to see the students of his students grow to become great shaykhs in their own right. Moreover, Muslims from the Levant and the Ḥijāz would travel to Cairo to study with him,[211] while every Egyptian scholar of repute was his student in one way or another, either directly, or indirectly through study with an earlier generation who had attended his lessons.[212] Even al-Sakhāwī, writing thirty years before al-Anṣārī's death,

207. N. al-Ghazzī, *Kawākib*, 1:201.

208. N. al-Ghazzī, *Kawākib*, 1:103.

209. N. al-Ghazzī, *Kawākib*, 1:295; al-Haytamī, *al-Fatāwā al-ḥadīthiyya*, 51.

210. N. al-Ghazzī, *Kawākib*, 1:199–201; al-Shaʿrānī, *al-Ṭabaqāt al-ṣughrā*, 37.

211. N. al-Ghazzī, *Kawākib*, 1:199.

212. N. al-Ghazzī, *Kawākib*, 1:201; al-Shaʿrānī, *al-Ṭabaqāt al-ṣughrā*, 37.

records that many notable scholars of various persuasions had studied under him, and all acknowledged his excellence as a teacher-scholar.[213] In a similar vein, al-ʿAlāʾī explains al-Anṣārī's popularity as a function of his uncanny ability to receive anybody while still giving everybody the attention that was due to them.[214]

Ibn al-Shammāʿ's (d. 936/1529) detailed encounter with al-Anṣārī in 921/1515–16 provides us with a helpful illustration of what al-ʿAlāʾī meant by this. Although he would ultimately cite al-Suyūṭī as his most influential teacher in Cairo, Ibn al-Shammāʿ nevertheless recalls an intimate conversation that he had with al-Anṣārī when he first joined the latter's study circle. When al-Anṣārī asked his name, Ibn al-Shammāʿ replied "ʿUmar," to which his teacher affectionately explained that he loved anyone named ʿUmar, as he held a profound love for ʿUmar b. al-Khaṭṭāb, the second caliph of Islam. Al-Anṣārī then proceeded to narrate a dream that he once had of the Caliph ʿUmar in which ʿUmar praised him; al-Anṣārī had woken up afterward in a state of delight that he had not experienced before. After describing his dream, al-Anṣārī next turned to the subject of ʿUmar Ibn al-Fāriḍ and detailed to those students present the facts of his involvement in the famous Ibn al-Fāriḍ controversy of so many decades earlier. Ibn al-Shammāʿ, for his part, would remember al-Anṣārī's words vividly and would repeat them to a later biographer. It is clear from his account that al-Anṣārī's genial demeanor had left a profound impression on him.[215]

Another scholar who stands out as one of al-Anṣārī's most influential pupils, particularly in the field of law, was Shihāb al-Dīn al-Ramlī (d. 957/1550), whom al-Ghazzī refers to as "the *faqīh* of Egypt."[216] Al-Anṣārī considered al-Ramlī to be his top student, and he gave the latter explicit permission to correct his writings during his own lifetime. It appears that no other student was allowed to do this.[217] Shihāb al-Dīn's son Shams al-Dīn

213. Al-Sakhāwī, *Ḍawʾ*, 3:236; cf. al-Sakhāwī, *Rafʿ*, 144–45.

214. N. al-Ghazzī, *Kawākib*, 1:200.

215. N. al-Ghazzī, *Kawākib*, 1:203; Ibn al-Ḥanbalī, *Durr al-ḥabab*, 1:1014–15. Ibn al-Shammāʿ would meet with al-Anṣārī for the last time in 924/1518; he studied several texts under him which he lists in full in his *thabat*. Ibn al-Shammāʿ, *al-Qabas al-ḥāwī*, 1:285.

216. N. al-Ghazzī, *Kawākib*, 1:199.

217. N. al-Ghazzī, *Kawākib*, 2:119; al-Shaʿrānī, *al-Ṭabaqāt al-ṣughrā*, 68. Al-Ramlī is specifically noted to have made changes to al-Anṣārī's commentary on the *Bahja* and his *Asnā l-maṭālib*. Al-Khaṭīb al-Shirbīnī (d. 977/1570) is recorded to have collected

al-Ramlī (d. 1004/1595)—"the second al-Shāfiʿī"—would emerge as one of the two highest authorities in the later Shāfiʿī *madhhab* along with Ibn Ḥajar al-Haytamī (d. 974/1567). Although he would have been no older than ten by the time of al-Anṣārī's death, Shams al-Dīn transmitted the latter's texts on the direct authority of an *ijāza* from al-Anṣārī that he received as a child. Another indirect *ijāza* through his father further authorized him in these same works.[218]

In fact, the primary sources abound with stories of other influential scholars who cite al-Anṣārī as one of their earliest teachers in various Islamic disciplines. A scholar named ʿAlī b. Ismāʿīl al-Shāfiʿī (d. 971/1563), for example, began his studies of the Qurʾān under al-Anṣārī before the age of ten.[219] Al-Anṣārī would give another seventeen-year-old student, Maḥmūd b. Muḥammad b. al-Raḍī (d. 956/1549–50), an *ijāza* in several texts in the year 919/1513–14.[220] Similarly, Badr al-Dīn al-Ghazzī (d. 984/1577), the father of Najm al-Dīn al-Ghazzī, was no older than seventeen when he completed his studies under al-Anṣārī.[221] These examples and many others like them suggest that al-Anṣārī's later students were both numerous and diverse in age; many attended al-Anṣārī's lessons as adolescents or even younger.[222]

Ibn Ḥajar al-Haytamī, "the muftī of the Ḥijāz,"[223] provides us with a good illustration of the sentiment that many of al-Anṣārī's later students displayed toward their teacher. Born in 909/1504, al-Haytamī was no older

---

al-Ramlī's fatwas, which are printed in the margins of al-Haytamī's *al-Fatāwā al-kubrā al-fiqhiyya* (Cairo: al-Maṭbaʿa al-Maymaniyya, 1891; repr. Beirut: Dār al-Fikr, 1983). Cf. *Encyclopaedia of Islam*, s.v. "al-Ramlī" (Aaron Zysow).

218. *Encyclopaedia of Islam*, s.v. "al-Ramlī."

219. N. al-Ghazzī, *Kawākib*, 3:182.

220. N. al-Ghazzī, *Kawākib*, 2:247.

221. N. al-Ghazzī, *Kawākib*, 3:4. Badr al-Dīn left Cairo before Rajab 921/August 1515, thus ending his studies with al-Anṣārī.

222. For examples of his later students of various ages who cite al-Anṣārī as a major influence, see, inter alia, N. al-Ghazzī, *Kawākib*, 1:199; 2:56; 3:51, 81, 90–91, 140, and passim; ʿAbd al-Qādir al-ʿAydarūs, *al-Nūr al-sāfir ʿan akhbār al-qarn al-ʿāshir* (Beirut: Dār Ṣādir, 2001), 186, 479, 523, and passim; al-Munāwī, *al-Kawākib al-durriyya*, 3:324. Also see F. de Jong, *Ṭuruq and Ṭuruq-Linked Institutions in Nineteenth Century Egypt* (Leiden: Brill, 1978), 10n12.

223. For this sobriquet, see N. al-Ghazzī, *Kawākib*, 1:199.

than sixteen when al-Anṣārī died.[224] Nevertheless, al-Anṣārī gave him a comprehensive *ijāza* to transmit on his authority,[225] and al-Haytamī would later elevate al-Anṣārī to the foremost position in his *muʿjam* (record of collected *ijāzas*). As he explains to his reader, "I have presented our shaykh Zakariyyā first because he is the most stately of those righteous scholars and prophetic inheritors (*al-aʾimma al-wārithīn*) upon whom I have laid my gaze, and because he is the highest of the sagacious and masterful jurists from whom I have narrated and learned."[226] According to al-Haytamī, "He lived a long life such that he became unrivaled in his time for the shortness of his *isnāds*. There remained no one in his day who had not taken from him directly (*mushāfahat*[an]) or from him through an intermediary or through multiple intermediaries. In fact, it so happened that one person took from him directly and then on another occasion took from another person who was seven intermediaries [removed from al-Anṣārī in his *isnād*]. This had no parallel among any of his contemporaries."[227] Al-Haytamī inserts personal anecdotes about al-Anṣārī into his writings and fatwas in many places, while he often references al-Anṣārī's defense of Sufis like Ibn ʿArabī and Ibn al-Fāriḍ as part of an argument from authority to counter those who leveled criticisms at them. In his collection of fatwas, for example, al-Haytamī records that he once entered into a debate with a person who had denied the existence of a hierarchy of saints on earth. With his disputant in attendance, al-Haytamī posed the matter to al-Anṣārī, who vindicated him decidedly in his belief in the hierarchy of saints. Al-Anṣārī then prayed for his young student, perhaps in recognition of their similar worldview.[228] In another fatwa, al-Haytamī reports that a trusted source once told him that he was introduced to the axial saint (*al-quṭb*) in Mecca, and the latter informed him that the highest saint of Egypt was from among the jurists. When the narrator later saw the axial saint again and asked

224. N. al-Ghazzī, *Kawākib*, 3:111–13; *Encyclopaedia of Islam*, s.v. "Ibn Ḥadjar al-Haytamī" (C. van Arendonk and J. Schacht).

225. Al-Kattānī, *Fihris al-fahāris*, 1:459.

226. ʿAbd al-Ḥayy Ibn al-ʿImād, *Shadharāt al-dhahab fī akhbār man dhahab*, 8 vols. (Beirut: Dār al-Fikr, 1994) 8:135; al-ʿAydarūs, *al-Nūr al-sāfir*, 176.

227. Al-Kattānī, *Fihris al-fahāris*, 1:458; cf. Ibn al-ʿImād, *Shadharāt al-dhahab*, 8:135; al-ʿAydarūs, *al-Nūr al-sāfir*, 177.

228. Al-Haytamī, *al-Fatāwā al-kubrā al-fiqhiyya*, 1:3–4.

him to specify who it was, he was told that it was currently Burhān al-Dīn Ibn Abī Sharīf, but after him it would be al-Anṣārī.[229] Al-Haytamī's role in establishing al-Anṣārī as the "renewer" (*mujjadid*) of the ninth Islamic century is discussed in more detail below in chapter 5.

If it were not for the intimate relationships that al-Anṣārī forged with his later students, our knowledge of his life today would be significantly less detailed than it is. In all likelihood it was around the time of the Ottoman conquest of Egypt, at the dawn of year 923/1517, when the blind al-Anṣārī, then approaching his ninety-fourth year of life, would ask al-Shaʿrānī if anyone else were present with them during a private conversation. When he was assured that the two were alone, he said to his student, "I will tell you my life's story, from its beginning to its end up to the present moment, so that you know it, and it will be as if you have lived with me since the very beginning." He then narrated the famous poverty-to-patronage story discussed above.[230]

Only from al-Shaʿrānī's writings do we learn that in his later years al-Anṣārī felt regret, if not inner turmoil, over his decision to accept the chief justiceship. As al-Anṣārī explains to his student, his career advancement had brought him into the public eye when he had previously lived in a state of spiritual concealment (*satr*).[231] Al-Anṣārī's habit of giving charity in secret is another theme from his private life that appears only in al-Shaʿrānī's biographies for him. As al-Shaʿrānī explains, al-Anṣārī made scheduled payments to a long list of supplicants according to varying pay scales and timetables. He did so, however, without the knowledge of his peers, who otherwise believed him to be tight-fisted. To explain this incongruity, al-Shaʿrānī records that whenever a beggar knocked at the door, his teacher would ask him if anybody else were present. If al-Shaʿrānī replied in the affirmative, al-Anṣārī would instruct the beggar to return later when there were no other witnesses.[232]

229. Al-Haytamī, *al-Fatāwā al-ḥadīthiyya*, 50–51.

230. Al-Shaʿrānī, *al-Ṭabaqāt al-kubrā*, 2:690; cf. al-Shaʿrānī, *al-Ṭabaqāt al-ṣughrā*, 40. It was also in the year 923/1517 that al-Anṣārī sold the plot of land that he had purchased five years earlier. Amīn, *Fihrist wathāʾiq al-Qāhira*, 239.

231. Al-Shaʿrānī, *al-Ṭabaqāt al-ṣughrā*, 41–42; al-Shaʿrānī, *al-Ṭabaqāt al-kubrā*, 2:690; N. al-Ghazzī, *Kawākib*, 1:200.

232. Al-Shaʿrānī, *al-Ṭabaqāt al-ṣughrā*, 43–44; al-Shaʿrānī, *al-Ṭabaqāt al-kubrā*, 2:692.

In another narration, we learn that a particular beggar from Upper Egypt would solicit a per diem from al-Anṣārī while relating fantastical stories of his daily visits with dead saints in far-off lands. When questioned by al-Shaʿrānī as to why he honored such fabricated stories with charity, al-Anṣārī replied, "It's possible that he's telling the truth, as the matter is conceivable when the whole world is but a single footstep for the believers."[233] But not always was al-Anṣārī so willfully naive toward beggars. In another of al-Shaʿrānī's narrations, for example, a professional Sufi from the family of the Prophet complained of having lost his turban to members of al-Anṣārī's entourage. When given another turban in lieu of monetary compensation, the man threw the object back in the face of his giver. When he was apprised of the event, al-Anṣārī explained to his students, "He is blind of heart."[234]

Other anecdotes of al-Anṣārī's sober piety abound in al-Shaʿrānī's biographies of his teacher. We learn, for example, that al-Anṣārī insisted on praying his supererogatory prayers in a full standing posture even when ill and at the very end of his life, which he explained by saying, "I fear that laziness will overcome me and that I will end my days in such a state."[235] Furthermore, al-Anṣārī's strategies for preserving his productivity were legendary, and he would tell those who spoke too long in his presence, "Hurry up, you've wasted our time!"[236] His admirers and critics alike also noted his distaste for gossip and backbiting; al-Sakhāwī describes al-Anṣārī as pious, goodnatured, and decent, though he notes that his efforts to remain agreeable with all walks of people bordered on the extreme at times. According to al-Sakhāwī, al-Anṣārī's irenic disposition constantly led him to praise people and pray for them, while he saved his strongest praise for al-Sakhāwī himself.[237]

Though certainly unusual, al-Anṣārī's ninety-seven-year lifespan is not impossible to fathom in light of his austere lifestyle, which was grounded in a simple diet and a predictable daily routine. Though blind and suffering

233. Al-Shaʿrānī, *al-Ṭabaqāt al-ṣughrā*, 44.

234. Al-Shaʿrānī, *al-Ṭabaqāt al-kubrā*, 2:692.

235. Al-Shaʿrānī, *al-Ṭabaqāt al-kubrā*, 2:688; cf. al-Shaʿrānī, *al-Ṭabaqāt al-ṣughrā*, 38.

236. Al-Shaʿrānī, *al-Ṭabaqāt al-kubrā*, 2:688.

237. Al-Sakhāwī, *Ḍawʾ*, 3:237; al-Sakhāwī, *Rafʿ*, 146. Cf. al-Shaʿrānī, *al-Ṭabaqāt al-ṣughrā*, 37; al-Shaʿrānī, *al-Ṭabaqāt al-kubrā*, 2:688.

from periodic infirmities, al-Anṣārī appears to have maintained his physical health until the very end of his life. He is reported to have drunk coffee on occasion to treat his hemorrhoids; if this story is true, it would make al-Anṣārī a very early adopter of coffee drinking.[238] Al-Munāwī elsewhere reports that Shams al-Dīn al-Ramlī had related to him an anecdote in which he witnessed Burhān al-Dīn Ibn Abī Sharīf and al-Anṣārī seated next to each other in a gathering. Still an uninhibited child at the time, al-Ramlī asked his father in astonishment why the younger Ibn Abī Sharīf sat hunched over and feeble while al-Anṣārī, then in his mid-nineties, held himself perfectly upright and appeared in far better health than his colleague. The boy's father replied that Ibn Abī Sharīf had lost his bodily health through his overindulgence in sexual intercourse, while al-Anṣārī was "entirely opposed to this."[239] Al-Anṣārī's mental health at this late stage also appears to have remained strong. He completed his theological commentary *Fatḥ al-raḥmān bi-sharḥ Luqṭat al-ʿajlān* in mid-924/1518,[240] for example, while we read of scholars who studied with him even in the year of his death.[241] Moreover, al-Anṣārī would be offered the head teaching position at the Jamāliyya School only four months prior to his death, when it was discovered that school's waqf deed stipulated that the post must go to the most learned Shāfiʿī in the land.[242]

In his account of al-Anṣārī's death in 926/1520, al-Shaʿrānī provides a fascinating narrative that seamlessly jumps between a vivid dream sequence and al-Anṣārī's burial, though the two events are separated by a gap of perhaps several years. Al-Shaʿrānī writes,

> Once I dreamt an agreeable vision of him which I did not relate to him. When I next sat in front of him to read over his commentary on al-Bukhārī, he said to me without any prompting,

---

238. Aḥmad Ibn Ḥajar al-Haytamī, *al-Īʿāb sharḥ al-ʿUbāb*, 2 vols., MS 5541, ف 1/1160, King Saud University, Riyadh, fol. 1:47v.

239. Al-Munāwī, *al-Kawākib al-durriyya*, 3:313.

240. Zakariyyā al-Anṣārī, *Fatḥ al-raḥmān bi-sharḥ Luqṭat al-ʿajlān wa-billat al-ẓamʾān*, MS Laleli 297.3/03671-005, Istanbul, fol. 128v.

241. For example, see N. al-Ghazzī, *Kawākib*, 2:56, in which the scholar Muḥammad b. ʿUmar al-Safīrī al-Ḥalabī (d. 956/1549–50) is recorded to have sat with al-Anṣārī in the year 927/1520–21, though this must be corrected to 926/1520 in light of al-Anṣārī's death that year.

242. Ibn Iyās, *Badāʾiʿ*, 5:343, 370.

> "Stop and tell me what you dreamt last night." I replied, "I dreamt that I was with you in a boat and you were seated to the left of Imām al-Shāfiʿī. You said to me, 'Greet the Imām with blessings of peace,' which I did, and he prayed for me. Our boat was sailing on the river like the waves of the Nile, and I saw that it was carpeted in green brocade. The sail and its riggings were similarly made of green silk, and the bolsters were green. We continued to sail until we reached a magnificent garden—its roots reached the shore of the river, and its fruits were hanging from the crockets of the garden wall. I then climbed up to the garden from the boat and saw beautiful slavegirls gathering saffron in white baskets on top of their heads; every bouquet of saffron in a basket was the size of a cluster of dates. Then I awoke." He said, "If your dream is true, I will be buried near to Imām al-Shāfiʿī, as the boat has linked me and him."[243]

On Wednesday, 3 Dhū l-Ḥijja 926/14 November 1520, Zakariyyā al-Anṣārī died.[244] Though little is recorded about his final hours,[245] the sources provide a detailed narration of the events surrounding his burial procession. Al-Anṣārī's body was washed on Thursday morning, and beginning from the Sābiqiyya School,[246] his pallbearers proceeded toward al-Azhar, where an unusually large collection of scholars, judges, notables, and commoners had gathered to pray over the deceased.[247] Meanwhile, a grave had been dug for al-Anṣārī near the al-Naṣr Gate. Hearing this, Jamāl al-Dīn al-Ṣānī and another colleague began to question al-Shaʿrānī about his purported vision, to which al-Shaʿrānī replied, "The shaykh merely said, 'If your dream

243. N. al-Ghazzī, *Kawākib*, 1:207; al-Shaʿrānī, *al-Ṭabaqāt al-ṣughrā*, 44–45. Cf. al-Shaʿrānī, *al-Ṭabaqāt al-kubrā*, 2:692.

244. The death date here is agreed upon by, inter alia, Ibn Iyās and al-Shaʿrānī in his *Kubrā*. The printed edition of al-Shaʿrānī's *Ṣughrā* records a death date of "Dhū l-Ḥijja of year 910 and then some" (*nayyif wa-ʿashar*), which is certainly a transcription error of the words *sitt* (six) and *ʿishrīn* (twenty). Al-Ghazzī records the correct year of death but places the event on the third of Dhū l-Qaʿda, exactly one month premature.

245. One contemporary author writes that al-Anṣārī died in the Manṣūrī Hospital. ʿAbd al-Mutaʿāl al-Ṣaʿīdī, *al-Mujaddidūn fī l-Islām min al-qarn al-awwal ilā l-rābiʿ ʿashar* (Cairo: Maktabat al-Ādāb, 1950), 452.

246. Ibn Iyās, *Badāʾiʿ*, 5:371.

247. N. al-Ghazzī, *Kawākib*, 1:206.

is true . . .' "[248] Then, in the midst of this conversation, a messenger arrived on behalf of the Ottoman Viceroy Khā'ir Bey (d. 928/1522) and presented fifty dinars and a fine shroud for preparation of the body.[249] Explaining that the viceroy was too weak to make the journey to al-Azhar, he requested that the pallbearers transport the body to the Mu'minī Fountain,[250] located beneath the Citadel and thus close to the viceroy's residence. The funeral prayer proceeded accordingly, and following the prayer, Khā'ir Bey ordered that al-Anṣārī's body be buried in the Lesser Qarāfa cemetery, in a newly constructed gravesite (*fisqiyya*) abutting the mausoleum of al-Shāfiʿī. The viceroy then joined in carrying the bier toward the cemetery, and leading an immense procession of Egypt's elite and common,[251] he would witness al-Anṣārī's interment in a grave that remains a shrine until this day.

Three months later, news of al-Anṣārī's death reached Mecca, and an absentee funeral prayer was held for him in the Holy Mosque after the Friday prayer. Afterward, a group of scholars and admirers gathered near the Zamzam well in the mosque and, with emotionally charged epitaphs, eulogized al-Anṣārī as "the Nawawī of his time" and "the sage of his day."[252] It was a few months after this event that the news of his death would reach Damascus, as a political crisis had slowed the spread of information between Egypt and the Levant. An absentee funeral prayer was similarly held for al-Anṣārī in the Umayyad Mosque after the Friday prayer.[253]

---

248. Al-Shaʿrānī, *al-Ṭabaqāt al-ṣughrā*, 45; al-Shaʿrānī, *al-Ṭabaqāt al-kubrā*, 2:292–93.

249. Ibn Iyās, *Badāʾiʿ*, 5:371.

250. The site was named after its founder, Sayf al-Dīn al-Mu'minī (d. 771/1369–70); it is often referenced incorrectly in the primary literature as "*sabīl al-mu'minīn*" (The Fountain of the Believers). See Daniel Crecelius and ʿAbd al-Wahhāb Bakr, trans., *al-Damurdashi's Chronicle of Egypt* (Leiden: Brill, 1991), 74n212.

251. Al-Shaʿrānī, *al-Ṭabaqāt al-ṣughrā*, 45; al-Shaʿrānī, *al-Ṭabaqāt al-kubrā*, 2:292–93; N. al-Ghazzī, *Kawākib*, 1:207; Ibn Iyās, *Badāʾiʿ*, 5:372. For the idiosyncratic use of *fisqiyya* here, which is used only by al-ʿAlāʾī in al-Ghazzī's recording, see Muḥammad Muḥammad Amīn and Laylā ʿAlī Ibrāhīm, *al-Muṣṭalaḥāt al-miʿmāriyya fī l-wathāʾiq al-mamlūkiyya* (Cairo: American University in Cairo Press, 1990), 85.

252. Ibn al-Shammāʿ, *al-Qabas al-ḥāwī*, 1:285–86.

253. Al-Sakhāwī, *Rafʿ*, 150 (likely recorded by Ibn Fahd); Ibn Ṭūlūn, *Mufākahat al-khillān*, 2:133; N. al-Ghazzī, *Kawākib*, 1:207; Ibn al-Ḥimṣī, *Ḥawādith al-zamān*, 546–48. For the event, Ibn Ṭūlūn and al-Ghazzī provide the date of Friday, 4 Jumādā II 927/10 May 1521.

Table 2.1. A Timeline of Zakariyyā al-Anṣārī's Life

Year	Age	Event
826/1423	0	Zakariyyā al-Anṣārī is born in the village of Sunayka in the Egyptian delta
~841/1437–38	~15	Zakariyyā's father Muḥammad dies; al-Anṣārī begins his studies at al-Azhar in Cairo
Before 849/1445	< 22	Journeys to al-Maḥalla al-Kubrā to study Sufism with Muḥammad al-Ghamrī (d. 849/1445)
850/1447	24	Performs the Ḥajj in Mecca and studies with various scholars in the Ḥijāz
852/1448–49	25	Returns from Mecca; offered position of imam at Zayniyya-Ustādāriyya School, which he does not take
852/1449	26	Ibn Ḥajar al-ʿAsqalānī dies; al-Anṣārī seeks but fails to take over the chief librarianship of the Maḥmūdiyya collection
After 852/1449	> 26	Al-Anṣārī is appointed "shaykh of *taṣawwuf*" at the mosque of al-ʿAlam b. al-Jīʿān
861/1457	34	Al-Anṣārī's son Muḥammad is born near al-Azhar
865/1461	38	Al-Ẓāhir Khushqadam (r. to 872/1467) ascends to the sultanate; he seeks out al-Anṣārī's blessings
866/1461	38	Al-Anṣārī is appointed to the head teaching post at the sultan's mausoleum
871/1466	43	The sultan offers the chief Shāfiʿī justiceship to al-Anṣārī but he refuses
872/1468	45	Qāytbāy (r. to 901/1495) ascends to the sultanate after a brief period of political turmoil
873/1469	46	The sultan appoints al-Anṣārī to the head teaching post at the Sābiqiyya School; he will live there until his death
874/1469	46	The Ibn al-Fāriḍ controversy erupts in Cairo
875/1470	47	Al-Anṣārī pens his fatwa in defense of Ibn al-Fāriḍ

continued on next page

Table 2.1. Continued.

Year	Age	Event
876/1471	48	Al-Anṣārī is overheard speaking with the sultan about employment opportunities for his son Muḥammad
876/1472	49	Al-Anṣārī is one recipient of the sultan's charitable giving during Ramaḍān
881/1476	53	The sultan appoints al-Anṣārī to the head teaching post at the Ṣāliḥiyya School and to oversight of various waqfs; al-Anṣārī's financial standing would improve significantly from this point forward
886/1481	58	Al-Anṣārī is appointed by the sultan to the chief Shāfiʿī justiceship; this time he accepts
887/1482	59	Beginnings of al-Anṣārī's waqf difficulties and loss of reverence in the public eye
888/1483	60	Al-Anṣārī deems a defendant legally insane, thereby further alienating the public
892/1487	64	Al-Anṣārī completes his *Asnā l-maṭālib* in substantive law
892/1487	64	Al-Anṣārī's officers are placed under *tarsīm*; some of his men are arrested; al-Anṣārī is relieved of the Qarāfa waqfs
893/1488	65	Al-Anṣārī completes his *Iḥkām al-dalāla* commentary on al-Qushayrī's *Risāla* in Sufism
897/1492	69	Al-Anṣārī's son Yaḥyā dies of the plague; his son Muḥammad performs the Ḥajj in this year; Columbus lands in the Americas
901/1496	73	Qāytbāy dies and his son Muḥammad al-Nāṣir (r. to 903/1498) ascends to the sultanate
~901/1496	~73	Al-Anṣārī's son Jamāl al-Dīn Yūsuf (d. 987/1579–80) is born
902/1497	74	Al-Sakhāwī dies
903/1497	74	The ʿAbbasid Caliph al-Mutawakkil dies and his son Yaʿqūb succeeds him with al-Anṣārī's intervention

Year	Age	Event
904/1499	76	Muḥammad b. Zakariyyā al-Anṣārī drowns in the Nile; al-Anṣārī begins to suffer from "infirmity" and blindness
905/1500	77	Al-Anṣārī is honored in the sultan's court
906/1500	77	Al-Anṣārī is removed from the chief justiceship by Sultan al-Ashraf Jān Bulāṭ during the latter's brief reign
906/1501	78	Al-Anṣārī is reinstated to the chief justiceship by Sultan al-ʿĀdil Ṭūmānbāy during the latter's hundred-day rule; al-Anṣārī defends al-Suyūṭī (d. 911/1505) before the sultan
906/1501	78	After twenty years of service, al-Anṣārī, now fully blind, is dismissed from the chief justiceship for the final time under the new Sultan Qānṣawh al-Ghawrī (r. to 922/1516); he retires to a life of full-time teaching and scholarship until his death
913/1507	84	Al-Anṣārī opposes Sultan al-Ghawrī's calls for the execution of an heretical sermonizer
914/1508	85	Al-Anṣārī vests ʿAbd al-Wahhāb al-Shaʿrānī (d. 973/1565) in the Sufi *khirqa*, thus beginning their close relationship
918/1512	89	Al-Anṣārī purchases a parcel land
919/1513	90	Al-Anṣārī and Sultan al-Ghawrī engage in a final, heated confrontation over a criminal case of adultery
921/1515–16	92	Ibn al-Shammāʿ (d. 936/1529) first meets with al-Anṣārī and later records their conversation from this meeting
923/1517	94	The Ottoman conquest of Egypt; al-Anṣārī is recorded to have sold land; he may have begun narrating autobiographical information to al-Shaʿrānī around this time
926/1520	97	Zakariyyā al-Anṣārī dies; absentee funerals are prayed for him in Mecca and Damascus in the months that follow

Table 2.2. A Bibliography of Texts Attributed to Zakariyyā al-Anṣārī

No.	Title	Genre	Comment./ Abridg.	Composition Date	Publisher (or location if MS)
1	*Al-Adab fī tablīgh al-arab*	Hadith/Ethics	Abridgment	900/1495	Ed. ʿAlī Ḥusayn al-Bawwāb. Oman: Dār al-Furqān, 1993.
2	*Al-Aḍwāʾ al-bahija fī ibrāz daqāʾiq al-Munfarija*	Poetry	Commentary	881/1477	Ed. ʿAbd al-Majīd Diyāb. In *al-Munfarijtān*. Cairo: Dār al-Faḍīla, 1999.
3	*Aqṣā l-amānī fī ʿilm al-bayān wa-l-badīʿ wa-l-maʿānī*	Rhetoric	Abridgment		Ed. Mushtāq al-Mashāʿilī. Kuwait: Maktabat Ahl al-Athar, 2017.
4	*Asʾila ḥawl āyāt min al-Qurʾān*	Exegesis			MS al-Taymūriyya 98, Dār al-Kutub al-Miṣriyya, Cairo.
5	*Asnā l-maṭālib: sharḥ Rawḍ al-ṭālib*	Shāfiʿī Fiqh	Commentary	892/1487	Ed. Maḥmūd Maṭrajī. 6 vols. Beirut: Dār al-Fikr, 2008
6	*Bulūgh al-arab bi-sharḥ Shudhūr al-dhahab*	Arabic Grammar	Commentary		Ed. Khalaf ʿAwda al-Qaysī. Amman: Dār Yāfā al-ʿIlmiyya, 2011.
7	*Al-Daqāʾiq al-muḥkama fī sharḥ al-Muqaddima al-Jazariyya*	Qurʾān Recitation	Commentary	883/1480-1	Ed. Nasīb Nashāwī. Damascus: Dār al-Maktabī, 1995.
8	*Dīwān*	Poetry			MS 7677 tāʾ, al-Asad National Library, Damascus.

9	*Al-Durar al-saniyya fī sharḥ al-Alfiyya*	Grammar	Commentary		Ed. Walīd al-Ḥusayn. Beirut: Dār Ibn Ḥazm, 2011.
10	*Fatḥ al-ʿallām bi-sharḥ al-Iʿlām bi-aḥādīth al-aḥkām*	Hadith/Fiqh	Commentary	910/1505	Beirut: Dār al-Kutub al-ʿIlmiyya, 1990.
11	*Fatḥ al-bāqī bi-sharḥ Alfiyyat al-ʿIrāqī*	Hadith	Commentary	896/1491	Beirut: Dār Ibn Ḥazm, 1999.
12	*Fatḥ al-ilāh al-mājid bi-īḍāḥ Sharḥ al-ʿAqāʾid*	Theology	Commentary		Ed. ʿArafa al-Nādī. Kuwait: Dār al-Ḍiyāʾ, 2013.
13	*Fatḥ al-jalīl bi-bayān khafī Anwār al-tanzīl*	Exegesis	Commentary	After 906/1501	MS tafsīr 3916, al-Asad National Library, Damascus.
14	*Fatḥ al-mubdiʿ fī sharḥ al-Muqniʿ*	Algebra	Commentary		MS 6008, al-Asad National Library, Damascus.
15	*Fatḥ mufarrij al-kurab*	Poetry	Commentary	After 881/1477	Ed. Jamīl ʿUwayḍa. Kuwait: Dār Ibn al-Nadīm, 1990.
16	*Fatḥ munazzil al-mathānī bi-sharḥ Aqṣā l-amālī*	Rhetoric	Commentary		Ed. Mushtāq al-Mashāʿīlī. Kuwait: Maktabat Ahl al-Athar, 2017.
17	*Fatḥ rabb al-bariyya bi-sharḥ al-Qaṣīda al-Khazrajiyya*	Prosody	Commentary		Cairo: al-Maṭbaʿa al-ʿĀmira al-ʿUthmāniyya, 1884 (printed in al-Damāmīnī's *al-ʿUyūn al-fākhira*).
18	*Fatḥ al-raḥmān bi-kashf mā yaltabis fī l-Qurʾān*	Exegesis			Ed. Muḥammad ʿAlī al-Ṣābūnī. Beirut: Dār al-Qurʾān al-Karīm, 1983.

continued on next page

Table 2.2. Continued.

No.	Title	Genre	Comment./ Abridg.	Composition Date	Publisher (or location if MS)
19	*Fatḥ al-raḥmān bi-sharḥ Luqṭat al-ʿajlān wa-billat al-ẓamʾān*	Uṣūl al-Fiqh	Commentary	924/1518	Cairo: Maṭbaʿat al-Nīl, 1328/1910
20	*Fatḥ al-raḥmān bi-sharḥ Risālat al-Walī Raslān*	Sufism	Commentary	After 893/ 1488	Ed. ʿIzzat Ḥuṣriyya. *Shurūḥ Risālat al-Shaykh Arslān.* Damascus: Maṭbaʿat al-ʿAlam, 1969.
21	*Fatḥ al-wahhāb bi-mā yajib taʿallumuh ʿalā dhawī l-albāb*	Theology			MS al-Taymūriyya 443, Dār al-Kutub al-Miṣriyya, Cairo.
22	*Fatḥ al-wahhāb bi-sharḥ al-Ādāb*	Rules of Investigation	Commentary	868/1463–64	Ed. ʿArafa al-Nādī. Kuwait: Dār al-Ḍiyāʾ, 2014.
23	*Fatḥ al-wahhāb bi-sharḥ Manhaj al-ṭullāb*	Shāfiʿī Fiqh			2 vols. Cairo: ʿIsā al-Bābī al-Ḥalabī, 1925.
24	*Fatḥ al-wahhāb bi-sharḥ Tanqīḥ al-Lubāb*	Shāfiʿī Fiqh	Commentary	881/1477 at latest	MS Landberg MSS 465, Beinecke Library, New Haven.
25	*Al-Fatḥa al-unsiyya li-ghaliq al-Tuḥfa al-qudsiyya*	Estate Division	Commentary	885/1461	MS Laleli 297.4/01304-002, Istanbul.
26	*Al-Futūḥāt al-ilāhiyya fī nafʿ arwāḥ al-dhawāt al-insāniyya*	Sufism		After 893/ 1488	A. H. Harley, "A Manual of Ṣūfism," Journal of the Asiatic Society of Bengal 20 (1924): 123–42.

27	*Ghāyat al-wuṣūl ilā ʿilm al-fuṣūl*	Estate Division	Commentary		Ed. Sirāj al-Ḥaqq b. Muḥammad Luqmān. MA diss., Medina, al-Jāmiʿa al-Islāmiyya, 2000.
28	*Ghāyat al-wuṣūl: sharḥ Lubb al-uṣūl*	Uṣūl al-Fiqh	Commentary	902/1497	Cairo: Muṣṭāfā al-Bābī al-Ḥalabī, 1941.
29	*Al-Ghurar al-bahiyya fī sharḥ al-Bahja al-Wardiyya*	Shāfiʿī Fiqh	Commentary	867/1463ff	5 vols. Cairo: al-Maṭbaʿa al-Maymaniyya, n.d.
30	*Ḥāshiya ʿalā l-Ḥawāshī al-mufahhima fī sharḥ al-Muqaddima*	Qurʾān Recitation	Commentary		
31	*Ḥāshiya ʿalā Jamʿ al-jawāmiʿ*	Uṣūl al-Fiqh	Commentary	Btw. 896/1491 and 902/1497	Ed. ʿAbd al-Ḥafīẓ al-Jazāʾirī. 4 vols. Riyadh: Maktabat al-Rushd, 2007
32	*Ḥāshiya ʿalā l-Nahja al-muḍiyya*	*Shāfiʿī Fiqh*	Commentary		
33	*Ḥāshiya ʿalā l-Talwīḥ fī kashf ḥaqāʾiq al-tanqīḥ*	Uṣūl al-Fiqh	Commentary		Delhi, 1875.
34	*Hidāyat al-mutanassik wa-kifāyat al-mutamassik*	Hadith		902/1497	MS A 1099, National Library of Ankara, Ankara.
35	*Al-Ḥudūd al-anīqa wa-l-taʿrīfāt al-daqīqa*	Legal Terminology			Ed. Māzin al-Mubarak. Beirut: Dār al-Fikr al-Muʿāṣir, 1991.
36	*Iḥkām al-dalāla ʿalā taḥrīr al-Risāla*	Sufism	Commentary	893/1488	4 vols. Cairo: Maktabat al-Īmān, 2007.

continued on next page

Table 2.2. Continued.

No.	Title	Genre	Comment./ Abridg.	Composition Date	Publisher (or location if MS)
37	*Al-Iʿlām wa-l-ihtimām bi-jamʿ fatāwā shaykh al-islām*	Fatwas			Ed. Qāsim al-Rifāʿī. Damascus: Dār al-Taqwā, 2007.
38	*ʿImād al-riḍāʾ bi-bayān Ādāb al-qaḍāʾ*	Judicial Procedure	Abridgment	Before 903/ 1498	Ed. ʿAbd al-Raḥmān Bakīr. 2 vols. Jeddah: Al-Dār al-Saʿūdiyya, 1986.
39	*Iʿrāb al-Qurʾān al-ʿaẓīm*	Grammar/ Exegesis			Ed. Mūsā ʿAlī Mūsā Masʿūd. Cairo: Dār al-Nashr li-l-Jāmiʿāt, 2010.
40	*Khulāṣat al-fawāʾid al-Muḥammadiyya*	Shāfiʿī Fiqh	Commentary		
41	*Lawāmiʿ al-afkār fī sharḥ Ṭawāliʿ al-anwār*	Theology	Commentary		Ed. ʿArafa al-Nādī. Cairo: Dār Uṣūl al-Dīn, 2018.
42	*Lubb al-uṣūl*	Uṣūl al-Fiqh	Abridgment		Cairo: Muṣṭāfā al-Bābī al-Ḥalabī, 1941.
43	*Al-Luʾluʾ al-naẓīm fī rawm al-taʿallum wa-l-taʿlīm*	Classification of Sciences		910/1504	Ed. ʿAbdallāh Nawwāra. Cairo: Dār al-Qalam li-l-Turāth, 1997.
44	*Manhaj al-ṭullāb*	Shāfiʿī Fiqh	Abridgment		2 vols. Cairo: ʿIsā al-Bābī al-Ḥalabī, 1925.
45	*Manhaj al-wuṣūl ilā takhrīj (taḥrīr) al-Fuṣūl*	Estate Division	Commentary	878/1473	MS 21264 bāʾ, Dār al-Kutub al-Miṣriyya, Cairo.

46	*Al-Manāhij al-kāfiya fī sharḥ al-Shāfiya*	Morphology	Commentary		In *Majmūʿat al-Shāfiya fī ʿilmay al-taṣrīf wa-l-khaṭṭ*. Beirut: Dār al-Kutub al-ʿIlmiyya, 2014.
47	*Al-Maqṣid li-talkhīṣ mā fī l-Murshid*	Qurʾān Recitation	Abridgment		Ed. Muḥammad al-Ṣabbāgh. Cairo: Dār al-Ṭibāʿa, 1863.
48	*Minḥat al-bārī bi-sharḥ Ṣaḥīḥ al-Bukhārī* (or *Tuḥfat al-bārī)*	Hadith	Commentary	After 914/1508	Ed. Sulaymān al-ʿĀzimī. 10 vols. Riyadh: Maktabat al-Rushd, 2005.
49	*Mulakhkhaṣ talkhīṣ al-Miftāḥ fī ʿulūm al-balāgha*	Rhetoric	Abridgment		Ed. Ilyās Qablān al-Turkī. Beirut: Dār Ṣādir, 2008.
50	*Muqaddima fī l-kalām ʿalā l-basmala wa-l-ḥamdala*	Exegesis	Commentary	Before 907/1501	Ed. Ṣāliḥ Mahdī al-Ghazāwī. *Al-Mawrid* 7, no. 3 (1978): 239–48.
51	*Al-Muṭṭalaʿ sharḥ al-Īsāghūjī*	Logic	Commentary	885/1480	Ed. ʿArafa al-Nādī. Kuwait: Dār al-Ḍiyāʾ, 2017.
52	*Nihāyat al-hidāya ilā taḥrīr al-Kifāya fī ʿilm al-farāʾiḍ*	Estate Division	Commentary	Before 862/1458	Ed. ʿAbd al-Rāziq ʿAbd al-Rāziq. 2 vols. Riyad: Dār Ibn Khuzayma, 1999.
53	*Risāla fī bayān al-alfāẓ al-latī yatadāwaluhā l-ṣūfiyya*	Sufism		After 893/1488	MS Taṣawwuf 83, Dār al-Kutub al-Miṣriyya, Cairo.
54	*Riṣālat fī karāmāt al-awliyāʾ*	Saintly Miracles			MS 6273, al-Maktaba al-Ẓāhiriyya, Damascus.
55	*Sharḥ al-Arbaʿīn al-Nawawiyya*	Hadith	Commentary		MS 2576/32991, Maktabat al-Azhar, Cairo.
56	*Sharḥ Ḍābiṭat al-ashkāl al-arbaʿa*	Logic	Commentary		India, 1875.

continued on next page

Table 2.2. Continued.

No.	Title	Genre	Comment./ Abridg.	Composition Date	Publisher (or location if MS)
57	*Sharḥ ʿImād al-riḍā bi-bayān Ādāb al-qaḍāʾ*	Judicial Procedure	Commentary		Ed. ʿAbd al-Raḥmān Bakīr. 2 vols. Jeddah: Al-Dār al-Saʿūdiyya, 1986.
58	*Sharḥ Minhāj al-wuṣūl ilā ʿilm al-uṣūl*	Uṣūl al-Fiqh	Commentary		
59	*Sharḥ Mukhtaṣar al-Muzanī*	Shāfiʿī Fiqh	Commentary	Before 910/1505	
60	*Sharḥ Ṣaḥīḥ Muslim*	Hadith	Commentary	After 914/1508	
61	*Sharḥ al-Shamsiyya*	Logic	Commentary		
62	*Sharḥ Tuḥfat al-qurrāʾ fī l-fatḥ wa-l-imāla bayn al-lafẓayn*	Qurʾān Recitation	Commentary		
63	*Taḥrīr Tanqīḥ al-Lubāb*	Shāfiʿī Fiqh	Abridgment		Cairo: Maktabat al-Īmān, 2019.
64	*Talkhīṣ al-Azhiyya fī aḥkām al-adʿiyya*	Supplication	Abridgment		Ed. ʿAbd al-Raʾūf b. Muḥammad al-Kamālī. Beirut: Dār al-Bashāʾir al-Islāmiyya, 2005.
65	*Talkhīṣ Taqrīb al-Nashr*	Qurʾān Recitation	Abridgment		Ed. Ibrāhīm ʿAṭwa ʿAwaḍ. *Journal of al-Azhar* 65, no. 2 (1992).
66	*Thabat*	Academic Register		Before 902/ 1497	Ed. Muḥammad Ibrāhīm al-Ḥusayn. Beirut: Dār al-Bashāʾir al-Islāmiyya, 2010.
67	*Al-Tuḥfa al-ʿaliyya fī l-khuṭab al-minbariyya*	Friday Sermons			Cairo: Maṭbaʿat al-Saʿāda, 1906.

68	*Tuḥfat nujabāʾ al-ʿaṣr*	Qurʾān Recitation			Ed. Muḥyī Hilāl al-Sarḥān. Baghdad: Baghdad University Press, 1986
69	*Tuḥfat al-qurrāʾ fī l-fatḥ wa-l-imāla bayn al-lafẓayn*	Qurʾān Recitation	Abridgment		MS 1/24 (365), Benghazi University, Benghazi.
70	*Tuḥfat al-rāghibīn fī bayān amr al-ṭawāʿīn*	Pandemics	Abridgment	After 918/1513	MS 56 Taṣawwuf Ḥalīm ʿArabī/443547, Dār al-Kutub al-Miṣriyya, Cairo.
71	*Tuḥfat al-ṭullāb bi-sharḥ Taḥrīr Tanqīḥ al-Lubāb*	Shāfiʿī Fiqh	Commentary	After 881/1477	Cairo: Maktabat al-Īmān, 2019.
72	*Al-Zubda al-rāʾiqa fī sharḥ al-Burda al-fāʾiqa*	Poetry	Commentary	914/1509	MS Adab 2166, Dār al-Kutub al-Miṣriyya, Cairo.

Table 2.3. A Table of Zakariyyā al-Anṣārī's *Ijāza*s

The table that follows lists al-Anṣārī's teachers, the texts that he studied with them, and the nature of the *ijāza*s (licenses) that connects him with these texts. This information has been gathered from al-Anṣārī's *thabat*—a word that finds no direct equivalence in English but which designates a catalogue of a particular individual's *ijāza*s that he acquired in the course of his education. Al-Anṣārī's *thabat*, like most others of its kind, furnishes us with some information on the means and method (Ar. *ṭarīqat al-taḥammul*) through which he obtained his *ijāza* from a teacher for any given text. An *ijāza* identified as "*samā*ʿ[an]," for example, implies that the teacher named read the text, or a specified part thereof, to the student who was subsequently granted an *ijāza* to transmit the text to his own students. Similarly, the qualifier "*qirāʾa*[t[an]]" implies that the student himself read the text back to his teacher who then granted him the *ijāza*. Both types of *ijāza*s reveal a higher degree of intimacy and time spent between the student and his teacher, at least as it concerns the particular text in question.

An *ijāza* described as "*idhn*[an]," on the other hand, reveals no such intimacy, though it does not definitively preclude it either. Rather, such a license may be bestowed at the teacher's discretion with or without having reviewed the particular text with the licensee. The teacher's knowledge of his student, in such an instance, may be based on his own experiences with the student or simply on the good reputation of the latter which preceded him. In either case, the license that is designated as "*idhn*[an]" provides the contemporary historian with less insight into the relationship between a student and his teacher than do the licenses designated as "*samā*ʿ[an]" or "*qirāʾa*[t[an]]." In light of all this, there exists an incentive to note the exact designation of a particular *ijāza* whenever possible, and thus the right-hand column of the table below notes the nature of the al-Anṣārī's *ijāza* for a given text, for which I have limited the classification scheme to the three categories that have been noted above, namely *samā*ʿ (aural reception of a text from a teacher), *qirāʾa* (reading of a text to a teacher), and *idhn* (generic permission to transmit a text – used synonymously with "*ijāza*[t[an]]").[1] Whenever the nature of an *ijāza* is left unspecified, I have designated it as "*idhn*" on the assumption that the author

1. In support of this simplified three-category classification system, see, *inter alia*, Khālid b. ʿAbdallāh Bāḥamīd al-Anṣārī, *Sharḥ Nukhbat al-Fikr* (Riyadh: Dār al-Iʿtiṣām, 2003-4), 73-78, esp. 78; Muḥammad Ḍiyāʾ al-Raḥmān al-Aʿẓamī, *Muʿjam muṣṭalaḥāt al-ḥadīth wa-laṭāʾif al-asānīd* (Riyadh: Maktabat Aḍwāʾ al-Salaf, 1999), 232-35 (s.v. "*ṣiyagh al-adāʾ*"). It should be noted here that the *samā*ʿ and *qirāʾa* classifications also denote a permission (*idhn*) to transmit a text. Though used occasionally by al-Anṣārī, a fourth classification of *mushāfaha* (orally) has not been included in the table below, as it is meant to define the physical nature of the *ijāza* itself (viz. an oral or written *ijāza* from the teacher). In support of this interpretation, see Bāḥamīd al-Anṣārī, *Sharḥ Nukhbat al-Fikr*, 76, 78; cf. al-Aʿẓamī, *Muʿjam muṣṭalaḥāt al-ḥadīth*, 234.

would have noted the classifications of *samāʿ* or *qirāʾa* had this been possible, as they carry more prestige within the *thabat* genre with *samāʿ* generally holding the highest rank according to the scholars of hadith.[2] Finally, I have designated the highly coveted "short *isnāds*" that the author references within his *thabat* with the symbol "(ʿā)" next to the teacher's name to signify the Arabic "*ʿāliyy*."

2. Bāḥamīd al-Anṣārī, *Sharḥ Nukhbat al-Fikr*, 73-75; cf. Messick, *The Calligraphic State*, 92.

List of Teachers and Texts that Defined Zakariyyā al-Anṣārī's Education

Text	Author	Genre	Teacher(s)	Ijāza
al-ḥadīth al-musalsal bi-l-awwaliyya	N/A	Individual musalsal hadith	Ibn Ḥajar al-ʿAsqalānī (d. 852/1449)	samāʿ
			Riḍwān al-ʿAqabī (d. 852/1448)	"
			Muḥammad al-Ḥukrī (d. 862/1458)	"
			Muḥammad al-Rashīdī (d. 854/1450)	qirāʾa
al-ṭarīq/talqīn al-dhikr/ lubs al-khirqa	N/A	The Sufi Path	Muḥammad al-Ghamrī (d. 849/1445)	N/A
			Aḥmad al-Itkāwī (d. ca. 845/1441–42)*	
			Muḥammad al-Fuwwī (d. 866/1461–62)	
			ʿUmar al-Nabatītī (d. 867/1462)	
			Aḥmad al-Zalabānī (d. ca. 877/1472–73)	
			ʿAbd al-Raḥmān al-Tamīmī (d. 876/1472)	
al-ḥadīth al-musalsal bi-l-muṣāfaḥa	N/A	Individual musalsal hadith	Riḍwān al-ʿAqabī	samāʿ
Various texts in Shāfiʿī law (including *Sharḥ al-Bahja* and *Mukhtaṣar al-Rawḍa* among other unidentified works)	Misc.	Fiqh (Shāfiʿī)	Muḥammad al-Qāyātī (d. 850/1446)	qirāʾa
			ʿUmar al-Bulqīnī (d. 868/1464)	"
			Ibn Ḥajar al-ʿAsqalānī	"
			Mūsā al-Subkī (d. 840/1437)	"
			Muḥammad al-Badrashī (d. 846/1443)	"
			Aḥmad Ibn al-Majdī (d. 850/1447)	"
			Muḥammad al-Wanāʾī (d. 849/1445)	"
			Muḥammad al-Ḥijāzī (d. 849/1445)	"
			al-Ḥasan al-Nassāba (d. 866/1461)	"
			ʿAbd al-Raḥmān al-Būtījī (d. 864/1460)	"

*Alternatively spelled "al-Idkāwī." See al-Sakhāwī, *Ḍawʾ*, 2:44; cf. 11:183.

al-ḥadīth al-musalsal bi-l-fuqahāʾ	N/A	Individual musalsal hadith	Ibn Ḥajar al-ʿAsqalānī Abū l-Fatḥ al-Marāghī (d. 859/1455) (ʿā)	idhn "
Qurʾānic recitations (*qirāʾāt*) and other works by Ibn al-Jazarī	N/A (see works of Ibn al-Jazarī below)	Qurʾān recitation	Riḍwān al-ʿAqabī ʿAlī al-Makhzūmī (d. 864/1459) Ṭāhir al-Nuwayrī (d. 856/1452) ʿA. al-Raḥmān Ibn ʿAyyāsh (d. 853/1449) Aḥmad al-Sikandarī (d. 857/1453)	qirāʾa " " " "
al-ḥadīth al-musalsal bi-qirāʾat sūrat al-Ṣaff	N/A	Individual musalsal hadith	Riḍwān al-ʿAqabī	samāʿ
Ṣaḥīḥ al-Bukhārī	Muḥammad b. Ismāʿīl al-Bukhārī (d. 256/870)	Hadith collection	Ibn Ḥajar al-ʿAsqalānī Muḥammad al-Qāyātī Ibrāhīm al-Ḥanbalī (d. 852/1448)	qirāʾa samāʿ "
Ṣaḥīḥ Muslim	Muslim b. al-Ḥajjāj (d. 261/875)	Hadith collection	Riḍwān al-ʿAqabī Muḥammad al-Qāyātī Ibn Ḥajar al-ʿAsqalānī ʿA. al-Raḥmān al-Zarkashī (d. 846/1442)	qirāʾa samāʿ " "
Sunan Abī Dāwūd	Abū Dāwūd al-Sijistānī (d. 275/889)	Hadith collection	Ibrāhīm al-Ḥanbalī Muḥammad al-Qāyātī ʿA. al-Raḥīm Ibn al-Furāt (d. 851/1448)	qirāʾa samāʿ "
al-Jāmiʿ al-ṣaḥīḥ li-l-Tirmidhī	Abū ʿĪsā al-Tirmidhī (d. 279/892)	Hadith collection	Muḥammad al-Qāyātī ʿAbd al-Raḥīm Ibn al-Furāt	samāʿ idhn

continued on next page

List of Teachers and Texts that Defined Zakariyyā al-Anṣārī's Education (Continued)

Text	Author	Genre	Teacher(s)	Ijāza
al-Sunan al-ṣughrā li-l-Nasaʾī	Aḥmad b. Shuʿayb al-Nasāʾī (d. 303/915)	Hadith collection	Riḍwān al-ʿAqabī	qirāʾa
al-Sunan al-kubrā li-l-Nasaʾī	"	Hadith collection	al-Ḥasan al-Nassāba Muḥammad al-Rashīdī ʿAbd al-Raḥīm Ibn al-Furāt (ʿā)	samaʿ " idhn
Sunan Ibn Mājah	Ibn Mājah al-Qazwīnī (d. 273/886–87)	Hadith collection	Ibn Ḥajar al-ʿAsqalānī	qirāʾa
al-Muwaṭṭaʾ (riwāyat Yaḥyā b. Yaḥyā)	Mālik b. Anas (d. 179/796)	Muṣannaf work	Ibrāhīm al-Ḥanbalī	samāʿ
al-Muwaṭṭaʾ (riwāyat Abī Muṣʿab)	"	Muṣannaf work	Ibrāhīm al-Ḥanbalī Ibn Ḥajar al-ʿAsqalānī	idhn "
Musnad al-Shāfiʿī	Muḥammad b. Idrīs al-Shāfiʿī (d. 204/820)	Hadith collection	Riḍwān al-ʿAqabī Ibn Ḥajar al-ʿAsqalānī ʿAbd al-Raḥīm Ibn al-Furāt (ʿā)	qirāʾa idhn "
al-Risāla	"	Uṣūl al-fiqh	Abū l-Fatḥ al-Marāghī ʿAbd al-Raḥīm Ibn al-Furāt (ʿā)	idhn "
Ikhtilāf al-ḥadīth	"	Hadith criticism	Ibn Ḥajar al-ʿAsqalānī	idhn
al-Sunan al-maʾthūra ʿan al-Shāfiʿī (riwāyat al-Muzanī)	"	Hadith collection	Abū l-Fatḥ al-Marāghī	idhn

Sharḥ Maʿānī al-āthār	Aḥmad al-Ṭaḥāwī (d. 321/933)	Hadith commentary	Riḍwān al-ʿAqabī Ibn Ḥajar al-ʿAsqalānī	samāʿ "
Musnad Abī Ḥanīfa li-l-Ḥārithī (d. 340/952)	ʿAbdallāh al-Ḥārithī	Hadith collection	ʿAbd al-Salām al-Baghdādī (d. 859/1455)	idhn
Musnad Aḥmad b. Ḥanbal	Aḥmad b. Ḥanbal (d. 241/855)	Hadith collection	ʿAbd al-Raḥīm Ibn Furāt	idhn
Musnad Abī Yaʿlā	Abū Yaʿlā al-Mawṣilī (d. 307/919)	Hadith collection	Ibn Ḥajar al-ʿAsqalānī ʿAbd al-Raḥīm Ibn al-Furāt (ʿā)	samāʿ idhn
al-Sunan al-kubrā li-l-Bayhaqī	Abū Bakr Aḥmad al-Bayhaqī (d. 458/1066)	Hadith collection	Muḥammad al-Rashīdī ʿAbd al-Raḥīm Ibn al-Furāt (ʿā)	idhn "
al-Sunan li-l-Dāraquṭnī	ʿAlī al-Daraquṭnī (d. 385/995)	Hadith collection	Abū l-Fatḥ al-Marāghī	idhn
Sīrat Ibn Hishām	ʿAbd al-Malik Ibn Hishām (d. 218/833)	Sīra	Riḍwān al-ʿAqabī Ibn Ḥajar al-ʿAsqalānī	samāʿ "
Sīrat Ibn Sayyid al-Nās	Ibn Sayyid al-Nās (d. 734/1334)	Sīra	Ibn Ḥajar al-ʿAsqalānī	qirāʾa
Dalāʾil al-nubuwwa	Abū Bakr Aḥmad al-Bayhaqī	Sīra	Muḥammad al-Rashīdī Ibrāhīm al-Ḥanbalī ʿAbd al-Raḥmān al-Zarkashī (ʿā)	idhn " "
al-Shifāʾ	al-Qāḍī ʿIyāḍ (d. 544/1149)	Sīra	Ibrāhīm al-Ḥanbalī Muḥammad al-Rashīdī Muḥammad al-Qāyātī (ʿā)	qirāʾa idhn samāʿ

continued on next page

List of Teachers and Texts that Defined Zakariyyā al-Anṣārī's Education (Continued)

Text	Author	Genre	Teacher(s)	Ijāza
al-Shamāʾil al-nabawiyya	Abū ʿĪsā al-Tirmidhī	Specialized hadith collection	Abū l-Fatḥ al-Marāghī ʿAbd al-Raḥīm Ibn al-Furāt (ʿā)	idhn "
ʿUrf al-taʿrīf fī l-mawlid al-sharīf	Ibn al-Jazarī (d. 833/1429)	Misc. treatises	Riḍwān al-ʿAqabī	samāʿ
al-Adab al-mufrad	Muḥammad b. Ismāʿīl al-Bukhārī	Specialized hadith collection	Ibrāhīm al-Ḥanbalī	idhn
ʿAmal al-yawm wa-l-layla	Aḥmad b. Muḥammad Ibn al-Sunnī (d. 364/974)	Specialized hadith collection	Riḍwān al-ʿAqabī ʿAbd al-Raḥīm Ibn al-Furāt	qirāʾa idhn
al-Duʿāʾ li-l-Maḥāmilī	al-Ḥusayn al-Maḥāmilī (d. 330/941)	Specialized hadith collection	Riḍwān al-ʿAqabī	samāʿ
al-Adhkār	Yaḥya b. Sharaf al-Nawawī (d. 676/1278)	Specialized hadith collection	Ibrāhīm al-Ḥanbalī Ibn Ḥajar al-ʿAsqalānī	qirāʾa idhn
ʿUddat al-Ḥiṣn al-ḥaṣīn	Muḥammad Ibn al-Jazarī	Specialized hadith collection	Ibn Fahd al-Hāshimī (d. 871/1466)	idhn

al-Muḥaddith al-fāṣil bayn al-rāwī wa-l-wāʿī	Ibn Khallād al-Rāmhurmuzī (d. 360/970)	Hadith criticism	Ibn Ḥajar al-ʿAsqalānī Ibrāhīm al-Ḥanbalī	samāʿ "
Sharaf aṣḥāb al-ḥadīth	al-Khaṭīb al-Baghdādī (d. 463/1072)	Hadith criticism	Muḥammad al-Rashīdī	idhn
al-Ashriba al-ṣaghīr	Aḥmad b. Ḥanbal	Misc. treatises	Muḥammad al-Rashīdī	idhn
al-Warʿa	Aḥmad al-Marwadhī (d. 275/888)	Specialized hadith collection	Ibrāhīm al-Ḥanbalī	idhn
al-Arbaʿūn li-l-Dāraquṭnī	Abū l-Ḥasan ʿAlī al-Daraquṭnī	Specialized hadith collection	Muḥammad al-Rashīdī	idhn
al-Arbaʿūn li-l-Juwaynī	ʿAbd al-Malik al-Juwaynī (d. 1085/478)	Specialized hadith collection	Muḥammad al-Rashīdī	idhn
al-Arbaʿūn li-l-Nīsābūrī	al-Ḥākim al-Nīsābūrī (d. 405/1014)	Specialized hadith collection	Muḥammad al-Rashīdī	idhn
al-Arbaʿūn li-l-Thaqafī	al-Qāsim al-Thaqafī (d. 489/1096)	Specialized hadith collection	Muḥammad al-Rashīdī	idhn
ʿUlūm al-ḥadīth	Ibn al-Ṣalāḥ (d. 643/1245)	Hadith criticism	Ibn Ḥajar al-ʿAsqalānī	samāʿ
al-Alfiyya fī ʿulūm al-ḥadīth (with author's commentary)	al-Ḥāfiẓ al-ʿIrāqī (d. 806/1404)	Hadith criticism	Ibn Ḥajar al-ʿAsqalānī Muḥammad al-Qāyātī M. Ibn Humām al-Ḥanafī (d. 861/1457)	samāʿ " qirāʾa

continued on next page

List of Teachers and Texts that Defined Zakariyyā al-Anṣārī's Education (Continued)

Text	**Author**	**Genre**	**Teacher(s)**	**Ijāza**
Nuzhat al-naẓar bi-sharḥ Nukhbat al-fikar	Ibn Ḥajar al-ʿAsqalānī	Hadith criticism	Ibn Ḥajar al-ʿAsqalānī	samāʿ
Ḥilyat al-awliyāʾ	Abū Nuʿaym al-Iṣfahānī (d. 430/1038)	Biographical dictionary	Riḍwān al-ʿAqabī ʿAbd al-Raḥīm Ibn al-Furāt (ʿā)	idhn "
al-Risāla al-Qushayriyya	ʿAbd al-Karīm al-Qushayrī (d. 465/1072)	Sufi Handbook	Abū l-Fatḥ al-Marāghī ʿAbd al-Raḥīm Ibn al-Furāt	idhn "
ʿAwārif al-maʿārif	ʿUmar al-Suhrawardī (d. 632/1234)	Sufi Handbook	Ibn Ḥajar al-ʿAsqalānī	idhn
Bidāyat al-hidāya	Abū Ḥāmid al-Ghazālī (d. 505/1111)	Sufism	Muḥammad al-Rashīdī	idhn
al-ʿAqīda li-l-Ghazālī	"	Theology	Ibn Ḥajar al-ʿAsqalānī	idhn
Iḥyāʾ ʿulūm al-dīn	"	Sufism	Riḍwān al-ʿAqabī	idhn
Riyāḍ al-ṣāliḥīn	Yaḥya b. Sharaf al-Nawawī	Specialized hadith collection	Ibrāhīm al-Ḥanbalī	qirāʾa
al-Targhīb wa-l-tarhīb	ʿAbd al-ʿAẓīm al-Mundhirī (d. 656/1258)	Specialized hadith collection	Muḥammad al-Qāyātī Ibn Ḥajar al-ʿAsqalānī	samāʿ idhn

Maṣābīḥ al-sunna; Sharḥ al-Maṣābīḥ; Maʿālim al-tanzīl	al-Ḥusayn b. Masʿūd al-Baghawī (d. 510/1117)	Hadith collection; tafsīr	Riḍwān al-ʿAqabī ʿAbd al-Raḥīm Ibn al-Furāt (ʿā)	idhn "
Mashāriq al-anwār	al-Ḥasan al-Ṣāghānī (d. 650/1252)	Hadith collection	Abū l-Fatḥ al-Marāghī	idhn
ʿUmdat al-aḥkām	ʿAbd al-Ghanī al-Jammāʿīlī (d. 600/1203)	Specialized hadith collection	Riḍwān al-ʿAqabī ʿAbd al-Raḥīm Ibn al-Furāt	qirāʾa idhn
Bulūgh al-marām	Ibn Ḥajar al-ʿAsqalānī	Specialized hadith collection	Ibn Ḥajar al-ʿAsqalānī	qirāʾa
al-Baʿth wa-l-nushūr	Abū Dāwūd al-Sijistānī	Specialized hadith collection	ʿAbd al-Raḥīm Ibn Furāt	samāʿ
al-Tadhkira fī aḥwāl al-mawtā wa-umūr al-ākhira	Muḥammad b. Aḥmad al-Qurṭubī (d. 671/1273)	Eschatology	ʿAbd al-Raḥīm Ibn Furāt	idhn
Faḍl Ramaḍān	Ibn Abī l-Dunyā (d. 281/894)	Misc. treatises	Riḍwān al-ʿAqabī	samāʿ
al-Muʿjam al-ṣaghīr	Sulaymān b. Aḥmad al-Ṭabarānī (d. 360/971)	Hadith collection	Riḍwān al-ʿAqabī	samāʿ

continued on next page

List of Teachers and Texts that Defined Zakariyyā al-Anṣārī's Education (Continued)

Text	**Author**	**Genre**	**Teacher(s)**	**Ijāza**
al-Muʿjam al-awsaṭ	"	Hadith collection	Ibn Ḥajar al-ʿAsqalānī	samāʿ
Mashyakhat al-Khaffāf	Yūsuf b. al-Mubārak al-Khaffāf (d. 601/1204)	Mashyakha	Riḍwān al-ʿAqabī	idhn
al-Arbaʿūn li-l-Mundhirī	ʿAbd al-ʿAẓīm al-Mundhirī	Specialized hadith collection	Riḍwān al-ʿAqabī	qirāʾa
al-Arbaʿūn li-l-Nawawī	Yaḥya b. Sharaf al-Nawawī	Specialized hadith collection	Ibrāhīm al-Ḥanbalī	qirāʾa
al-Arbaʿūn li-l-Dhahabī	Muḥammad al-Dhahabī (d. 748/1348)	Specialized hadith collection	Riḍwān al-ʿAqabī	samāʿ
Fawāʾid al-Thaqafī	al-Qāsim b. al-Faḍl al-Thaqafī	Hadith collection	Riḍwān al-ʿAqabī	samāʿ
Juzʾ Sufyān b. ʿUyayna	Sufyān b. ʿUyayna (d. 198/814)	Hadith collection	Riḍwān al-ʿAqabī	samāʿ
Juzʾ al-Shaḥḥādhī	Abū Bakr b. Ismāʿīl al-Shaḥḥādhī	Hadith collection	Riḍwān al-ʿAqabī	samāʿ
al-Mujālasa wa-jawāhir al-ʿilm	Aḥmad b. Marwān al-Dīnawarī (d. 333/915)	Hadith collection	Ibn Ḥajar al-ʿAsqalānī	samāʿ

Mukhtaṣar Sunan Abī Dāwūd	ʿAbd al-Aẓīm al-Mundhirī	Hadith collection	Ibn Ḥajar al-ʿAsqalānī	idhn
al-Maḥāmiliyyāt	al-Ḥusayn al-Maḥāmilī	Hadith collection	Ibn Ḥajar al-ʿAsqalānī	samāʿ
al-Tibyān fī ādāb ḥamalat al-Qurʾān	Yaḥya b. Sharaf al-Nawawī	Misc. treatises	Ibrāhīm al-Ḥanbalī	qirāʾa
al-Taysīr fī l-qirāʾāt al-sabʿ	ʿUthmān b. Saʿīd al-Dānī (d. 444/1053)	Qurʾān recitation	Riḍwān al-ʿAqabī	samāʿ
ʿUnwān al-sharaf al-wāfī	Ismāʿīl Ibn al-Muqriʾ (d. 455/1063)	Misc.	Aḥmad al-Sikandarī ʿAbd al-Raḥīm Ibn al-Furāt (ʿā)	idhn "
Ḥirz al-amānī (al-Shāṭibiyya)	al-Qāsim al-Shāṭibī (d. 590/1194)	Qurʾān recitation	Riḍwān al-ʿAqabī Aḥmad al-Sikandarī	qirāʾa idhn
ʿAqīlat atrāb al-qaṣāʾid (al-Rāʾiya)	"	Qurʾān orthography	Riḍwān al-ʿAqabī	qirāʾa
Ṭayyibat al-Nashr/ al-Nashr	Muḥammad Ibn al-Jazarī	Qurʾān recitation	Muḥammad Ibn Fahd al-Hāshimī	idhn
al-Tanbīh fī l-fiqh	Ibrāhīm b. ʿAlī al-Shīrāzī (d. 476/1083)	Fiqh (Shāfiʿī)	Ṣāliḥ al-Bulqīnī (d. 868/1464)	idhn
Minhāj al-ṭālibīn	Yaḥya b. Sharaf al-Nawawī	Fiqh (Shāfiʿī)	Ibn Ḥajar al-ʿAsqalānī Ṣāliḥ al-Bulqīnī	idhn "

continued on next page

List of Teachers and Texts that Defined Zakariyyā al-Anṣārī's Education (Continued)

Text	Author	Genre	Teacher(s)	Ijāza
al-Ḥāwī al-ṣaghīr	ʿAbd al-Ghaffār al-Qazwīnī (d. 665/1266)	Fiqh (Shāfiʿī)	ʿAbd al-Raḥīm Ibn Furāt	idhn
Bahjat al-Ḥāwī	ʿUmar Ibn al-Wardī (d. 749/1349)	Fiqh (Shāfiʿī)	Ibn Ḥajar al-ʿAsqalānī	idhn
al-Nahja al-marḍiyya	Abū Zurʿa al-ʿIrāqī (d. 826/1423)	Fiqh (Shāfiʿī)	Muḥammad al-Qāyātī Ṣāliḥ al-Bulqīnī	qirāʾa "
Various unidentified works by al-Muzanī	Ismāʿīl b. Yaḥyā al-Muzanī (d. 264/878)	Fiqh (Shāfiʿī)	ʿAbd al-Raḥīm Ibn Furāt Ibn Ḥājar al-ʿAsqalānī	idhn "
Ghāyat al-ikhtiṣār	Abū Shujāʿ al-Aṣfahānī (d. ca. 488/1095)	Fiqh (Shāfiʿī)	Ibn Ḥajar al-ʿAsqalānī	idhn
Mukhtaṣar al-Qudūrī	Aḥmad b. Muḥammad al-Qudūrī (d. 328/1037)	Fiqh (Ḥanafī)	Abū l-Yaman al-Nuwayrī (d. 853/1449)	idhn
al-Hidāya	ʿAlī al-Marghīnānī (d. 593/1197)	Fiqh (Ḥanafī)	Ibn Ḥajar al-ʿAsqalānī	idhn

Kanz al-daqāʾiq; Manār al-anwār	ʿAbdallāh b. Aḥmad al-Nasafī (d. 710/1310)	Fiqh (Ḥanafī); uṣūl al-fiqh	Ibn Ḥajar al-ʿAsqalānī	idhn
al-Mukhtār li-l-fatwā; al-Ikhtiyār; etc.	ʿAbdallāh al-Mawṣilī (d. 683/1284)	Fiqh (Ḥanafī)	ʿAbd al-Salām al-Baghdādī	idhn
Majmaʿ al-baḥrayn	Aḥmad Ibn al-Sāʿātī (d. 694/1295)	Fiqh (Ḥanafī)	ʿAbd al-Salām al-Baghdādī	idhn
al-Mudawwana	Saḥnūn ʿAbd al-Salām (d. 240/854)	Fiqh (Mālikī)	Muḥammad al-Qāyātī	idhn
al-Risāla li-Ibn Abī Zayd	Ibn Abī Zayd al-Qayrawānī (d. 386/996)	Fiqh (Mālikī)	Ibrāhīm al-Ḥanbalī	idhn
Jāmiʿ al-ummahāt; Mukhtaṣar al-Muntahā; al-Kāfiya	ʿUthmān Ibn al-Ḥājib (d. 646/1249)	Fiqh (Mālikī); uṣūl al-fiqh; grammar	Abū l-Fatḥ al-Marāghī	idhn
Mukhtaṣar al-shaykh Khalīl	Khalīl b. Isḥāq al-Jundī (d. 776/1374)	Fiqh (Mālikī)	Riḍwān al-ʿAqabī	idhn
Mukhtaṣar al-Khiraqī	ʿUmar b. al-Ḥusayn al-Khiraqī (d. 334/945)	Fiqh (Ḥanbalī)	Ibrāhīm al-Ḥanbalī	idhn
al-Muḥarrar fī l-fiqh	Ibn Taymiyya (d. 652/1254)	Fiqh (Ḥanbalī)	ʿAbd al-Salām al-Baghdādī Ibrāhīm al-Ḥanbalī	idhn "

continued on next page

List of Teachers and Texts that Defined Zakariyyā al-Anṣārī's Education (Continued)

Text	**Author**	**Genre**	**Teacher(s)**	**Ijāza**
al-Muqniʿ	ʿAbdallāh Ibn Qudāma (d. 620/1223)	Fiqh (Ḥanbalī)	ʿAbd al-Raḥīm Ibn Furāt	idhn
Ṭawāliʿ al-anwār	ʿAbdallāh al-Bayḍāwī (d. 685/1287)	Theology	Ibn Ḥajar al-ʿAsqalānī	idhn
Minhāj al-wuṣūl	"	Uṣūl al-fiqh	Ibn Ḥajar al-ʿAsqalānī	idhn
Jamʿ al-jawāmiʿ (and other works)	Tāj al-Dīn al-Subkī (d. 771/1370)	Uṣūl al-fiqh	ʿAbd al-Raḥīm Ibn Furāt	idhn
Mulḥat al-iʿrāb	al-Qāsim b. ʿAlī al-Ḥarīrī (d. 516/1122)	Grammar	ʿAbd al-Raḥīm Ibn Furāt	idhn
Alfiyyat Ibn Mālik	Muḥ. b. ʿAbdallāh Ibn Mālik (d. 672/1274)	Grammar	Muḥammad al-Rashīdī	idhn
al-Ājurrūmiyya	Muḥammad Ibn Ājurrūm (d. 723/1323)	Grammar	Muḥammad al-Rāʿī (d. 853/1450)	idhn
Various unidentified works by Ibn Hishām	ʿAbdallāh Ibn Hishām (d. 761/1360)	Grammar	Ibn Ḥajar al-ʿAsqalānī	idhn

Talkhīṣ al-Miftāḥ	Muḥammad al-Qazwīnī (d. 739/1338)	Rhetoric	Riḍwān al-ʿAqabī	idhn
al-Burda	Muḥammad b. Saʿīd al-Būṣīrī (d. 696/1296)	Poem	Ibrāhīm al-Ḥanbalī ʿAbd al-Raḥīm Ibn al-Furāt	qirāʾa idhn
Various unidentified works by Ibn al-Hāʾim (d. 715/1412)	Aḥmad Ibn al-Hāʾim	Estate division; mathematics	ʿAbd al-Raḥmān al-Tamīmī	idhn
al-Majmūʿ fī l-farāʾiḍ	Muḥammad b. Sharaf al-Kallāʾī (d. 777/1375)	Estate division	Abū l-Jūd al-Banabī (d. 863/1459)	qirāʾa
al-Waraqāt	ʿAbd al-Malik b. Yūsuf al-Juwaynī	Uṣūl al-fiqh	Ibn Ḥajar al-ʿAsqalānī Muḥammad al-Rashīdī	idhn "
al-Kāmil and other works by al-Mubarrad	Muḥ. al-Mubarrad (d. ca. 285/898)	Literature (adab)	Ibn Ḥajar al-ʿAsqalānī	idhn
Various works by al-Zamakhsharī	Maḥmūd b. ʿUmar al-Zamakhsharī (d. 538/1143)	Tafsīr; grammar; etc.	ʿAbd al-Raḥīm Ibn Furāt	idhn

Chapter Three

The *Iḥkām* and the Rhetoric of the Sufi Commentary

The present chapter and the chapter that follows examine Zakariyyā al-Anṣārī's commentaries in the disciplines of Sufism and law, respectively, as case studies to illustrate the literary mechanics and rhetorical processes that defined Muslim commentary writing. In the present chapter, I focus my analysis on the *Iḥkām al-dalāla ʿalā taḥrīr al-Risāla* (*The Bolstering of Guidance in Rendering the Epistle*), al-Anṣārī's running commentary on ʿAbd al-Karīm al-Qushayrī's (d. 465/1072) famous Sufi handbook the *Risāla* (*Epistle*).[1] Of al-Anṣārī's four works devoted to the discipline of Sufism, the *Iḥkām* represents his most substantive Sufi text, both in its length and in its depth of content. Moreover, al-Anṣārī himself appears to have preferred his *Iḥkām* as a final word of sorts for his readership, as each of his other Sufi texts, at one point or another, refers the reader to this earlier commentary for more detailed discussions of various matters of Sufi thought and practice.[2]

---

1. Al-Anṣārī relates his own reading of al-Qushayrī's *Risāla* on the authority of multiple parties (*jamaʿāt*), while the one *isnād* to al-Qushayrī that he cites in full is through Muḥammad al-Marāghī (d. 859/1455), which al-Anṣārī obtained in 850/1447 while studying with the latter in Mecca. Zakariyyā al-Anṣārī, *Iḥkām al-dalāla ʿalā taḥrīr al-Risāla*, 4 vols. (Cairo: Maktabat al-Īmān, 2007), 1:15; al-Sakhāwī, *Ḍawʾ*, 3:235; al-Sakhāwī, *Rafʿ*, 144; al-Kattānī, *Fihris al-fahāris*, 1:319.

2. ʿIzzat Ḥuṣriyya, *Shurūḥ Risālat al-Shaykh Arslān* (Damascus: Maṭbaʿat al-ʿAlam, 1969) (hereupon cited as: al-Anṣārī, *Fatḥ al-raḥmān*), 187; Harley, "Manual of Ṣūfism," 135, 138; Zakariyyā al-Anṣārī, *Risāla Fī Bayān al-alfāẓ al-latī yatadāwaluhā l-ṣūfiyya*, MS Taṣawwuf 83, Dār al-Kutub al-Miṣriyya, Cairo, fol. 1r.

Because al-Anṣārī and al-Qushayrī lived with over four and a half centuries and three thousand kilometers separating their lives, a comparison of the *Iḥkām* and the base text that it is built upon promises to shed much needed light on various textual and institutional developments that took place in the history of the Sufi commentary. In other words, as he wrote his *Risāla*, al-Qushayrī's audience, milieu, objectives, and motives were starkly different from those of al-Anṣārī in the writing of the latter's *Iḥkām*. How then did al-Anṣārī adapt an eleventh-century Nīshāpūrī handbook in Sufism to his own fifteenth-century Egyptian context?

In answering this question, this chapter begins with a broader rhetorical analysis of the *Iḥkām* to show how al-Anṣārī redirects al-Qushayrī's *Risāla* through three essential techniques: a recasting in content, a recasting in form, and a recasting in tone and objective of the original base text. It then shifts to an examination of those instances in the *Iḥkām* in which al-Anṣārī employs a legal hermeneutic and legal language to relieve tensions between his worldview and the worldviews of the Sufis who appear in al-Qushayrī's original *Risāla*. Here I argue that such a commentarial approach effectively treats the lives of these Sufis as a form of scripture, and is made possible—if not necessary—by the inextricable integration of the legal, theological, and mystical realms within the worldview of Muslim scholars from the later Islamic middle period. Finally, the chapter considers the commentarial form in which the *Iḥkām* was written—namely, as an interwoven commentary (*sharḥ mamzūj*)—and its affective impact on al-Anṣārī's readership. As I argue in this section, the interwoven commentary endowed commentators like al-Anṣārī with new and subtle forms of control over the received tradition. It may also have influenced the reception and appreciation of commentaries like the *Iḥkām* by increasing their processing fluency, a term borrowed from the field of psychological aesthetics.

Al-Anṣārī clearly intended his *Iḥkām* for a student readership, and the analysis below must be framed in light of this fact, as it helps to explain the author's consistent drive toward clarity and harmonization. Al-Anṣārī's repeated cautioning against aberrant theological readings of al-Qushayrī's base text and his encouraging, if not paternalistic, tone when addressing elementary matters of spiritual practice would suggest that his reader is not an intellectually mature scholar but is rather deficient in many fundamentals of the scholarly disciplines.[3] Nevertheless, this reader already possesses a basic

3. See, for example, al-Anṣārī, *Iḥkām al-dalāla*, 2:7, 113–14.

yearning to pursue the Sufi Path, as at no point does al-Anṣārī attempt to persuade him or her of the merits of this Path. In other words, al-Anṣārī and his intended reader share common assumptions about the validity of Sufism as an object of academic study. As is seen below, when apologetics do occur in the *Iḥkām*, they are directed at an audience of sympathetic insiders, and they serve to enhance the consistency of a Sufi worldview that is otherwise accepted as axiomatic.

Today the *Iḥkām* exists in multiple published editions and reprints. Among countless existing manuscripts of it, a draft (*musawwada*) holograph manuscript of the text has survived until the present day and is held by the Chester Beatty Library. Although a microfilm of this manuscript has been consulted for the present study, the author's frequent corrections, deletions, and dislocated addenda severely undermine the clarity of the artifact.[4] The present chapter rather cites a reprint of what is likely the most widespread published edition of *Iḥkām*, namely a Būlāq print from 1873. Filling the center of the page of this four-volume edition is the supercommentary of the Egyptian scholar Muṣṭafā al-ʿArūsī (d. 1876), titled *Natāʾij al-afkār al-qudsiyya fī bayān maʿānī Sharḥ al-Risāla al-Qushayriyya* (*The Harvests of Holy Contemplations in Clarifying the Meanings of the Commentary on al-Qushayrī's Epistle*). Al-Anṣārī's *Iḥkām* circumscribes al-Qushayrī's parenthetical base text in the margins of the book, which also contains a few scattered editorial comments (*taqrīrāt*) throughout by a nineteenth-century editor named Ibrāhīm ʿAbd al-Ghaffār al-Dasūqī.[5] Comparing the holograph manuscript to this published version of the text suggests that the latter is based on a sound collation of the manuscript record, while Richard Gramlich argues that it contains the best of the printed editions of al-Qushayrī's *Risāla* at the time of his writing in 1988.[6] This assessment

4. MS Arabic 3843, Chester Beatty Library, Dublin, fols. 1b-294a. See Arberry, *Handlist*, 4:27–28, and plate 114 for a reproduction of fol. 260b. Arberry mistakenly identifies the author as "Ibn al-Anṣārī."

5. Al-Anṣārī, *Iḥkām al-dalāla*, 4:228–29, 232–33. Al-Qushayrī's original *Risāla* was completed in the early part of 438/middle of 1045; al-Anṣārī's commentary was completed in Jumādā I 893/April 1488; al-ʿArūsī's supercommentary was completed in Jumādā II 1271/March 1855.

6. He does note, however, that the published edition suffers from misplaced brackets that cause the text and commentary to appear to run together. Richard Gramlich, *Das Sendschreiben al-Qušayrīs über das Sufitum* (Wiesbaden, Germany: Franz Steiner Verlag, 1989), 18. Richard M. Frank similarly notes that the Būlāq edition "remains the best available" for al-Qushayrī's original base text. Richard M. Frank, "Two Short

should not come as a surprise in light of the fact that al-Anṣārī was collating several manuscripts of al-Qushayrī's *Risāla*—perhaps as many as five—when he wrote his *Iḥkām* commentary.[7]

Subtle Intellectual Innovation in the *Iḥkām al-dalāla*

Within his *Iḥkām al-dalāla*, al-Anṣārī's direct contradictions of al-Qushayrī's base text are rare.[8] It is not difficult to understand why this is the case: overt confrontation with an inherited text would undermine the claims of a later scholar to stand within the same intellectual tradition of the author of that inherited text. This rule would apply particularly in the case of medieval Sufism, where a connection to past masters through institutions like the *silsila* served as the foundation of authority. However, the fifteenth- and sixteenth-century reader of al-Anṣārī's *Iḥkām* would have intellectual needs that could not be met by a simple gloss on a four-hundred-and-fifty-year-old text like al-Qushayrī's *Risāla*. How then does al-Anṣārī meet the needs of his readership while maintaining a deferential tone toward an early Sufi master like al-Qushayrī and his text? In answering this question, my analysis of the *Iḥkām* here deemphasizes those portions of the commentary in which al-Anṣārī closely parallels al-Qushayrī's base text, and emphasizes his more glaring divergences from it. Such an analysis, in other words, focuses on areas of tension between the commentary and the base text in order to reveal those arenas in which al-Anṣārī is willing to forgo deference toward al-Qushayrī in favor of his own voice. Because al-Anṣārī saw an incentive in maintaining the integrity of an authority like al-Qushayrī, his tensions with the latter—subtle though they may be—must be given their due consideration.

Dogmatic Works of Abū l-Qāsim al-Qushayrī," *Mélanges de l'Institut Dominicain d'Etudes Orientales du Caire* 15 (1982): 57–58.

7. References to multiple manuscripts ("*nusakh*," *pace* "*nuskha*") can be found at al-Anṣārī, *Iḥkām al-dalāla*, 1:39, 61 (three cited), 74 (at least five cited), 109 (two cited), 182 (at least three cited); 2:5 (at least three cited), 142; 3:228 (two cited); 4:122. Beyond these references, I have counted nearly three hundred additional citations of variant readings that are based on collation with a one alternate manuscript ("*wa-fī l-nuskha* . . .").

8. For a few examples of al-Anṣārī's direct contradictions of the *Risāla*, see al-Anṣārī, *Iḥkām al-dalāla*, 2:148, 4:126, 127, 129, 153.

A rhetorical recasting or redirecting of a base text enables a commentator to strike a careful balance between deference toward, and control over, the received tradition, and it should therefore come as little surprise that this is exactly what al-Anṣārī does to the *Risāla* within his *Iḥkām*. While maintaining an implicit and explicit veneer of allegiance to al-Qushayrī's original base text, al-Anṣārī nevertheless retains considerable control over the substance of his commentary through a variety of techniques and devices. More specifically, in the quest to adapt al-Qushayrī's base text to accord better with al-Anṣārī's own thought and the needs of his audience, the *Iḥkām* employs three broad categories of rhetorical conventions to redirect the *Risāla*: (1) conventions that recast the actual content of the original text; (2) conventions that recast its form; and (3) conventions that recast its tone and objective.

As for al-Anṣārī's recasting the content of al-Qushayrī's *Risāla*, one means through which he does this is by limiting or qualifying the intention of the original text. In other words, the author acknowledges the literal meaning of al-Qushayrī's text but immediately confines this meaning to specific cases and instances that do not represent the entirety of experience. Thus, for example, to a particular Sufi's blanket condemnation of self-contentment with one's spiritual standing, al-Anṣārī confirms the validity of this sentiment but adds the qualifier, "That is, whenever one refrains from seeking an increase in [one's spiritual standing]." Otherwise, he argues, it is good to be content with one's lot, as the scholars who are pleased with God's decree never cease from asking for His increase.[9] In another instance, al-Qushayrī cites an unattributed interpretation of two verses of the Qur'ān to posit that the grateful believer has a constant eye toward God's increase (*al-mazīd*), while the patient believer remains always fixated on God. Al-Anṣārī would appear to disagree with the sweeping nature of this exegesis, as he counters that both cases describe the *predominant* situation, while there are certainly grateful believers who do not have an eye toward God's increase, just as there are patient believers who do not have an eye toward God throughout their tribulation.[10] In a third example, al-Qushayrī explains that the friend of God is the "son of his present moment" (*ibn*

9. Al-Anṣārī, *Iḥkām al-dalāla*, 2:5.

10. Al-Anṣārī, *Iḥkām al-dalāla*, 3:72. The verses cited by al-Qushayrī are Qur'ān 14:7 and 2:153.

waqtih) such that this person experiences no fear, no hope, and no sadness. To this al-Anṣārī counters that such a description applies to *some* of God's friends in *some* of their spiritual states. In fact, the opposite may be closer to the truth in that *most* of God's friends experience these states *most* of the time![11] What is perhaps most interesting about this final example is that al-Anṣārī has chosen to conclude al-Qushayrī's chapter on *wilāya* with it.[12] He thereby frames the chapter within a new interpretative scaffolding—a technique that is discussed below.

Another way that al-Anṣārī recasts the content of the *Risāla* is through his subtle, if not disguised, contradiction of the base text by means of a terse commentary that serves to ease it in new directions. Al-Anṣārī thus avoids a direct confrontation with the *Risāla* in favor of a token affirmation of it that is followed by an immediate abrogation. For example, when al-Qushayrī explains that the highest aspiration of the Sufis is to be effaced from witnessing themselves and never returned to their selves/senses again, al-Anṣārī immediately adds, "And when He returns them to their selves/senses to fulfill His due and hope for His bounty, this is not a deficiency on their part" (*Wa-matā raddahum ilayhim li-qiyām ḥaqqih wa-rajā' faḍlih lam yakun dhālik naqṣ*[an]).[13] Similarly, to al-Qushayrī's austere counsel that a Sufi aspirant should have no fixed income, al-Anṣārī adds the qualification "in excess of what suffices him or her" (*fāḍil*[un] *ʿan kifāyatih*), thereby changing the import of the original text entirely and perhaps reconciling it with the predilections of his own society.[14] In another example, al-Qushayrī counsels the Sufi aspirant to separate from all worldly people, as "keeping their company is a proven poison" (*samm mujarrab*). Al-Anṣārī, in turn, affirms this counsel, but only at the early stages of the Path, for "when asceticism has established itself in one's heart and one's desire for virtue (*al-khayr*) has grown strong and one's experiential knowledge (*maʿrifa*) has been perfected, one will not be bothered by keeping their company, as one's asceticism and knowledge will preserve him or her from inclining toward their lot."[15] The

11. Al-Anṣārī, *Iḥkām al-dalāla*, 3:218.

12. For the best treatment of the term *wilāya* and a summary of reasons for my leaving it untranslated here, see Vincent Cornell, *Realm of the Saint: Power and Authority in Moroccan Sufism* (Austin, TX: University of Texas Press, 1998), xvii–xliv.

13. Al-Anṣārī, *Iḥkām al-dalāla*, 2:77.

14. Al-Anṣārī, *Iḥkām al-dalāla*, 4:226.

15. Al-Anṣārī, *Iḥkām al-dalāla*, 4:226–27.

text of the original base text is thus undermined, and al-Anṣārī's own religious ethic replaces that of the master al-Qushayrī. Writing in the context of Qur'ānic exegesis, Walid Saleh refers to a comparable methodology of "neutralizing the impact of the verse," in which Muslim exegetes would layer new interpretations of a Qur'ānic verse on top of older interpretations that contradicted them. The reader would be left with nothing to validate one interpretation over the others, and the exegete would have succeeded in diluting what was seen as problematic in the received tradition without having to contradict it directly.[16]

Another technique that al-Anṣārī employs frequently to recast the content of the *Risāla* can be found in his idiosyncratic readings of al-Qushayrī's base text. Ranging from mildly counterintuitive to bizarre interpretations, these readings function to redeploy the *Risāla* in a variety of directions to meet various ends. At the most basic level, al-Anṣārī frequently interprets al-Qushayrī's text in an idiosyncratic manner in order to reconcile it with his own mystical worldview. For example, in two instances in the *Risāla*, specific Sufi masters warn against the dangers of *ta'wīl*—here most likely meaning to interpret the Qur'ān "in a manner not according to the obvious meaning."[17] Perhaps because an allegorical interpretation of scripture does not represent as practical and immediate a danger in al-Anṣārī's thinking as does immoderation in matters of law, the author interprets al-Qushayrī's *ta'wīl* as meaning to talk oneself into legally dubious matters. He thus uses the base text of the *Risāla* as a launching point to warn his reader against actions and behaviors that do not accord with the most precautious interpretations of the law.[18]

In a similar vein, al-Anṣārī would appear unwilling to accept the obvious reading of al-Qushayrī's statement that supplication (*du'ā'*) is for the beginners on the Path while the tongues of the advanced travelers are silent. Rather, al-Anṣārī reads al-Qushayrī to mean that either their tongues are silent for everything *except* what knowledge tells them is the most beloved thing to God—a subtle contradiction of al-Qushayrī's text—or their silence comes only at those particular times when silence is preferred. Even in the

16. Saleh, *Formation of the Classical Tafsīr Tradition*, 143–44.

17. E. W. Lane, *An Arabic-English Lexicon*, 8 vols. (Beirut: Librairie du Liban, 1968), 1.1:126–27 (s.v. أ - و - ل); cf. Abū Ḥafs 'Umar al-Suhrawardī, *'Awārif al-ma'ārif*, reprinted in *Mulḥaq Iḥyā' 'ulūm al-dīn* (Egypt: al-Maktaba al-Tijāriyya al-Kubrā, n. d.), 50.

18. Al-Anṣārī, *Iḥkām al-dalāla*, 2:16, 157.

latter case, God knows the contents of their hearts and can answer their prayers without the movement of their tongues. In both cases, however, al-Anṣārī avoids the obvious reading that supplication might be obsolete for the advanced travelers on the Sufi Path, as such a reading runs counter to his views on the merits of supplication at any spiritual stage.[19]

On several occasions al-Anṣārī employs idiosyncratic readings of al-Qushayrī's base text in order to maintain the authority of Sunni scholars over orthodoxy and orthopraxy. A particularly illustrative example of this appears in his commentary on the words of al-Junayd (d. 297/910), "The veracious Sufi aspirant has no need for the knowledge of the scholars." Here, al-Anṣārī explains that al-Junayd is referring to that knowledge that is not necessary for correct religious practice. Otherwise, should there exist a deficiency in the aspirant's knowledge of correct practice, then it would become obligatory for him or her to gather it from the scholars.[20] The author thus eschews the obvious reading of al-Junayd's words as they appear in the *Risāla* in favor of a creative reading that upholds the authority of the scholars.

Idiosyncratic readings are also employed to advance an agenda that is completely independent of the original base text. In other words, al-Anṣārī reserves the right to take al-Qushayrī's text in whichever direction he chooses through his readings of it. For example, to a statement of Dhū l-Nūn al-Miṣrī (d. ca. 243/857), "Whoever learns to be content finds peace from the people of his or her time," al-Anṣārī adds the qualifier "in the markets and so forth," thereby recasting the quote to meet the needs of his own urban setting.[21] In another example, al-Qushayrī cites an ambiguous story in which a party of children is reported to have been playing near a group of elders. When questioned about their lack of shame in playing in such a manner, one child responds that because these elders have few legal scruples (*warʿa*), they are viewed with little reverence in the children's eyes. In his commentary, al-Anṣārī explains that the story represents a confirmation of the sound hadith that orders Muslims "to discipline children and order them to pray when they are seven years old and spank them [for missing

19. Al-Anṣārī, *Iḥkām al-dalāla*, 3:226–27; al-Anṣārī, *Talkhīṣ al-Azhiyya fī aḥkām al-adʿiyya* (Beirut: Dār al-Bashā'ir al-Islāmiyya, 2005), 25–29.

20. Al-Anṣārī, *Iḥkām al-dalāla*, 3:121.

21. Al-Anṣārī, *Iḥkām al-dalāla*, 3:44.

prayer] when they are twelve."[22] In fact, because the story appears in al-Qushayrī's chapter on *warʿa* (pious scrupulosity), the focus of it would appear to fall on the elders described therein, while the behavior of the children remains vague. Nevertheless, al-Anṣārī uses the occasion to comment on the proper discipline of children, and the original text of the *Risāla* is coaxed in a new direction. Again, a parallel here can be found in the Muslim exegetical tradition. Through a technique that Saleh refers to as "functional hermeneutics," an exegete might use a verse of the Qurʾān "as the trigger for an exposition of Muslim norms," and the resulting exegesis remains no longer "about explaining the linguistic syntax, rather it is about explaining the moral syntax" of its Qurʾānic base text.[23]

These idiosyncratic readings of the *Risāla*, in addition to al-Anṣārī's limiting and qualifying of the base text, and his disguised contradictions of it, comprise the three primary techniques through which the author recasts the *Risāla*'s content. Al-Anṣārī's recasting of the text's form represents a secondary means through which he achieves objectives both similar to, and independent of, those that inform his content-based redirections of al-Qushayrī's original text. Specifically, al-Anṣārī superimposes a framework over the text in order to systematize it, to reconcile it with his own theory and definitions, and to allow it to function better as a textbook for his student readers. He accomplishes these ends through a variety of strategies.

One form-based technique that al-Anṣārī uses throughout his commentary appears as a general scaffolding that reconciles perceived discrepancies within the *Risāla*, particularly terminological discrepancies. While al-Qushayrī would appear to hold few reservations about presenting materials on a single theme that espouse a variety of opinions, including contradictory opinions, al-Anṣārī aims to systematize the text to the best of his ability. This goal of systematization lends credence to the theory that al-Anṣārī intended his *Iḥkām* as a textbook for students, who we can assume are less comfortable with contradictions than are advanced scholars. The author's commentary on al-Qushayrī's chapter on love (*maḥabba*) provides good examples of this scaffolding technique. Here, al-Anṣārī consolidates al-Qushayrī's four disparate definitions of God's love into two general categories: love that stems from God's will (*irāda*), and love that stems from

22. Al-Anṣārī, *Iḥkām al-dalāla*, 2:159.

23. Saleh, *Formation of the Classical Tafsīr Tradition*, 167–78.

God's speech.[24] In a similar vein, al-Anṣārī posits three general categories of love from the human perspective: love out of compassion and affection, love out of appreciation for gifts bestowed by the beloved, and love out of admiration of qualities in the beloved.[25] These categories are then read into the *Risāla* at various points in order to maintain its theoretical consistency throughout the chapter. Thus, for example, to a Sufi's statement, "[There exists] a love that necessitates the sparing of blood and a love that necessitates the spilling of it," al-Anṣārī identifies the former love with appreciation of the beloved's bounty and identifies the latter love with complete immersion in remembrance of the beloved.[26] The two types of love are thus reconciled with al-Anṣārī's previous, tripartite division of love (matching the second and third categories of love, respectively), and the author thereby imposes a higher standard of consistency onto al-Qushayrī's *Risāla*.

Al-Anṣārī's preambles to each new chapter of the *Risāla* represent another important vehicle for his formal recasting of the text. Though they vary considerably in length, detail, and content, al-Anṣārī's preambles frequently provide a linguistic and terminological definition for a new chapter's subject, alternative opinions on it, proximate causes and upshots of it, and finally its legal ruling (viz. praiseworthy, unlawful, etc.). In effect, these introductory additions frame the original text and thereby shape the chapter so that it resembles a chapter in a standard work of Islamic substantive law.[27] Moreover, framing the original base text in such a manner allows it to function as a standardized textbook that might appear more accessible to a reader who is familiar with the teaching texts used in madrasa study circles.

A final vehicle for al-Anṣārī's formal recasting of the *Risāla* that is worth mentioning appears in the author's reconciling the disparate definitions of the Sufis by positioning them within a larger causal nexus. Specifically, al-Anṣārī identifies areas of al-Qushayrī's text that appear to contradict previously stated definitions, and he recasts these problematic passages as

24. Al-Anṣārī, *Iḥkām al-dalāla*, 4:86.

25. Al-Anṣārī, *Iḥkām al-dalāla*, 4:87–88.

26. Al-Anṣārī, *Iḥkām al-dalāla*, 4:92.

27. Good examples of these preambles can be found at al-Anṣārī, *Iḥkām al-dalāla*, 2:110, 147, 187–88, 213, 230, 3:31–32, 36, 46, 64, 74, 83, 93, 98–99, 107, 125–26, 131, 137, 144, 150, 174, 195, 202–3, 208, 219, 4:2–3, 13, 122, 146–47, 190. Additional, shorter examples can be found at 3:40, 115, 155, 168, 185, 4:31, 37, 61, 78, 105, 190.

either effects (*thamarāt*, literally "fruits") or causes of a standardized definition that thereupon subsumes them. This approach serves to maintain the consistency of the *Risāla* without directly contravening the statements of the Sufi masters that comprise it. An example can be found in al-Qushayrī's discussion of patience, where to a Sufi's statement that "patience is to abandon complaining," al-Anṣārī writes, "This is among the signs of patience but not patience itself."[28] In another example, Sahl al-Tustarī (d. 283/896) remarks, "Repentance is to abandon procrastination," to which al-Anṣārī explains, "This is not repentance but rather one of its causes."[29] In each case, al-Anṣārī's commentary functions as a scaffolding to redirect the original base text seamlessly into a consistent, textbook-styled mold.

Beyond these form-based techniques, al-Anṣārī's recasting of the tone and objective of al-Qushayrī's *Risāla* appears as the third vehicle through which he redirects the original base text within his commentary. One of al-Anṣārī's primary methods of redirecting the text in such a way is through his employing an unmistakably legal lens in his commentary to recast the *Risāla* into a mold that is more legal in its tone and substance than al-Qushayrī had originally intended. The examples of this are many. For instance, when al-Qushayrī explains that the Sufis do not leave their daily litanies (*awrād*) during their spiritual travels (*asfār*), as "dispensations are for the person whose travel is out of necessity," al-Anṣārī provides an especially legalistic addition to this passage, noting that the Sufis take no dispensations in their travels because the legal conditions for dispensations are not fulfilled. However, if we postulate a situation in which the Sufis intended to visit a particular shaykh and had thus specified a particular direction for their travel, which must cover a minimum distance to constitute a longer travel, then taking dispensations would be permissible.[30] In another example, which is almost comical in its blending of the genres of law and Sufism, al-Qushayrī remarks, "It is said that the Sufi does not change [in his state], though if he changes, [his soul] does not become soiled." To this al-Anṣārī adds, "This change does not remain long with him—rather he returns to God's [remembrance] quickly, as a slight change

28. Al-Anṣārī, *Iḥkām al-dalāla*, 3:86.

29. Al-Anṣārī, *Iḥkām al-dalāla*, 2:117.

30. Al-Anṣārī, *Iḥkām al-dalāla*, 4:27. Cf. al-Anṣārī, *Fatḥ al-wahhāb bi-sharḥ Manhaj al-ṭullāb*, 2 vols. (Cairo: ʿĪsā al-Bābī al-Ḥalabī, 1925), 1:70.

disappears with a large amount of water quickly" (*al-taghayyur al-yasīr yazūl bi-l-māʾ al-kathīr bi-surʿa*).[31] Here al-Anṣārī has analogized a legal ruling to the content of al-Qushayrī's base text to derive a novel reading of the text. In fact, al-Anṣārī employs the terms and critical methodology of a legist throughout his commentary. For example, to al-Qushayrī's presenting the opinions of two Sufis on whether experiential knowledge of God (*maʿrifa*) is superior to love of God or vice versa, al-Anṣārī comments that both opinions are sound (*ṣaḥīḥ*) from the perspective of their respective orientations (*tawjīhayn*), though the first opinion (in which love of God is given priority over knowledge of him) is more suitable (*awfaq*) according to the later specialists (*muḥaqqiqūn*), as al-Qushayrī himself alludes to in his weighing (*tarjīḥ*) of the matter.[32] Similar examples of al-Anṣārī's legal methodology and tone that he interjects throughout the text are too many to list in detail here.

A final means by which al-Anṣārī recasts al-Qushayrī's *Risāla* appears in his softening and tempering of the tone of the base text, particularly in those areas that anathematize other Muslims or appear to limit the mercy of God. Once again, al-Anṣārī's approach would suggest that the author intended his work to be read by students or, in any case, nonscholars. His avoidance of the anathema (*takfīr*) appears in various forms and contexts. For example, to a Sufi's harsh theological judgment against the Qadariyya theological sect, al-Anṣārī cites the statement that "the Qadariyya are the Magi of this Muslim Nation," though he is then quick to remind his reader that they are not deemed disbelievers according to later experts.[33] In another example, a theologian who subscribed to the Muʿtazilite position on the eternity of God's punishment is seen in a dream saying, "We have found the [hereafter] easier than we imagined." In his commentary on this story, al-Anṣārī leaves open the possibility that God may have forgiven this individual in spite of his heretical beliefs.[34] In a similar vein, to al-Qushayrī's citation of the famous hadith "He or she will not enter paradise in whose heart is an atom's weight of arrogance," al-Anṣārī tempers the literal read-

31. Al-Anṣārī, *Iḥkām al-dalāla*, 4:12.

32. Al-Anṣārī, *Iḥkām al-dalāla*, 4:103.

33. Al-Anṣārī, *Iḥkām al-dalāla*, 1:55. For the Qadariyya, see, inter alia, W. M. Watt, *Free Will and Predestination in Early Islam* (London: Luzac, 1948), passim.

34. Al-Anṣārī, *Iḥkām al-dalāla*, 2:208.

ing of the text by qualifying damnable arrogance to that which leads to disbelief, while anything less than this will merely prevent a believer from entering paradise with the "truly successful" (*al-fā'izīn*).[35] In a final example, to a Sufi's stern warning that no good will ever come of the person who has tasted the pleasures of the soul, al-Anṣārī adds the important qualifier "unless God should reach you with His mercy."[36] The uncompromising tone of the Sufi's original statement is thus mitigated, and al-Qushayrī's text is thereby eased in a more lenient direction.

Reading the Sufis as Scripture

According to a story in al-Qushayrī's *Risāla*, the Sufi master Sarī al-Saqaṭī (d. 251/865), grabbing the skin of his arm, exclaimed, "By the glory of God exalted! If I said that this skin had gone dry on the bone out of love of Him, I would be telling the truth!" In his commentary on Sarī's words, al-Anṣārī writes in his *Iḥkām*, "In this story is a permission (*wa-fīh jawāz*) for shaykhs to manifest their praiseworthy qualities and to speak of them to their students in order to perfect [the latter's] emulation of [their masters]."[37] Later Sufis, in other words, can not only look to Sarī's words as a source of personal inspiration as they go about their own spiritual travels and toils, but they should also view his precedent as a ethical/legal benchmark for defining the boundaries of the permissible—here as it relates to ostentation (*riyā'*) and its avoidance. Al-Anṣārī's very wording in this passage—"in this story is a permission"—might be better suited to a traditional work of hadith commentary, as examples of this expression within such commentaries are too numerous to mention.

In fact, al-Anṣārī's *Iḥkām* repeatedly attempts to reconcile all of the Sufis' words and actions, as they appear in the *Risāla*, with the entirety of the Islamic legal tradition as it existed in the later Islamic middle period. In the eyes of al-Anṣārī, the Sufis are not only free of sin but their behavior consistently conforms to even the minutia of Islamic jurisprudence. It is particularly for reasons such as this that the *Iḥkām* became famous around

35. Al-Anṣārī, *Iḥkām al-dalāla*, 3:10.

36. Al-Anṣārī, *Iḥkām al-dalāla*, 1:164.

37. Al-Anṣārī, *Iḥkām al-dalāla*, 1:85–86.

the world for its "insistence on the conformity of Sufism to the *sharīʿah*," in the words of one scholar who has documented its later reception in Southeast Asia.[38]

In one story of the *Risāla*, for example, a Sufi shaykh replaces a Qurʾān recitation circle with a poetry session. Although al-Qushayrī cites the story as an example of dutiful submission to one's shaykh, al-Anṣārī nevertheless adds the explanation that perhaps the shaykh cancelled the recitation circle in light of Mālik b. Anas's (d. 179/796) opinion that such circles are legally disliked (*makrūh*).[39] In another example, a Sufi attests to his unconditioned pleasure with God's decree by recalling, "Never have I been as happy with anything as the time that I was sitting and a man came and urinated on me." Unwilling to disregard the legal implications of such an anecdote, al-Anṣārī explains in his commentary that one cannot condemn this Sufi for failing to censure the sin of the urinator, as "it is conceivable that he was incapable of changing [the situation] through action or word so he [aspired] to change it in his heart without revealing this. It is also conceivable that he [tried] to change it through his words (*bi-lisānih*), while there was no need to mention this to others in order for them to transmit it from him [when recounting his story]."[40]

Even to the anecdote of a Sufi who would lock himself indoors during the month of Ramaḍān in ascetical exercises so that "not a single *rakʿa* of prayer would escape him," as the text of the *Risāla* assures us, al-Anṣārī feels compelled to add, "Perhaps he had a valid excuse in abandoning the Friday prayer and the [regular] congregational prayer. It is also conceivable that he did not abandon these and his wife merely *thought* that he had not left the house."[41] In another example, the *Risāla* reports the story of al-Ḥasan

38. Azyumardi Azra, *The Origins of Islamic Reformism in Southeast Asia* (Honolulu: University of Hawai'i Press, 2004), 36–37.

39. Al-Anṣārī, *Iḥkām al-dalāla*, 4:120.

40. Al-Anṣārī, *Iḥkām al-dalāla*, 3:19; cf. 3:189. The three means of changing a bad deed cited in al-Anṣārī's words are in reference to the hadith "Whoever among you sees a bad deed (*munkar*), then let him change it with his hand, and if he cannot, then with his tongue, and if he cannot, then with his heart—and that is the weakest of faith." The original text can be found, inter alia, in Muslim b. al-Ḥajjāj, *Ṣaḥīḥ Muslim*, Kitāb al-Īmān, "Bāb Bayān kawn al-nahī ʿan al-munkar min al-īmān," no. 186.

41. Al-Anṣārī, *Iḥkām al-dalāla*, 4:171 (italics are mine).

al-Baṣrī's (d. 110/728) receiving a reprimand in his dream for his refusal to pray behind a non-Arab imam out of fear that the latter would mispronounce the Qur'ān. To this, al-Anṣārī in his *Iḥkām* adds the legal disclaimer that in fact the imam's prayer must have been sound and his pronunciation not extreme enough to nullify al-Ḥasan's prayer.[42] What is implied in this disclaimer is that al-Ḥasan would not have received his oneiric reprimand had his decision been sound according to Islamic jurisprudence.

Apologetic explanations like the abovementioned examples abound within the *Iḥkām*, and all of them serve to demonstrate—however anachronistically—the unfailing ability of the early Sufis to uphold the detailed injunctions of Islamic jurisprudence as defined by later Muslim scholars like al-Anṣārī. The lives of these Sufis thus function as a scriptural text that must be interpreted to accord with the normative standards of each generation. As scholars of religion have noted, the term "scripture" describes neither a genre of literature nor texts that display certain characteristics but rather texts that are defined by their function within the eyes of a community and that somehow participate in a revelation from God.[43] In this light, al-Anṣārī's approach to the lives of the Sufis in the *Risāla* reflects those same commentarial assumptions that exegetes bring to their studies of scripture within any tradition. Here, specifically, we find in al-Anṣārī's commentary the assumption that the scriptural text (i.e., the lives of the Sufis) is self-consistent and eschews contradiction, and the assumption that it is morally sound and upholds the commentator's own standards of decency.[44] In fact, as has been mentioned above, in several places al-Anṣārī even employs interpretive strategies in his approach to the *Risāla* that find direct parallels in classical Qur'ānic exegesis.

---

42. Al-Anṣārī, *Iḥkām al-dalāla*, 4:167, 196.

43. David Tracy, "Writing," in *Critical Terms for Religious Studies*, ed. Mark C. Taylor (Chicago: University of Chicago Press, 1998), 383; *Encyclopedia of Religion*, s.v. "Scripture" (William A. Graham), 12:8195.

44. For these commentarial assumptions, see John B. Henderson, *Scripture, Canon, and Commentary: A Comparison of Confucian and Western Exegesis* (Princeton, NJ: Princeton University Press, 1991), 115–16, 121–29, 158, 160, 162, 168–77. Cf. Jonathan Brown's review discussion of the principle of charity and its usefulness to the study of canonization processes within Muslim intellectual history. Jonathan A. C. Brown, *The Canonization of Bukhārī and Muslim: The Formation and Function of the Sunnī Ḥadīth Canon* (Leiden: Brill, 2007), 42–46.

To understand why al-Anṣārī would work so hard to uphold a reading of the *Risāla* that treats the lives of the Sufis as a form of de facto scripture, it is helpful to consider a few historical variables. First, texts like the *Risāla* served to elevate the specific Sufi personalities found within them into all-but-infallible mystical exemplars for later generations of Sufi thinkers. By al-Anṣārī's time, the *Risāla* itself, "one of the most widely read books in the history of Sufism," according to one contemporary scholar,[45] had attained a canonical status as evidenced by nothing more than its broad reception within Muslim intellectual circles.[46] If we consider Gerald Sheppard's useful continuum between what he calls "canon 1," the criteria for determining the normative standards of a community, and "canon 2," the catalogue of authoritative texts that a community establishes for itself, the *Risāla* might be said to fall closer to the former pole in the absence of a centralized institution to give it official canonicity. However, organic processes, such as the text's incorporation into the personalized teaching curricula of Muslim scholars and its prominence in *thabat* works by the fifteenth century, pull it toward the "canon 2" pole, albeit not entirely.[47]

As the text's reception increased in its momentum with the passage of time, the Sufi personalities contained within it would increase accordingly in their perceived integrity and irreproachability. Such a process of gradual apotheosis similarly made the transmission chains (sing. *isnād*) of

45. Jawid Ahmad Mojaddedi, *The Biographical Tradition in Sufism: The Ṭabaqāt Genre from al-Sulamī to Jāmī* (Richmond: Curzon Press, 2001), 100. See also Ahmet T. Karamustafa, *Sufism: The Formative Period* (Edinburgh: Edinburgh University Press, 2007), 99.

46. Also consider in this context the words of Gerald Bruns, "The distinction between canonical and noncanonical . . . is a distinction between texts that are forceful in a given situation and those which are not." Gerald L. Bruns, "Canon and Power in the Hebrew Scriptures," *Critical Inquiry* 10, no. 3 (1984): 464. Cf. James Sanders, who explains that the needs of a community determine its conceptions of a text's authority and thus its canonicity. James A. Sanders, *Canon and Community: A Guide to Canonical Criticism* (Philadelphia, PA: Fortress Press, 1984), 30ff.

47. *The Encyclopedia of Religion*, ed. Lindsay Jones, 15 vols., 2nd ed. (New York: Macmillan, 2005), s.v. "Canon" (Gerald T. Sheppard), 3:1407–10. For an example of its use in a personalized teaching curriculum, see al-Shaʿrānī, *al-Ṭabaqāt al-kubrā*, 2:689; for an example of its appearance in a *thabat* work, see Matthew B. Ingalls, "Subtle Innovation within Networks of Convention: The Life, Thought, and Intellectual Legacy of Zakariyyā al-Anṣārī (d. 926/1520)" (PhD diss., Yale University, 2011), 298–99.

the *Risāla* beyond reproach for later commentators like al-Anṣārī. In fact, late-Sunni textual criticism tended to view *any* evidence of an authentic "origin" (*aṣl*) for a tradition to be sufficient to raise that tradition above accusations of forgery,[48] and this tendency no doubt influenced scholarly attitudes toward transmitted texts used in the study of Sufism as well. The end effect of these two factors was that a later scholar could not uphold the integrity of the Sufi masters simply by dismissing their controversial behavior or words on the grounds of misattribution. In fact, at no point in his *Iḥkām* does al-Anṣārī offer a defense of the Sufis on such grounds.

But perhaps more helpful to understanding al-Anṣārī's scriptural reading of the Sufis' lives as they appear in the *Risāla* is to consider the intellectual integration of Ashʿarism, late-Sunni *madhhabism*, and Sharīʿa-bound Sufism that characterized the dominant scholarly worldview of al-Anṣārī's fifteenth-century Egypt.[49] The theological, legal, and mystical elements in this integration would become so inextricably intertwined that to question one element would have immediate ramifications for the others, as the legitimacy of each rested on common institutional structures, such as the *isnād*, as was mentioned above. In other words, if the "happy marriage between Sufism and legal-theological scholarship is the hallmark" of al-Qushayrī's *Risāla*, as Karamustafa describes it,[50] then the spheres of thought had become even more tightly fused by the time that al-Anṣārī's Sufi writings made their appearance.

As an example of al-Anṣārī's fusing the theological and mystical realms in his *Iḥkām*, consider the author's commentary on an elliptical statement that appears toward the beginning of the *Risāla*. Here the author analogizes the Ashʿarī position on God's creating an ability in the eye to behold the beatific vision in the hereafter with His creating knowledge of Him in the hearts of those who know God experientially (*ʿārifūn*). Just as the beatific vision transcends direction when encompassing a directionless God, so too does the knowledge of the *ʿārifūn* know no direction. Then, further fusing

48. Jonathan A. C. Brown, "Even If It's Not True, It's True: Using Unreliable Ḥadīths in Sunni Islam," *Islamic Law and Society* 18 (2011): 16–17; also see Jonathan A. C. Brown, *Hadith: Muhammad's Legacy in the Medieval and Modern World* (Oxford: Oneworld, 2009), 106–10, esp. 108.

49. In other texts al-Anṣārī adopts an attitude that is antagonistic toward the discipline of *kalām*. See, for example, al-Anṣārī, *Asnā l-maṭālib*, 6:268.

50. Karamustafa, *Sufism*, 99.

the mystical and the theological spheres, al-Anṣārī cites the verse of the Qur'ān "And whoever is blind in this world will also be blind in the hereafter," suggesting that those who fall short of the *ʿārifūn* in their experiential knowledge of God will be deficient in their theological understandings of Him as well.[51] In a similar vein, al-Anṣārī applies a novel theological reading to two separate Sufi aphorisms and thereby utilizes mystical experience as a means of resolving the sticky freewill-predestination debate.[52] Elsewhere in his commentary, he explains that the Sufis should be considered "to be part of the larger body of religious scholars" (*min jumlat ṭawāʾif al-ʿulamāʾ*) and expressly analogizes their discipline and its terms of art with those of the theologians (*ahl uṣūl al-dīn*).[53] In this manner, al-Anṣārī links Sufism and theology as mutually inclusive spheres of scholarly insight.

Legal thought is similarly fused with mystical thought in al-Anṣārī's Sufi writings, as has been seen already in several examples from the *Iḥkām* above. According to al-Anṣārī, legal knowledge (*al-ʿilm al-sharʿī*) must serve as a final reference and barometer for all actions, spiritual states, and mystical realities;[54] he even extends al-Junayd's position that Sufism "is bound by the Qur'ān and Sunna" to encompass scholarly consensus and analogy, the other two "roots" of Islamic jurisprudence.[55] Demonstrating how the commentator's thinking transitions seamlessly from legal language to mystical language, one particularly illustrative example from the *Iḥkām* appears in al-Anṣārī's outline of the various substations of repentance (*maqāmāt al-tawba*). Here he writes, "If one is provided with [the passion for repentance], it will carry this person through all of the substations of repentance, such as repentance from disliked deeds, to repentance from abandoning praiseworthy deeds, to repentance from abandoning the best deeds, to repentance from heedless states, to repentance from seeing one's righteous works [as emanating from oneself]."[56] The repentance continuum that he cites thus begins in the jurist's world of the five legal rulings (*aḥkām*) and ends in the mystic's world of spiritual poverty (*faqr*).

51. Al-Anṣārī, *Iḥkām al-dalāla*, 1:48. The verse cited here is a partial rendering of Qur'ān 17:72.

52. Al-Anṣārī, *Iḥkām al-dalāla*, 4:12, 142–43.

53. Al-Anṣārī, *Iḥkām al-dalāla*, 2:21.

54. Al-Anṣārī, *Iḥkām al-dalāla*, 3:98.

55. Al-Anṣārī, *Iḥkām al-dalāla*, 1:143.

56. Al-Anṣārī, *Iḥkām al-dalāla*, 2:117–18; cf. 2:121.

In another example of this subtle transition between mystical and legal language, al-Anṣārī writes,

> This discipline [of Sufism] is "knowledge by bestowal" (*ʿilm al-wirātha*), which is the result of action referred to in the Tradition, "Whoever acts [righteously] according to their knowledge, God will bestow upon them knowledge of what they did not know." Knowledge by bestowal, in turn, is deep understanding of religion (*al-fiqh fī l-dīn*)—that is wisdom, the recipient of which *has received a great good.* It was said to al-Ḥasan al-Baṣrī, "The *fuqahāʾ* (jurists) have said such-and-such," to which he replied, "Have you ever seen a true *faqīh*? The true *faqīh* is but he who renounces the world, stands at night [in prayer], fasts during the day, and who neither deceives nor disputes [but] spreads God's wisdom. If it is accepted from him, he praises God; if it is rejected, he praises God."[57]

Here, both al-Ḥasan and al-Anṣārī use the words *fiqh* and *faqīh* (pl. *fuqahāʾ*) as a self-conscious play on words. That al-Anṣārī immediately quotes al-Ḥasan's take on the "true *faqīh*" after his own reference to *fiqh* suggests that the author's distinction between *fiqh* in its technical register (i.e., practical jurisprudence) and in its conventional register (i.e., deep understanding) is intentionally blurred.

One particularly novel crossover between law and Sufism within the author's thought appears in his analogizing spiritual maladies with physical diseases in order to find new areas of legal flexibility. Three instances of this are found in the *Iḥkām* that al-Anṣārī uses for apologetic purposes. In one example, al-Qushayrī records an anecdote in which a Sufi throws away his money in fulfillment of his companion's request. To this, al-Anṣārī comments that while throwing away money is unlawful in its essence, it becomes lawful if done for the sake of medical treatment (*al-tadāwī*). He then explains, "If it is permissible for a servant to waste large amounts of money for the sake of bodily diseases which might not go away, then

57. Al-Anṣārī, *Iḥkām al-dalāla*, 1:69–70. The Tradition cited here is found in Abū Nuʿaym al-Iṣfahānī, *Ḥilyat al-awliyāʾ wa-ṭabaqāt al-aṣfiyāʾ*, 10 vols. (Cairo: Maktabat al-Khānjī, 1932ff), 10:15. The verse cited (in English italics) is a partial rendering of Qurʾān 2:269.

how much more so in the case of spiritual diseases such that through [this wasting of money] the training and suppression of one's soul takes place and [these diseases] never return!"[58] In another very similar example, the author offers the same defense to al-Shiblī's (d. 334/946) burning of his clothes on ascetical grounds—an ostensibly unlawful act when done without reason.[59] In a third example, in which al-Shiblī shaves his beard to distract others from using God's name in vain, al-Anṣārī explains, "He did this as a treatment for the maladies of his heart, thus in his case, it is not blameworthy."[60] In all three examples, al-Anṣārī's legal reasoning conflates the worlds of externalities and internal states in a novel manner. While a fatwa collection or a standard work in Islamic substantive law might be expected to take physical maladies into consideration in the course of legal reasoning, the same cannot be said of spiritual maladies. Al-Anṣārī, however, makes an analogy between the two classes of maladies in order to expand the existing understandings of legally valid behavior. This approach and the results obtained once again reflect al-Anṣārī's scriptural reading of the Sufis lives as they appear in al-Qushayrī's *Risāla*.

One important upshot of (and further evidence for) al-Anṣārī's scriptural reading of the Sufis' lives appears in his quest to reconcile the statements and opinions of the Sufis with each other just as an exegete would reconcile verses of the Qur'ān. Through his efforts, the words of the Sufis form a single, consistent text. Perhaps the author's most successful means of achieving such consistency appears in his appealing to the spiritual states of the Sufis as a means of making their words and deeds relative to their specific circumstances. In other words, while a Sufi's particular statement or action may appear strange when taken in its absolute sense, it can be justified within the context of this Sufi's particular state and station along the Sufi Path. Thus, in one anecdote in the *Risāla*, a Sufi explains that persistently knocking on God's door will eventually lead to its opening, to which another Sufi objects that the door, in fact, has never been closed. Here, al-Anṣārī explains that the first Sufi was speaking according to the "station of acquisition and servitude" (*maqām al-kasb wa-l-ʿubūdiyya*), while the second was speaking according to "the station of divine oneness"

58. Al-Anṣārī, *Iḥkām al-dalāla*, 3:142.

59. Al-Anṣārī, *Iḥkām al-dalāla*, 3:180.

60. Al-Anṣārī, *Iḥkām al-dalāla*, 3:207.

(*maqām al-tawḥīd*).[61] Their understandings, though not wholly equal at the absolute level, nevertheless reflect saintly perspectives on a single truth.[62]

The abovementioned variables then—the gradual apotheosis of the early Sufi masters with the passage of time, the wholesale acceptance of their words and deeds as authentic, and the irreducible integration of the intellectual realms within the worldview of scholars from the later Islamic middle period—require us to expand our definition of Muslim scripture to include de facto sources like al-Qushayrī's *Risāla* and the saintly stories contained within it. Or, stated from the perspective of commentators like al-Anṣārī: God manifests His will within the actions of His friends (*awliyā'*), and hence the lives of God's friends, as enshrined in texts like the *Risāla*, demand a scriptural reading. But such a reading will flow in two directions because of the seamless integration of the intellectual realms that has been described. Thus, the lives of the early Sufi masters will set an ethical standard for the inheritors of their tradition, while later theological and legal understandings will be read back into the words and behavior of these early masters. Moreover, legal language plays a crucial role in this scriptural reading of the Sufis' lives. Expressions such as "in this story is a permission . . ." (*wa-fīh jawāz*), of which there are many in al-Anṣārī's *Iḥkām*, serve the same function as they do in hadith commentaries and *muṣannaf* works, among other genres: they impute scriptural integrity to a foundational text while simultaneously structuring a reader's own social realities and normative standards.

The Aesthetic and Rhetorical Impact of the Interwoven Commentary

Formal devices particular to the later Islamic middle period provided Muslim commentators like al-Anṣārī with unique tools with which to harness their creative potential in order to display their own voices and personal concerns within their commentaries. As has been mentioned above, al-Anṣārī relied especially on the form of the interwoven commentary (*sharḥ mamzūj*) when writing commentaries like the *Iḥkām*, in addition to most of his legal com-

61. Al-Anṣārī, *Iḥkām al-dalāla*, 3:225.

62. A similar methodology can be found in several other instances in the *Iḥkām*. See, for example, al-Anṣārī, *Iḥkām al-dalāla*, 2:76, 118–19; 3:105, 244; 4:29, 145, 194.

mentaries, and his use of this particular device will serve here to illustrate the connections between form, creativity, and reception within commentary writing during this period. As the interwoven commentary has already been described above in chapter 1, the present analysis focuses on the rhetorical and aesthetical impact of the interwoven commentary from a theoretical perspective, which is then connected to examples from al-Anṣārī's *Iḥkām*.

According to contemporary theories from the field of psychological aesthetics, the interwoven commentary should lead to an increase in what is known as a text's "processing fluency." According to these theories, "Aesthetic experience is a function of the perceiver's processing dynamics" whereby "the more fluently the perceiver can process an object, the more positive is his or her aesthetic response."[63] Or, to phrase it in terms that should improve on the concept's own processing fluency: the ease of processing information positively affects a person's appreciation for the medium of this information. The relative ease of processing a particular stimulus (here, an interwoven commentary) induces subjective pleasure, or simply positive affect, in the subject (here, the premodern reader). In turn, this subjective experience informs the subject's evaluative judgments of the stimulus, thereby linking fluency and evaluation.[64] The subjective experience may also motivate the subject and reinforce the processing strategies that he or she has employed—a dynamic that may help to account for the large and motivated student readership that al-Anṣārī's texts attracted.[65] Nevertheless, how subjects attribute the fluency of a stimulus, and whether they are self-conscious of it, still figure into their assessments of the stimulus. If the source of the fluency is unknown or processed subconsciously, then it has the strongest effect on the evaluation of its medium; if it is recognized and deemed irrelevant, then it has the least effect.[66] As an example of the latter phenomenon, consider that a person is more likely to evaluate a clear argument negatively if he or she perceives it to be patronizing in its extreme

63. Rolf Reber, Norbert Schwarz, and Piotr Winkielman, "Processing Fluency and Aesthetic Pleasure: Is Beauty in the Perceiver's Processing Experience?," *Personality and Social Psychology Review* 8, no. 4 (2004): 365.

64. Reber et al., "Processing Fluency and Aesthetic Pleasure," 365–68.

65. Piotr Winkielman et al., "Fluency of Consistency: When Thoughts Fit Nicely and Flow Smoothly," in *Cognitive Consistency: A Fundamental Principle in Social Cognition*, ed. Bertram Gawronski and Fritz Strack, 89–111 (New York: Guilford Press, 2012), 94–95. For al-Anṣārī's large student readership, see, inter alia, N. al-Ghazzī, *Kawākib*, 1:201.

66. Reber et al., "Processing Fluency and Aesthetic Pleasure," 372–75.

degree of clarity. This person would no longer view the argument as clever and persuasive but would rather see it as an attempt to manipulate his or her better judgment.

If we assume that the subject reader is not self-conscious of the dynamics behind processing fluency, then any quality in the object that facilitates its conceptual processing will increase its processing fluency and hence the likelihood that the subject will evaluate it positively.[67] General qualities that facilitate processing fluency in an object include symmetry, visual clarity, and perceived familiarity. These qualities all require a subject to process less information in evaluating a stimulus when compared with similar stimuli that lack these qualities. For example, a symmetrical object offers a subject less information to process than an asymmetrical object of comparable measure. The symmetrical object is thus easier to process conceptually and therefore can be expected to elicit a more positive affect in, and a better evaluation from, a subject.[68] By presenting both base text and commentary together as one text, the interwoven commentary improves on the symmetry and visual clarity of the commentarial form and absolves the reader of the disruptions entailed in jumping between the two component texts. In all aspects, then, and with all other variables held constant, the interwoven commentary relies on less information to communicate its message.

An inverse relationship between the qualities of an object and its processing fluency holds as well. A higher processing fluency, in other words, cues a subject to expect other valued qualities within an object. The perceived familiarity of an object, for example, often stems not from actual familiarity, which might be entirely imagined, but rather from the positive affect generated by fluency.[69] This correlation between fluency and perceived familiarity is worth mentioning in the present context as it might help us to account for subtle intellectual innovation among Muslim scholars like al-Anṣārī whose credentials were otherwise grounded, at least rhetorically, in their fidelity to the received tradition. Were the writings of these scholars to be high in processing fluency in the eyes of their readership, then we can expect them to elicit a positive affect in this readership that, in turn, is often misidentified as a sense of familiarity. For its part, this sense of

67. Reber et al., "Processing Fluency and Aesthetic Pleasure," 366.

68. Reber et al., "Processing Fluency and Aesthetic Pleasure," 368–72; Winkielman et al., "Fluency of Consistency," 98–99.

69. Winkielman et al., "Fluency of Consistency," 95–96, 99.

familiarity might conceivably lower the inhibitions of its subjects toward content that breaks from the received tradition, particularly if this content is presented through a subtle rhetoric like that described above. One psychological study, moreover, has demonstrated a convincing link between a subject's mood (their "affective context") and the degree to which they value familiarity. According to this study, familiarity is especially valued by subjects in a negative mood, which signals an unsafe environment.[70] Thus, in a historical context of political turmoil and the perceived breakdown of moral authority—as is the dominant metanarrative of many generations but particularly that of al-Anṣārī—the familiar rises in value and is conjured up through processing fluency.[71]

Beyond generating a sense of familiarity, processing fluency also influences our perceptions of truth: the more coherent and fluent the form of the information presented to us is, the higher a "perceived truth value" we assign to it. Although the parts of a competing truth claim might be complex, if the whole of it can be processed with relative ease and constitutes a single, coherent structure or narrative, we are more likely to give it precedence over rival truth claims that are presented less coherently.[72] In this light, to the degree that an interwoven commentary improves on processing fluency when compared with other commentarial forms, it should enjoy a comparable advantage in its claims to truth. In the final analysis, then, the increased ease of processing a written form that combines two original texts into an easily digested amalgamated text should predictably increase the chance that a reader will find this latter text to be clearly argued and convincing, familiar and true, and—most importantly—superior to other texts that are not as aesthetically pleasing (see figure 3.1).[73]

70. Marieke de Vries et al., "Happiness Cools the Warm Glow of Familiarity: Psychophysiological Evidence That Mood Modulates the Familiarity-Affect Link," *Psychological Sciences* 21, no. 3 (2010): 326.

71. See Mark C. Taylor, *After God* (Chicago: University of Chicago Press, 2009), chapter 5–6.

72. Winkielman et al., "Fluency of Consistency," 96, 105–7; Rolf Reber and Norbert Schwarz, "Effects of Perceptual Fluency on Judgments of Truth," *Consciousness and Cognition* 8 (1999): 338–42, esp. 339.

73. Consider in this context what Saleh writes on Qur'ān commentaries: "The length and style of a commentary are as important as the content. . . . [One] that is impossible to read is useless no matter how insightful the content." Saleh, *Formation of the Classical Tafsīr Tradition*, 83.

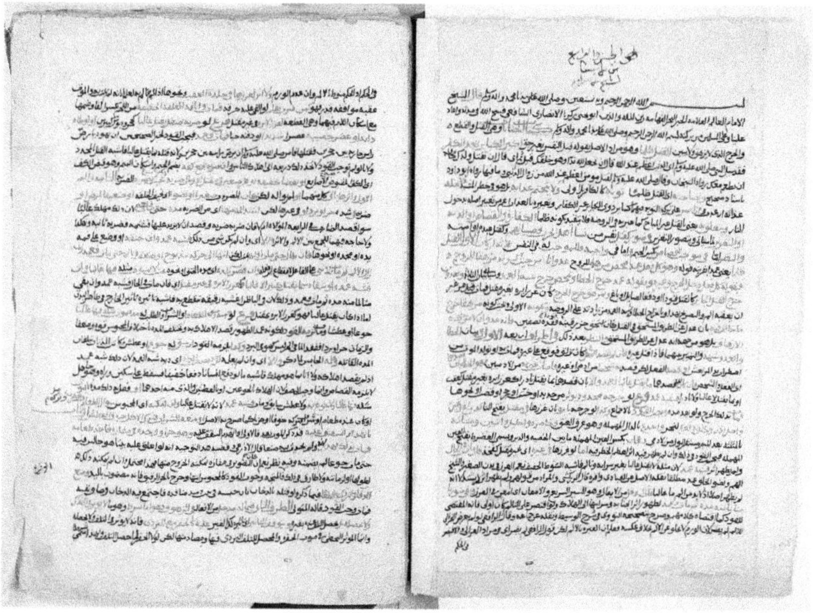

Figure 3.1. A sample folio from a manuscript of al-Anṣārī's interwoven commentary *Asnā l-maṭālib: Sharḥ Rawḍ al-ṭālib*, Umm al-Qurā University, Mecca, fols. 1v-2r. *Source*: Brill. Used with permission.

But the increased processing fluency generated by the interwoven commentary does not represent this form's only advantage over other commentarial forms. By weaving commentary into a base text, a commentator exercises a unique measure of control over the latter text and is able to redeploy it subtly into the interpretive direction of his choosing. Such control would allow a commentator like al-Anṣārī to maintain his scriptural reading of the lives of the Sufis even in the face of textual evidence that might otherwise undermine his favorable expectations of these Sufis. It is perhaps for this reason that al-Anṣārī was especially famous for his reliance on the interwoven commentarial form.[74]

To demonstrate how the interwoven commentary enhances the control of a commentator over a base text, let us consider three examples from the *Iḥkām*, a quintessential example of the interwoven commentary from

74. B. al-Ghazzī, *al-Durr al-naḍīd*, 465–66; Ḥājjī Khalīfa, *Kashf al-ẓunūn*, 1:882n1.

the Muslim manuscript tradition. The first appears within the context of al-Qushayrī's chapter on self-denial (*al-zuhd*)—here the interwoven text has been translated with al-Anṣārī's commentary represented in boldface:

> Aḥmad b. Ḥanbal said, "Self-denial is according to three stages. The first is to abandon the unlawful **with one's heart**; this is the self-denial of the common people. The second is to abandon what is superfluous of the lawful **with one's heart**; this is the self-denial of the elect **of these people**. The third is to abandon anything that distracts the servant from God, the exalted, **with one's heart**; this is the self-denial of those who know **God, the exalted." These are the elect of the elect. As for abandoning such things with the limbs, this is from the fruits of self-denial but not self-denial itself, as has been discussed.**[75]

Whereas Ibn Ḥanbal's (d. 241/855) original statement reflects an early ninth-century understanding of *zuhd*, which very much centered around an abandonment of material possessions and physical comforts, al-Anṣārī's commentary qualifies Ibn Ḥanbal's statement to reconcile it with the commentator's own metaphorical understanding of *zuhd*, namely "to turn away from the world in one's heart."[76] However, what is significant to the present discussion is the means through which the interwoven commentary enables al-Anṣārī to contradict his predecessor without doing so overtly. The amalgamated text here seamlessly bends the original base text with the selective addition of a few sparse words—in fact, only a single phonological word in Arabic (*bi-l-qalb*) thrice repeated in the first half of the text—to generate a meaning that suits the commentator's worldview, though not necessarily that of the base text's author.

A similar phenomenon can be found a few pages later within a chapter on fear of God. The interwoven text reads as follows: "Abū Ḥafṣ said,[77] 'Fear

75. Al-Anṣārī, *Iḥkām al-dalāla*, 2:175–76.

76. Al-Anṣārī, *Iḥkām al-dalāla*, 2:164. See Christopher Melchert, "The Transition from Asceticism to Mysticism at the Middle of the Ninth Century C.E.," *Studia Islamica* 83 (1996): 51–70.

77. Abū Ḥafṣ al-Ḥaddād (d. ca. 265/878–79). The other narrators in al-Qushayrī's transmission chain for this quote have been omitted.

is the heart's lantern through which it perceives **via the intermediary of knowledge** all the good and evil that is in it.' **Thus in reality, fear drives [the heart] to circumspection in order for it to discern good from evil, while its discernment is through knowledge not fear.**"[78]

Through his interjection of two phonological words (*bi-wāsiṭat al-ʿilm*) into the first sentence of the base text, al-Anṣārī succeeds in shifting the meaning of Abū Ḥafṣ' statement to accord with his own scholarly worldview. Now fear of God no longer acts as the final arbiter to distinguish good from evil, but rather knowledge serves in this capacity, while fear merely facilitates the deliberative process behind the use of knowledge. But the amalgamated text never emphasizes these differences in worldviews between Abū Ḥafṣ and his fifteenth-century commentator. Instead it maintains the syntactical cohesion of the original statement, and without gainsaying the conceptual units that inform this statement, it eases the larger meaning of the text into a direction of the commentator's choosing.

A third example of this approach can be found in al-Anṣārī's commentary on al-Qushayrī's discussion of modesty (*al-ḥayāʾ*). In this instance, to a Sufi's statement that "the greatest knowledge (*ʿilm*) is awe and modesty," al-Anṣārī interjects only a few words to yield a completely new reading: "The greatest knowledge, **which is the experiential knowledge (*maʿrifa*) of God, the exalted, its fruit** is awe and modesty."[79] The text now conforms to al-Anṣārī's own understanding that the experiential knowledge of God trumps awe and modesty, which are now merely aftereffects of *maʿrifa*. More importantly, however, the author communicates his contravening position while successfully avoiding a direct confrontation with the opinion of an earlier Sufi master. In the final analysis, then, the interwoven commentary functions as a highly effective medium through which al-Anṣārī gives voice to his own idiosyncratic interpretations of Sufism while maintaining a scriptural deference toward the outward words and actions of the Sufis.

But why bend, patch, and qualify a base text, as al-Anṣārī does, when it would be so much simpler to refute an earlier text or simply rewrite the tradition? It would seem that ascribing authority to a canonical base text functions to preserve social efficiency and cohesion inasmuch as the canon's deficiencies can be sidestepped through commentary, thereby obviating the

78. Al-Anṣārī, *Iḥkām al-dalāla*, 2:191.

79. Al-Anṣārī, *Iḥkām al-dalāla*, 3:145.

need to reascribe authority elsewhere.[80] Metaphorically stated, if canon is the rusty anchor that binds successive societal ships within a larger canonical tradition, then commentary is the solder on this anchor that forestalls any search for a new mooring.

Commentators, for their part, usually occupy a space that is close to the central institutions of power within a society. Their unique standing grants them special access to the canon, which in turn they interpret to reinforce these same institutions of power, regulating through their scholarly discourse who has access to them.[81] In many ways, then, commentaries function as "buffers in defense of sanity and civilization," in the words of one scholar.[82] Their buffering in defense of civilization can be found in their very attitudes toward the past whereby the canonical text is valued for its creative potential to maintain the order of society.[83] Similarly, their buffering in defense of sanity emerges in their ability to create a more immediate order at the level of meaning. Commentary, that is, creates a new canonical text by narrowing the spectrum of interpretive possibility that is available to a given audience.[84]

Commentary, in other words, makes sense of—and thus orders—the present through a taxonomy that is rooted in the canonical past; it is the medium through which a community determines its relationship to its past. The present, for its part, is frequently perceived as distant from the center of the tradition, both temporally and spatially. This distance from the center becomes even more pronounced in the face of social turmoil, such as the perceived breakdown of societal morals, as is reflected in the "corruption of the times" (*fasād al-zamān*) metanarrative that informed the discourse of later Muslim scholars like al-Anṣārī.[85] In response to such

80. Glenn W. Most, "Preface," in *Commentaries—Kommentare*, ed. Glenn W. Most, vii–xv (Göttingen, Germany: Vandenhoeck and Ruprecht, 1999), viii; Smith, *Imagining Religion*, 49–52.

81. Most, "Preface," ix.

82. Henderson, *Scripture, Canon, and Commentary*, 222.

83. Aaron Hughes, "Presenting the Past: The Genre of Commentary in Theoretical Perspective," *Method and Theory in the Study of Religion* 15 (2003): 164.

84. Cutler, "Interpreting *Tirukkuṟaḷ*," 561; also see Kraus, "Introduction," 9.

85. For examples of this metanarrative within the *Iḥkām*, see al-Anṣārī, *Iḥkām al-dalāla*, 1:193, 2:173, 3:11, 147.

disruptions, commentary seeks to relieve the present of its uncanniness through its redeployments of the past, while the discourse that emerges is frequently the locus of impressive creativity.[86]

Al-Anṣārī's *Iḥkām* certainly reflects such creativity and imagination. His scriptural reading of the Sufis' lives in the *Risāla*, though clearly a function of his intellectual context, demands creative solutions from him throughout his commentary. Although the interwoven commentarial form would make his task easier, it would never completely free him of the need for ingenuity in his use of language. In the end, the rhetorical power of commentaries like the *Iḥkām* remains very much connected to the mind of the commentator no matter how much agency we ascribe to contextual considerations. Scholarly conventions like the interwoven commentary, in other words, are not the only means of accounting for the large readership that the *Iḥkām* continues to enjoy. Rather, the text's popularity is, in no small way, a testament to creativity of its author.

86. Hughes, "Presenting the Past," 159, 162–66.

Chapter Four

Fanning the Fire of Islamic Legal Change with the *Mukhtaṣar-Sharḥ* Bellows

The present chapter adjusts the methodology of the previous chapter to examine the literary mechanics that defined the discipline of Islamic law in the later Islamic middle period. As in the previous chapter, I have taken the writings of Zakariyyā al-Anṣārī as my case study, though for reasons that become clear below, the present chapter's analysis must encompass both al-Anṣārī's legal commentaries *and* his abridgments (sing. *mukhtaṣar*) to derive any conclusions about the textual record and what it means for the study of Islamic law. After a few words on the idiosyncrasies that characterized al-Anṣārī's legal texts, the chapter documents all of al-Anṣārī's works in Islamic substantive law (*furūʿ al-fiqh*) and how they figure into the textual genealogies that preceded them. Part 2 of the chapter then examines three generations of texts from one of these genealogies to show how the antipodal processes of commentary (*sharḥ*) and abridgment (*ikhtiṣār*) affect the rhetoric of Islamic law and legal change within the textual tradition. Part 3 next extends these findings to an entire textual genealogy through the lens of a single passage from one of al-Anṣārī's commentaries; tracing this passage back through the textual record illuminates the major structural changes that transformed this particular textual genealogy over its seven-hundred-year history. Finally, with the help of a figure, a concluding section summarizes the lessons that can be gleaned from the analyses of parts 2 and 3 as they apply to the operations of commentary and abridgment within the literary history of Islamic law.

As chapter 5 describes in more depth below, al-Anṣārī's legal commentaries would play an integral role in shaping the later Shāfiʿī *madhhab*, and to understand why this was the case, it is helpful to begin with a few words on the stylistics that characterized these commentaries. Here my analysis gives particular weight to al-Anṣārī's two legal commentaries that received the most attention from later commentators, namely his *Tuḥfat al-ṭullāb* (*The Students' Gift*) and the *Fatḥ al-wahhāb* (*Epiphany from God, the Bestower*). What is unique about the stylistics of commentaries like the *Tuḥfat al-ṭullāb* and the *Fatḥ al-wahhāb* that might have made them worthy of the attention of later commentators, scholars, and students?

The first obvious characteristic shared by these two texts that hints at an answer to this question is their relative terseness. The *Tuḥfat al-ṭullāb* and the *Fatḥ al-wahhāb* stand as al-Anṣārī's shortest complete commentaries in substantive law, which, on the one hand, makes them particularly useful in later teaching circles while creating, on the other, the need for subsequent commentaries to unpack their pithy prose. The *Fatḥ al-wahhāb*, moreover, represents a commentary on the author's own *mukhtaṣar* of Yaḥyā b. Sharaf al-Nawawī's (676/1277) *Minhāj al-ṭālibīn* (*The Students' Program*)—a base text that carries with it the highest degree of cachet within the later Shāfiʿī *madhhab*.[1]

But beyond the mere terseness of these two texts, several other methodological idioms characterize al-Anṣārī's legal writings and might help to explain the pedagogical—and thus commentarial—attention that at least some of these writings would receive. The first is the author's unfailing concern with identifying where a given text adds to, or differs from, the foundational text from which it derives (that is, through either the process of abridgment or commentary). This theme, and examples of it, is taken up in the analysis that follows, but it is worth noting for now that al-Anṣārī's tone is consistently irenic throughout this process, as he applies the most charitable reading possible whenever he attempts to reconcile two texts within a textual genealogy.[2]

---

1. On the theoretical position of the *Minhāj* within al-Nawawī's larger oeuvre, see Ibn Ḥajar al-Haytamī, *Tuḥfat al-muḥtāj bi-sharḥ al-Minhāj* [printed in the margins of ʿAbd al-Ḥamīd al-Shirwānī and Aḥmad b. Qāsim al-ʿAbbādī's *Ḥawāshī ʿalā Tuḥfat al-muḥtāj bi-sharḥ al-Minhāj*], 10 vols. (Cairo: al-Maktaba al-Tijāriyya al-Kubrā, 1938), 1:39.

2. For an example, see al-Anṣārī, *Asnā l-maṭālib*, 1:148, in which al-Anṣārī eschews the most obvious explanation for a discrepancy in a base text (that the author Ibn al-Muqrī misread al-Nawawī's original text) by positing that the base text author must

Al-Anṣārī's legal writings also demonstrate consistent concern for providing scriptural or other textual evidence for the legal positions within a base text; they do so in a succinct language that tends toward a single piece of evidence per legal ruling.[3] To be sure, al-Anṣārī wrote in an age in which legal interpretation was expected to be justified on the basis of evidence from the inherited textual tradition,[4] and yet the low ratio of evidence to ruling suggests that al-Anṣārī's name carried authority in its own right within the later *madhhab*. In other words, the objective of his rhetoric is less about convincing his reader of his position than in clearing his reader's conscience of deference to a postformative authority like himself. Here, instead, deference returns to the textual evidence that has been provided, although it is al-Anṣārī who retains final authority by determining which piece of evidence merits such deference.

Similarly, the author references the works of al-Nawawī and ʿAbd al-Karīm al-Rāfiʿī (d. 623/1226) whenever possible to justify his ruling on a legal question or to undermine an opposing position. Of course, a tenth/sixteenth-century Shāfiʿī legist like al-Anṣārī could not stand outside the authority of these two masters. But because their collected works as a whole contain conflicting rulings on many questions of Islamic law and remain silent on even more questions that would occupy the minds of later generations, al-Anṣārī would retain considerable autonomy as he worked to identify the "relied upon" (*muʿtamad*) position of the *madhhab* even within al-Nawawī and al-Rāfiʿī's shadow of authority.[5] As for his own authority, al-Anṣārī frequently refers his reader to his other texts either for a more detailed treatment of a subject if it is legal in nature or for a nonlegal

have preferred a different position of al-Nawawī that he took from an outside source. Also see Ṭāriq Yūsuf Ḥasan Jābir, "Shaykh al-Islām Zakariyyā al-Anṣārī wa-atharuh fī l-fiqh al-Shāfiʿī" (MA thesis, University of Jordan, 2004), 80–83.

3. For an illustrative handful of examples, which are otherwise legion, see Jābir, "Shaykh al-Islām Zakariyyā al-Anṣārī," 73–78.

4. See Sherman A. Jackson, "Literalism, Empiricism, and Induction: Apprehending and Concretizing Islamic Law's *Maqāṣid al-Sharīʿah* in the Modern World," *Michigan State Law Review* (2006): 1473.

5. Jābir counts over one hundred instances in which al-Anṣārī would exercise his independent legal reasoning to weigh between the positions of al-Nawawī and al-Rāfiʿī or break from their precedent. The ten examples of this that he provides as case studies cover matters from across the branches of Islamic law. Jābir, "Shaykh al-Islām Zakariyyā al-Anṣārī," 152–67.

discussion if the subject touches on a field outside the sphere of law.[6] This self-referentiality would function to buttress al-Anṣārī's authority while increasing the momentum of canonicity that was ascribed to his various works in the decades and centuries that followed him. It also hints at his pedagogical concerns, as it would be students of law who were most likely to follow up on such citations in the course of their studies.

Two final qualities that characterize al-Anṣārī's legal writings may help in explaining their popularity and scholarly reception. The first is the author's careful eye for precision and economy of speech; these define the stylistic essence of al-Anṣārī's *Fatḥ al-wahhāb* and *Tuḥfat al-ṭullāb*.[7] In fact, al-Anṣārī is uncharacteristically quick to criticize his predecessors in their choice of language whenever he deems it inaccurate, vague, maundering, or otherwise uninspired, as precision of language would be one of the few safe arenas in which a later scholar like al-Anṣārī could claim superiority over his predecessors without having to ground his originality—at least rhetorically—in their authority. A second and final quality worth mentioning in this context appears in the author's frequent inclusion of supplementary "useful points" (*fawāʾid*) and ancillary applications of the matters discussed in a base text. Most often these come in the concluding sections of subchapters; they function to scaffold the material at hand or summarize it for the benefit of students of law.[8]

Part I: Al-Anṣārī's Works in Islamic Substantive Law

If we exclude his four works devoted to estate division (*farāʾiḍ*) and his commentary on the celebrated *Mukhtaṣar* of Ismāʿīl b. Yaḥyā al-Muzanī (d.

6. For an example of the former, see al-Anṣārī, *Fatḥ al-wahhāb bi-sharḥ Manhaj al-ṭullāb*, 1:114; for an example of the latter, see al-Anṣārī, *al-Ghurar al-bahiyya*, 1:136.

7. Jābir holds that it is precision of speech (*al-tadqīq fī l-ʿibāra*) that has made the *Fatḥ al-wahhāb* and the *Tuḥfat al-ṭullāb* so popular among Shāfiʿī scholars. Jābir, "Shaykh al-Islām Zakariyyā al-Anṣārī," 99.

8. For an example, see al-Anṣārī, *Asnā l-maṭālib*, 1:495. Elsewhere the author defines a "useful point" as "every beneficial thing that accrues from an action." Zakariyyā al-Anṣārī, *Tuḥfat al-ṭullāb bi-sharḥ Taḥrīr Tanqīḥ al-Lubāb* (Mecca: al-Maṭbaʿa al-Mīriyya, 1310 [1892–93]), 3.

264/877–78), which appears to be lost to us today,[9] we can group al-Anṣārī's texts in substantive law into the four textual genealogies that follow. Whenever possible, al-Anṣārī's motives in writing each text is noted below.

Texts That Derive from al-Nawawī's *Minhāj al-ṭālibīn*

The texts that derive from al-Nawawī's *Minhāj al-ṭālibīn* are al-Anṣārī's *Manhaj al-ṭullāb* (*The Students' Course*), a *mukhtaṣar* of al-Nawawī's *Minhāj*; and his *Fatḥ al-wahhāb*, a commentary on this same *mukhtaṣar*. In the introduction to his *Manhaj*, al-Anṣārī explains that he replaced the non-*muʿtamad* positions in al-Nawawī's original text with their *muʿtamad* equivalents while also removing the details of scholarly disagreement (*al-khilāf*).[10] Subsequently, in the introduction to his *Fatḥ al-wahhāb*, the author writes that it was "someone dear to me, from the learned folk (*al-fuḍalāʾ*) who visit me frequently," who requested that he write this commentary on his abridgment of the *Minhāj*.[11] It is worth noting here that al-Anṣārī does not identify his intended audience as students per se, although the text would certainly appear designed to help students in digesting al-Nawawī's much longer work,[12] and it has been used in such a way by students of Islamic law until the present time (see figure 4.1).[13]

9. Al-Shaʿrānī records that he studied the text with al-Anṣārī. ʿAbd al-Wahhāb al-Shaʿrānī, *Laṭāʾif al-minan wa-l-akhlāq fī wujūb al-taḥadduth bi-niʿmat Allāh ʿalā l-iṭlāq*, ed. Aḥmad ʿIzzū ʿInāya (Damascus: Dār al-Taqwā, 2004), 73. Also see al-Malījī al-Shaʿrānī, *Manāqib al-Shaʿrānī*, 55, where it is suggested that the text was a partial commentary. For al-Anṣārī's own references that confirm the text's one-time existence, see al-Anṣārī, *Fatḥ al-ʿallām*, 33, 140, 195, 266.

10. Al-Anṣārī, *Fatḥ al-wahhāb bi-sharḥ Manhaj al-ṭullāb*, 1:3.

11. Al-Anṣārī, *Fatḥ al-wahhāb bi-sharḥ Manhaj al-ṭullāb*, 1:2.

12. Jābir shares this assessment. Jābir, "Shaykh al-Islām Zakariyyā al-Anṣārī," 71. The *Manhaj* identifies its audience with the generic "those who are desirous" (*al-rāghibūn*). Al-Anṣārī, *Fatḥ al-wahhāb bi-sharḥ Manhaj al-ṭullāb*, 1:3.

13. For an account of how the text figures into contemporary Shāfiʿī-*madhhab* curricula in various places around the world today, see Muhammad Nabeel Musharraf, *A Roadmap for Studying Fiqh: An Introduction to the Key Texts of the Four Madhhabs* (Perth: Australian Islamic Library, 2017), 46–47.

A Textual Geneaology for the
Manhaj al-ṭullāb and *Fatḥ al-wahhāb*

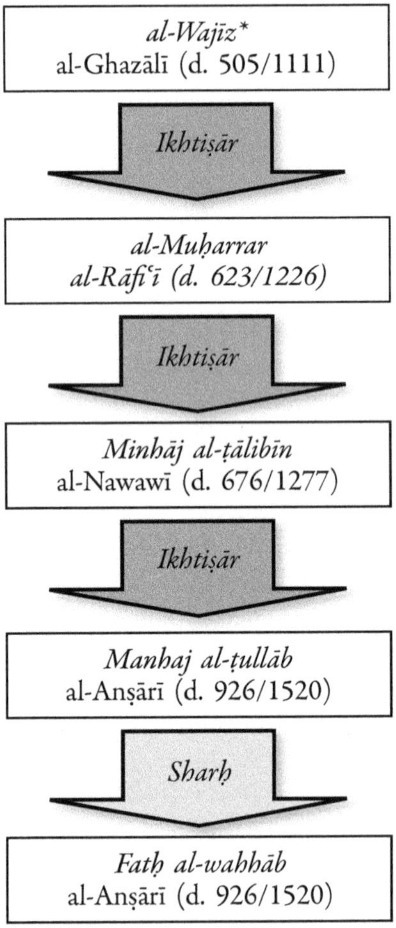

*Muslim scholars are divided on whether al-Rāfiʿī's *Muḥarrar* should be viewed as a *mukhtaṣar* of al-Ghazālī's *Wajīz* or as an autonomous beginning to its own textual genealogy. For the former position, see al-Bujayrimī, *al-Tajrīd li-nafʿ al-ʿabīd*, 1:16; for the latter position, see al-Haytamī, *Tuḥfat al-muḥtāj bi-sharḥ al-Minhāj*, 1:35.

Figure 4.1. A textual genealogy for the *Manhaj al-ṭullāb* and *Fatḥ al-wahhāb*. *Source*: Author provided.

Texts That Derive from Abū Zurʿa al-ʿIrāqī's *Tanqīḥ al-Lubāb*

The texts that derive from Abū Zurʿa al-ʿIrāqī's *Tanqīḥ al-Lubāb* are al-Anṣārī's *Taḥrīr Tanqīḥ al-Lubāb* (*The Rendering of the Revision of the Quintessence*), a *mukhtaṣar* of al-ʿIrāqī's *Tanqīḥ*; his *Tuḥfat al-ṭullāb*, a commentary on this same *mukhtaṣar*; and his *Fatḥ al-wahhab*, a direct commentary on al-ʿIrāqī's *Tanqīḥ*. I refer to the latter text as al-Anṣārī's direct commentary on the *Tanqīḥ* to avoid confusion with his other *Fatḥ al-wahhāb,* which has been discussed above.

In the text of his *Taḥrīr Tanqīḥ al-Lubāb*, the author once again notes that he replaced the non-*muʿtamad* positions in the original text with their *muʿtamad* equivalents while also removing the details of scholarly disagreement. Here, however, he explicitly intends students as his primary readership.[14]

As for the third text, al-Anṣārī's direct commentary on the *Tanqīḥ*, some of the secondary literature to date has referenced its existence but are otherwise at a loss as to its contents.[15] In his *Tuḥfat al-ṭullāb*, al-Anṣārī himself refers his reader to this "*sharḥ al-aṣl*" (commentary on the original source) to find further details on various discussions at hand,[16] which also confirms that he wrote his *Tuḥfat al-ṭullāb* after his direct commentary on the *Tanqīḥ*. I was fortunate enough to stumble across a complete manuscript of this direct commentary in the Beinecke Library's Landberg Collection, and since this appears to be one of only a few copies of the text in existence today,[17] a few words about the manuscript are worth mentioning here.

Landberg MSS 465 comprises 370 bound folios, copied in a clear *naskhī* hand, with folios 1 through 10 written by a different copyist and followed by a lacuna on the subsequent folio. Al-ʿIrāqī's base text is copied in red ink, with al-Anṣārī's interwoven commentary in black ink. Alternate

14. Al-Anṣārī, *Tuḥfat al-ṭullāb*, 3.

15. For example, see Jābir's terse references to "*Sharḥ al-aṣl*." Jābir, "Shaykh al-Islām Zakariyyā al-Anṣārī," 61, 72; ʿAbd al-Qādir b. ʿAbd al-Muṭṭalib al-Mandaylī, *al-Khazāʾin al-saniyya min mashāhīr al-kutub al-fiqhiyya li-aʾimmatinā al-fuqahāʾ al-Shāfiʿiyya* (Beirut: Muʾassasat al-Risāla, 2004), 60. Cf. al-Ḥabashī, who does not seem to know of the text's existence. Al-Ḥabashī, *Jāmiʿ al-shurūḥ wa-l-ḥawāshī*, 3:1522.

16. See, for example, al-Anṣārī, *Tuḥfat al-ṭullāb*, 11.

17. Copied in 881/1477, another manuscript of the text is held by the Chester Beatty Library. Arberry, *Handlist*, 7:36 (MS 5111).

opinions that al-Anṣārī presents in his commentary are designated with a short overlining in red above the first word (e.g., *wa-qīl* or *qāl*); the same is done when al-Anṣārī inserts a new clause or consideration into the discussion at hand. As for dating the manuscript, which otherwise bears no date or copyist's name in its colophon, Leon Nemoy traces it back to around the year 1800,[18] although the original purchaser of the manuscript, Count Carlo Landberg (d. 1924), dates it closer to 1700.[19] The manuscript and its relationship to al-Anṣārī's *Taḥrīr Tanqīḥ al-Lubāb* and *Tuḥfat al-ṭullāb* plays a central role in the analysis of part 2 that follows.

As for why he wrote this direct commentary on the *Tanqīḥ*, the author explains in his introductory remarks that his commentary aims to "unpack [the base text's] terms, clarify its intended meaning, verify its legal topics (*masāʾil*), and pinpoint its evidences. [It does as much and is] accompanied with important principles and manifold useful points, while being neither redundantly long nor abstrusely short, with the objective thereby to help students and in the hopes [in writing it] of abundant recompense and reward [in the hereafter]."[20] Here we see again that, as with the other two texts by the author within this particular genealogy, it is students of Islamic law who comprise al-Anṣārī's intended audience (see figure 4.2).

Asnā l-maṭālib, a Commentary on Ibn al-Muqrī's *Rawḍ al-ṭālib*

Al-Anṣārī completed his *Asnā l-maṭālib* (*The Most Brilliant of Pursuits*) in the year 892/1487, when he was in his midsixties.[21] Along with *al-Ghurar al-bahiyya* (mentioned below), the text stands as one of his two longest

18. Leon Nemoy, "Arabic Manuscripts in the Yale University Library," *Transactions of the Connecticut Academy of Arts and Sciences* 40 (1956): 108. Nemoy describes the manuscript as follows: "990 (L-465): *Fatḥ al-wahhāb bi-sharḥ Tanḳīḥ al-Lubāb*. 370 ff. 21 x 15½ cm. *ca.* 1800. Commentary on the *Tanḳīḥ al-Lubāb* (manual of Shāfiʿī law, by Aḥmad al-ʿIrāḳī, being an abridgement of *al-Lubāb fī l-fiḳh* of Aḥmad ibn al-Maḥāmilī)."

19. Carlo Landberg, writing in or around the year 1900, refers to the manuscript as "ca. 200 J. alte MS." Carlo Landberg, *Kurzes Verzeichniss der Sammlung arabischer Handschriften des Grafen C. von Landberg*, 6 vols., Landberg MSS 0 (vol. 4), Beinecke Library, Yale University, New Haven; see volume 1 for the author's reference to the year 1900.

20. Al-Anṣārī, *Fatḥ al-wahhāb bi-sharḥ Tanqīḥ al-Lubāb*, fol. 2r.

21. Al-Sakhāwī, *Ḍawʾ*, 2:295.

A Textual Genealogy for the
Taḥrīr Tanqīḥ al-Lubāb, Tuḥfat al-ṭullāb, and *Fatḥ al-wahhāb*

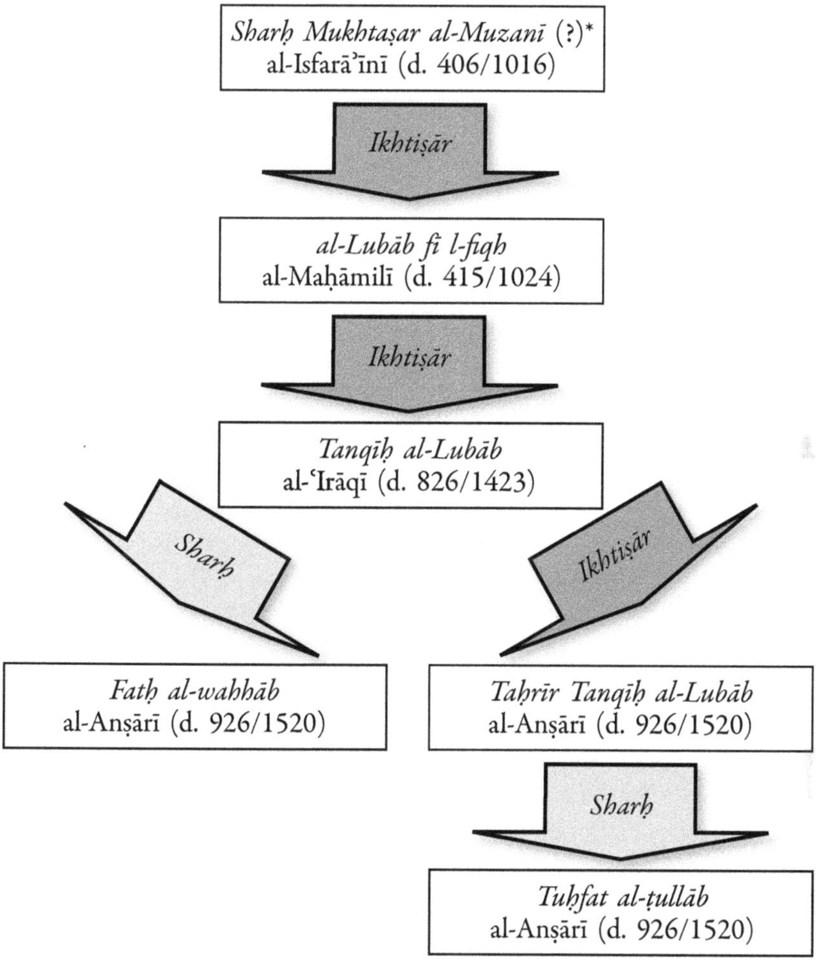

*The relationship between this text and the *Lubāb* is speculative, and the latter likely took its material from several sources, none of which it mentions explicitly in its introduction. In this light, the *Lubāb* is a *mukhtaṣar* in that it anticipates a future *sharḥ*, but it does not do *ikhtiṣār* to a single base text as do the *Tanqīḥ al-Lubāb* and *Taḥrīr Tanqīḥ al-Lubāb* in this particular genealogy.

Figure 4.2. A textual genealogy for the *Taḥrīr Tanqīḥ al-Lubāb, Tuḥfat al-ṭullāb*, and *Fatḥ al-wahhāb*. *Source*: Author provided.

works in substantive law. Although the author wrote no other commentaries or abridgments related to Ibn al-Muqrī's *Rawḍ al-ṭālib* (*The Training of the Student*) except this text, the textual genealogy that the *Asnā l-maṭālib* ties into arguably represents the most direct line back to al-Shāfiʿī's original *Umm* (*The Foundation*) of the four genealogies here. This is not to suggest that the legal positions found in the book are closest to those of al-Shāfiʿī. Rather, when viewed as a discrete text, the *Asnā l-maṭālib* directly traces its existence back to its textual ancestor the *Umm*, as figure 4.3 illustrates.

As for Ibn al-Muqrī's base text, the *Rawḍ al-ṭālib* is an abridgment of al-Nawawī's *Rawḍat al-ṭālibīn wa-ʿumdat al-muftiyīn* (*The Students' Garden and the Muftis' Reference*), which, for its part, later Shāfiʿīs would consider the foremost abridgment within al-Nawawī's oeuvre.[22] The normative status of the latter text would, in turn, transfer onto Ibn al-Muqrī's *mukhtaṣar* of it, thus making the *Rawḍ al-ṭālib* essential and popular reading for students of the Shāfiʿī *madhhab* during and after the ninth/fifteenth century.[23] It is with the interests of such students in mind that al-Anṣārī took to writing his commentary on the *Rawḍ al-ṭālib* and thereby restore what he considered to be essential details and alternate positions that had been lost in Ibn al-Muqrī's abridgment.[24] This approach comes as the exact opposite approach that al-Anṣārī adopted when penning his *Manhaj al-ṭullāb* and *Taḥrīr Tanqīḥ al-Lubāb* abridgments. In the case of the latter two texts, the author removed details that he considered nonessential in his inherited base texts in favor of concise prose to suit the needs of his students.

Texts That Derive from Ibn al-Wardī's Didactic Poem *al-Bahja*

The texts that derive from Ibn al-Wardī's didactic poem *al-Bahja* are al-Anṣārī's extended commentary on the *Bahja*, which he completed in

22. For an example of this assessment, see al-Haytamī, *Tuḥfat al-muḥtāj bi-sharḥ al-Minhāj*, 1:39.

23. Jābir, "Shaykh al-Islām Zakariyyā al-Anṣārī," 69. For the commentarial attention that the *Asnā l-maṭālib* would receive, see page 110; al-Ḥabashī, *Jāmiʿ al-shurūḥ wa-l-ḥawāshī*, 2:990.

24. Al-Anṣārī, *Asnā l-maṭālib*, 1:25.

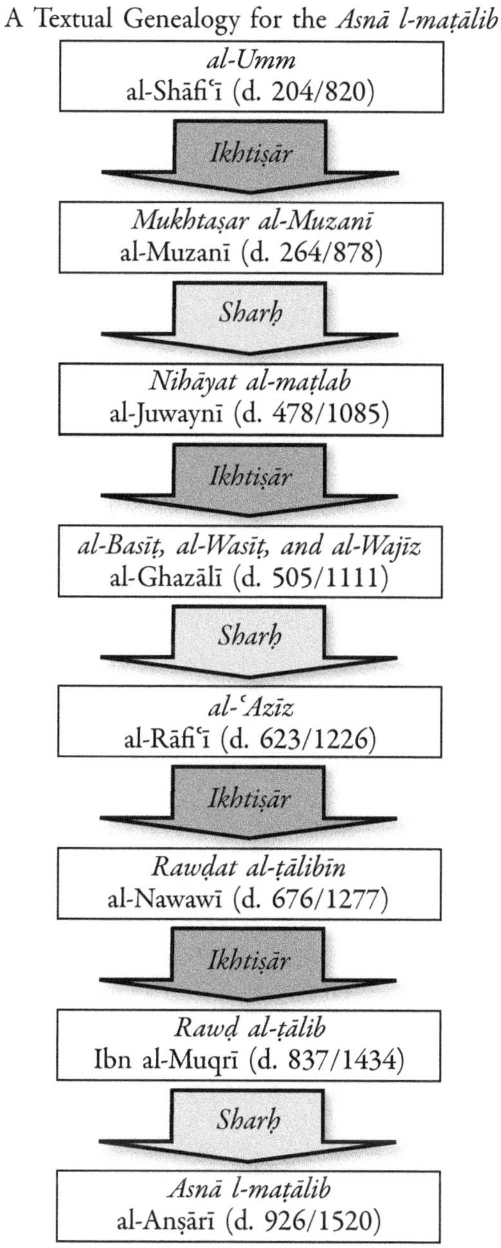

Figure 4.3. A textual genealogy for the *Asnā l-maṭālib*. *Source*: Author provided.

867/1463;[25] the *Khulāṣat al-fawāʾid al-Muḥammadiyya* (*The Summary of the Muhammadan Lessons*), his shorter commentary on the same base text; and his *Ḥāshiya* (supercommentary) on Abū Zurʿa al-ʿIrāqī's commentary on the *Bahja*.[26]

The *Bahja al-Wardiyya* (*The Wardian Splendor*) itself is Ibn al-Wardī's versification of ʿAbd al-Karīm al-Qazwīnī's (d. 665/1266) influential text in Shāfiʿī substantive law *al-Ḥāwī al-ṣaghīr* (*The Lesser Collection*). For the purposes of the present study, in which I limit my analysis to those dynamics that occur within a textual genealogy via the alternating processes of commentary and abridgment, the additional process of versification (*naẓm*) adds too complex a variable to the discussion to fit within the scope of this chapter. For this reason, al-Anṣārī's three commentaries on Ibn al-Wardī's *Bahja* await a future study (see figure 4.4).

Part II: Commentarial Dynamics of Law figwithin a Limited Textual Genealogy

How do the antipodal processes of commentary (*sharḥ*) and abridgment (*ikhtiṣār*) affect the interpretation of a legal text and the rhetorical power (or authority) that lies behind this interpretation? To answer this question, it helps to start with a limited scope of descendent texts and then extend the findings that they reveal to an entire textual genealogy. Part 3 below takes up such an extended analysis, while the present section considers three examples from purity law (*ṭahāra*) as they evolve across four generations within a single textual genealogy—specifically, the genealogy sketched in figure 4.2. Al-Anṣārī's legal commentaries and abridgments form the crux of the analysis in both this part and part 3 below.

Writing in Baghdad at some point around the turn of the fifth/eleventh century, Abū l-Ḥasan Aḥmad b. Muḥammad al-Maḥāmilī (d. 415/1024) intended his *al-Lubāb fī l-fiqh al-Shāfiʿī* (*The Quintessence of Shāfiʿī Law*) to

25. Al-Anṣārī, *al-Ghurar al-bahiyya*, 5:334.

26. For a few comments on the confusion surrounding the first two texts, see al-Mandaylī, *al-Khazāʾin al-saniyya*, 76n4; cf. al-Ḥabashī, *Jāmiʿ al-shurūḥ wa-l-ḥawāshī*, 2:802–3, which confirms the titles as they have been listed here and mentions two commentaries on the *Ghurar*—for the latter of these, read ʿAbd al-Raḥmān al-Shirbīnī (d. 1326/1908) for al-Khaṭīb al-Shirbīnī; see El Shamsy, "*Ḥāshiya* in Islamic Law," 312.

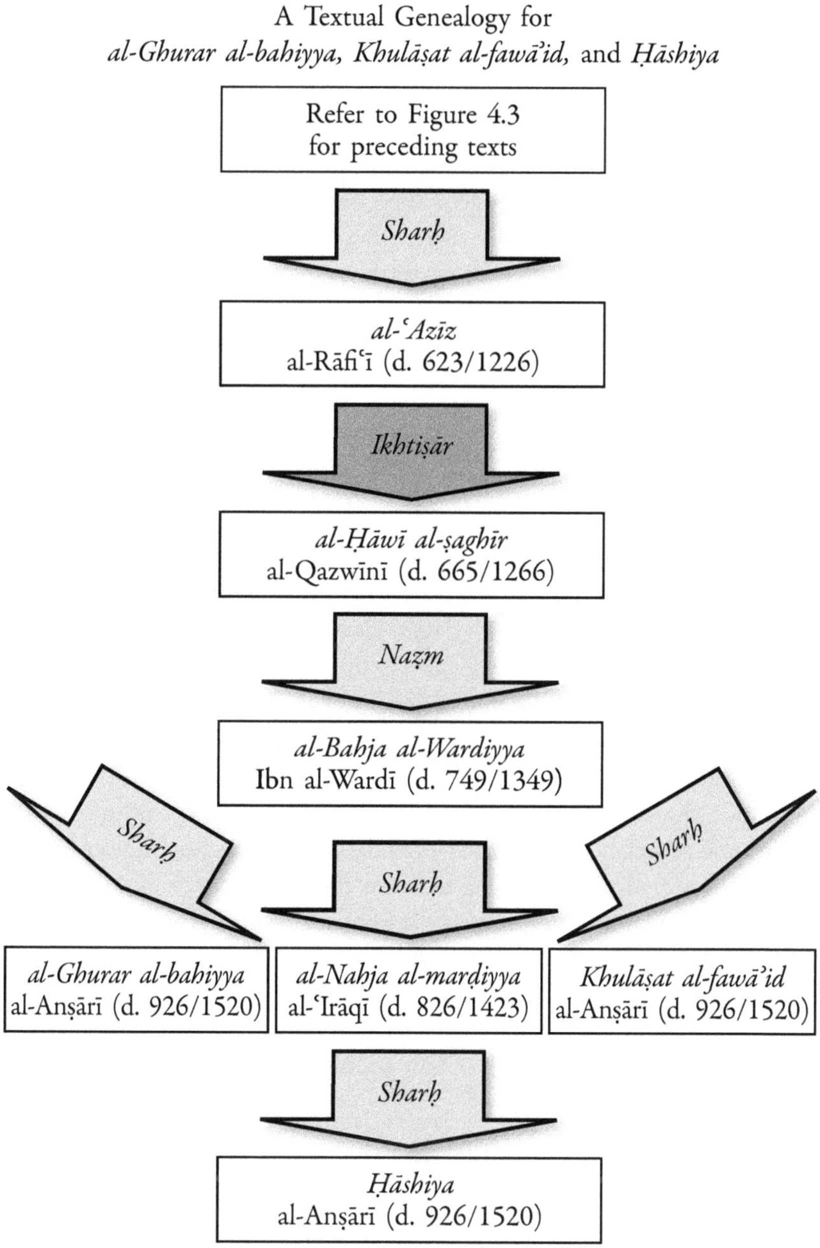

Figure 4.4. A textual genealogy for *al-Ghurar al-bahiyya*, *Khulāṣat al-fawā'id*, and *Ḥāshiya*. *Source*: Author provided.

serve as a simplified condensation of Shāfiʿī substantive law. The text reads like an annotated outline and attempts to render complicated legal discussions into numbered categories and subheadings to facilitate their retention. Al-ʿIrāqī wrote his *Tanqīḥ al-Lubāb* (*The Revision of the Quintessence*) as an abridgment of al-Maḥāmilī's *Lubāb*, and thus the latter text serves as the first generation in the textual genealogy discussed here, while the *Tanqīḥ al-Lubāb* and al-Anṣārī's direct commentary on it (*Fatḥ al-wahhāb*) serve as generations two and three, respectively.

Example 1: On Ritual Ablution and Compromised Boot Wiping

In his chapter "Those Things That Negate One's Ritual Ablution" (*Bāb mā yanquḍu l-wuḍūʾ*), al-Maḥāmilī writes, "The seventh thing [that negates one's ritual ablution] is the nullification of a provision for wiping over one's boots (*al-khuffayn*); here there is another opinion of al-Shāfiʿī (*qawl*) that one might limit themselves to washing their feet."[27] In this statement the author addresses the case of those who have opted to pass their wet hands over the tops of their boots while making their ritual ablution in lieu of fully washing their bare feet.[28] Because wiping over the boots is generally considered a legal dispensation (*rukhṣa*), it carries with it additional stipulations that would not affect those who wash their feet with each ritual ablution.

But the text of the *Lubāb* does not address these conditions and provisions expressly. Moreover, it provides two conflicting opinions on a legal question without deciding between them. The first opinion implies that if a provision for wiping over the boots is nullified, then the one who wiped is required to repeat every step of the ritual ablution if they wish to perform a ritual act that stipulates ablution. The second opinion, however, requires that they merely wash their feet completely and thus perform only the last step of the ritual ablution that wiping over the boots had otherwise supplanted.

---

27. Aḥmad b. Muḥammad al-Maḥāmilī, *al-Lubāb fī l-fiqh al-Shāfiʿī*, ed. ʿAbd al-Karīm b. Ṣunaytān al-ʿAmrī (Medina: Dār al-Bukhārī, 1416 [1995–96]), 64.

28. See *Encyclopaedia of Islam*, s.v. "al-Masḥ ʿAlā ʾl-Khuffayn" (Ch. Pellat); *al-Mawsūʿa al-fiqhiyya*, 45 vols. (Kuwait: Kuwaiti Ministry of Awqāf and Islamic Affairs, 1997), 37:261–71.

For a Muslim who wishes to pray in a correct state of ritual purity, the difference between the two opinions is stark, as al-Maḥāmilī was certainly aware. We can only conclude then that he intended his indecisive text to serve as a *prompt* to foment commentarial exposition, if not debate. Here I follow in the footsteps of Asad Ahmed, who published an analysis in 2013 of two eighteenth-century commentaries and one nineteenth-century supercommentary on Muḥibballāh al-Bihārī's (d. 1118/1707) *Sullam al-ʿulūm* (*The Scale of the Disciplines*) in logic. Among Ahmed's conclusions in this article is that the author of the base text and its commentators would intend specific lemmata in their works to function as arenas for the philosophical debate of students and later commentators.[29] The more allusive their language—or, in the case of the *Lubāb*, the more indecisive—the more likely that their text would attract commentarial attention from later generations, and the more likely that it would be integrated into premodern teaching circles that thrive off of debate and, in the case of law, the opportunity for *taṣḥīḥ*, or "rule-review," as Al-Azem has cleverly translated it.[30]

In fact, I would argue that works of Islamic substantive law function even *more* readily as arenas for commentarial debate, as the pedagogical imperative behind the teaching of law in the premodern Muslim world and the plurality of opinion that was assumed to undergird the discipline were more pronounced than in most other areas of scholarship. And although it is the commentator who ultimately decides which lemmata warrant commentary, as Ahmed and many others before him have noted,[31] consider the case of the jurist of some renown who presents his reader with multiple positions on a legal question without weighing their relative merits, or who leaves his text ambiguous in places, or who adopts contrarian positions

29. Ahmed, "Post-Classical Philosophical Commentaries/Glosses," 320, 323, and 343.

30. Talal Al-Azem, "Precedent, Commentary, and Legal Rules in the Madhhab-Law Tradition: Ibn Quṭlūbughā's (d. 879/1474) *al-Taṣḥīḥ wa-al-tarjīḥ*" (PhD diss., University of Oxford, 2011), 8–9, 119–22, and passim. Also see Lutz Wiederhold, "Legal Doctrines in Conflict: The Relevance of *Madhhab* Boundaries to Legal Reasoning in the Light of an Unpublished Treatise on *Taqlīd* and *Ijtihād*," *Islamic Law and Society* 3, no. 2 (1996): 244–47; Hallaq, *Authority, Continuity, and Change in Islamic Law*, 133–65.

31. For more on this theme, see, inter alia, Roland Barthes, *S/Z: An Essay*, trans. Richard Miller (New York: Hill and Wang, 1974), 15; Cutler, "Interpreting *Tirukkuṟaḷ*," 552–53; Frank Kermode, *The Genesis of Secrecy: On the Interpretation of Narrative* (Cambridge, MA: Harvard University Press, 1979), 20; Kraus, "Introduction," 13–16, and passim.

that may be enticing to a student readership: each author has effectively challenged a future commentator to respond, and thereby retains considerable control in setting the agenda of the future discourse. Moreover, the twenty-first-century cliché that no publicity is bad publicity might still apply to such premodern texts, as the more commentarial attention that a text foments—even if it be the refutations of adversaries—the more its canonicity within the later tradition is likely to grow.

The text of the *Lubāb* thus presents future commentators with a prompt-lemma, and both al-ʿIrāqī in his abridgment of the text and al-Anṣārī in his commentary on this abridgment respond accordingly, if not in a diametrical manner. The corresponding section of the interwoven commentary text reads as follows (with the *Tanqīḥ*'s base text in bold):

> **The seventh [thing that negates one's ritual ablution] is the nullification of a provision for wiping over one's boots. That is, through the exposure of the foot** or part of it, or exposure of the cloth that is over it, or part of it, **or the elapsing of the duration**, i.e., the duration [allowed] for wiping,[32] or uncertainty as to its elapsing. All of these require the performing of [a complete] ritual ablution, as one's entire purity is nullified with the nullification of part of it, as in the case of ritual prayer. The author's words from "that is" until the end of his words here is one of his own additions [to the original text of the *Lubāb*], and as you recognize, it is insufficient in detail. **In another opinion of al-Shāfiʿī (*qawl*) it is sufficient to wash the feet,** as their purity alone is nullified through exposure or through the elapsing of time. **My position (*qultu*) is that this is the most obvious reading of al-Shāfiʿī (*al-aẓhar*);**[33] **and God knows best.** Thus, such things are not cause for compromising the ritual purity of anything other than the feet. There are two positions attributed to al-Shāfiʿī on this matter (*wa-huwa*

32. The dispensation of wiping over one's boots remains valid in itself for up to one day for the nontraveler, and up to three days for the traveler.

33. On the terms *qawl* and *al-aẓhar*, see, inter alia, al-Khaṭīb al-Shirbīnī, *Mughnī l-muḥtāj ilā maʿrifat maʿānī alfāẓ al-Minhāj*, 4 vols. (Beirut: Dār al-Maʿrifa, 1997), 1:35–36.

> *ʿalā l-qawlayn*) owing to the compromised purity of the feet. In his *Majmūʿ*, al-Nawawī has chosen the position that this necessitates nothing and that one may pray with their existing state of purity as they see fit.[34]

If we take the base text of the *Tanqīḥ* by itself, we find that al-ʿIrāqī remains faithful to the original wording of the *Lubāb*, although he adds some detail to the initial discussion which al-Anṣārī in his commentary criticizes as insufficient. More significant to the application of the law, however, is al-ʿIrāqī's act of *taṣḥīḥ*, which comes in response to the *Lubāb*'s prompt-lemma and weighs decisively in favor of one of the two opinions attributed to al-Shāfiʿī, namely that worshippers need only rewash their feet in the situation described. The *Lubāb*'s original prompt-lemma effectively disappears in its second-generation iteration, and a practicable ruling appears in its place.

But the story does not end there. Al-Anṣārī's commentary on the *Tanqīḥ* initially explains the rationale behind al-ʿIrāqī's *taṣḥīḥ* but concludes the discussion by adding to it a third position—that worshippers need not do anything to their feet and they would still retain their state of ritual purity—which the author expressly links to al-Nawawī's *Majmūʿ* and the authority implied therein. A new prompt-lemma has now emerged, as al-Anṣārī does not weigh between al-ʿIrāqī's position and the third opinion that the commentator has tacked onto the text.[35] It is also worth mentioning in this context that the *Taḥrīr Tanqīḥ al-Lubāb*, al-Anṣārī's abridgment of al-ʿIrāqī's *Tanqīḥ* that marks a parallel branch of the textual genealogy under analysis, limits its treatment of the things that negate one's ritual ablution to the first six items mentioned in the *Lubāb*'s original text. Thus, the author excludes the entire debate that has been detailed above, thereby restricting the ability of a future commentator to reintegrate it, albeit not in an absolute sense, as is discussed below.[36]

---

34. Al-Anṣārī, *Fatḥ al-wahhāb bi-sharḥ Tanqīḥ al-Lubāb*, fol. 20r.

35. On the authoritative status of the *Majmūʿ* in the later Shāfiʿī *madhhab*, see al-Haytamī, *Tuḥfat al-muḥtāj bi-sharḥ al-Minhāj*, 1:39.

36. Cf. al-Anṣārī, *Tuḥfat al-ṭullāb*, 8–10.

Example 2: On the Age of Menopause

As a woman's menstrual cycle factors into many aspects of family law and Islamic ritual as they appear in works of substantive law, Muslim jurists throughout the centuries have proposed various estimates for an average woman's "age of despair" (*sinn al-ya's*)—a premodern dysphemism for the age of menopause after which a woman should despair of becoming pregnant. For these jurists, an estimate for the age of menopause would help older Muslim women in distinguishing between what is likely to be menstrual bleeding and what is likely to be indeterminate vaginal bleeding (*istiḥāḍa*), as the latter generally holds very little legal influence on a woman's participation in Islamic rituals, for example.

It is with such background information in mind that we consider the various estimates of an average age of menopause that appear within the textual genealogy under discussion. In the chapter "Menstruation" (*Bāb al-ḥayḍ*) of his *Lubāb*, al-Maḥāmilī writes, "The earliest that women menstruate is upon completing nine years of age; the time that menstruation ceases is sixty years of age."[37]

Although he will replace al-Maḥāmilī's oblique reference to menopause with the less-than-sympathetic idiom "age of despair," al-ʿIrāqī, for his part, shows fidelity to his predecessor's original text before adding his own voice. The interwoven text of the *Tanqīḥ* (in bold) with al-Anṣārī's commentary reads:

> **The age of despair** from menstruation. According to what the majority of jurists (including al-Nawawī) have deemed to be the correct position based on the information available and on what is [generally] known: the [age of] despair for all women **is** considered **at age sixty**; it is also said fifty; and it is also said seventy. **My position (*qultu*) is that the more correct position (*al-aṣaḥḥ*) is sixty-two years,**[38] **and God knows best.**

---

37. Al-Maḥāmilī, *al-Lubāb fī l-fiqh al-Shāfiʿī*, 87.

38. If we assume that al-ʿIrāqī is self-aware in his use of Shāfiʿī terms-of-art here, then his wording *al-aṣaḥḥ* implies that he is deciding between two or more opinions (here, *wujūh*) of the early Shāfiʿī jurists (*al-aṣḥāb*) who came after al-Shāfiʿī, and that at least one of these unstated dissenting opinions that he has considered is comparatively strong in its own right. See, inter alia, al-Shirbīnī, *Mughnī l-muḥtāj*, 1:36–39. On the

> According to what [al-Shāfiʿī] has determined in his *Umm* and which al-Rāfiʿī deems to be the correct position, "The thing to be considered is the age of despair of a woman's closest female relatives through her parents, in the order of their closeness to her (*al-aqrab fa-l-aqrab*), owing to their closeness in habitus (*ṭabʿ*). If these relatives should differ in the age that is customary for them, then on this issue, consideration should be given to the lowest age that is customary among them; it is also said the highest age that is customary, which is the more likely opinion (*al-ashbah*)." Thus ends [the text of al-Shāfiʿī].[39]

In summary, then, the text of the *Lubāb* relays a definitive opinion on the age of menopause that the *Tanqīḥ* retains but amends with its own opinion that it deems legally superior. But, by citing al-Nawawī, al-Anṣārī's commentary on this second-generation abridgment provides a persuasive argument from authority for the original position of the first-generation text, while simultaneously adding two weaker opinions to the discussion in passing. The latter text then appends an additional opinion that traces back to al-Shāfiʿī's *Umm* and is sanctioned by al-Rāfiʿī—the other gatekeeper for legitimacy within the later *madhhab*. In the end, what al-ʿIrāqī's text updates and narrows to a single position, al-Anṣārī's text opens to the two conflicting positions of al-Nawawī and al-Rāfiʿī, thus leaving later generations with a prompt-lemma.

However, al-Anṣārī appears to have had a change of heart on the issue if we trace his treatment of it through the other branch of the textual genealogy under analysis. On the issue of menopause, al-Anṣārī's abridgment of the *Tanqīḥ* (in bold) with the author's interwoven *Tuḥfat al-ṭullāb* commentary simply reads: "**The age of despair** from menstruation **is sixty-two years**."[40] Here then, for reasons unexplained, al-Anṣārī has reproduced the position of al-ʿIrāqī without reference to any other position including that of the original *Lubāb*. Within this limited textual genealogy, al-Anṣārī's third-generation abridgment and fourth-generation commentary have thrown their weight behind a particular opinion from which the author had previously distanced

aṣḥāb al-wujūh, see Hallaq, *Authority, Continuity, and Change in Islamic Law*, 48–50.

39. Al-Anṣārī, *Fatḥ al-wahhāb bi-sharḥ Tanqīḥ al-Lubāb*, fol. 20r. On the term *al-ashbah*, see Hallaq, *Authority, Continuity, and Change in Islamic Law*, 155.

40. Al-Anṣārī, *Tuḥfat al-ṭullāb*, 20.

himself. From the vantage of a would-be commentator on the interwoven text, the opinion that menopause hits the average woman at sixty-two years of age has earned the approval of two legal authorities (al-ʿIrāqī and al-Anṣārī) and three generations of texts (the *Tanqīḥ al-Lubāb*, the *Taḥrīr Tanqīḥ al-Lubāb*, and the *Tuḥfat al-ṭullāb*). And while approval such as this would certainly figure into the reception of the opinion and its normative value in the eyes of later generations, al-Anṣārī's direct commentary on the *Tanqīḥ* shows us that the matter is hardly closed.

Example 3: On Removing Filth with Difficulty

A third and final example worthy of consideration here appears in the context of filth and its removal from one's person and clothing as a condition for certain Islamic rituals like prayer (*ṣalāt*). When introducing the subject, al-Maḥāmilī, as is his wont, leaves his reader with a prompt-lemma when he writes, "Removing filths is according to ten types [of filth]: First, filth that occurs on the body or clothing. Its ruling is that one wash [it off]. If its trace does not disappear, then there are two positions of the early Shāfiʿī scholars on this" (*fa-ʿalā wajhayn*).[41] The author provides no further details on what these two positions are nor on how to weigh between them, and thus the reader of his text must wait for the assistance of a future commentator or teacher.

It should come as little surprise then that al-ʿIrāqī and al-Anṣārī's treatment of the lemma, as it appears in the former's abridgment of the *Lubāb* and in the latter's interwoven commentary on it, offers such assistance to their respective readers. In fact, their texts work in tandem to knead the original lemma into a number of corollary directions like glutinous dough. The interwoven commentary text reads:

> **Filth**, based on where it occurs and how it is removed (while the wording of the *Lubāb* is "removing filth" [*sic*]) **is** ten **types. First is that which occurs on the body or clothing** or similar things.[42] If it be de jure [in nature] in that no trace of taste, color,

41. Al-Maḥāmilī, *al-Lubāb fī l-fiqh al-Shāfiʿī*, 79–80.

42. I have left untranslated a portion of the text here in which al-Anṣārī provides the correct short vowels on a word (*tashkīl*) for his reader, though of course the author's commentary has informed my translation of the word.

or odor of it can be perceived—like dried urine that leaves no trace—it suffices to run water over it once. If it is substantive in that a trace of it can be perceived, **then it is washed until its trace fades. If** its trace **does not vanish even with difficulty**, in that it does not fade with extreme rubbing or cutting, **then there are two statements of al-Shāfiʿī (*fa-qawlān*)**: the first is that it is purified because of the extreme difficulty involved; the second is that it is not purified because the thing that points to the very substance of the filth still remains. Rubbing and cutting here are praiseworthy; and it is also said that they are a legal condition for removal of the filth. Yes, if it is possible to remove the filth through such actions then they are legally required, just as using potash and similar things would be required. His qualification "with difficulty," which is an addition to the text of the *Lubāb*, excludes whatever filth could be easily removed because no extreme difficulty [is implied therein]. **My position (*qultu*) is that the most obvious reading of al-Shāfiʿī (*al-aẓhar*) is legal amnesty (*al-ʿafw*) for the complete removal of both odor and color** because of what has already been mentioned. The effect of his words is like the two positions of the early Shāfiʿī scholars (*ka-l-wajhayn*): that [1] the spot is pardonably impure—and this is a position of the early scholars;[43] and [2] the correct position (*al-ṣaḥīḥ*), in [al-Nawawī's] *Rawḍa* which was transmitted by al-Rāfiʿī from the majority of scholars, that [the spot] is pure in actuality.[44] **And** the most obvious reading of al-Shāfiʿī is that **combining of the two [traces] is [legally] harmful**—that is, odor and color because of their testifying decidedly to the presence of the filth's very substance. The latter does no [legal] harm owing to the extreme difficulty in removing both of them, nor is there legal harm if they are each in a separate spot. **And** it is [legally] harmful **for taste in itself**

43. "And this is a position of the early scholars" (*wa-huwa wajh*ᵘⁿ): al-Anṣārī is correcting al-ʿIrāqī here to suggest that this position does not trace back to al-Shāfiʿī but rather to the *aṣḥāb* who came after him.

44. The author's use of *al-ṣaḥīḥ* implies that, in this particular example, the contrasting *wajh*-position is weak in its own right; the term is rhetorically stronger than *al-aṣaḥḥ* as it was used in example 2.

> **to remain present, and God knows best**, owing to the ease of removing it in most cases, and because its remaining presence testifies to the presence of the filth's very substance. The obvious reading of his words, like those of the *Lubāb* (*ka-aṣlih*), is that the disagreement centers around the presence of taste, while there is no disagreement in al-Nawawī's *Majmūʿ* and other texts that it is [legally] harmful.[45]

In summarizing the operations of the two texts above at the individual level, we first notice that al-ʿIrāqī's *Tanqīḥ al-Lubāb* adds "with difficulty" as a qualification to the *Lubāb*'s original discussion. It also converts the two *wajh*-positions in the latter text to two *qawl*-positions and thereby raises their rhetorical weight by linking them back to the authority of al-Shāfiʿī himself. Moreover, the *Tanqīḥ* is first to broach the question of whether tenacious traces of filth are merely a forgivable offense or whether they are pure in actuality, although it never expressly mentions the latter position. Rather, as the text does not provide the reader with details of the "two statements of al-Shāfiʿī" (*qawlān*) that it ultimately decides between, it has effectively generated its own prompt-lemma for a future commentator (here, al-Anṣārī) who might disagree with its author's legal reasoning.

Al-Anṣārī's commentary on the *Tanqīḥ* hence picks up on this prompt-lemma by identifying to the reader where al-ʿIrāqī has performed *taṣḥīḥ* in his abridgment and then reverses this act by integrating the counter position into the interstices of the base text and declaring it to be the correct position. The author of the commentary does so, moreover, using the strongest designation possible (viz. *al-ṣaḥīḥ*) while relaying it through al-Nawawī, al-Rāfiʿī, and the majority of Shāfiʿī scholars. These names imply an argument from authority that would supersede the authority of al-Shāfiʿī himself to al-Anṣārī's late-medieval readership, although to be safe, the author nonetheless returns the *qawl*-positions in al-ʿIrāqī's text back to their original *wajh*-position form and thereby removes al-Shāfiʿī from the discussion altogether.

Finally, in the alternate textual lineage that runs through al-Anṣārī's abridgment of the *Tanqīḥ* and onto his *Tuḥfat al-ṭullāb* commentary, al-Anṣārī's opinion that tenacious traces of filth are pure in actuality assumes an even more unequivocal form. The interwoven commentary text reads:

45. Al-Anṣārī, *Fatḥ al-wahhāb bi-sharḥ Tanqīḥ al-Lubāb*, fols. 48r–v.

> **Its removal**, that is, filth, **even from one's boot, is** legally required **by washing** (except in some cases that follow, such as the case of the male infant's urine) **whereby its qualities** of taste, color, and odor **disappear, except what** disappears **with difficulty of color or odor.** Removing one of these is then not legally required. Rather, the spot is purified, *pace* [the case in which color and odor] combine because of their testifying decidedly to the presence of the filth's very substance. Similar to the latter case is that in which the filth's taste remains owing to the ease of removing it in most cases.[46]

Al-Anṣārī has thus integrated the qualification "with difficulty" into his own abridgment, while his commentary ignores completely the *Tanqīḥ*'s original position that tenacious traces of filth represent a forgivable offense in favor of the author's own verdict that they are pure in actuality. A single, uncontested position—that belonging to al-Anṣārī—has now displaced what was originally two contradictory positions in the al-ʿIrāqī/al-Anṣārī interwoven commentary text. Here, by abridging (*ikhtiṣār*) al-ʿIrāqī's text first instead of commenting on it directly, al-Anṣārī has assumed stronger control over the textual discourse. Moreover, within the context of teaching, his position is carried primarily by the base text of his abridgment and thus becomes the position that student readers would memorize and take as a starting point for debate. In the end, then, al-Anṣārī has washed all traces (tenacious or otherwise) of al-ʿIrāqī's position away, leaving his reader with a terse text that posits his own position as the only one worthy of consideration and not merely the better of two alternatives.

Part III: Commentarial Dynamics of Law within a Complete Textual Genealogy

How might extending the textual scope of our analysis affect our understanding of some of the processes described above? To begin answering this question I turn my attention here to a complete textual genealogy—that is, a lineage of legal texts that stretches back to a source that the authors of these texts viewed as foundational. In the case of the Shāfiʿī *madhhab*,

46. Al-Anṣārī, *Tuḥfat al-ṭullāb*, 16.

the *Kitāb al-Umm* of al-Shāfiʿī represents the most obvious foundational text, at least within the subdiscipline of substantive law, while out of all of al-Anṣārī's legal writings, the author's *Asnā l-maṭālib* commentary enjoys the closest thing to an uninterrupted genealogical connection back to the *Umm* (see figure 4.3). In this light, it stands as the most promising starting point for analysis.

But on the question of which lemma to analyze, the choice is not quite as obvious. One potentially fruitful lead appears in a passing comment in Wael Hallaq's *Authority, Continuity, and Change in Islamic Law* in which the author notes that a premodern jurist's rationale for weighing one legal position over another is likely as much a function of his sociolegal background as it is a function of his hermeneutics. However, the scholar's task of proving this, Hallaq explains, is formidable.[47]

With an eye toward this formidable task, I began my analysis in the *Asnā l-maṭālib*'s chapter on the judgeship,[48] as it represents an area of Islamic law that intersected quite differently with the practical lives of al-Anṣārī and Ibn al-Muqrī, the author of the *Rawḍ al-ṭālib* that the *Asnā l-maṭālib* comments on. According to al-Sakhāwī's biography for him, the Yemeni Ibn al-Muqrī was appointed to serve as a diplomatic envoy to Mamlūk Egypt on behalf of the Rasūlid state but would delay his travels in the hopes of attaining the chief justiceship in his homeland. He ultimately failed to obtain the post, and thus we might assume that his knowledge of the legalities and practicalities surrounding the judgeship were to remain strictly theoretical throughout his life.[49] Al-Anṣārī, however, held the chief justiceship for an unprecedented duration of twenty years. This and the fact that al-Anṣārī completed his *Asnā l-maṭālib* six years into his chief justiceship might lead us to expect a much more pragmatic approach to his commentarial discussions of the judgeship.

Can we then identify differences in the legal attitudes of these two authors in their writings on the judgeship that parallel differences in their biographical relationship to the office? Second, and more important to the present study, can we trace these differences back through the textual

47. Hallaq, *Authority, Continuity and Change in Islamic Law*, 145.

48. Al-Anṣārī, *Asnā l-maṭālib*, 6:264–356.

49. Al-Sakhāwī, *Ḍawʾ*, 2:292–95; cf. Ṭāhā Aḥmad Abū Zayd, *Ismāʿīl al-Muqrī: Ḥayātuh wa-shiʿruh* (Ṣanʿāʾ, Yemen: Markaz al-Dirāsāt wa-l-Buḥūth al-Yamanī; Beirut: Dār al-Ādāb, 1986), 49–51.

genealogy under analysis to derive any larger conclusions about Muslim legal commentary and the formal and rhetorical devices that define it? These were the specific questions that guided my analysis of the chapter on the judgeship in Ibn al-Muqrī's *Rawḍ al-ṭālib* and al-Anṣārī's *Asnā l-maṭālib* commentary on it, and I had hoped that answering them would shed more light on Muslim legal hermeneutics. What I found instead is that the formidability that Hallaq notes in linking sociobiographical influences with an author's legal thinking owes less to a paucity of textual data—as I had been anticipating—and more to the speculative nature of the exercise. In other words, as a legal commentator strives to convince his reader and presumably himself that it is only his knowledge of the law and its scriptural foundations that determine how he diverges from a base text, then how much leeway do we later generations have in reading personal motives into these divergences before we enter into the realm of cynicism?

Here let us consider an example. In his base text, Ibn al-Muqrī writes, "Whoever specifically the [obligation of the judgeship] falls upon, both his requesting and accepting [the post] are obligatory for him." The remainder of the section provides general qualifications that a person must fulfill in order to be considered appropriate for the judgeship, but it does not provide any details about the theoretical candidate for the judgeship on whom this communal obligation falls.[50] The problem thus remains that, were we to read Ibn al-Muqrī's text in isolation, we might be led to believe that any person who fulfills the *general* qualifications for the judgeship that he lists would be considered sinful were this person not to request and accept the post whenever the situation called for it. In this light, al-Anṣārī's earlier refusal to accept the judgeship in 871/1466 when the Mamlūk sultan insisted that he do so would be highly problematic in light of Ibn al-Muqrī's text.[51] With this biographical detail in mind, it is noteworthy that al-Anṣārī's commentary on the text shifts the obligation from seemingly every qualified person to, effectively, nobody. The base text (in bold) with al-Anṣārī's interwoven commentary reads, "**Whoever specifically the [obligation of the judgeship] falls upon**, in that there exists no one suitable for the judgeship other than him in his district, **both his requesting and accepting [the post] are obligatory for him**, as his assuming this authority owes to

50. Al-Anṣārī, *Asnā l-maṭālib*, 6:265.

51. Al-Anṣārī fled the scene and the post remained unoccupied for twenty-seven days. Al-Maqrīzī, *al-Sulūk li-maʿrifat duwal al-mulūk*, 3 (1): 197–98.

the district's need of him."[52] The interwoven commentary text now implies that only a suitable person (*ṣāliḥ*) who lives in a district devoid of any other suitable candidates would be held accountable for refusing the judgeship, and al-Anṣārī's own refusal of the post can no longer be seen as a sinful action if we assume that he lived surrounded by other suitable candidates.

Notwithstanding the plausibility of the explanation above, it hardly seems responsible, or even fair, to read personal motives into the rulings of scholars who lived five centuries ago—motives that would have likely emerged in the deepest recesses of their subconscious if they even existed in the first place. In this particular example, such a reading implies that al-Anṣārī viewed the base text through the lens of his own life decisions and used his commentary to redirect it in a manner that assuaged his feelings of cognitive dissonance.

An alternate explanation—one that demands far less speculation and that better aligns with the analysis in part 2 above—might suggest that Ibn al-Muqrī anticipated the qualifications of later commentators as he penned this section of his *Rawḍ al-ṭālib* abridgment, and he thus intended his base text here as a prompt-lemma to trigger the pen of a later commentator. This latter explanation certainly finds resonance when seen in light of the remainder of the author's chapter, which includes prompt-lemmata at almost every turn. Consider as an example Ibn al-Muqrī's list of a muftī's necessary qualifications as it appears in his chapter on the judgeship. On the question of whether a muftī must of necessity know arithmetic in order to determine the correct answer to any inquiry related to it, the author simply notes that there are two positions of the early Shāfiʿī masters (*wajhayn*), though he provides no details as to what these positions are. The reader of the text is therefore left with a statement that is meaningless for all practical purposes and is certainly redundant. That is to say, a qualification either exists or it does not exist, and to hedge one's bets, as Ibn al-Muqrī might appear to

52. Al-Anṣārī, *Asnā l-maṭālib*, 6:265. Noteworthy also is Shihāb al-Dīn al-Ramlī's commentary on this lemma (at al-Anṣārī, *Asnā l-maṭālib*, 6:265) in which he adds a further qualification that, in the case of a tyrannical political leadership, the obligation to request the judgeship is lifted if a candidate has a strong conviction (*law ghalaba ʿalā ẓannih*) that his request would go unheeded. The obligation is thus subjected to the reasonable expectations of the candidate, which further erodes the compulsion behind it. Al-Anṣārī's top pupil, al-Ramlī, never held the judgeship himself but nonetheless read al-Anṣārī's commentary on the judgeship with his teacher while the latter was still serving as chief justice. Al-Sakhāwī, *Ḍawʾ*, 2:295.

be doing, in no way helps the student of law who reads such a text in the hope of finding concrete answers (or at least details that point him or her in the right direction). The only conclusion to be drawn here is that Ibn al-Muqrī intentionally left the task of explication to a later commentator. We should not be surprised then to find that, without missing a beat, al-Anṣārī provides us with just such an explication, describing in his commentary each position and its originator, determining which one he deems the better position (*al-aṣaḥḥ*), and providing the legal reasoning behind the contrary opinion, presumably for the benefit of later students and commentators.[53]

If it is a *choice*, then, between explaining a commentator's decisions on the grounds of biography and context or on the grounds of the genre-specific conventions and the structural imperatives of legal literature, the latter is the safer bet for the contemporary scholar. But it nonetheless remains possible to trace lemmata like those cited above back through a complete textual genealogy to generate results that shed much needed light on the actual nature of these conventions and imperatives. To do so let us reconsider the interwoven commentary text on the obligation of the judgeship above: "**Whoever specifically the [obligation of the judgeship] falls upon**, in that there exists no one suitable for the judgeship other than him in his district, **both his requesting and accepting [the post] are obligatory for him**, as his assuming this authority owes to the district's need of him." Beginning with the *Kitāb al-Umm* of al-Shāfiʿī, we find no equivalent discussion on the obligation of the judgeship and the means of determining it, while it is conspicuously absent from the first subsection, "[On] the Conduct and Commendable Actions of the Judge" (*Adab al-qāḍī wa-mā yustaḥabb li-l-qāḍī*) of the author's larger "Book of Judgments" (*Kitāb al-aqḍiya*).[54] Similarly, al-Muzanī in his famous abridgment (*Mukhtaṣar al-Muzanī*) of the *Kitāb al-Umm* includes no mention of the discussion in his corresponding "Book on the Conduct of the Judge" (*Kitāb adab al-qāḍī*).[55] Rather, both

53. Al-Anṣārī, *Asnā l-maṭālib*, 6:275.

54. Muḥammad b. Idrīs al-Shāfiʿī, *Kitāb al-Umm*, 7 vols. (Cairo: Dār al-Shaʿb, 1968), 6:201; for the complete *Kitāb al-aqḍiya*, see 6:199–237. Ahmed El Shamsy makes a convincing case that al-Shāfiʿī himself titled many (if not most) of the chapters of his *Kitāb al-Umm*. Ahmed El Shamsy, "Al-Shāfiʿī's Written Corpus: A Source-Critical Study," *Journal of the American Oriental Society* 132, no. 2 (2012): 214.

55. Ibrāhīm b. Yaḥyā al-Muzanī, *Mukhtaṣar al-Muzanī* (printed in the margins of the edition of *Kitāb al-Umm* cited above), 5:241.

al-Shāfiʿī's subsection and al-Muzanī's book jump immediately into questions concerning where a judge should and should not sit to adjudicate cases, which we can take as a helpful bookmark as we follow the emergence of the discussion through the remainder of the textual genealogy.

For its part, al-Muzanī's *Mukhtaṣar* would receive a detailed and excursive commentary in ʿAbd al-Malik b. ʿAbdallāh al-Juwaynī's (d. 478/1085) *Nihāyat al-maṭlab fī dirāyat al-madhhab* (*The Conclusion of the Search in Knowledge of the Madhhab*),[56] the third link in our genealogy under analysis. One of the first texts that would attempt to collect the various approaches (*ṭuruq*) and opinions (*wujūh*) of the early Shāfiʿī scholars in one place,[57] the *Nihāya* adds an extensive introduction of its own to its "Book on the Conduct of the Judge" before reaching its first subsection (*faṣl*), which corresponds with al-Muzanī's discussion of where a judge should and should not sit to adjudicate cases.[58] After citing a handful of Qurʾānic verses and several hadith texts to establish both the necessity of the judgeship and the grave responsibility that it entails, al-Juwaynī warns his reader that the early Shāfiʿī scholars were haphazard in their rulings on the judgeship, while he intends his introductory words to guide an otherwise ungrounded jurist to the essentials of the institution.[59] It is in this introductory section where we first encounter the germ that will grow into the passage constructed by Ibn al-Muqrī and al-Anṣārī in their interwoven commentary.

In fact, in al-Juwaynī's introduction we find the earliest signs in our genealogy of an author who is painfully aware of the inherent ethical

56. The sheer breadth of al-Juwaynī's *Nihāya*, which reaches twenty volumes in the published edition used here, often makes it difficult to recognize the outline of al-Muzanī's *Mukhtaṣar* that forms its core. Nevertheless, al-Juwaynī himself notes in his introduction that the *Nihāya* is fully premised on the structure of al-Muzanī's text, its choice of legal topics (*masāʾil*), and its recension of al-Shāfiʿī's original words. ʿAbd al-Malik b. ʿAbdallāh al-Juwaynī, *Nihāyat al-maṭlab fī dirāyat al-madhhab*, ed. ʿAbd al-ʿAẓīm al-Dīb, 20 vols. (Jeddah, Saudi Arabia: Dār al-Minhāj, 2007), 1:4.

57. ʿAlī Jumʿa, *al-Madkhal ilā dirāsat al-madhāhib al-fiqhiyya* (Cairo: Dār al-Salām, 2004), 41.

58. The subsection (*faṣl*) begins at al-Juwaynī, *Nihāyat al-maṭlab*, 18:466, leaving the author's introduction to run for ten pages of the printed edition of the *Nihāya* cited here. For more on the phenomenon of commentators' commandeering of subchapter headings (*tarājim*), see Joel Blecher, "In the Shade of the *Ṣaḥīḥ*: Politics, Culture and Innovation in an Islamic Commentary Tradition" (PhD diss., Princeton University, 2013), 105–38.

59. Al-Juwaynī, *Nihāyat al-maṭlab*, 18:457–61.

tension at the heart of the judgeship: although the institution represents a clear communal obligation whose executor deserves the highest reward for his service to the Muslim community, the power wielded by a judge and the potential for inequity (if not iniquity) that he must constantly ward off are nevertheless very real dangers that a God-fearing Muslim should rightfully avoid. In the ideal world of the jurists, then, the political ruler (*imām*) will appoint only the most knowledgeable and incorruptible candidate to the judgeship, while only the latter will accept the position, albeit begrudgingly and fully aware of his soul's potential for deceit. The jurists, however, allow such an ideal candidate to request the judgeship from the ruler as a pragmatic concession that acknowledges the likelihood of information asymmetries in society.

It is within the context of such considerations that al-Juwaynī cites the opinions of al-Qāḍī al-Ḥusayn b. Muḥammad al-Marwarrūdhī (d. 462/1069), among which is the latter's statement, "If there is no one in the district suitable [for the judgeship] other than [a particular candidate], then it becomes obligatory for him to offer himself [for the position]."[60] Although the wording here is slightly different than that used by al-Anṣārī in his *Asnā l-maṭālib*, the meanings of the two statements are in essence the same, and we have identified one possible source of written inspiration—either direct or indirect—for the qualification that al-Anṣārī would interject into Ibn al-Muqrī's base text almost four hundred years later. Moreover, the introduction to al-Juwaynī's discussion on the judgeship, when viewed in its totality, remains overwhelmingly suspicious of those who might request the judgeship, and in his concluding sentences the author defaults to the position that requesting the judgeship is "legally disliked" (*al-karāhiyya*) should any question as to a candidate's suitability or propensity for venality exist. In fact, al-Juwaynī's warnings on the judgeship are so emphatic in the end that he forces himself to consider a situation in which no suitable candidate presents himself for the post for fear of its dangers. Just as the Sharīʿa sees no need to oblige a man to have intercourse with his wife, al-Juwaynī analogizes, so too the obligation to seek the judgeship: the matter always seems to take care of itself.[61]

After al-Juwaynī's *Nihāya* we come to the most tenuous link in our textual genealogy—namely, the link between the *Nihāya* and Abū Ḥāmid

60. Al-Juwaynī, *Nihāyat al-maṭlab*, 18:462; cf. 463 (top).

61. Al-Juwaynī, *Nihāyat al-maṭlab*, 18:466.

al-Ghazālī's (d. 505/1111) three famous works in substantive law. The first and largest of these, al-Ghazālī's yet unpublished *al-Basīṭ fī l-madhhab* (*The Extended Treatment of the Madhhab*), has been viewed by Shāfiʿī scholars since at least the seventh/thirteenth century as an abridgment of the *Nihāya*,[62] and later Shāfiʿīs until contemporary times would repeat this assertion seemingly without question.[63] However, al-Ghazālī does not refer to his text as an abridgment of the *Nihāya* per se. Moreover, although he claims to include in his *Basīṭ* all that al-Juwaynī included in his *Nihāya*, al-Ghazālī relies on his own system of structuring his text and arranging the legal topics that appear within it.[64] To call the *Basīṭ* a *mukhtaṣar* of the *Nihāya* then is to sap the term of most of its semantic value. Nonetheless, al-Ghazālī's text shows obvious connections to the text of the *Nihāya* on almost every page, and we should be cautious before dismissing the views of the later Shāfiʿīs here, as their seven-hundred-year-old understanding of the tradition brings its own ontological realities to the discussion.

What is not debatable is that al-Ghazālī intended *al-Wasīṭ fī l-madhhab* (*The Medial Treatment of the Madhhab*)—his second, middle-length text in substantive law—to stand as an abridgment of his *Basīṭ*; his third and shortest text in substantive law titled *al-Wajīz fī l-madhhab* (*The Concise Treatment of the Madhhab*) he likewise wrote as an abridgment of the *Wasīṭ*. If we then compare the *Nihāya*'s chapter on the judgeship with the analogous chapters in these two latter texts, we discover significant shifts in the structuring of the discussion as it appears in the textual genealogy at hand. In his *Wasīṭ*, al-Ghazālī breaks his "Book on the Conduct of Rendering a Judgment" (*Kitāb adab al-qaḍāʾ*) into four subchapters (*abwāb*), the first of which tackles the rules surrounding both the appointment and discharge of

62. ʿAbd al-ʿAẓīm al-Dīb, the editor of the 2007 edition of the *Nihāya*, has traced this view back as far as al-Nawawī and Ibn al-Ṣalāh (d. 643/1245). See al-Juwaynī, *Nihāyat al-maṭlab*, "muqaddimāt" (introductory volume), 242–43.

63. For example, see Abū Bakr b. Aḥmad Ibn Qāḍī Shubha, *Ṭabaqāt al-Shāfiʿiyya*, 4 vols. (Hyderabad: Dāʾirat al-Maʿārif al-ʿUthmāniyya, 1979), 1:327; al-Jamal, *Ḥāshiyat al-Jamal ʿalā Sharḥ al-Manhaj*, 1:23–24; Alawī b. Aḥmad al-Saqqāf, *Mukhtaṣar al-Fawāʾid al-Makkiyya fī-mā yaḥtājuh ṭalabat al-Shāfiʿiyya*, ed. Yūsuf b. ʿAbd al-Raḥmān al-Marʿashlī (Beirut: Dār al-Bashāʾir al-Islāmiyya, 2004), 65; al-Mandaylī, *al-Khazāʾin al-saniyya*, 28n2; Jumʿa, *al-Madkhal*, 51.

64. For the text of al-Ghazālī's introduction to his *Basīṭ*, see al-Juwaynī, *Nihāyat al-maṭlab*, "muqaddimāt" (introductory volume), 243.

judges and is divided into two sections accordingly. The first of these sections ("On Appointment") comprises six legal topics (*masāʾil*); it is in the second of these ("On the Permissibility of Requesting the Judgeship and Positions of Rule") that al-Ghazālī approaches the matter that would form the crux of Ibn al-Muqrī and al-Anṣārī's interwoven commentary passage above.[65]

Here al-Ghazālī cites four situations (*aḥwāl*) that affect the legality of requesting and accepting the judgeship. The first is the situation in which there exists only one person suitable for the position, although the author provides no further details as to how far the zone of candidacy might stretch. Such a person is legally obligated to request the judgeship and make himself known to the ruler, and it is unlawful for him to refuse the post even if he fears the treachery of his soul. In the remaining three situations al-Ghazālī discusses the complex legalities of requesting and accepting the judgeship by those candidates who are surpassed in suitability, who are suitable but outperformed by another, and who are equaled in suitability and excellence in their respective locales.[66] What is significant here is the author's addition of the qualification "in his district" to the circumstances that he considers, and the wording that we later find in Ibn al-Muqrī and al-Anṣārī's amalgamated text would appear to be a blend of this qualification with the words that al-Ghazālī uses in the first situation noted above.

At this point in our textual genealogy, the *Wasīṭ* has provided us with the most detailed and methodically structured treatment of the issue under analysis.[67] For its part, al-Ghazālī's *Wajīz* parallels the exact structure of his *Wasīṭ* here, though it does so while shedding many details of the latter text, including the significant "in his district" qualification.[68] The published edition of the *Wajīz* in fact condenses into one paragraph what the *Wasīṭ* required three published pages to resolve; it represents an abridgment in the most obvious sense of the term.

---

65. Abū Ḥāmid Muḥammad b. Muḥammad al-Ghazālī, *al-Wasīṭ fī l-madhhab*, ed. Aḥmad Maḥmūd Ibrāhīm, 7 vols. (Cairo: Dār al-Salām, 1997), 7:287–89.

66. Al-Ghazālī, *al-Wasīṭ fī l-madhhab*, 7:288–89.

67. That is, if we exclude the author's unpublished *Basīṭ*, which is likely to contain even more detail on the issue.

68. Abū Ḥāmid Muḥammad b. Muḥammad al-Ghazālī, *al-Wajīz fī l-fiqh al-imām al-Shāfiʿī*, ed. ʿAlī Muʿawwaḍ and ʿĀdil ʿAbd al-Mawjūd, 2 vols. (Beirut: Dār al-Arqam, 1997), 2:237.

Writing about a century after al-Ghazālī, al-Rāfiʿī would intend his *al-ʿAzīz* (*The Precious Book*) to serve as a commentary on the *Wajīz*, and his text—which appears next in our genealogy—would ultimately surpass the length and detail of al-Ghazālī's *Wasīṭ*. Although al-Rāfiʿī's text binds itself to the original base text of the *Wajīz*, it nevertheless provides its own organizational structure to whatever material it brings to the discussion and, in that way, bears little resemblance to the text of the *Wasīṭ*. Al-Rāfiʿī's discussion of the conditions for requesting and accepting the judgeship provides us with a good example here. The author considers the case of a particular candidate by asking, first, whether such a person is suitable for the judgeship or not. If he is suitable, then either the communal obligation falls on him alone, or there exists someone other than him who is also suitable. If the communal obligation falls on him alone, then al-Rāfiʿī rules, just like al-Ghazālī in his *Wasīṭ*, that this candidate must accept the judgeship regardless of his desires or fears. In the second case, the communal obligation does not fall on him alone because there exists another suitable candidate who is better, equal, or inferior to him. The author only then broaches the question of whether the judgeship of the one surpassed in ability is valid, and how this ties into the various rulings on requesting the judgeship and the discharge of the office as a communal obligation.[69]

What is significant to the present analysis is that al-Rāfiʿī's commentary restructures and reconceptualizes the corollary considerations that al-Ghazālī had left out of his *Wajīz* but that appear in his *Wasīṭ* within a different framework. Whereas al-Ghazālī's *Wasīṭ* treats the number of qualified candidates and the relative ranking of candidates as equally essential considerations, al-Rāfiʿī's *ʿAzīz* treats only the number of candidates as an essential consideration, while their relative ranking appears as a secondary consideration that admits a difference of scholarly opinion into the discussion (notwithstanding the author's willingness to weigh between these scholarly opinions). Moreover, it is only in a later section that al-Rāfiʿī mentions the important "in his district" qualification when he writes, "The early Shāfiʿī scholars (*al-aṣḥāb*) are agreed in their approaches (*ṭuruq*) that a person's assuming sole responsibility for the obligation of the judgeship or not assuming sole responsibility for it is based on considerations of land and

69. ʿAbd al-Karīm b. Muḥammad al-Rāfiʿī, *al-ʿAzīz: Sharḥ al-Wajīz*, ed. ʿAlī Muʿawwaḍ and ʿĀdil ʿAbd al-Mawjūd, 14 vols. (Beirut: Dār al-Kutub al-ʿIlmiyya, 1997), 12:411–13.

district and no more."[70] The qualification thus appears as an afterthought in al-Rāfiʿī's text and does not enjoy the same degree of prominence and essentiality that it does in al-Juwaynī's *Nihāya* and al-Ghazālī's *Wasīṭ*.

We find almost the exact same treatment in al-Rāfiʿī's *ʿAzīz* reproduced in al-Nawawī's *Rawḍat al-ṭālibīn*, an abridgment of the *ʿAzīz* that comes as the next text in our genealogy. On the relevant discussion of the conditions for requesting and accepting the judgeship, al-Nawawī's wording and the structure of his argument appear nearly identical to those of al-Rāfiʿī, albeit they are replicated in a slightly abbreviated form. In fact, al-Nawawī reproduces al-Rāfiʿī's exact quote above on "considerations of country and district" and places it in the same position relative to the rest of his text.[71]

It is at this point in our textual genealogy that we finally reach the *Rawḍ al-ṭālib*, Ibn al-Muqrī's highly condensed abridgment of al-Nawawī's *Rawḍat al-ṭālibīn*, and with the background discussions of the earlier texts now in mind, it is easy to see how Ibn al-Muqrī's text—when taken on its own—leaves us with insufficient information. In his treatment of the conditions for requesting and accepting the judgeship, Ibn al-Muqrī distills al-Nawawī's original text into a few terse sentences that, through their pithiness, forfeit the clear structure and detail that informed al-Nawawī's treatment of the discussion and that of al-Rāfiʿī and al-Ghazālī before him. While all previous texts in our genealogy link the obligation of the judgeship to the number of candidates (viz. one or more than one) who meet the bar of suitability for the office and the spatial range (viz. district or land) in which to assess this number of candidates, Ibn al-Muqrī provides us with no such details when he writes, "Whoever specifically the [obligation of the judgeship] falls upon, both his requesting and accepting [the post] are obligatory for him." In fact, the text here represents an indirect abridgment of the first and most stringent case that al-Ghazālī had originally considered of his four theoretical situations (*aḥwāl*), though now it appears without the clear structure and orientating sentences of the latter text to contextualize it. In the first interwoven commentary to appear in our genealogy, al-Anṣārī is thus forced to interject an essential qualification—"in that there exists no one suitable for the judgeship other than him in his district"—into the

70. Al-Rāfiʿī, *al-ʿAzīz*, 12:414. Read *taʿayyun al-shakhṣ* for *taʿyīn al-shakhṣ*.

71. Yaḥyā b. Sharaf al-Nawawī, *Rawḍat al-ṭālibīn wa-ʿumdat al-muftiyīn*, ed. ʿAlī Muʿawwaḍ and ʿĀdil ʿAbd al-Mawjūd, 8 vols. (Beirut: Dār al-Kutub al-ʿIlmiyya, 2000), 8:79–82.

otherwise ambiguous statement found in Ibn al-Muqrī's base text. Al-Anṣārī pieces this qualification together from various places in the textual tradition that preceded Ibn al-Muqrī, although the exact wording of it would appear to be his own.[72]

With that we have arrived back at the original passage of Ibn al-Muqrī and al-Anṣārī's interwoven commentary text. But what larger lessons then can we learn in the end from this exercise? Perhaps most important is that by tracing a particular lemma through an entire textual genealogy, we gain a better understanding of the structural changes that each text in this genealogy imposes on the subsequent textual tradition. Thus, in as far as they discuss the legalities for requesting and accepting the judgeship, the ten texts of the genealogy above can be grouped into five structural stages as follows:

1. Stage One—the foundational texts: *al-Umm* of al-Shāfiʿī; the *Mukhtaṣar* of al-Muzanī. These two texts are the first in the *madhhab* to approach the conduct of the judge—and thus, implicitly, the institution of the judgeship—as a subject that merits inclusion in a book of Islamic substantive law.

2. Stage Two—the systematic laying down of all practical and ethical concerns related to the judgeship as a formal office and institution: the *Nihāyat al-maṭlab* of al-Juwaynī. Written when the judgeship had routinized into its most complex form as an institution, al-Juwaynī's *Nihāya* appends to the discussion in stage one a detailed introduction on the ethics and legalities related to attaining and assigning the office. The concerns raised here define the parameters of the discourse from this point forward and the relative positions in the texts (viz. in the introductions to chapters) in which they are articulated.

3. Stage Three—the systematic restructuring of the concerns raised in stage two and their corollary concerns: *al-Basīṭ*, *al-Wasīṭ*, and *al-Wajīz* of al-Ghazālī; *al-ʿAzīz* of al-Rāfiʿī; *Rawḍat al-ṭālibīn* of al-Nawawī. Following the precedent

72. Al-Anṣārī, *Asnā l-maṭālib*, 6:265–66.

of al-Ghazālī, the texts in this stage rearrange the concerns of stage two, tease out their inferences, and superimpose on them a rational scaffolding. Al-Rāfiʿī in his *ʿAzīz* revises al-Ghazālī's original structure slightly, and thus his text and al-Nawawī's *Rawḍa* could be viewed as a substage of stage three.

4. Stage Four—the reproduction of stage three in a highly abbreviated form: the *Rawḍ al-ṭālib* of Ibn al-Muqrī. Ibn al-Muqrī's *Rawḍ* abridges the text that it receives from stage three to produce a text that is unnavigable without a commentary; such an extreme form of abridgment is unprecedented within this textual genealogy even though four of the preceding texts were written as abridgments (or five if we include al-Ghazālī's *Basīṭ*).
5. Stage Five—the systematic expansion of stage four through an interwoven commentary: the *Asnā l-maṭālib* of al-Anṣārī. Al-Anṣārī's interwoven commentary on the text of stage four utilizes material from antecedent texts in the genealogy (or from parallel genealogies) to produce an amalgamated stage four/stage five text. Because of the extreme abridgment that occurred in stage four, the final amalgamated text bears little resemblance to the texts of stage three.

Moving past the formative two stages for now, we can identify the essential operations that account for the shifts to stages three, four, and five as follows.

The texts of stage three are grouped together on the basis of their attempts to systematize their contents within a rational framework that aims for comprehensiveness. It does not matter here if a given text is an abridgment of, or a commentary on, the previous text in the genealogy, as it is the *arrangement* of the texts' contents that defines the essence of this stage. The text of stage four, however, is characterized by the *degree* to which it abridges the preceding text in the genealogy. Because it removes so much content from the stage three text that it abridges, the clear, rational structure of the latter text is effectively lost, and we can no longer group the new text with the texts of the previous stage. In this light, the operation of *ikhtiṣār* defines the essence of stage four. Finally, it is the "interweavement" (*mazj*) of the commentary in stage five that defines this stage, as the operation makes the stage four text comprehensible once again and generates an amalgamated stage four/stage five text that is not beholden to the structural imperatives that would define stage three. In other words, by inheriting a text that has been unhinged from its structure in stage four, the stage five commentator is free to embed a new structure into his interwoven commentary as he sees fit.

In light of the terseness of Ibn al-Muqrī's stage four abridgment and the scholarly customs of his time, we must assume that the author anticipated a commentary for his *Rawḍ* when he wrote it. In order to benefit from his text, a reader must have familiarity with the textual tradition that preceded it—either direct familiarity, as would be the case of a scholar like al-Anṣārī, or indirect familiarity, as would be the case of a student who might study the text with a living teacher. Without this contextual background, it is easy to read personal motives into the decisions of a commentator on the *Rawḍ* such as al-Anṣārī. This is not to say that such personal motives were entirely absent. Rather, in the analysis above, I hope to have demonstrated some of the methodological advantages of moving away from speculative questions into an author's biases and motives in favor of questions that link an author's text back to the textual tradition from which it claims to descend.

Conclusion: The Operations of *Ikhtiṣār* and *Sharḥ* in Comparison

In various places in the analyses of parts 2 and 3 above we find that the operation of *ikhtiṣār* in one generation of a textual genealogy provides a commentator in a subsequent generation with more control over the substance and structure of the legal discourse that he inherits. Two variables influence the degree of control that such a commentator assumes. First is the relationship between an abridgment author and a commentator. Or, to put it differently in light of the examples just seen, we might ask, are the abridgment's author and its later commentator one and the same individual? As demonstrated in the examples of part 2 (especially example 3), a legal commentator enjoys far broader control over the inherited discourse when he first abridges a base text himself rather than comment on it directly. As the operation of *ikhtiṣār* strips a base text of all substance and structure that the abridgment author considers superfluous, when this same author, through his commentary, later expands on those lemmata of his abridgment that he deems worthy of excursive treatment, he has effectively redefined the conversation and its fundamental agenda. The effect is compounded in the case of the interwoven commentary, as this commentarial form enables a commentator to rend his base text into pieces as small as individual letters (*ḥurūf*, including *ḥurūf al-ʿaṭf* and *ḥurūf al-jarr*) and then expand his interwoven commentary text in infinite possible directions, adding detail and structure of his own all along the way. It is perhaps for just such a reason that al-Anṣārī wrote all six of his legal commentaries listed in part 1 as interwoven commentaries.[73]

The second variable that influences a later commentator's control over the received discourse is the severity in degree to which a preceding abridgment has abridged its base text: the more extreme the operation of *ikhtiṣār*, the more control a later commentator enjoys. However, this equation is not absolute. We must remember that a commentator's professed aim is to explain to a reader the meaning of what cannot be understood intuitively in a base text. In this way, the more enigmatic a base text appears, the more the commentator's pen is forced to render it understandable. An abridgment author thus retains *some* control over the commentarial reception of his text, as his extreme acts of *ikhtiṣār* function almost like prompt-lemmata in setting the agenda of the commentarial discourse. With this important qualification in mind, we might summarize the second variable of commentarial control by saying: the scale of *ikhtiṣār* is proportional to the scale of subsequent commentarial control over the received textual tradition, and to the perceived need for commentary to elucidate that tradition.

One additional consideration that figures into the question of textual control is the fact that, unlike a commentary, and particularly an interwoven commentary, an abridgment is not bound to the skeleton of its base text. In order to illustrate how this difference might affect the different strategies of rule-review (*taṣḥīḥ*) available to an abridgment author *pace* those available to a commentator, let us consider figure 4.5 below, which attempts to render some of the complex processes described above into a simple graphic form.

73. Here I exclude al-Anṣārī's *ḥāshiya* on al-ʿIrāqī's commentary on the *Bahja*.

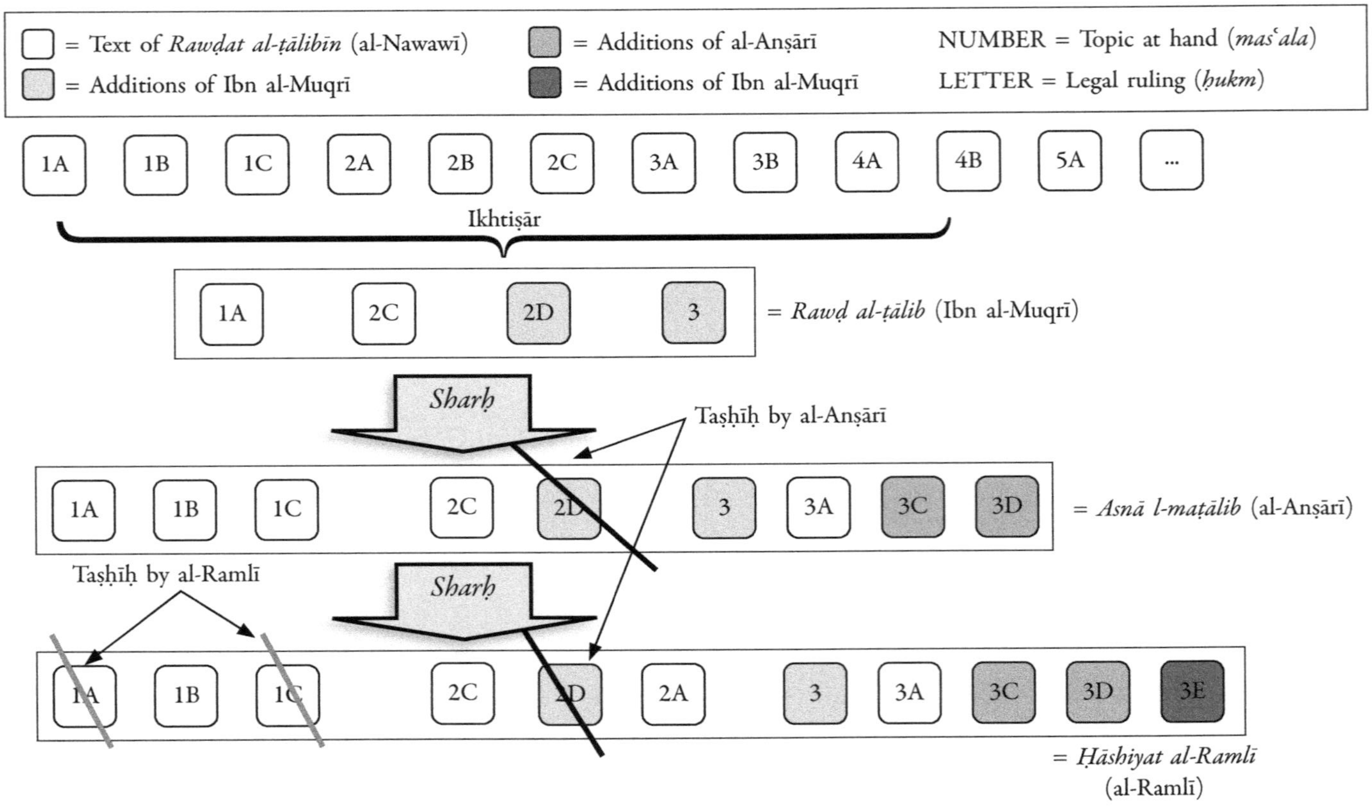

Figure 4.5. A visual representation of the processes of *sharḥ* and *ikhtiṣār*. *Source*: Author provided.

Depicted as blocks arranged horizontally into rectangular "texts" here, each of four generations of legal texts appears as a composite of discrete textual units, with each unit comprising a generic legal topic (represented by a number) and a scholarly ruling thereto (represented by a capital letter). A block that contains only a number but no letter thus symbolizes a prompt-lemma like that seen in the text of the *Lubāb* in example 3 of part 2:[74] the text mentions a legal topic (*masʾala*) but otherwise provides us with no specific ruling (*ḥukm*) on it. Although three of the four textual generations of the figure correspond with actual texts discussed in part 3 above,[75] I have intended the model to stand in for any textual genealogy in Islamic substantive law that alternates between works of commentary and abridgment.

Within this figure, then, if we compare the individual units that together symbolize the text of al-Nawawī's *Rawḍat al-ṭālibīn* with those that symbolize Ibn al-Muqrī's *Rawḍ al-ṭālib*, we can identify at least three operations that are particular to the process of *ikhtiṣār* that have been demonstrated in the textual examples already discussed. First, the abridgment might perform an act of "tacit *taṣḥīḥ*" through its selective reproduction of a base text, as we find in examples 2 and 3 of part 2 with al-Anṣārī's ruling on menopause in his *Taḥrīr Tanqīḥ al-Lubāb mukhtaṣar* and his removal of al-ʿIrāqī's ruling of divine amnesty (*al-ʿafw*) from this same text. Thus, the three original rulings ("1A," "1B," and "1C") on the first topic in al-Nawawī's *Rawḍa* of the figure are reduced to a single ruling ("1A") in Ibn al-Muqrī's abridgment, while the latter text would then carry no rhetorical obligation to justify its choice or even identify it as an act of *taṣḥīḥ* to its reader. Second, the abridgment might reduce the number of rulings of its base text and then add additional rulings of its own to these, leaving later commentators with a prompt-lemma that is quite different from the prompt-lemma that it originally inherited from its base text. This process is represented in al-Nawawī and Ibn al-Muqrī's treatment of

74. That is, as seen in the last clause of al-Maḥāmilī's text: "Filth that occurs on the body or clothing. Its ruling is that one wash [it off]. If its trace does not disappear, then there are two positions of the early Shāfiʿī scholars on this." Al-Maḥāmilī, *al-Lubāb fī l-fiqh al-Shāfiʿī*, 79–80.

75. The fourth textual generation of the diagram corresponds with Shihāb al-Dīn al-Ramlī's supercommentary on al-Anṣārī's *Asnā l-maṭālib*; it bears the generic title provided by a later scribe *Ḥāshiyat al-Ramlī*.

topic "2" in the figure and finds a parallel in our textual examples when we compare al-ʿIrāqī's *Tanqīḥ al-Lubāb* with al-Anṣārī's abridgment thereof in example 3 of part 2 above. Finally, an abridgment might strip its base text of all scholarly rulings on a particular legal topic, leaving its reader with only a passing mention of the topic itself to serve as a prompt for future commentarial exposition. Ibn al-Muqrī's reducing units "3A" and "3B" of al-Nawawī's base text to an unlettered "3" unit symbolizes this operation in the figure. Although it is admittedly messier than any diagram might ever hope to depict, the text of Ibn al-Muqrī's actual *Rawḍ al-ṭālib* that was analyzed in part 3 provides a practical illustration of this operation.

When compared with *ikhtiṣār*, we can also identify three operations that are particular to the process of *sharḥ*, as are seen in the textual examples of parts 2 and 3 and illustrated in the figure above. First, *sharḥ* expands the number of legal opinions available whenever it identifies to its reader an instance of *taṣḥīḥ* in its base text. This process is depicted in the figure in the reexpansion of unit "1A" of Ibn al-Muqrī's *Rawḍ* to units "1A," "1B," and "1C" in al-Anṣārī's *Asnā l-maṭālib*; it is also seen in *Ḥāshiyat al-Ramlī*'s reintroduction of unit "2A" to the discussion following the *Asnā*'s act of *taṣḥīḥ* in the previous textual generation. As has been noted in the introduction, al-Anṣārī in his commentaries is always quick to point out where a base text has broken from the foundational text that it derives from, either through acts of *taṣḥīḥ* in the base text or through its other "additions" (*ziyādāt*) to the received discussion (also see examples 1 and 3 of part 2 above). In the case of an abridgment, such additions and acts of *taṣḥīḥ* would otherwise remain invisible to an uninitiated reader were it not for the assistance of a commentator in identifying them. Moreover, these efforts of the commentator to add alternate positions to the text without weighing one over another, and to draw attention to those areas where a base text has narrowed the scope of legal options that were previously available in the textual tradition, both serve to open the door once again to new instances of *taṣḥīḥ* within future commentaries. While the former operation generates a prompt that effectively forces the hand of a later commentator at some future juncture to perform *taṣḥīḥ* and thereby provide a definitive legal ruling, the latter operation throws into question the canonicity of a ruling that has been transmitted as definitive and thus inscribes it with the potential to serve as a prompt-lemma for future debate once again.

Second, *sharḥ* performs its own acts of *taṣḥīḥ*, particularly where prompt-lemmata appear in the base text; this operation is depicted in the *Asnā*'s treatment of topic "2" and *Ḥāshiyat al-Ramlī*'s treatment of topic "1" in the figure. Although al-Anṣārī's wording is sometimes subtle,[76] his direct commentary on al-ʿIrāqī's base text in examples 2 and 3 of part 2 includes instances of *taṣḥīḥ* by the commentator in response to both prompt-lemmata and previous acts of *taṣḥīḥ* by al-ʿIrāqī.

Finally, *sharḥ* generates its own prompt-lemmata in a manner that differs slightly from that of *ikhtiṣār*. Because a commentary remains beholden to the skeleton of its base text, as has already been mentioned, it cannot distill its base text down before adding its own voice to the discussion, as can an abridgment. In a way, then, the entropy of a theoretical commentary is always higher than that of an equivalent abridgment, as each generation of commentary adds new layers of detail and alternate opinions to the base text that it receives. This snowballing effect is shown in the expanding treatment of topic "3" between the second, third, and fourth textual generations of the figure, while it can also be seen in all three examples analyzed above in part 2.

This last operation also reminds us that no textual generation is ever closed to a future commentator, although the texts of great middle period consolidators like al-Nawawī and al-Rāfiʿī would function as semipermeable membranes standing between the preceding tradition and later commentators like al-Anṣārī.[77] Just as the *Asnā* circumvents Ibn al-Muqrī's *Rawḍ* to reintroduce unit "3A" and *Ḥāshiyat al-Ramlī* circumvents two textual generations to reintroduce unit "2A" from al-Nawawī's foundational text in the figure,[78] so too is al-Anṣārī able to check the fidelity of al-ʿIrāqī to the original text of the *Lubāb* by referencing the latter text directly. And although the analysis above has limited itself—in the interest of space—to

76. The subtlety with which al-Anṣārī often performs *taṣḥīḥ* may explain why al-Ramlī in his supercommentary on the *Asnā l-maṭālib* must constantly explain to his reader, "His words [such and such] indicate an act of *taṣḥīḥ* by him" (*wa-qawluh . . . ashār ilā taṣḥīḥih*). Al-Ramlī resorts to this exact phrase dozens, if not hundreds, of times in the course of his *ḥāshiya*.

77. See El Shamsy, "*Ḥāshiya* in Islamic Law," 295.

78. For a parallel phenomenon from the Muslim exegetical tradition, see Saleh, *Formation of the Classical Tafsīr Tradition*, 20.

the diachronic change that occurs in the vertical shift between generations of a textual genealogy, this is not to discount the very real influence of parallel commentaries on a base text which authors like al-Anṣārī would read while writing their own commentaries on this same base text.[79]

In the final analysis, then, the permanent ossification of any particular detail of the law as it appears in premodern works of Islamic substantive law would appear unlikely, as the legal "canon" here displays a unique tolerance for reopening itself and exposing itself to revision. In that regard, it is certainly a different animal from canonical texts in Sufism, which often demand a scriptural reading, as has been discussed in the previous chapter. Rather than signaling a baroque or static tradition, as was the misperception of many twentieth-century scholars, the later literature of Islamic law indicates a tradition that was dynamic and intellectually immersive. The movement from abridgment to commentary to abridgment to commentary (or some permutation thereof) would always produce lemmata that left space for change and development in the legal tradition; the very form of the texts and the structures that define the processes of *sharḥ* and *ikhtiṣār* made this change both possible and inevitable. To summarize the relationship between these processes with a concluding metaphor, we might say that the pens of commentators and abridgment authors run along the lines of a textual tradition like passive-aggressive janitors in a long corridor of windows: with each window that one janitor opens, a different janitor closes another, producing through their perpetual and antithetical operations a climate that is both free of stagnant air and yet never too drafty as to drown out an intelligible conversation.

79. For the titles of the commentaries that al-Anṣārī relied on in writing his *Asnā l-maṭālib*, see Jābir, "Shaykh al-Islām Zakariyyā al-Anṣārī," 80. For more on the diachronic vs. synchronic study of Muslim commentaries, see Ahmed, "Post-Classical Philosophical Commentaries/Glosses," esp. 344–45.

Chapter Five

The Legacy of al-Anṣārī

Within a few years of his death, speculation began to circulate within the Sunni scholarly community that perhaps Zakariyyā al-Anṣārī had been the "renewer" (*mujjadid*) of the ninth Islamic century. This idea of a renewer traces back to a hadith in which the Prophet states, "At the turn of every hundred years, God will send to this Umma a person who will renew its religion (*dīn*) for it." Sunni scholars have traditionally understood this hadith to refer to centenary figures who would emerge to inspire the global community of Muslims through a charisma grounded in their intellect, piety, or skill at political leadership.[1] Aḥmad Ibn Ḥajar al-Haytamī may have been the first to suggest this designation for his teacher al-Anṣārī.[2] Nevertheless, the idea spread rapidly,[3] and writing within a century of al-Anṣārī's death, the Indian

1. The hadith can be found, inter alia, at Abū Dāwūd Sulaymān al-Sijistānī, *Sunan Abī Dāwūd*, "Kitāb al-Malāḥim: Bāb Mā yudhkar fī qarn al-mi'a," #4291. For the *mujaddid* tradition in Islamic thought and discussions of al-Anṣārī's place therein, see Ella Landau-Tasseron, "The 'Cyclical Reform': A Study of the *Mujaddid* Tradition," *Studia Islamica* 70 (1989): 84, 90, 93–94.

2. Al-Kattānī, *Fihris al-fahāris*, 1:458, citing al-Haytamī's hadith commentary on *al-Mishkāt*.

3. The Yemeni jurist ʿAbdallāh b. ʿUmar Bāmakhrama (d. 972/1565), for example, follows al-Haytamī in classifying al-Anṣārī as the *mujaddid* of the ninth Islamic century in lieu of Jalāl al-Dīn al-Suyūṭī, who expressly claimed *mujaddid* status and is typically pitted against al-Anṣārī in scholarly speculation on the *mujaddid* of this century. Muḥammad Amīn al-Muḥibbī, *Khulāṣat al-athar fī aʿyān al-qarn al-ḥādī ʿashar*, 4 vols. (Beirut: Maktabat al-Khayyāṭ, 1966), 3:346–47. For an example of a scholar who favored al-Suyūṭī as the *mujaddid* over al-Anṣārī, see Mullā ʿAlī al-Qārī, *Mirqāt al-mafātīḥ sharḥ Mishkāt al-maṣābīḥ*, 9 vols. (Beirut: Dār al-Fikr, 2002), 1:321.

scholar ʿAbd al-Qādir al-ʿAydarūs (d. 1037/1628) would even make the bold claim that there existed a consensus of the scholarly community (*ijmāʿ*) on al-Anṣārī's *mujaddid* status.[4] What, then, did later scholars like these find in al-Anṣārī's life and writings that compelled them to make such weighty claims?

The remainder of this chapter aims to answer this question. It begins in its treatment with al-Anṣārī's most tangible legacy, namely his later descendants and his most distinguished students within the Shāfiʿī *madhhab* who would secure for their teacher a prominence in that legal school that endures until today. The remaining majority of the chapter below next examines al-Anṣārī's more abstract influence on conceptual shifts that took place within fifteenth- and sixteenth-century Sunni thought. These shifts fall roughly into two broad categories, both of which are connected to Sufism. The first category describes what we can call formalization trends within scholarly treatments of Sufism, whereby Sufism would gradually be reconceived as an area of scholarly study and inquiry akin to other subfields of exoteric scholarship such as jurisprudence, Qurʾānic exegesis, and hadith criticism, among others. In turn, these formalization trends would parallel the second category of conceptual shifts: the willingness of scholars to embrace the cross-fertilization between Sufism and Islamic law that would characterize the period. The relationship between these two categories is not always clear, however, and it is perhaps best to view them as contemporaneous fruits of a common Zeitgeist without forcing them into a causal nexus. Nevertheless, al-Anṣārī's influence frequently appears at the epicenter of each of their intellectual trajectories, and his thought functions as an anchoring point between them.

The Anṣārī Dynasty

We can trace the genealogical lines that proceeded from al-Anṣārī's two surviving male descendants for several generations. Both lines produced several Egyptian scholars who were highly regarded by their scholarly peers, and through these lines a small "Anṣārī dynasty" of scholars emerged that we can track for at least two hundred years after the death of their famous forefather.

The first line is through al-Anṣārī's grandson, Zakariyyā (d. 959/1552), the child of al-Anṣārī's son Yaḥyā, who died of the plague in 897/1492.

4. Al-ʿAydarūs, *al-Nūr al-sāfir*, 177; cf. 307, 577.

After studying under his grandfather for many years in addition to other noteworthy scholars of his time, including Burhān al-Dīn Ibn Abī Sharīf (d. 923/1517) and al-Shaʿrānī's Sufi master ʿAlī al-Marṣafī (d. 930/1524), Zakariyyā would eventually hold his own teaching circles and would issue fatwas. Additionally, he served as a judge for the Egyptian Ḥajj delegation in the year 947/1541. Having undertaken the pilgrimage with this same delegation, al-Shaʿrānī records that Zakariyyā issued legal judgments all day and would circumambulate the Kaʿba all night. He is also noted to have given much in charity to the poor during his stay near the Two Holy Sanctuaries.[5] The twentieth-century scholar ʿAbd al-Ḥayy al-Kattānī (d. 1962), moreover, records an *ijāza* to the complete works of al-Anṣārī through a grandson of this younger Zakariyyā named Jamāl al-Dīn.[6] Another son of Zakariyyā named Shams al-Dīn Muḥammad is recorded to have been on the payroll ledgers of multiple waqfs around the years 992–93/1584–85.[7]

The more noteworthy line of descent, however, traces back to al-Anṣārī's son Jamāl al-Dīn Yūsuf (d. 987/1579–80), the scion of a black concubine and al-Anṣārī who was born toward the end of the latter's life, as has been mentioned in chapter 2. Jamāl al-Dīn would pursue a scholarly career like his father, and al-Shaʿrānī records that he eventually taught at the same prestigious Ṣāliḥiyya School that his father had superintended so many years earlier. In the aftermath of al-Anṣārī's death in 926/1520, Jamāl al-Dīn is reported to have confined himself to his home in pious seclusion, venturing out periodically only to visit his father's grave.[8]

Jamāl al-Dīn Yūsuf, in turn, begot a scholar by the name of Walī l-Dīn Aḥmad, who died no earlier than about 1008/1600, and who, at least for

---

5. Al-Shaʿrānī, *al-Ṭabaqāt al-ṣughrā*, 90; N. al-Ghazzī, *Kawākib*, 2:145.

6. Al-Kattānī, *Fihris al-fahāris*, 1:459. Al-Ghazzī records a miraculous anecdote involving this Jamāl al-Dīn and a Jewish debtor. N. al-Ghazzī, *Kawākib*, 2:238–39; also see Egyptian National Archives document no. 1003-000007-0709, signed in year 980/1573, which appears to correspond with the story. Accessed online at http://nationalarchives.gov.eg/nae/ar/home.jsp on 25 February 2009.

7. Egyptian National Archives, document nos. 1001-000072-1107, 1001-000072-1109, and 1001-000075-0769.

8. Al-Shaʿrānī, *al-Ṭabaqāt al-ṣughrā*, 133–34; N. al-Ghazzī, *Kawākib*, 3:221. Also see al-Kattānī's biography for him for more on the students of Jamāl al-Dīn, who transmitted on his authority, and for the existence of a large *fahrasa* (catalogue of teachers and chains of transmission) that was compiled by one of his students. Al-Kattānī, *Fihris al-fahāris*, 1:298–99. Other examples of *isnād*s in which Jamāl al-Dīn transmits on the direct authority of his father are found at 1:89, 216, 459, 2:810, 923, and 1064.

a time, held a teaching position at the Ṣāliḥiyya School as well.[9] From this Walī l-Dīn was born a scholar of distinction named Muḥyī l-Dīn ʿAbd al-Qādir (d. 1043/1634), who studied with his grandfather, Jamāl al-Dīn Yūsuf, and was known for his breadth of expertise in the various scholarly disciplines. We learn also from his biographers that Muḥyī l-Dīn would be buried near the gravesite of his great-grandfather al-Anṣārī—a tradition that would continue for at least the next three generations.[10]

The next descendant in this genealogical line is arguably the most significant scholar within al-Anṣārī's family tree, namely Zayn al-ʿĀbidīn Yūsuf (d. 1068/1657). Known for his piety, Zayn al-ʿĀbidīn studied with his father and would leave behind several texts that have survived in manuscript form until the present day. Among these are a supercommentary on al-Anṣārī's commentary on the *Jazariyya* in Qurʾānic recitation (*tajwīd*) titled *al-Nukat al-lawdhaʿiyya* (*Sagacious Allusions*); a commentary on the sixth/twelfth-century poem "*Lāmiyat al-ʿajam*" that he completed in 1064/1654; a commentary titled *al-Minaḥ al-Rabbāniyya* (*The Lordly Benefactions*) on al-Anṣārī's *al-Futūḥāt al-ilāhiyya* text in Sufism; and—perhaps most important to the present study—an extensive biographical text on al-Anṣārī's life titled *Tuḥfat al-aḥbāb bi-faḍāʾil aḥad al-aqṭāb* (*The Gift for the Beloved Ones Regarding the Merits of One of God's Axial Saints*). Originally written in 1025/1616 when the author was twenty-four years old, this latter text contains anecdotes and information on al-Anṣārī that have been passed through the generations of his descendants and that often cannot be found in any other biographical source.[11]

9. For his name Aḥmad, see Zayn al-ʿĀbidīn al-Anṣārī, *Tuḥfat al-aḥbāb*, fol. 4v. For the Ṣāliḥiyya post, see fol. 11v.

10. For his first name ʿAbd al-Qādir, see Zayn al-ʿĀbidīn al-Anṣārī, *Tuḥfat al-aḥbāb*, fol. 4v. For the remainder of his biography, see al-Muḥibbī, *Khulāṣat al-athar*, 4:332–33.

11. Al-Muḥibbī, *Khulāṣat al-athar*, 2:199; al-Kattānī, *Fihris al-fahāris*, 1:502; Karl Vollers, *Katalog der islamischen, christlich-orientalischen, jüdischen, und samaritanischen Handschriften der Universitäts-Bibliothek zu Leipzig* (Leipzig: O. Harrassowitz, 1906), 70 (s.v. "Leipzig 253"); Ismāʿīl Pāshā al-Baghdādī, *Īḍāḥ al-maknūn fī l-dhayl ʿalā Kashf al-ẓunūn ʿan asāmī l-kutub wa-l-funūn*, ed. M. Şerefettin Yaltkaya and Rifat Bilge Kilisli, 2 vols. (Istanbul: Milli Eğitim Basımevi, 1945), 2:397–98, 542–43, 677; Ismāʿīl Pāshā al-Baghdādī, *Hadiyyat al-ʿārifīn: asmāʾ al-muʾallifīn wa-āthār al-muṣannifīn*, ed. Rifat Bilge and İbnülemin Mahmut Kemal İnal, 2 vols. (Istanbul: Milli Eğitim Basımevi, 1951), 1:379. The composition date of Zayn al-ʿĀbidīn's commentary on the "*Lāmiya*" was taken from the colophon of MS Adab 2838/41248, al-Maktaba al-Azhariyya, Cairo.

Zayn al-ʿĀbidīn was the father and teacher of another well-regarded scholar named Sharaf al-Dīn Yaḥyā (d. 1092/1681), who wrote many books of his own, including a biographical dictionary of his teachers and scholarly peers. Three documents held in the Egyptian National Archives and signed in the years 1071/1660 and 1075/1664 reveal that Sharaf al-Dīn was employed by various waqfs and possessed property near al-Azhar.[12] His wealth also enabled him to amass a vast collection of books, for which he was famous, while he was especially concerned with gathering manuscripts of texts written by his great-great-great-grandfather al-Anṣārī.[13]

Finally, the last scholar in this lineage that I can trace with certainty is the son of Sharaf al-Dīn named ʿAbd al-ʿAẓīm (d. 1136/1723–24), whose necrology is included by ʿAbd al-Raḥmān al-Jabartī (d. 1237/1825) in the latter's *ʿAjāʾib al-āthār*. Beyond a few general comments about ʿAbd al-ʿAẓīm's upright nature and the respect afforded to him by his peers, al-Jabartī leaves us with very few specific details on his life. We do learn, however, that each descendant in al-Anṣārī's family tree took his primary education from his respective father,[14] thus preserving a common transmission chain running backward through time to various texts that functioned almost as an Anṣārī family curriculum.

Two additional idiosyncrasies in the Anṣārī family are worth mentioning in this context. The first is that al-Anṣārī's tradition of sheltering his children indoors away from public scrutiny—which he initiated with his later-life son Jamāl al-Dīn Yūsuf—appears to have continued for at least another three generations, if not more. In fact, Zayn al-ʿĀbidīn records that his maternal grandfather had attempted to inquire about Muḥyī l-Dīn ʿAbd al-Qādir for the sake of marrying his daughter off to the latter, and the locals who he asked were unaware that this great-grandson of al-Anṣārī

The original composition date of the *Tuḥfat al-aḥbāb* is found in the colophon on fol. 42v of the manuscript, which was copied in 1032/1623.

12. Document nos. 1001-000265-1698, 1001-000265-2092, and 1001-000268-1181, accessed online at http://nationalarchives.gov.eg/nae/ar/home.jsp on 25 February 2009. These documents are also the source from which I have learned the first names, viz. Yūsuf and Yaḥyā, for Zayn al-ʿĀbidīn and Sharaf al-Dīn respectively.

13. Al-Muḥibbī, *Khulāṣat al-athar*, 2:222–23; al-Kattānī, *Fihris al-fahāris*, 2:675, 1064–65. Also see 2:298–99 in which two copies of the *fahrasa* of Jamāl al-Dīn Yūsuf cited above are traced back to the library of Sharaf al-Dīn.

14. ʿAbd al-Raḥmān al-Jabartī, *ʿAjāʾib al-āthār fī l-tarājim wa-l-akhbār*, 4 vols. (Cairo: Dār al-Ṭibāʿa, 1880), 1:85–86.

even existed.[15] Zayn al-ʿĀbidīn also records a second tradition in the family that we can call the "Anṣārī curse," in which al-Anṣārī is reported to have invoked the wrath of God on anybody who would harm his son Jamāl al-Dīn Yūsuf, who in turn transferred the force of the invocation to his line of descendants. The effects of the invocation would endure and were frequently severe, according to Zayn al-ʿĀbidīn. For example, when Zayn al-ʿĀbidīn's grandfather Walī l-Dīn lost his position at the Ṣāliḥiyya School to another scholar, the latter died soon thereafter. In another story, Walī l-Dīn would face persecution from an unnamed oppressor who also died. The deceased would later tell him in a dream vision that Walī l-Dīn had in fact killed him through the power of the Anṣārī curse but that he would not be held accountable for this action in the hereafter. Zayn al-ʿĀbidīn reports similar tales of God's vengeance on those who oppressed his father, Muḥyī l-Dīn.[16]

Al-Anṣārī and the Later Shāfiʿī *Madhhab*

Above all Zakariyyā al-Anṣārī is remembered to this day for his legal acumen, while scholars who considered him the *mujaddid* of the ninth Islamic century were often explicit in according him this status on the basis of his legal writings and their influence in shaping the Shāfiʿī *madhhab* as it was to appear in later centuries.[17] In fact, scholars of the later Shāfiʿī *madhhab* view him as one of the four most influential Shāfiʿī jurists of the generations following Yaḥyā b. Sharaf al-Nawawī (d. 676/1277) and ʿAbd al-Karīm b. Muḥammad al-Rāfiʿī (d. 623/1226).[18] As is shown in figure 5.1 below, the

15. Zayn al-ʿĀbidīn al-Anṣārī, *Tuḥfat al-aḥbāb*, fols. 11v–12r. Zayn al-ʿĀbidīn's maternal grandfather was named Abū ʿAbdallāh Muḥammad al-Naḥrīrī al-Ḥanafī; his name appears in various *ijāza*s transmitted through Jamāl al-Dīn Yūsuf, suggesting that he was connected to the Anṣārī family through study and scholarship.

16. Zayn al-ʿĀbidīn al-Anṣārī, *Tuḥfat al-aḥbāb*, fols. 11v–12v.

17. Bāmakhrama, for example, who would have identified al-Anṣārī as the *mujaddid* soon after al-Haytamī did, is clear in linking this status to al-Anṣārī's "writings and the dependency of most people on them, especially as it relates to *fiqh* and revising the *madhhab*." Al-Muḥibbī, *Khulāṣat al-athar*, 3:346.

18. See, inter alia, al-Mandaylī, *al-Khazāʾin al-saniyya*, 171–78; cf. Muḥammad b. Sulaymān al-Kurdī al-Madanī, *al-Fawāʾid al-Madaniyya fī-man yuftā bi-qawlih min aʾimmat al-Shāfiʿiyya* (Lebanon: Dār Nūr al-Ṣabāḥ & Dār al-Jaffān wa-l-Jābī, 2011), 61–63, 286–87.

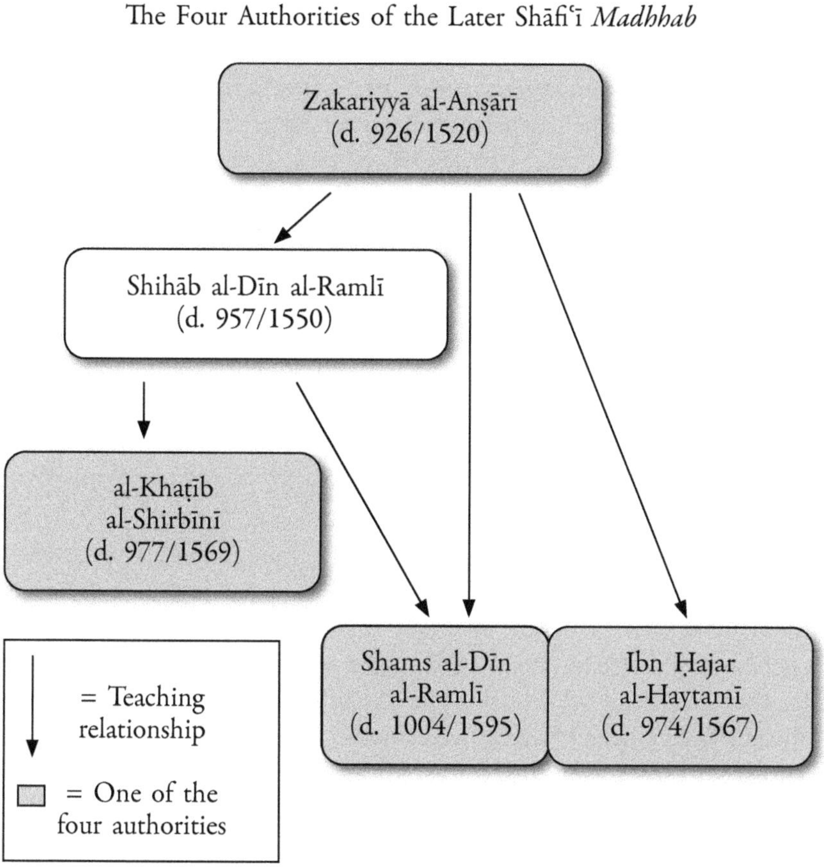

Figure 5.1. The four authorities of the later Shāfiʿī *Madhhab*. *Source*: Author provided.

remaining three jurists—Ibn Ḥajar al-Haytamī (d. 974/1567), al-Khaṭīb al-Shirbīnī (d. 977/1569), and Shams al-Dīn al-Ramlī (d. 1004/1595)—were either direct students of al-Anṣārī (al-Haytamī and al-Ramlī) or students of his students (al-Shirbīnī via Shihāb al-Dīn al-Ramlī [d. 957/1550]).

The most significant division of the later *madhhab* until the present day would pit those scholars who prioritize the legal opinions of al-Haytamī—namely Shāfiʿī scholars of Yemen, Ḥaḍramawt, the Ḥijāz, the Levant, Southeast Asia, and the Indian Ocean basin—against those who prioritize the opinions of Shams al-Dīn al-Ramlī—namely Shāfiʿī scholars of Kurdistan and Egypt.[19] Within this framework, al-Haytamī's opinions are seen to correspond overwhelmingly with al-Anṣārī's stated opinions, while al-Ramlī's opinions correspond more closely to those of his father Shihāb al-Dīn to the extent that the latter differ from, or supplement, the positions of al-Anṣārī (the teacher of both Ramlīs).[20] When neither al-Haytamī nor al-Ramlī touches on a particular legal question, however, al-Anṣārī's position on it, should it exist, becomes the *madhhab*'s default position for use in fatwas.[21] According to Zayn al-ʿĀbidīn al-Anṣārī in his *Tuḥfat al-aḥbāb*, al-Anṣārī's scholarly peers began to accord his fatwas legal precedence during his own lifetime around the time that he turned sixty.[22]

Such accounts for al-Anṣārī's theoretical status within the later Shāfiʿī *madhhab* as we find it in the writings of Shāfiʿī scholars after the tenth/sixteenth century. These same writings rank al-Anṣārī's smaller commentary on the *Bahja* of Ibn al-Wardī (d. 749/1349) as his most authoritative legal text, followed closely by his commentary on his own *Manhaj al-ṭullāb* (*The Students' Course*).[23] But to gauge the historical prominence—or canonicity—of al-Anṣārī's legal writings, it is perhaps more helpful to consider the commentarial attention that they received from later scholars. If we applied such a metric, we would find that two of the author's texts stand far above the others. The first is the *Tuḥfat al-ṭullāb* (*The Students' Gift*), al-Anṣārī's commentary on his own *mukhtaṣar* (abridgment) titled *Taḥrīr Tanqīḥ al-Lubāb* (*The Rendering of the Revision of the Quintessence*), which accumulated at least twenty-two supercommentaries, mainly in the eleventh/seventeenth century, with some appearing in the two centuries that followed.[24] The second is the *Fatḥ al-wahhāb* (*Epiphany from God,*

19. Al-Kurdī al-Madanī, *al-Fawāʾid al-Madaniyya*, 59–64.

20. Al-Mandaylī, *al-Khazāʾin al-saniyya*, 173. For more on the legal relationship between the two Ramlīs, see Hallaq, *Authority, Continuity, and Change*, 182, 189.

21. Hallaq, *Authority, Continuity, and Change*, 177. For the term *madhhab* as it is used in this sentence, see page 193; Makdisi, *Rise of Colleges*, 111.

22. Zayn al-ʿĀbidīn al-Anṣārī, *Tuḥfat al-aḥbāb*, fol. 8r.

23. For an example of this ranking, see al-Mandaylī, *al-Khazāʾin al-saniyya*, 177 (and the sources cited there in note 5). Cf. Jābir, "Shaykh al-Islām Zakariyyā al-Anṣārī," 107–9.

24. Al-Ḥabashī, *Jāmiʿ al-shurūḥ wa-l-ḥawāshī*, 1:543–47. One of these supercommentaries would receive four commentaries of its own, while al-Anṣārī's original *mukhtaṣar* would be versified at least three times and thereupon ramify into new commentarial genealogies.

the Bestower), al-Anṣārī's commentary on his own *Manhaj al-ṭullāb* and the same text that the later Shāfiʿī scholars would rank as his second most authoritative legal work. The *Fatḥ al-wahhāb* received at least twenty-one supercommentaries between the tenth/sixteenth and thirteenth/nineteenth centuries, with the majority appearing around the middle of this time span.[25] In Southeast Asia in particular it was an essential reference for scholars and textbook for students, and is still in use today within various traditional curricula.[26] None of the author's other works in substantive law garnered anything close to the commentarial attention that these two texts received, including his smaller commentary on the *Bahja*.[27]

However, the later prominence of al-Anṣārī's writings was not limited to the legal disciplines. For example, one of his texts that would receive an especially high degree of attention from later commentators was his *Muṭṭalaʿ* (*Investigation*), a commentary on Athīr al-Dīn al-Abharī's (d. 663/1264) *Īsāghūjī* (*Isagoge*) in logic. In his handlist of Arabic philosophical commentaries, Robert Wisnovsky documents no fewer than ten supercommentaries on al-Anṣārī's *Muṭṭalaʿ*, while most of these were written in the seventeenth and eighteenth centuries.[28] The breadth of al-Anṣārī's scholarship, and the manuscript record that it produced, would also affect twentieth-century editors when choosing what texts to publish for the first time. Writing in 1908, for example, the Syrian scholar Muḥammad Jamāl al-Dīn al-Qāsimī (d. 1914) notes that the only commentary on Badr al-Dīn al-Zarkashī's (d. 794/1392) *Luqṭat al-ʿajlān* (*Gleanings for the One in a Rush*) in logic and the roots of law (*uṣūl al-fiqh*) that he could locate was that of al-Anṣārī (titled *Fatḥ al-raḥmān*). The latter text both aided al-Qāsimī in his own commentary and motivated him to publish al-Zarkashī's text in the first place.[29]

25. Al-Ḥabashī, *Jāmiʿ al-shurūḥ wa-l-ḥawāshī*, 3:1942–47. For its part, the original *Manhaj al-ṭullāb* would receive at least twelve direct commentaries and would be abridged at least six times and versified at least once, making it the third most popular legal text written by al-Anṣārī as gauged by the commentarial attention that it received.

26. Azra, *Origins of Islamic Reformism*, 63, 79, 81, 129–30; G. W. J. Drewes, *Directions for Travellers on the Mystic Path* (The Hague: Martinus Nijhoff, 1977), 26–28, 180.

27. See al-Ḥabashī, *Jāmiʿ al-shurūḥ wa-l-ḥawāshī*, 2:802–3 and 990; cf. Jābir, "Shaykh al-Islām Zakariyyā al-Anṣārī," 109–16; El Shamsy, "The *Ḥāshiya* in Islamic Law," 305–12.

28. Wisnovsky, "Arabic Philosophical Commentary," 162.

29. Badr al-Dīn al-Zarkashī, *Luqṭat al-ʿajlān*, ed. and annotated by Muḥammad Jamāl al-Qāsimī al-Dimashqī (Cairo: Maṭbaʿat Madrasat Wālidat ʿAbbās al-Awwal, 1908), 4.

Al-Anṣārī's influence on Muslim posterity is also apparent in scholarly *isnāds* (chains of transmission) and *ijāzas* (licenses to transmit texts) that stretch unto the present day and are global in their reach. In his study of the impact of Middle Eastern scholarly networks on seventeenth and eighteenth-century Malay-Indonesian scholarship and reformism, for instance, Azra places al-Anṣārī within a small elite of fifteenth-century Egyptian scholars who transmitted hadith *isnāds* that later generations of scholars prized above all others. In seeking out these particular *isnāds* from one another, hadith scholars widened the scope of Muslim scholarly networks—a trend that began in Arabia and North Africa but would eventually expand into Southeast Asia (among other lands). These scholarly hadith networks, in turn, would foster other forms of intellectual exchange and emergent creativity among scholars that ultimately tied into Islamic renewal and reform in Southeast Asia on the eve of the colonial period.[30]

Similarly, we can examine the *Fihris* (*Catalogue*) of the twentieth-century Moroccan scholar ʿAbd al-Ḥayy al-Kattānī (d. 1962) as a case study to shed light on how modern Muslim scholars from around the world have connected themselves to al-Anṣārī through *isnād* and *ijāza* chains. From the *Fihris*, for example, we learn that al-Kattānī appears to value his *isnāds* through al-Anṣārī to various hadiths (or hadith collections) especially where they demonstrate al-Anṣārī's direct connection to the great hadith master Ibn Ḥajar al-ʿAsqalānī (d. 852/1449).[31] As for al-Kattānī's *isnāds* to the entirety of al-Anṣārī's written works, these are relayed through ten particular students of al-Anṣārī, including the three illustrated in figure 5.1 above, in addition to ʿAbd al-Wahhāb al-Shaʿrānī.[32] The *isnāds* of other scholars mentioned in the *Fihris* back to al-Anṣārī are too numerous to list here.

Sufism and the *Taṣnīf al-ʿulūm* Genre

The ninth/fifteenth century marks a critical juncture in cementing the scholarly legitimacy of Sufism among Sunni scholars, and manifestations

30. Azra, *Origins of Islamic Reformism*, 19, 25, 35–37, 125, and passim.

31. Al-Kattānī, *Fihris al-fahāris*, 1:87, 93, 111, 112, 190, 326–37. At page 328, al-Anṣārī himself is reported to have praised any student of his who was fortunate enough to have met Ibn Ḥajar and could transmit on his direct authority.

32. Al-Kattānī, *Fihris al-fahāris*, 1:459.

of this cementing process appear in multiple genres of Sunni scholarship. While pinpointing a single ninth/fifteenth-century author as the agent of such intellectual shifts is not possible, the differences in scholarly attitudes toward Sufism nonetheless remain stark when we compare works within specific genres of writing from before and after this century.

One genre of writing that provides unique insights into this shift in attitudes toward Sufism is that of *taṣnīf al-ʿulūm*, the enumeration and classification of the intellectual sciences, both religious and profane, often within a hierarchy of relative prominence.[33] Though not the first text on the subject, the *Mafātīḥ al-ʿulūm* of Muḥammad b. Aḥmad al-Khʷārazmī (d. 387/997) stands as a preeminent example of the earliest writings in *taṣnīf al-ʿulūm*.[34] Written soon after the year 366–67/977,[35] the *Mafātīḥ* enumerates both the intellectual sciences and their respective terms of art, though it fails to include Sufism (*taṣawwuf* or any semblance thereof) within its treatment. This lacuna is not difficult to explain in light of Sufism's precarious standing in the eyes of the late fourth/tenth-century Sunni scholarly establishment.[36] However, the *Epistles* (*Rasāʾil*) of the Ikhwān al-Ṣafāʾ, written around the same time of the *Mafātīḥ al-ʿulūm*, lists Sufism as one of the "conventional Sharīʿa disciplines" (*al-ʿulūm al-sharʿiyya al-waḍʿiyya*) and thus puts it on the same level as jurisprudence, for example, though not exactly on the same level as certain philosophical disciplines, which otherwise transcend the world of human constructs and conventions.[37] Nevertheless, if the point here is to trace the emergence of Sufism within Sunni writings on *taṣnīf al-ʿulūm*, then al-Khʷārazmī's *Mafātīḥ al-ʿulūm* might serve us as a better baseline from which to compare later developments in the genre, while the *Epistles* of the Ikhwān al-Ṣafāʾ would appear as an outlier that emerged about two centuries ahead of its time.

33. For more on this genre, see Franz Rosenthal, *The Classical Heritage in Islam*, trans. Emile and Jenny Marmorstein (London: Routledge and Kegan Paul, 1975), 55–73.

34. That is, according to C. E. Bosworth's assessment. C. E. Bosworth, "A Pioneer Arabic Encyclopedia of the Sciences: Al-Khawārizmī's Keys of the Sciences," *Isis* 54, no. 1 (1963): 101 and passim. Al-Khʷārazmī's death date is taken from al-Ziriklī, *al-Aʿlām*, 5:312. I have consulted a 1930 Egyptian edition of the *Mafātīḥ*, which is based on Gerlof van Vloten's critical edition of 1895.

35. Bosworth, "Pioneer Arabic Encyclopedia," 100.

36. See Karamustafa, *Sufism*, 89–108.

37. Godefroid de Callataÿ, "The Classification of the Sciences according to the *Rasaʾil Ikhwan al-Safaʾ*," *Institute of Ismaili Studies* (2003): 4–5.

Works in *taṣnīf al-ʿulūm* from the fifth/eleventh century similarly demonstrate little consideration of Sufism as a religious discipline in the tradition of jurisprudence, exegesis, and theology. Thus, the *Risālat Marātib al-ʿulūm* of Ibn Ḥazm (d. 456/1064) identifies four subcategories of the religious sciences (here, *ʿilm sharīʿat al-islām*), namely the science of the Qur'ān, the science of hadith, the science of jurisprudence, and the science of theology. The remaining disciplines within the author's framework concern matters profane or derivative, while Sufism, as a subcategory of knowledge, is nowhere to be found.[38] Abū Ḥāmid al-Ghazālī's (d. 505/1111) classification of the intellectual disciplines, in contrast, displays a stronger emphasis on esoteric knowledge, though it too avoids mention of Sufism proper as a formal subcategory of scholarly study. Here, al-Ghazālī subsumes what could be called Sufi practice within the "science of morals" (*ʿilm al-akhlāq*), while the "science of unveiling" (*ʿilm al-mukāshafa*) appears as the esoteric half of the "science of the path to the hereafter" (*ʿilm ṭarīq al-ākhira*) within the author's classification system. For its part, this latter science comprises the personally obligatory portion of the religious disciplines when taken in their entirety.[39]

The earliest schema to treat Sufism (*taṣawwuf*) as an autonomous science within the religious disciplines would appear in the Persian encyclopedia *Yawāqīt al-ʿulūm wa-darārī l-nujūm* of Bahā' al-Dīn al-Najjār (d. ca. 575/1180), which was composed for the Seljuq governor of Qazvin before 573/1177.[40] This text would remain an outlier for at least another century;

38. ʿAlī b. Aḥmad Ibn Ḥazm, "Risālat Marātib al-ʿulūm," in *Rasā'il Ibn Ḥazm al-Andalusī*, ed. Iḥsān ʿAbbās (Cairo: Maktabat al-Khānjī; Baghdād: Maktabat al-Muthannā, 1954), 78ff. It is worth noting here that Abū Naṣr al-Sarrāj (d. 378/988), writing in the fourth/tenth century, divides the sciences of Sharīʿa (*ʿulūm al-sharīʿa*) into the four larger categories of hadith sciences, legal sciences, rational and rhetorical sciences, and the esoteric sciences (i.e., Sufism). Nevertheless, al-Sarrāj's schema is noted, somewhat in passing, within the context of a larger defense of the Sufis and *not* within a discussion of *taṣnīf al-ʿulūm*. For this reason, it has not been included within the analysis above. Abū Naṣr al-Sarrāj, *Kitāb al-Lumaʿ fī l-taṣawwuf*, ed. Reynold A. Nicholson (Leiden: Brill, 1914), 378–81.

39. Osman Bakar, *Classification of Knowledge in Islam* (Cambridge: Islamic Texts Society, 1998), 203–26.

40. Matthew S. Melvin-Koushki, "The Quest for a Universal Science: The Occult Philosophy of Ṣā'in al-Dīn Turka Iṣfahānī (1369–1432) and Intellectual Millenarianism in Early Timurid Iran" (PhD diss., Yale University, 2012), 211.

a cotemporaneous Persian text by Fakhr al-Dīn al-Rāzī (d. 606/1210) in the *taṣnīf al-ʿulūm* genre, titled *Jāmiʿ al-ʿulūm*, includes no separate discipline of Sufism within its schema of sixty intellectual disciplines.[41]

It is not until around the eighth/fourteenth century that Sufism begins to appear regularly within works of *taṣnīf al-ʿulūm*. Some of the earliest examples are the Persian encyclopedia *Durrat al-tāj li-ghurrat al-dībāj* of Quṭb al-Dīn al-Shīrāzī (d. 710/1311) and the Arabic encyclopedia of unknown authorship *Masālik al-mubtadiʾ wa-masāʾil al-muqtaḍī*, which exists only in a unicum manuscript that was copied in 712/1312.[42] More noteworthy to the present discussion is the *Irshād al-qāṣid ilā asnā l-maqāṣid fī anwāʿ al-ʿulūm* of Ibn al-Akfānī (d. 749/1348); al-Anṣārī would borrow heavily from this text while composing his own work in *taṣnīf al-ʿulūm*,[43] as is discussed below. Written no later than 734/1334, the *Irshād* does not contain a separate subentry for the "science of Sufism" within its classification system,[44] although Sufism figures prominently within the author's discussion of the "science of metaphysics" (*al-ʿilm al-ilāhī*), which to him represents the acme of the intellectual disciplines.[45] Here, Ibn al-Akfānī posits both a theoretical and a practical component to the study of metaphysics, while the Sufis stand as the foremost authorities in the latter sphere. In fact, the author reserves his highest praise for the *mujtahid* who begins his intellectual path with the theoretical treatments of the philosophers and who ends with the practical purification exercises of the Sufis. This, in the author's estimation, was the methodology of Socrates, Plato, and Shihāb al-Dīn Yaḥyā al-Suhrawardī (d. 587/1191).[46]

---

41. Fakhr al-Dīn al-Rāzī, *Jamiʿ al-ʿulūm (sittīnī)*, ed. Sayyid ʿAlī Āl Dāwūd (Tehran: Bunyād-i Mawqūfāt-i Duktar Maḥmūd Afshār, 2003), 458–63.

42. Melvin-Koushki, "Quest for a Universal Science," 212. The *Masālik al-mubtadiʾ* refers to Sufism as *ʿilm al-ṭarīqa* (the science of the Sufi Path).

43. ʿAbdallāh Nadhīr Aḥmad, ed., *Khizānat al-ʿulūm fī taṣnīf al-funūn al-islāmiyya wa-maṣādirihā* (Beirut: Dār al-Bashāʾir al-Islāmiyya, 1998), 12.

44. On the date of composition, see Muḥammad b. Ibrāhīm Ibn al-Akfānī, *Irshād al-qāṣid ilā asnā l-maqāṣid fī anwāʿ al-ʿulūm*, ed. ʿAbd al-Munʿim Muḥammad ʿUmar (Cairo: Dār al-Fikr al-ʿArabī, 1990), 228.

45. Ibn al-Akfānī, *Irshād al-qāṣid*, 132.

46. Ibn al-Akfānī, *Irshād al-qāṣid*, 133–34. Also see Gerhard Böwering, *The Mystical Vision of Existence in Classical Islam: The Qurʾānic Hermeneutics of the Sufi Sahl al-Tustarī (d. 283/896)* (Berlin: Walter de Gruyter, 1980), 52–54.

But it is two works from the eighth/fourteenth century that would play a more lasting role in incorporating Sufism as a formal science within the larger *taṣnīf al-ʿulūm* framework.[47] The first of these is the Persian encyclopedia *Nafāʾis al-funūn fī ʿarāʾis al-ʿuyūn* of Shams al-Dīn Muḥammad b. Maḥmūd al-Āmulī, which was composed partly in 735/1335 and completed between 743/1342 and the author's death in 753/1352, according to C. A. Storey.[48] The *Nafāʾis* employs two major classification divisions (*qism*): that encompassing the ancient (*awāʾil*) sciences, and that encompassing the Islamic (here, *awākhir*) sciences. Within the latter division, the author lists eighty-five specialized sciences (*ʿilm*), which are grouped into thirty-six arts (*fann*), and these into four larger categories (*maqālat*), namely the literary sciences (*adabiyyāt*), the religious sciences (*sharʿiyyāt*), Sufism (*ʿilm-i taṣawwuf*), and "the sciences of daily discourse" (*ʿulūm-i muḥāwarī*).[49] The category of Sufism, for its part, encompasses the following five "arts": the science of mystical wayfaring (*ʿilm-i sulūk*), the science of the mystical reality (*ʿilm-i ḥaqīqat*), the science of inner processes (*ʿilm-i marāṣid*), the science of letters (*ʿilm-i ḥurūf*), and the science of chivalrous behavior (*ʿilm-i futuwwat*).[50] Within al-Āmulī's schema, then, Sufism figures as a broad and autonomous category of knowledge that stands on an equal footing with the *entirety* of the other religious sciences (*sharʿiyyāt*) when taken together. It thus enjoys a privileged position when juxtaposed with any single science from the religious disciplines, such as theology (*ʿilm-i kalām*) or jurisprudence (*ʿilm-i fiqh*).

47. Fritz Meier identifies the eighth/fourteenth century as a period in which scholars had already begun associating Sufism "with the generally recognized religious disciplines"; Ibn Khaldūn and al-Āmulī thus conform to this assessment. Fritz Meier, "Khurāsān and the End of Classical Sufism," in *Essays on Islamic Piety and Mysticism*, ed. Fritz Meier (Leiden: Brill, 1999), 189.

48. C. A. Storey, *Persian Literature: A Bio-Bibliographical Survey*, 5 vols. (London: Luzacs, 1927ff.), 2:355–57; cf. Seyyed Hossein Nasr, *Islamic Science: An Illustrated Study* (London: World of Islam Festival, 1976), 14–16, where the work is traced to the ninth/fifteenth century, and Ibn Khaldūn's *taṣnīf al-ʿulūm* framework thus appears as the earlier precedent to that of al-Āmulī.

49. Thus, from largest to smallest division, the schema runs: *qism* → *maqālat* → *fann* → *ʿilm*. The translation for *ʿulūm-i muḥāwarī* here is taken from Nasr, *Islamic Science*, 16.

50. Shams al-Dīn al-Āmulī, *Nafāʾis al-funūn fī ʿarāʾis al-ʿuyūn*, ed. Mīrzā Abū l-Ḥasan Shaʿrānī, 3 vols. (Tehran, Kitābfurūshī-i Islāmiyya, 1958–60), 1:161–99. The five *fanns*, in turn, encompass forty *ʿilms*, which, in the interest of space, need not be enumerated here.

A better theoretical treatment of this eighth/fourteenth-century trend can be found in Ibn Khaldūn's (d. 808/1406) subchapter on the science of Sufism within his celebrated *Muqaddima*, which he wrote between 776/1375 and 780/1379. Here, Ibn Khaldūn situates Sufism within the "traditional, conventional sciences," which "depend upon information based on the authority of the given religious law," and which stand in opposition to the "philosophical sciences."[51] A human being, the author explains, possesses two types of perception: one to perceive "matters of knowledge," and another to perceive his or her own internal states (*aḥwāl*). As a formal science, Sufism refers to the study of these states and their dynamic relationship with an individual's actions.[52] According to Ibn Khaldūn, "[Sufism] is concerned with pious exertion, self-scrutiny with regard to it, discussion of the different kinds of mystical and ecstatic experience occurring in the course of (self-scrutiny), the mode of ascent from one mystical experience to another, and the interpretation of the technical terminology of mysticism in use among [the Sufis]."[53] Ibn Khaldūn explains that because the religious law of the jurists failed to consider the subjective processes and states that afflict a person, the larger "science of the religious law" ultimately split to encompass two subfields: the law of the jurists and the spiritualism of the Sufis. Moreover, the author traces the formalization of Sufism into a discipline of systematic study back to al-Ghazālī, before whom Sufism "had merely consisted of divine worship, and its laws had existed in the breasts of men."[54]

In fact, Ibn Khaldūn's own treatment of Sufism may have played an equally important role in the formalization of Sufism as that of al-Ghazālī. About a century after the composition of the *Muqaddima*, two additional works in *taṣnīf al-ʿulūm* would be written in Egypt, both of which treat Sufism as another formal discipline within the larger gamut of the traditional Islamic sciences. The first of these texts is Jalāl al-Dīn al-Suyūṭī's

51. ʿAbd al-Raḥmān Ibn Khaldūn, *The Muqaddimah: An Introduction to History*, trans. Franz Rosenthal, 3 vols. (Princeton, NJ: Princeton University Press, 1967), 2:436. Chapter 6 of the *Muqaddima*, stretching between volumes 2 and 3 of the translated edition cited here, functions as a text in *taṣnīf al-ʿulūm*. For the composition date of the *Muqaddima*, see *Encyclopaedia of Islam*, s.v. "Ibn Khaldūn, Walī al-Dīn" (M. Talbi).

52. Ibn Khaldūn, *Muqaddimah*, 3:77–78.

53. Ibn Khaldūn, *Muqaddimah*, 3:80.

54. Ibn Khaldūn, *Muqaddimah*, 3:79–80.

(d. 911/1505) *Itmām al-dirāya li-qurrā᾽ al-Nuqāya*, a commentary on the author's own *Nuqāya* that enumerates fourteen Islamic sciences and provides a description of their most salient principles and objectives. Written in the year 873/1468, al-Suyūṭī's text lists the "science of Sufism" as the last of the fourteen intellectual disciplines, which encompass both religious and profane subjects.[55] For every science other than Sufism, the author provides a terse definition of what its *ʿilm* (science/knowledge) encompasses. According to al-Suyūṭī, for example, the "science of anatomy" (*ʿilm al-tashrīḥ*) is "an *ʿilm* in which the human organs and the manner of their arrangement are studied."[56] In the case of Sufism, however, al-Suyūṭī provides a description of the science's "terminus" (*ḥadd*)—namely "devoting (*tajrīd*) one's heart to God [alone] and scorning everything other than Him"—without defining its *ʿilm*. In accounting for such a decision, the author explains that the Sufi, once he or she has understood the purpose of Sufism, is more in need of an objective (viz. the *ḥadd* of Sufism) in his or her undertaking than in an academic definition of it (viz. the *ʿilm* of Sufism) because of this person's "lack of concern for the latter which is the prerogative of the experts in externalities."[57] Al-Suyūṭī's treatment of Sufism is thus distinct from his treatment of the other intellectual sciences, although his novel placement of the subject within his *taṣnīf al-ʿulūm* framework represents a further development in a formalization trend that began at least a century earlier.

Writing only a few years after al-Suyūṭī, Zakariyyā al-Anṣārī demonstrates an even more casual attitude toward the "science of Sufism" within his own work in *taṣnīf al-ʿulūm*, titled *al-Luʾluʾ al-naẓīm fī rawm al-taʿallum wa-l-taʿlīm*.[58] In al-Anṣārī's text, Sufism is given no special designation within the author's succinct enumeration of the intellectual sciences. Rather, it

55. For the date of composition cited here, see Jalāl al-Dīn al-Suyūṭī, *Itmām al-dirāya li-qurrā᾽ al-Nuqāya* (Beirut: Dār al-Kutub al-ʿIlmiyya, 1985), 185.

56. Al-Suyūṭī, *Itmām al-dirāya*, 147.

57. Al-Suyūṭī, *Itmām al-dirāya*, 163.

58. A manuscript of the text that I have consulted bears the composition date of 3 Jumādā II 910/10 November 1504. Zakariyyā al-Anṣārī, *al-Luʾluʾ al-naẓīm fī rawm al-taʿallum wa-l-taʿlīm*, MS al-Maʿārif al-ʿĀmma 17621/3413, al-Maktaba al-Azhariyya, Cairo, fol. 6r. For more on the manuscript, see *Fihris al-kutub al-mawjūda bi-l-Maktaba al-Azhariyya*, 6 vols. (Cairo: Maṭbaʿat al-Azhar, 1962), 6:271. Cf. Aḥmad, *Khizānat al-ʿulūm*, 12–13, where the author places al-Suyūṭī's *Itmām* after al-Anṣārī's *Luʾluʾ* chronologically, which would appear mistaken in light of the evidence here.

emerges in a perfunctory manner within a grouping of the "regimen-based sciences" (*al-ʿulūm al-riyāḍiyya*), which include the mathematical and engineering sciences in addition to the "science of politics" and "the science of morals" (*ʿilm al-akhlāq*). Sufism is not, however, grouped with the three "Sharīʿa sciences" (*al-ʿulūm al-sharʿiyya*)—namely jurisprudence, Qurʾānic exegesis, and hadith studies—nor does it appear within the "rational sciences" (*al-ʿulūm al-ʿaqliyya*), which cover metaphysics, theology, and philosophy, among others.[59] Such a schema is made all the more idiosyncratic by the fact that al-Anṣārī would appear to have used Ibn al-Akfānī's *Irshād* as a template for much of the material in his *Luʾluʾ*.[60] Nevertheless, al-Anṣārī has removed the connections to Greek philosophy that characterized Ibn al-Akfānī's treatment of Sufism, which appears within the latter's chapter on metaphysics. He also presents Sufism within an autonomous chapter of its own. When we compare this treatment of Sufism with earlier treatments like that of al-Āmulī, we find that al-Anṣārī's nonchalant attitude toward "the science of Sufism" and his placement of it within an intellectual grouping of otherwise profane subjects demonstrate a new degree of routinization in scholarly attitudes toward Sufism within the *taṣnīf al-ʿulūm* genre during the later Islamic middle period.

The position of Sufism within ninth/fourteenth-century *taṣnīf al-ʿulūm* works such as those of al-Suyūṭī and al-Anṣārī reflects a larger shift in perceptions of Sufism's scholarly legitimacy and propensity for academic (*pace* experiential) study.[61] Al-Anṣārī's casual placement of Sufism within his *Luʾluʾ* represents part of his efforts to promote, perhaps inadvertently, an academic treatment of Sufism in an effort to bolster its scholarly standing. But it is the positing of an autonomous technical vocabulary for the study of Sufism that would provide al-Anṣārī with arguably the most powerful weapon in his scholarly defense of the Sufis.

---

59. Zakariyyā al-Anṣārī, *al-Luʾluʾ al-naẓīm fī rawm al-taʿallum wa-l-taʿlīm* (Cairo: Maṭbaʿat al-Mawsūʿāt, 1901/2), 7–8.

60. Compare, for example, al-Anṣārī's twelve conditions for teaching and learning the intellectual sciences (*al-Luʾluʾ*, 5–7) with the twelve of Ibn al-Akfānī (*Irshād al-qāṣid*, 99–105). Cf. Aḥmad, ed., *Khizānat al-ʿulūm*, 12.

61. Geoffroy, *Le soufisme*, 90–93, 155; Berkey, *Transmission of Knowledge*, 59; Leonor Fernandes, *The Evolution of a Sufi Institution in Mamluk Egypt: The Khanqah* (Berlin: Klaus Schwarz Verlag, 1988), 33–34, 101–2.

A Technical Terminology for Sufism

As Éric Geoffroy has noted, scholars of Sufism in the later Islamic middle period devoted much energy to deciphering the technical terminology of the Sufis. For its part, this technical terminology (*muṣṭalaḥāt*; alternatively, *iṣṭilāḥ/iṣṭilāḥāt*) arose out of a need felt by Sufi intellectuals to ascribe a human vocabulary to their otherwise ineffable experiences and visions. Moreover, while the famous "allusions" (*ishārāt*) of the Sufis had previously encouraged discretion—if not reticence—among the Sufis whenever they faced threats of hostility from the outside or empty posturing from within,[62] their developing a technical terminology of their own would assist in countering these threats, as it demanded a formal study of Sufism from those members of the scholarly establishment who wished either to appreciate or condemn the mystical experiences of the Sufis.

In other words, through their *muṣṭalaḥāt*, the Sufis claimed a semantic autonomy for their speech that consequently demanded a rigorous study from any would-be critic, just as would be the case for a critic of any other Islamic discipline. In its functionality, then, the technical terminology of Sufism played an important apologetic role. But can we also view the emergence of a Sufi technical vocabulary as a function of the routinization of Sufism that inspired the developments discussed above within the *taṣnīf al-ʿulūm* genre? At first glance, this might seem to be obvious: as any intellectual discipline evolves, its interpretive community relies on a shared terminology that expands and becomes more precise and technical with the forward movement of time.

In the case of Sufism, however, one problem with this view is that the technical terminology of Sufism functions quite differently from the terminologies of other Islamic disciplines. Perhaps owing to the subjective nature of mystical experience, the terms of art of the Sufis admit far more variance in their meanings than would be deemed acceptable in any of the exoteric sciences.[63] In fact, a multitude of contradictory definitions might

62. Geoffroy, *Le soufisme*, 393.

63. For a brief take on the polysemous nature of Sufi technical terminology when compared with those of other Islamic sciences, see the editor's introduction to ʿAbd al-Razzāq al-Kāshānī, *Muʿjam iṣṭilāḥāt al-ṣūfiyya*, ed. ʿAbd al-ʿĀl Shāhīn (Cairo: Dār al-Manār, 1992), 11–12.

apply to a single term of art within a single Sufi text,[64] while such a high degree of polysemy would remain impractical in most other Islamic disciplines. Within the various genres of Islamic law, hadith studies, and exegesis, for example, technical vocabularies serve to facilitate communication among specialists through a highly precise language that endeavors to function as an agreed-upon convention. We therefore find a careful balance between pithiness and precision within these vocabularies. The technical vocabulary of Sufism, however, originates in the *ishāra* (mystical allusion) background, and because of this, it tends to favor pithiness *over* precision in order to uphold the enigma of mystical experience.

In contradistinction to other technical vocabularies, then, the organic development of a technical vocabulary for Sufism to meet practical, scholarly needs would seem unlikely. Rather, apologetic objectives were the primary driving force behind ascribing formal *muṣṭalaḥāt* to the Sufis; this act of ascribing *muṣṭalaḥāt* to the Sufis stands at the crux of al-Anṣārī and al-Suyūṭī's respective defenses of them, as is discussed below.

In this light, it is significant that earlier Sufi writers such as Abū Naṣr al-Sarrāj (d. 378/988), ʿAbd al-Karīm al-Qushayrī (d. 465/1072), and Ibn ʿArabī (d. 638/1240) refer to the "vocables" (*alfāẓ*) of the Sufis and not to their "technical terminology."[65] In other words, the use of *muṣṭalaḥāt/iṣṭilāḥāt* to describe the Sufis' specialized vocabulary is significant in itself, as it would serve apologetic objectives while sharing few developmental or functional parallels with the technical vocabularies of other scholarly fields. So where do we find its earliest appearances?

While it is difficult to identify an unequivocal origin for the ascription of formal *muṣṭalaḥāt* to the Sufis, a passage found in al-Suyūṭī's apologetic treatise *Taʾyīd al-ḥaqīqa al-ʿaliyya wa-tashyīd al-ṭarīqa al-Shādhiliyya* and attributed to Quṭb al-Dīn al-Qasṭallānī (d. 686/1287) certainly stands as a very early precedent. As al-Qasṭallānī explains, every *ṭāʾifa* (community) of people possesses a particular *muṣṭalaḥ*, as is the case, for example, within the

64. For an interesting example of this phenomenon, see al-Anṣārī's definitions of *taṣawwuf* in *Iḥkām al-dalāla*, 4:2–3; cf. 1:69 and 2:5.

65. Al-Anṣārī, *Iḥkām al-dalāla*, 2:19, 21; Rafīq al-ʿAjam, "*al-Taʿrīfāt* li-Ibn ʿArabī," *al-Abḥāth* 36 (1988): 11; cf. al-Anṣārī, *Risāla Fī Bayān al-alfāẓ*, fol. 1r; al-Sarrāj, *Kitāb al-Lumaʿ fī l-taṣawwuf*, 3, 333, 374. Also, cf. Abū ʿAbd al-Raḥmān al-Sulamī, *Sufi Treatises of Abū ʿAbd al-Raḥmān al-Sulamī*, ed. Gerhard Böwering and Bilal Orfali (Beirut: Dār el-Machreq, 2009), 23–24.

ṭāʾifa of traders and that of weavers, among other professional communities.[66] The author's use of *muṣṭalaḥ* (singular) in this passage does not refer to a technical vocabulary in the scholarly sense of the term, however. Rather, a more generic "agreed-upon convention" is intended here,[67] as is attested to by al-Qasṭallānī's comparing of the Sufis' *muṣṭalaḥ* with those of other nonscholarly communities, and his subsequent reference to the *alfāẓ* of the Sufis that they "have agreed upon [among themselves]" (*aṣṭalaḥū*) and that parallel, almost exactly, the *alfāẓ* listed by al-Qushayrī in his *Risāla*.[68] In fact, al-Qasṭallānī's passage on the *muṣṭalaḥ* of the Sufis stands as a middle point between al-Qushayrī's introductory remarks on the *alfāẓ* of the Sufis in his *Risāla* and al-Anṣārī's commentary on the *Risāla*. In the latter text, al-Anṣārī has extended the logic of al-Qasṭallānī's argument in two ways. First, he likens the Sufis, through their use of language, to a particular *scholarly* community—namely the theologians—by noting that both groups apply idiosyncratic meanings to their respective terms and expressions. And second, he qualifies al-Qasṭallānī's generic usage of *ṭāʾifa* by asserting in no unclear terms that the *ṭāʾifa* of the Sufis is "from the larger body of scholars" (*min jumlat ṭawāʾif al-ʿulamāʾ*).[69] According to this reading, al-Anṣārī has adopted the framework of al-Qasṭallānī's argument, either through a direct or indirect familiarity with it, but he amends it to emphasize the scholarly standing of the Sufis.

For its part, the *muṣṭalaḥ* of the Sufis, according to al-Qasṭallānī, serves two very practical purposes: it enables the Sufis to communicate

66. For al-Qasṭallānī's biography, see, inter alia, Jamāl al-Dīn ʿAbd al-Raḥīm al-Isnawī, *Ṭabaqāt al-Shāfiʿiyya*, ed. ʿAbdallāh al-Jubūrī, 2 vols. (Baghdad: Iraqi Ministry of Awqāf, Maṭbaʿat al-Irshād, 1970–71), 2:326–27; Tāj al-Dīn al-Subkī, *Ṭabaqāt al-Shāfiʿiyya al-kubrā*, ed. Maḥmūd Muḥammad al-Ṭanāḥī and ʿAbd al-Fattāḥ Muḥammad al-Ḥilw, 10 vols. (Cairo: ʿĪsā al-Bābī al-Ḥalabī, 1964ff), 8:43–44; al-Ziriklī, *al-Aʿlām*, 5:323–24. The text quoted by al-Suyūṭī here is al-Qasṭallānī's unpublished *Iqtidāʾ al-ghāfil bi-htidāʾ al-ʿāqil*, which is noted in passing by al-Ziriklī though not found in Brockelmann (*Geschichte der arabischen Litteratur*).

67. For this translation, see Lane, *Arabic-English Lexicon*, book 1, part 4:1714–15 (s.v. ص - ل - ح). Elias Muhanna, in a personal communication, has also suggested the meaning "best practices" for *muṣṭalaḥ*, at least within an administrative context.

68. Jalāl al-Dīn al-Suyūṭī, *Taʾyīd al-ḥaqīqa al-ʿaliyya wa-tashyīd al-ṭarīqa al-Shādhiliyya* (Cairo: al-Maṭbaʿa al-Islāmiyya, 1934), 43; cf. al-Anṣārī, *Iḥkām al-dalāla*, 2:21.

69. Al-Anṣārī, *Iḥkām al-dalāla*, 2:21.

with one another, and it functions as a shibboleth to exclude pretenders from the Sufis' ranks.[70] These two themes of specialized communication and the exclusion of outsiders would persist within scholarly treatments of the Sufis' language in the centuries that were to follow al-Qasṭallānī. As can been seen in al-Anṣārī's treatment above, however, the subsequent generations of scholars who viewed Sufism favorably and who sought to defend it from its critics would ascribe a higher degree of intellectual authority to the Sufis and their language. Thus, the generic *muṣṭalaḥ* used by al-Qaṣṭallānī would evolve into *muṣṭalaḥāt/iṣṭilāḥāt* proper. These later treatments, in turn, would elevate the Sufis' standing to that of de facto scholars, and consequently, their specialized language was viewed as even more exclusivist, recondite, and—most importantly—irreproachable.

In tracing this shift from *muṣṭalaḥ* to *muṣṭalaḥāt*, then, we must consider the *Iṣṭilāḥāt al-ṣūfiyya* of ʿAbd al-Razzāq al-Kāshānī (d. 736/1335), about whom little is known. It represents perhaps the earliest scholarly treatise dedicated to an examination of the formal, technical nomenclature of Sufism.[71] In explaining the impetus for writing his text, al-Kāshānī cites the ignorance and confusion of the traditional scholarly establishment (*ahl al-ʿulūm al-manqūla wa-l-maʿqūla*) toward the Sufis' *iṣṭilāḥāt* that appear throughout his writings. In fact, according to al-Kāshānī, some of his scholarly peers had requested that he compile such a text to aid them in their reading of his other commentaries and exegetical works, while his introductory remarks suggest that a technical reading of the Sufis' words—*pace* a literary reading—was an unfamiliar concept, at least within his own eighth/fourteenth-century context.[72] No earlier precedent for ascribing a

70. Al-Suyūṭī, *Taʾyīd al-ḥaqīqa al-ʿaliyya*, 43

71. For the death date cited here, see Majīd Hādīzāda, ed., *Majmūʿa-yi rasāʾil wa-muṣannafāt-i shaykh Kamāl al-Dīn ʿAbd al-Razzāq-i Kāshānī* (Tehran: Mīrās-i Maktūb, 2000), 123–26; cf. *Encyclopaedia of Islam,* 3rd ed., s.v. "ʿAbd al-Razzāq al-Kāshānī" (Pierre Lory); *Encyclopaedia of Islam,* s.v. "ʿAbd al-Razzāḳ Kamāl al-Dīn b. Abū ʾl-Ghanāʾim al-Ḳāshānī" (D. B. MacDonald). It is also worth noting here that al-Āmulī, writing just around the time of al-Kāshānī's death, includes a science on the *iṣṭilāḥāt* of Sufis (*arbāb-i sulūk*) within the larger category (*maqālat*) of Sufism of his *taṣnīf al-ʿulūm* schema. Shams al-Dīn al-Āmulī, *Nafāʾis al-funūn fī ʿarāʾis al-ʿuyūn*, 1:170–72. Beyond his extensive list of the Sufis' technical vocabulary however, the author provides no further information to assist the analysis here.

72. Al-Kāshānī, *Muʿjam iṣṭilāḥāt al-ṣūfiyya*, 46.

technical vocabulary to the Sufis is referenced in al-Kāshānī's treatise, and we are left cautiously identifying the *Iṣṭilāḥāt al-ṣūfiyya* as a pioneering work on the subject. Written a few decades after al-Kāshānī's text, a fatwa by the Maghrebi jurist Aḥmad b. Qāsim al-Qabbāb (d. 778/1377) similarly references the Sufis' *iṣṭilāḥāt* in passing. However, here al-Qabbāb warns his inquirer that "most of the [Sufis'] technical terms are inexplicit and, rather, are cited in a symbolic or metonymical fashion."[73]

In the century that followed al-Kāshānī, al-Sayyid al-Sharīf al-Jurjānī (d. 816/1413) would compose his celebrated *Taʿrīfāt*, a comprehensive, albeit succinct, glossary of key scholarly definitions (*taʿrīfāt*) and technical terms (*iṣṭilāḥāt*) that were gathered by the author to aid Muslim students of knowledge. The text includes dozens of Sufi terms and definitions within its pages, and in a few instances, al-Jurjānī refers to the *iṣṭilāḥ* of the Sufis (*ahl al-ḥaqīqa*).[74] But a more detailed treatment of the subject can be found in the *Muqaddima* of Ibn Khaldūn, a contemporary of al-Jurjānī. Within his subchapter on the science of Sufism, Ibn Khaldūn writes, "Furthermore, the Sufis have their peculiar form of behavior and a (peculiar) linguistic terminology [*iṣṭilāḥāt*] which they use in instruction. Linguistic data apply only to commonly accepted ideas. When there occur ideas not commonly accepted, technical terms facilitating the understanding of those ideas are coined to express them. Thus, the Sufis have their special discipline, which is not discussed by other representatives of the religious law."[75] What is perhaps most pertinent in this passage to the present analysis is the author's linking of the Sufis' technical terminology to their unique position of authority within "their special discipline" of Sufism. In other words, the *iṣṭilāḥāt* of the Sufis function as a scholarly translation of their mystical ideas (*maʿānī*) while simultaneously legitimizing their discipline as a formal, religious science and preserving their exclusive claims to authority

73. Aḥmad b. Qāsim al-Qabbāb, *Fatwā l-Qabbāb fī sulūk ṭarīq al-ṣūfiyya*, appended to ʿAbd al-Raḥmān Ibn Khaldūn, *Shifāʾ al-sāʾil wa-tahdhīb al-masāʾil*, ed. Muḥammad Muṭīʿ al-Ḥāfiẓ (Damascus: Dār al-Fikr, 1996), 199.

74. Al-Sayyid al-Sharīf al-Jurjānī, *Kitāb al-Taʿrīfāt* (Beirut: Maktabat Lubnān, 1985), 172 (s.v. "*al-firāsa*"), 244 (s.v. "*al-maqām*").

75. Ibn Khaldūn, *Muqaddimah*, 3:79. Other passing references to the Sufis' *iṣṭilāḥāt* can be found at 3:80, 100.

within it.[76] In another text of his, *Shifāʾ al-sāʾil wa-tahdhīb al-masāʾil*, Ibn Khaldūn glosses several of the technical terms of the Sufis but also breaks the ideas of the Sufis into two categories: those that can be understood through reflection by employing one's rational and sensory faculties, and those that can be understood only through subjective experience and that "cannot be determined precisely through academic conventions nor through terminological expressions."[77]

Ibn Khaldūn's brief words above reflect a subtle change in scholarly attitudes toward the language of the Sufis, and they form an early precedent for apologetic adaptations of his reasoning that would emerge in the ninth/fifteenth and tenth/sixteenth centuries. According to these adaptations, any would-be critic of the Sufis must necessarily possess an intimate knowledge of the latter's *iṣṭilāḥāt* before even approaching their texts, let alone censuring them. Although it was al-Anṣārī's students who would provide the most detailed treatments of this argument,[78] we find its earlier and more influential articulations in the fatwas of Jalāl al-Dīn al-Suyūṭī and al-Anṣārī himself.

Within a text titled *al-Ḥāwī li-l-fatāwī*, al-Suyūṭī would arrange a collection of his own fatwas, which he had ceased issuing by the year 891/1486.[79] It is in this text that we find a subsection of "Fatwas Pertaining to Sufism" (*al-Fatāwā al-mutaʿallaqa bi-l-taṣawwuf*), which Geoffroy cites as "the first time that *taṣawwuf* figures as a science of its own within a

76. For an early precedent to this reasoning, albeit one that predates the ascription of formal *iṣṭilāḥāt* to the Sufis, see al-Sarrāj, *Kitāb al-Lumaʿ fī l-taṣawwuf*, 379.

77. Ibn Khaldūn, *Shifāʾ al-sāʾil wa-tahdhīb al-masāʾil*, 88–95, 129–30, 151–52. The quoted material is taken from page 130.

78. See, for example, al-Shaʿrānī, *al-Ṭabaqāt al-kubrā*, 1:55–56; ʿAbd al-Wahhāb al-Shaʿrānī, *al-Yawāqīt wa-l-jawāhir fī bayān ʿaqāʾid al-akābir*, 2 vols. (Beirut: Dār al-Maʿrifa, 1974), 1:11, quoting Sirāj al-Dīn al-Makhzūmī (d. 885/1480) (on the latter, see al-Ziriklī, *al-Aʿlām*, 6:238); al-Haytamī, *al-Fatāwā al-ḥadīthiyya*, 210.

79. Sartain, *Jalāl al-Dīn al-Suyūṭī*, 80–86. Though the author's introduction does suggest that he arranged his collection after a careful review of his entire corpus of fatwas from years past, neither this section nor the colophon at the conclusion of the printed edition of the work reveal any definitive date for the *Ḥāwī*'s compilation. Jalāl al-Dīn al-Suyūṭī, *al-Ḥāwī li-l-fatāwī*, 2 vols. (Beirut: Dār al-Kutub al-ʿIlmiyya, 1988), 1:5; 2:346. One fatwa from the subsection under discussion here (at 2:255) carries an original dating of Muḥarram 883/April 1478.

collection of fatwas."[80] Whether an earlier precedent can be found or not, al-Suyūṭī's subsection certainly demonstrates a new degree of routinization that would define the scholarly discourse surrounding Sufism in the late ninth/fifteenth century. Moreover, the first of the six fatwas contained here reflects an important shift in how Sufi legists from this period—legists like al-Suyūṭī and al-Anṣārī—would extend the *iṣṭilāḥāt* argument of scholars like Ibn Khaldūn in apologetic directions. In this fatwa, al-Suyūṭī responds to the discomfort of a questioner regarding the statement of an early Sufi, "A person who settles for *fiqh* to the exclusion of self-denial has sown sin." Al-Suyūṭī explains,

> This is the speech of a Sufi speaking according to his spiritual station. The elect often use the words "disbelief" and "sinfulness" in ways unknown to the jurists. One of the saintly forerunners has similarly said, "The good deeds of the righteous are the sins of God's intimates." He has thus deemed the good deeds [of the former] sinful in relation to the high station of God's intimates. Likewise, Ibn al-Fāriḍ (may God be pleased with him) has said, "If there should appear a desire for other than You/ on my mind inadvertently, I would pronounce myself apostate." It is obvious that this is not true apostasy. Also in this manner are the words of the Sufis, "Backbiting breaks the fast of the fasting person." All of this is according to the path of the elect, who impose on themselves what is not to be imposed on the general public.[81]

According to al-Suyūṭī, then, the language of the Sufi elect cannot be viewed through the same legal prism that is applied to the speech of everyday people. He affords the Sufis room for exaggeration in their speech that is not afforded to others, while elsewhere in his text he defends even their most controversial statements on similar grounds.

For example, within a subsection of the *Ḥāwī* titled "Theological Fatwas" (*al-Fatāwā al-uṣūliyya*), al-Suyūṭī considers the case of al-Ḥusayn b. Manṣūr al-Ḥallāj's (d. 309/922) famous utterance "I am God, the Truth" (*anā*

80. Geoffroy, *Le soufisme*, 154. For a detailed treatment of the development of the "Sufi fatwa," see Ingalls, "Between Center and Periphery."

81. Al-Suyūṭī, *al-Ḥāwī li-l-fatāwī*, 2:234.

l-ḥaqq), for which al-Ḥallāj was executed on the grounds of heresy and later accused, more specifically, of espousing monism (*al-ittiḥād*). Al-Suyūṭī begins his defense of al-Ḥāllāj on the familiar grounds of legal insanity—that is, that the Sufi's state of ecstasy rendered him temporarily insane and therefore beyond the reproach of the law. The author's approach here hardly marks the first time that a later scholar had defended al-Ḥallaj on such grounds, as it is simple and appeals to the logic of the legists in their own language.[82]

But it is al-Suyūṭī's subsequent defense of al-Ḥallāj's words that reflect a more profound shift in how Sufi jurists would construct a legal barrier around the words and actions of those who society deemed to be saintly figures.[83] According to him, the charge of monism has been cast unjustly at true Sufis over the centuries, when in fact the Arabic term for "monism"—*al-ittiḥād*—is a polyseme (*lafẓ mushtarak*), which the Sufis use according to its technical (*iṣṭilāḥī*) register to signify the less controversial concept of annihilation in God (*al-fanāʾ*). In other words, the Sufis employ a precising definition when using the term *al-ittiḥād* within their scholarly discipline and thereby render all other definitions of the term strictly lexical or conventional.[84] These lexical definitions of the term hold no authority within theological disputes, as any benign example of the word *al-ittiḥād* will attest. The example from everyday speech that al-Suyūṭī uses to demonstrate this is the sentence "Between me and my friend Zayd is an *ittiḥād*" (here, "accord"). No theologian would take offense at such a statement. At the same time, al-Suyūṭī does not appear to recognize a precising definition for *al-ittiḥād* within the discipline of theology.[85] Therefore, Muslim theologians who use the term must be relying on one of its lexical definitions, which cannot result in legal repercussions.

Al-Suyūṭī's argument in defense of al-Ḥallāj's words would remain academic, and it was al-Anṣārī's fatwa in defense of Ibn al-Fāriḍ around the

82. Al-Suyūṭī, *al-Ḥāwī li-l-fatāwī*, 2:130. Al-Ḥallāj is not mentioned by name. Cf. al-Suyūṭī, *Taʾyīd al-ḥaqīqa al-ʿaliyya*, 100–105. Also see Alexander D. Knysh, *Ibn ʿArabi in the Later Islamic Tradition: The Making of a Polemical Image in Medieval Islam* (Albany: State University of New York Press, 1999), 119–20; Geoffroy, *Le soufisme*, 473.

83. For an example of this shift from the following century, see al-Haytamī, *al-Fatāwā al-ḥadīthiyya*, 210–11.

84. See William T. Parry and Edward A. Hacker, *Aristotelian Logic* (Albany: State University of New York Press, 1991), 90–95.

85. Al-Suyūṭī, *al-Ḥāwī li-l-fatāwī*, 2:134.

year 875/1470—as has been discussed in chapter 2—that would insert a very similar argument directly into the Mamlūk sociopolitical sphere. In fact, al-Anṣārī's fatwa likely preceded that of al-Suyūṭī, while the wording of the latter suggests that al-Suyūṭī may have begun with al-Anṣārī's fatwa as his template, which he then reworked into a more elaborate and systematic tract.

Al-Anṣārī's fatwa would also find academic permanence within the discipline of Shāfiʿī substantive law (*furūʿ al-fiqh*). Writing around the year 892/1497,[86] al-Anṣārī revised and incorporated his Ibn al-Fāriḍ fatwa into his *Asnā l-maṭālib* commentary on Ibn al-Muqrī's (d. 837/1433) *Rawḍ al-ṭālib*. The relevant passage from the *Asnā l-maṭālib* represents a unique—if not unprecedented—example of how Sufi jurists like al-Anṣārī integrated Sufism into the discipline of *fiqh*, and is thus worth reproducing here in full. It is also illustrative of how scholars assimilated fatwas into works of substantive law, as Wael Hallaq has documented convincingly, while such works of substantive law would then function to revise the *madhhab* incrementally and would shape subsequent fatwas that scholars issued from within it.[87] In this light, by integrating his Ibn al-Fāriḍ fatwa into a work of substantive law, al-Anṣārī would set a new precedent for later Shāfiʿī scholars, as can be seen in the fatwas of some of his students.

Ibn al-Muqrī was a bitter opponent of the Andalusian mystic Ibn ʿArabī and his partisans, and for that reason he would insert the following words into his discussion of apostasy within the *Rawḍ al-ṭālib*: "[One has committed an act of disbelief who] doubts the established disbelief of the Jews, the Christians [. . .], and Ibn ʿArabī's community" (*ṭāʾifa*). With the aim of countering Ibn al-Muqrī's anathema, al-Anṣārī would make a few minor edits to the wording of his Ibn al-Fāriḍ fatwa and would then integrate this revised material into his commentary on Ibn al-Muqrī's text—this time in the defense of Ibn ʿArabī and his supporters. The final interwoven commentary found in the *Asnā l-maṭālib* appears as follows:

> [**One has committed an act of disbelief who**] **doubts the established disbelief of the Jews, the Christians** [. . .], **and Ibn ʿArabī's community**, whose words might suggest monism and

86. Al-Sakhāwī, *Ḍawʾ*, 2:292–95; Arberry, *Handlist*, 7:121 (MS 5406).

87. See Wael B. Hallaq, "From Fatwās to *Furūʿ*: Growth and Change in Islamic Substantive Law," *Islamic Law and Society* 1 (1994): 29–65.

other such things to outsiders when taken at face value. This [last category] is an addition by [Ibn al-Muqrī to al-Nawawī's *Rawḍat al-ṭalibīn*, which the *Rawḍ al-ṭālib* is an abridgment of], and it is based on what he, and others like him, have understood from the outward meanings of their speech. The truth is that they are an elect group of Muslims, and their speech functions according to their own technical vocabulary (*iṣṭilāḥ*), as is the case with the rest of the Sufis. Among themselves their speech is truth according to what they intend, even though it might otherwise demand an outsider's allegorical interpretation if such a person committed an act of disbelief were he or she to believe in its outward meaning, as a technical term is a truth in its technical sense [only] and is a metaphor in other contexts. Thus, the person among them who believes in this technical sense believes in a meaning that is sound. A group of scholars—intimately knowledgeable of God—have explicitly written about the sanctity of Ibn ʿArabī; among them are the shaykh Tāj al-Dīn Ibn ʿAtāʾ Allāh [(d. 709/1309)] and the shaykh ʿAbd Allāh al-Yāfiʿī [(d. 768/1367)]. When cited among non-Sufis, the outward meanings in the speech of Ibn ʿArabī and his community does not diminish the status of the latter, for the reasons we have said. Also, owing to the deficiency of language in explaining the state to which such a person has ascended, expressions that *seem* to reflect incarnationism or monism might issue forth from the knower of God as this person becomes immersed in the sea of God's oneness and intimate knowledge, whereby his or her essence and attributes vanish into God's essence and attributes, and he or she is oblivious to everything other than God. But there is nothing of the sort here [of true incarnationism and monism], as the master al-Saʿd al-Taftāzānī [(d. 793/1390)] and others have said.[88]

88. Al-Anṣārī, *Asnā l-maṭālib*, 5:632–33; cf. the wording of al-Anṣārī's original fatwa at Zakariyyā al-Anṣārī, *al-Iʿlām wa-l-ihtimām bi-jamʿ fatāwā shaykh al-islām*, ed. Qāsim al-Rifāʿī (Damascus: Dār al-Taqwā, 2007), 389–90. Al-Anṣārī's fatwa collection was arranged posthumously in 986/1578 by a scholar from Upper Egypt named Khalīl b. ʿUmar. Al-Anṣārī, *al-Iʿlām wa-l-ihtimām*, 13, 407.

Al-Anṣārī's defense of both Ibn al-Fāriḍ and Ibn ʿArabī would echo in the fatwas of his students, though none would include this defense within a work of substantive law, as their teacher had done. Nevertheless, by incorporating the position above into his *Asnā*, al-Anṣārī canonized it—to the limited extent that this verb applies to the history of Islamic law—by imbuing it with a higher degree of permanence within the *madhhab* than what his original fatwa could have attained on its own. Incorporating this position into the *Asnā* through a direct contradiction of Ibn al-Muqrī's base text, moreover, reflected a new tone of self-assurance within the ranks of Sufi scholars, and more so than the specific details of his argument, it was arguably the confidence that al-Anṣārī instilled in his students through this act that would serve as his most direct and abiding influence on later generations.

An example of this confidence can be seen in the fatwa collection of al-Anṣārī's student Shihāb al-Dīn al-Ramlī, which was collected and arranged by al-Khaṭīb al-Shirbīnī.[89] Within a concluding chapter of this text titled "Miscellaneous Matters" (*Masāʾil shattā*), an unnamed fatwa solicitor asks al-Ramlī about the intended addressee in Ibn al-Fāriḍ's verse:

> My heart keeps telling me that you are my destroyer;
> My spirit is your ransom: Did you know this or did you not?

As the question in the second hemistich here suggests that the addressee might possess incomplete knowledge, it would seem inappropriate for Ibn al-Fāriḍ to be addressing God, as ostensibly he is doing. In his fatwa, al-Ramlī confirms that the poet is, in fact, addressing God, though the second hemistich must be interpreted metaphorically to mean "My spirit is your ransom: Did you requite this or did you not?" Al-Ramlī then cites the story of another poet who took offense at this particular verse, upon which he experienced a dream vision of Ibn al-Fāriḍ, who explained that he had intended a sudden shift to an addressee other than God when he penned the last clause of the second hemistich.[90]

89. Al-Shaʿrānī, *al-Ṭabaqāt al-ṣughrā*, 68; N. al-Ghazzī, *Kawākib*, 1:199, 2:119. Cf. *Encyclopaedia of Islam*, s.v. "al-Ramlī" (A. Zysow); and Yūsuf Sarkīs, *Muʿjam al-maṭbūʿāt al-ʿarabiyya wa-l-muʿarraba*, 2 vols. (Cairo: Maktabat al-Thaqāfa al-Dīniyya, n. d.), 1:952, where Shams al-Dīn al-Ramlī is misidentified as the compiler of his father's fatwas.

90. Shihāb al-Dīn al-Ramlī, *Fatāwā al-Ramlī*, printed in margins of al-Haytamī, *al-Fatāwā al-kubrā al-fiqhiyya*, 4:214–15.

In the final analysis of the fatwa, then, al-Ramlī has preferred his own interpretation of the verse over that of the poet in the dream vision, but he nonetheless includes the story in his fatwa to justify the broader imperative to interpret Ibn al-Fāriḍ metaphorically. This imperative owes at least part of its existence to the precedent set, and obligation felt, by al-Anṣārī in penning his own defense of Ibn al-Fāriḍ's poetry. However, al-Ramlī's fatwa no longer relies on the measured reasoning that we find in the fatwas of al-Anṣārī and al-Suyūṭī. The latter fatwas were clearly written with an eye toward placating an antagonistic audience, as individual fatwas against Ibn ʿArabī and his teachings still lingered in the Mamlūk collective consciousness after having reached their apogee in the eighth/fourteenth century.[91] Rather, al-Ramlī's fatwa assumes much less hostility from its audience, while its incorporating a dream vision into its argument reflects what Geoffroy has identified as the "[legal] validation of 'intuitive unveiling' and 'inspiration' of the Sufis" that now characterized Muslim scholarship.[92]

An ever starker example of this latter phenomenon can be found in the fatwas of Ibn Ḥajar al-Haytamī, al-Anṣārī's star pupil, who would have an outsized influence on the later Shāfiʿī *madhhab*. Al-Haytamī's fatwas on Sufism appear scattered throughout a separate volume of "hadith fatwas" within a larger collection of his fatwas that was arranged by one of his students.[93] Here we find al-Haytamī to be far more outspoken in his sympathies for the Sufis than any of his Egyptian predecessors. In one relevant passage, for example, a fatwa solicitor asks al-Haytamī for his opinion on Ibn al-Fāriḍ and Ibn ʿArabī, to which al-Haytamī responds with a lengthy defense of these figures.[94] His fatwa here builds primarily on an argument from authority, in which the author cites the many scholarly supporters of Ibn al-Fāriḍ and Ibn ʿArabī and in this context includes a lengthy digression on al-Anṣārī and Burhān al-Dīn Ibn Abī Sharīf. Al-Haytamī also integrates into his fatwa a dream narration of Jamāl al-Dīn al-Ṣānī (d. 931/1525), al-Anṣārī's student and chief deputy during his days as chief justice. According to this narration, al-Ṣānī at one point considered himself an opponent of Ibn al-Fāriḍ but then experienced a dream in

---

91. Knysh, *Ibn ʿArabi*, 75ff, 120–28, 135–39, 170, 174, 191–96, 210–18, and 252ff.

92. Geoffroy, *Le soufisme*, 477.

93. See Lamyāʾ Aḥmad ʿAbdallāh Shāfiʿī, *Ibn Ḥajar al-Haytamī al-Makkī wa-juhūduh fī l-kitāba al-taʾrīkhiyya* (Giza: Maktabat al-Ghadd, 1998), 65–66; 160–62; 173–76.

94. Al-Haytamī, *al-Fatāwā al-ḥadīthiyya*, 50–55.

which he saw himself in a disheveled state on the Day of Judgment while riding on the back of Ibn al-Fāriḍ. A heavenly voice thereupon called to the party of Ibn al-Fāriḍ and instructed them to enter Paradise, but when al-Ṣānī attempted to follow this party, he was turned back, as he was not of their ranks. Al-Ṣānī reports that he then awoke from this dream in a state of extreme anxiety and interpreted the vision as a sign to repent for his censure of Ibn al-Fāriḍ and to affirm his belief in the latter's holiness. At a later stage, al-Ṣānī would experience a very similar dream as before, though in this version he was permitted to enter Paradise with the party of Ibn al-Fāriḍ, as he was now considered of their ranks.

Al-Haytamī concludes this story with a note that al-Ṣānī was a jurist and not a Sufi, and his dream visions were meant to reconnect him with the authority and blessing of his master al-Anṣārī,[95] who had always taught in support of Ibn al-Fāriḍ. In other words, al-Ṣānī's visions provide al-Haytamī with legal evidence to support the notion that Ibn al-Fāriḍ was not only a saintly figure in his own right but also that to disconnect oneself from him would serve to disconnect oneself from a broader tradition of authority upon which an individual's very legitimacy as a scholar rests. Al-Ṣānī's two dreams thus demonstrate what can happen if one questions the larger argument from authority that fills the rest of the fatwa's lines. When compared with earlier fatwas in defense of figures like Ibn al-Fāriḍ and Ibn ʿArabī, what becomes immediately apparent from al-Haytamī's fatwa is the increased epistemic validity of subjective evidence such as that provided by a dream vision. While al-Ramlī had previously referenced a dream narration as a secondary argument in support of a metaphorical interpretation of a single verse of Sufi poetry, al-Haytamī extends the jurisdiction of this method by taking a dream narration as the glue that binds the pieces of his broader argument in defense of Ibn al-Fāriḍ.

Although his name appears in al-Haytamī's fatwa and forms an integral part of its reasoning, it is difficult to imagine al-Anṣārī citing a dream vision in his own fatwas or legal texts. Even when he relies on an argument from authority within the abovementioned passage of the *Asnā*, as we see with his references to Ibn ʿAṭāʾ Allah, al-Yāfiʿī, and al-Taftāzānī, this argument appears in passing and is secondary to al-Anṣārī's *iṣṭilāḥāt* argument, which

95. Al-Haytamī, *al-Fatāwā al-ḥadīthiyya*, 52; cf. Henderson, *Scripture, Canon, and Commentary*, 65–66.

pivots on conventions and analogies that might ring more familiar to the legal scholars of his time. To be sure, the liberties that al-Haytamī could take within his fatwa demonstrate that Sufi scholars had acquired sufficient interpretive authority by early Ottoman times, and gone were the days of careful apologetics and reasoning that built on the assumptions of outsiders. What is significant here is how quickly the tide had shifted in favor of Sufi scholars like al-Haytamī—perhaps as little as thirty to forty years separated his fatwa from al-Anṣārī's *Asnā* passage. As the genealogy of texts above suggests, it was the intellectual space carved out by al-Anṣārī (along with scholarly peers like al-Suyūṭī) that furnished al-Ramlī and al-Haytamī's generation of Egyptian Sufi scholars with the self-assurance that we find in their legal treatments of Sufism.

Conclusion

Commentary, Canonization, and Creativity: A New Case for the "Era of Commentaries and Supercommentaries"

When attempting to draw larger lessons on originality and intellectual change from the study of Islamic commentary works written by even a single author, perhaps the biggest challenge facing contemporary historians of Islam is the sheer volume of comparisons that they must perform between the lemmata of a given commentary, the base text that these build on, and the passages of later-order or parallel-order commentaries that are relevant to the discussions under examination. If we hope to move the study of Muslim intellectual history past the thirteenth century within a reasonable timeframe, this challenge creates an incentive for studies of Islamic commentaries to begin at the level of lemmata and not at the level of complete books or multiple books within the written corpus of an author.[1] Most of the analyses conducted and conclusions reached in the study above have stemmed from a close reading of particular lemmata in Zakariyyā al-Anṣārī's commentaries, which I have then extended outward through comparisons with antecedent and subsequent texts. After making these comparisons, I have attempted to derive broader conclusions about the nature of Islamic commentaries by assessing the role of these lemmata in shifting the contours of the Islamic intellectual discourse during the later middle period.

1. Matthew B. Ingalls, "Zakariyyā al-Anṣārī and the Study of Muslim Commentaries from the Later Islamic Middle Period," *Religion Compass* 10, no. 5 (2016): 126.

To conclude my study while maintaining this methodology, the Ibn ʿArabī passage of al-Anṣārī's *Asnā l-maṭālib* cited in the previous chapter functions as a useful launch point for a discussion of two final themes that are essential to an appreciation of Islamic commentary texts during this period. The first is the theme of canonization—both canonization *of* commentary and canonization *through* commentary—and the idiosyncrasies at play when we attempt to apply this term within the context of Islamic commentary texts. The second is the theme of creativity. What is the nature of creativity, or originality, in Islamic commentary texts when we are willing to acknowledge its existence? What are the challenges posed in assessing it when the very form of commentary texts has come to symbolize the epitome of unoriginality in the minds of many modern critics, both Muslim and non-Muslim? I address these two themes in the space below; I begin with the abovementioned text of the *Asnā* and then expand into a broader consideration of the material that preceded it, which I put into conversation with some recent scholarship from the field of commentary studies.

Canonization in the Context of the Islamic Commentary

When looking backward from the perspective of sixteenth-century texts like those of al-Ramlī and al-Haytamī, we notice that the *Asnā*'s commentary on Ibn al-Muqrī functioned to canonize al-Anṣārī's earlier fatwa on Ibn ʿArabī and Ibn al-Fāriḍ. Once the fatwa was integrated into a work of commentary that was subsequently received by a large enough readership to give it momentum through time, its agency in shaping the later tradition increased exponentially. Later generations of Shāfiʿī commentators and scholars would now be forced to contend with it either through acceptance or rejection; this would not be the case had the fatwa not found permanence within the commentary of the *Asnā*. Al-Haytamī, for example, references the text of the *Asnā* as his leading argument against those who might question his decision to favor the position of Ibn ʿArabī and Ibn al-Fāriḍ's scholarly defenders over that of their detractors. In other words, al-Haytamī's strongest defense of these mystics is to establish that a defense of them exists within a legal commentary in Islamic substantive law (*furūʿ al-fiqh*), as scholarly fatwas on them are divided. As he then explains to his reader and theoretical interlocutor, "What [al-Anṣārī] relates in [his *Asnā*] is clear, so seek it there."[2]

In light of al-Anṣārī's status within the later Shāfiʿī *madhhab*, it is tempting to assume that it was his commanding authority that enabled him to contradict Ibn al-Muqrī's base text by inserting his fatwa into the *Asnā*. In fact, the line of causality may run in the opposite direction. Commentary, that is, functions to redistribute the authority of an earlier author within a new context in which that author's voice in no longer self-explanatory.[3] In this way, a commentator can disjoin the authority of an author like Ibn al-Muqrī from his base text and reclaim it for himself whenever he is able to demonstrate a forceful—even contradictory—interpretation of that base text.[4] The power to disjoin the authority of an author from his base text would be amplified through the form of the interwoven commentary, which lemmatizes the base text and thereby undermines its ideology of coherence and the organizational methodology of its author.[5] Al-Anṣārī's authority thus borrows and redeploys the authority of Ibn al-Muqrī, particularly in those places where his commentary challenges the positions of the latter. The end effect of this dynamic is the augmentation of al-Anṣārī's status within the collective Muslim imagination and, ultimately, later scholars' affirmation of him as an authority within the *madhhab*.

Without overstating the power of this *particular* passage of the *Asnā* in shaping the worldview of Sufi scholars like al-Ramlī and al-Haytamī, who of course were influenced more by their personal relationships with their teacher than by his texts alone, the passage certainly increased the intellectual cachet of an argument that was novel in its day. The canonization of this argument through a widely read commentary like the *Asnā* illustrates what Henderson has described as the "apotheosis" of commentary within

2. Al-Haytamī, *al-Fatāwā al-ḥadīthiyya*, 52.

3. Most, "Preface," x.

4. Vallance, "Non-Submissive Commentary," 241.

5. Kraus, "Introduction," 15. As Kraus explains (at page 7), "[Commentary] takes on an authority that can compromise, challenge, and even replace the authority of the commented text." For an illustrative example of this phenomenon within medieval Tamil commentaries, see Cutler, "Interpreting *Tirukkuṟaḷ*," 552–53.

a particular historical context.[6] As he explains, "The elevation of . . . commentary to the level of canon, may seem quaint and peculiar to moderns influences by Romantic notions of genius and originality and Protestant conceptions of *sola scriptura*. But even canons are as much the products of editing and exegesis as they are of poetry and prophecy."[7] By juxtaposing "Romantic notions of genius" with the activities of editors and exegetes, whose mundane decisions have as much of an impact on the canonization of texts as do any other factors, Henderson's words highlight the accidents of history that shape the processes of canonization—a major theme in canonization studies for several decades now.[8] In contrast, as it relates to the creative merits of al-Anṣārī's commentary texts that attained something resembling a canonical status, my analysis above has stressed the role of commentarial form and rhetoric over the unfiltered substance of these commentaries, though here I would argue that substance and rhetoric are inseparable if not synonymous for all practical purposes.

Notwithstanding this focus, it would be naïve of me to downplay the role of chance accidents of history that lead one text to be treated as canonical instead of another. Even within the premodern Islamic tradition we can find subtle acknowledgments of the factors that influenced canonization that are separate from the internal merits of a text. In his *Tadhkirat al-sāmiʿ wa-l-mutakallim* (*Reminder for the Hearer and the Speaker*), for example, Ibn Jamāʿa (d. 733/1332) provides an order for determining how a student should prioritize the placement of multiple texts and accord each the ritual respect that it is due relative to the others. Within his schema, the author lists as his third consideration that priority should be given to "whichever text is more popular among the scholars and the righteous."[9] Although his order for the placement of texts is not a perfect stand-in for the relative canonicity of these texts, his willingness to ascribe value to a text's popularity indicates that he views the reception of a text to be

6. Henderson, *Scripture, Canon, and Commentary*, 84, 87, and passim. The de facto canonization of Parimēlaḻakar's commentary on the *Tirukkuṟaḷ* provides a helpful example of this process. See Cutler, "Interpreting *Tirukkuṟaḷ*," 553, 565.

7. Henderson, *Scripture, Canon, and Commentary*, 87.

8. See, inter alia, Frank Kermode, *Pleasure and Change: The Aesthetics of Canon* (Oxford University Press, 2004), 34.

9. Ibn Jamāʿa, *Tadhkirat al-sāmiʿ*, 233.

a variable that is at least as important as the text's own inherent virtues. Moreover, the accidental forces of canonization even continue at the meta-level within academic studies of Islamic commentaries. Robert Wisnovsky's handlist of philosophical commentaries lists only those sixty-five philosophical base texts that received commentaries during the Islamic middle and early modern periods, for example, and in this way, it points later scholars toward those texts that might be worthier of their research attention.[10] I would be demonstrating a profound lack of self-awareness were I to claim that my present study does not participate in this same process in relation to al-Anṣārī's commentaries.

But, without succumbing to the temptations of romanticism, it would be equally mistaken to overemphasize accidental factors—or factors *wholly* external to the text—when explaining the links between commentary and canonization. As Gerald Bruns explains it, the distinction between canonical and noncanonical is "a distinction between texts that are forceful in a given situation and those which are not."[11] The rhetoric of commentary, the opportunities that it affords, and the constraints that it imposes are all essential factors in determining its forcefulness within a given historical context and thus its potential to canonize a base text or become canonical in its own right. This forcefulness certainly connects with external forces, but rarely can these be completely severed from the text and its author. A sense of cultural upheaval, for example, often leads a community to canonize a text that is symbolically valuable to its identity,[12] while this symbolic value ascribed to the text links to the authority of its author and to the text's earlier capacity to have resonated with the community's heroic forebears. We can explain the enduring popularity al-Anṣārī's *Iḥkām al-dalāla* today in light of these factors, for instance. One reason that the text remains the most widely read and influential commentary on al-Qushayrī's *Risāla* is because the Grand Shaykh of al-Azhar Muṣṭafā al-ʿArūsī (d. 1876) wrote a supercommentary on it and published both his and al-Anṣārī's texts at a critical moment in the history of the Egyptian printing press. In turn, his decision to apply his energies

10. Wisnovsky, "Arabic Philosophical Commentary," 158, 160–90.

11. Bruns, "Canon and Power in the Hebrew Scriptures," 464.

12. Ahmed El Shamsy, *The Canonization of Islamic Law: A Social and Intellectual History* (New York: Cambridge University Press, 2013), 9 (citing the scholarship of Aleida and Jann Assmann).

to the *Iḥkām* owes to a confluence of factors, both internal and external to the text, including the sense of dislocation felt by many Egyptian *ʿulamāʾ* at the time, the availability of new printing technologies, the accessibility of al-Anṣārī's prose, the particular dogmas that the *Iḥkām* upheld, and the symbolic value that al-ʿArūsī ascribed to a text that was written four hundred years earlier by an iconic "Azharī" like al-Anṣārī.

In itself, the forcefulness of a text could hardly be equated with canonicity if it fails to extend through time, and it would thus be misguided to view al-ʿArūsī's publication of the *Iḥkām* in the late nineteenth century as an atavistic event. Though the perception of a text's canonicity may ebb and flow with the passage of time, there must remain some echo of it at any given moment if the word "canonical" is to have any meaning at all in the context of the Islamic commentary tradition. Nevertheless, within this particular context, the echo of canonicity sometimes assumes an abstract form in which what persists in the collective imagination after the "heroic first readings" of a base text, as Edward Said refers to them, is not the canonicity of a particular text but rather the "schools" of discourse that distill from this first reading and structure the limits and possibilities of future generations of commentators.[13] In such a case, the canonicity of a first-order commentary persists in the subconscious of the community and might be glimpsed obliquely, for example, in the choices of later-order commentators to gloss certain words instead of others or to augment the exposition here instead of there. Moreover, the power of these schools of discourse in shaping the content, conventions, and rhetoric of subsequent commentaries often eclipses the power of the individual commentator, which helps to explain, at least partially, why commentaries tend to rely on the rhetoric of anonymity that has been described in chapter 1.[14]

Commentary, Creativity, and Subtle Innovation

When assessing al-Anṣārī's creativity and the role of his thought in shepherding the intellectual tradition in novel directions, it is helpful to consider

13. Edward W. Said, *Humanism and Democratic Criticism* (New York: Columbia University Press, 2004), 67–69; Stanley Fish, "Literature in the Reader: Affective Stylistics," *New Literary History* 2, no. 1 (1970): 141; White, *Tropics of Discourse*, 127–28; Ahmed, "Post-Classical Philosophical Commentaries/Glosses," 346.

14. Gumbrecht, *Powers of Philology*, 43–44, 47.

Robert Sternberg's "propulsion model" of creativity. According to this theory, a creative contribution to a field is defined as anything that propels the field from an existing place to a new place through the agency—wilful or not—of the contributor. The model thus analyses shifts in an intellectual tradition over time and views creativity as synonymous with an individual's impact in driving those shifts or in fortifying preexisting shifts.[15] Replication, for example, can serve in the latter capacity, as it might "establish the validity or invalidity of contributions" and "ensure that an approach is robust and can generate a number and variety of works."[16] In this light, even something as ostensibly unoriginal as the replication of an artistic technique might exhibit forms of creativity.

Sternberg's model identifies eight categories of creative contributions that an author or artist might make, and when the analyses of the previous chapters are filtered through the lens of his model, al-Anṣārī's creative contributions would fall into at least two of these categories. The first category—"forward incrementation"—obtains when a contributor succeeds in propelling a field forward in the trajectory that it is already following until it is taken up by other receptive contributors.[17] The previous chapter has demonstrated, for example, how al-Anṣārī's thought incrementally shifted the *iṣṭilāḥāt* argument until it was received with aplomb by scholars like al-Haytamī and al-Ramlī. A second category—"integration"—occurs when a contributor shifts a field by integrating two or more ideas that were previously seen as disparate or antithetical.[18] An obvious example here is al-Anṣārī's legal reading of the *Risāla* and the Sufis' lives that are documented within it, as has been discussed in various places in chapter 3. Another example is the Ibn ʿArabī passage of the *Asnā l-maṭālib*, which we can cautiously identify as the first instance in which a commentator introduced what I have defined elsewhere as the Sufi fatwa into a work of Islamic substantive law.[19] As has been shown in the previous chapter, this event symbolized a

15. Robert J. Sternberg, "A Propulsion Model of Types of Creative Contributions," *Review of General Psychology* 3, no. 2 (1999): 83–100.

16. Robert J. Sternberg, James C. Kaufman, and Jean Pretz, "The Propulsion Model of Creative Contributions Applied to the Arts and Letters," *Jour. of Creative Behavior* 35, no. 2 (2001): 80.

17. Sternberg et al., "Propulsion Model," 85–87.

18. Sternberg et al., "Propulsion Model," 95–97.

19. See Ingalls, "Between Center and Periphery," 145–63.

new degree of cross-pollination between Sufism and Islamic law and could be framed as a turning point that afforded later Sufi scholars the confidence that they needed to blend these two disciplines in unprecedented ways.[20]

Al-Anṣārī's texts exhibited creativity through their effecting forward incrementation and integration, to be sure. But in light of the author's *mujaddid* status in the collective memory of many later Muslims, we might also be tempted to read some degree of nonconformity toward the received tradition within his thought, as a *mujaddid* presumably embodies the daring spirit needed to confront the mistakes of the received tradition and thereby redirect it and make it a source of inspiration for the Muslim community once again. The creative contributions of such a person would correspond with Sternberg's categories of "redirection," "reconstruction," and "reinitiation"; they are the first things that come to mind when we consider creative individuals in history.

However, to limit creativity to these categories reflects romantic understandings that—though attractive—are more harmful than helpful in assessing the creativity of the Muslim commentarial tradition. Ideas, the determinants of creativity, are not discreet entities that reside in, and emerge from, individuals. Rather, they are communications between individuals who are arranged within social networks of groups, intergenerational chains, and rivalries. The ideas of an individual like al-Anṣārī are thus a product of the chains of social encounters that have defined his life up until the juncture in which these ideas are reified in the form of a text like the *Asnā*.[21] For its part, each social encounter varies in the intensity that it enacts solidarity between the individuals involved, while the interaction rituals that accompany it focus the attention and collective emotions of these actors to generate the emotional energy needed for social well-being.[22]

The substratum of all ideas are therefore social networks, which constitute the building blocks of society. If we simplify our model so that a

---

20. Consider, as an example, ʿAbd al-Wahhāb al-Shaʿrānī's *al-Mīzān al-kubrā*, a text in comparative Islamic law (*ikhtilāf al-madhāhib*) that filters the legal discourse through a Sufi epistemology. See Pagani, "Meaning of the *Ikhtilāf al-madhāhib*," 181–83, 185, and especially 190ff. Also see Geoffroy, *Le Soufisme*, 485–97; Ahmed Fekry Ibrahim, "Al-Shaʿrānī's Response to Legal Purism: A Theory of Legal Pluralism," *Islamic Law and Society* 20, no. 1/2 (2013): 110–40.

21. Randall Collins, *The Sociology of Philosophies: A Global Theory of Intellectual Change* (Cambridge, MA: Harvard University Press, 1998), 1–8.

22. Collins, *Sociology of Philosophies*, 20–24.

given society is equated with a single, overarching network of individuals, then subnetworks (and subcultures) emerge through variations in the degree to which individuals are bounded within this larger network. In turn, the lines that that separate subnetworks fluctuate and are determined by the degree to which individuals are bounded within them or by the perspective of the observer, who may be inside or outside of the system.[23] The more bounded and hermetic a network is, the more likely are its members to view the network's values as universal values, to view its classification of the world as a reflection of the natural order of reality, and to rely on taboos and moral prohibitions to reify the network's core institutions in order to stem heresy and dissent. Within this context, innovation must assume the subtlest of forms if it is to be tolerated at all.[24]

But the vagaries of history inevitably lead all tightly bounded networks to loosen at some future juncture. In sociological terms, another way of describing this process is to say that space will be created within which second-level observations can emerge to throw the first-level observations of the network into question. If first-level observations constitute what the network ascribes to the world (*pace* to the subjective observer) and that form its commonsense perceptions of the world and the internal logic of the group, then second-level observations describe not what the in-network member observes about the world, but *how* this observer does so, and how his or her mode of observation is different from that of members of other networks. Typically, second-level observations would be the domain of outside observers who claim to function disinterestedly vis-à-vis the observed network outside of which they stand, though *not* vis-à-vis their own social network into which they feed their observations. Because these outside observers share not the intuitive, first-level observations of their objects of study but espouse second-level observations, they read the commonsense world of the object network as a series of social constructs that are contingent on historical and sociological forces.[25]

Nevertheless, it remains possible for second-level observations to emerge *within* networks, particularly by way of individuals who are linked to multiple networks that overlap to varying degrees. These in-network

23. Stephan Fuchs, *Against Essentialism: A Theory of Culture and Society* (Cambridge, MA: Harvard University Press, 2001), 51, 66, 91–92.

24. Fuchs, *Against Essentialism*, 17, 61.

25. Fuchs, *Against Essentialism*, 27, 42, 39, and passim.

second-level observations can lead to the shifting of network boundaries while also enabling paradigm shifts within society and a new spirit of openness toward innovation that assumes less subtle forms. History teaches us that at least two particular catalysts drive this process. The first is public controversy, which allows first-level observations to be questioned, and thus opens the door of possibility for individuals within the network to espouse second-level observations about their world.[26] Here, we should consider the Ibn al-Fāriḍ controversy during al-Anṣārī's life, which played a pivotal role both in generating the text that al-Anṣārī would later insert into his *Asnā* commentary, and in establishing al-Anṣārī's career, renown, and, ultimately, his intellectual legacy. Admittedly, however, there is no way to know for sure whether it is the public controversy that enables such shifts in a network or if the public controversy represents the breaking point of fissures that were already present within a highly bounded network.

Another means of loosening a highly bounded network occurs when that network is exposed to greater cosmopolitanism. As its lines of demarcation become more opaque and it increases its contacts with outside networks, a formally hermetic network decentralizes and simultaneously merges its core—in part or in whole—with that of the other network.[27] At the global level, for example, we glimpse an extreme version of these processes at play in the urbanization trends of the past century. As regards the present study, this model applies if we separate the network of scholarly specialists in the exoteric sciences, as represented by a figure like Burhān al-Dīn al-Biqāʿī, from the network of peripheral mystical authorities, as represented by a figure like Muḥammad al-Iṣṭanbūlī. Within this particular case study, al-Anṣārī would function as a translator between the two networks and would eventually find himself at the center of a new, amalgamated network of Sufi scholars. This new network would experience the act of translating between disciplines like law and Sufism to be far easier than it was in the previous context, as it would espouse different first-level observations about the world, most notably in the form of new epistemological schemas and new rhetorical and methodological conventions to communicate these schemas.[28]

26. Fuchs, *Against Essentialism*, 29, 61.

27. Fuchs, *Against Essentialism*, 61–62, 81.

28. Fuchs, *Against Essentialism*, 81.

Within the broader context of Islamic commentaries, we notice an abstract cosmopolitanism at play in the interactions of commentators and texts. My study above has tended to focus on diachronic developments within the genealogies of commentary texts, as tracking these developments generates starker results that are easier to connect to ideological shifts in Islamic intellectual history. Nevertheless, as Asad Ahmed states at the conclusion of his 2013 study of two postclassical Muslim commentaries in logic, the genre of commentary "even when assessed over time, must be understood as synchronic."[29] Though diachronic developments clearly shaped the backbone of the commentarial record, a commentator would always dedicate his rhetorical and dialectical energies to the concerns of his *contemporary* readers and rivals, while the massive textual tradition that he borrowed from to address these concerns was effectively detached from the variables of temporality and geographical distance—variables that are otherwise essential to shaping the diachronic development of a textual genealogy. In other words, the demands of their own intellectual contexts forced commentators into a relationship with a truly massive body of texts, written by both ancients and contemporaries, by next-door neighbors and by Muslims in far-off lands.[30] Their relationship with, and redeployments of, this body of texts exposed Muslim commentators to a textual cosmopolitanism that would rival that of any other civilization.

In addition to their boundedness within networks of living peers, this textual cosmopolitanism meant that Muslim commentators were bounded to disembodied, horizontal networks that transcended time and space. The diversity of perspective that these more abstract networks afforded them would certainly function as a wellspring for commentarial creativity.[31] As can be seen time and again in al-Anṣārī's commentaries, however, this creativity was frequently camouflaged and presented in the form of selective citation of the received tradition. On the rhetorical power that lies within this method

---

29. Ahmed, "Post-Classical Philosophical Commentaries/Glosses," 344.

30. Hallaq, *Authority, Continuity, and Change*, 222, 233; Saleh, *Formation of the Classical Tafsīr Tradition*, 14.

31. For a contemporary study of the connections between creativity and diverse, horizontal networks, see Martin Reuf, "Strong Ties, Weak Ties and Islands: Structural and Organizational Predictors of Organizational Innovation," *Industrial and Corporate Change* 11, no. 3 (2002): 443.

of creative expression, Mikhail Bakhtin explains, "The context embracing another's words is responsible for its dialogising background, whose influence can be very great. Given the appropriate methods for framing, one may bring about fundamental changes even in another's utterance accurately quoted."[32] By uprooting an authority's words from their original context, a commentator would wield considerable influence over the later reception of these words and over their signification within the context of his commentary. For this reason, it is common to find highly subversive redeployments of a past scholar's words within later commentaries.[33] In the context of Islamic law especially, Hallaq has argued that "selective appropriation and manipulation of earlier juristic discourse" was the hallmark of the jurist's craft.[34] In fact, were commentators *not* to couch their creativity within a selective reframing of the received tradition, their words would run the risk of becoming inappreciable to the reader or "perceivable only as an absurdity."[35]

Though it is unmistakable to anyone who analyzes Islamic commentary texts closely enough, the subtle creativity that defined these texts remains difficult to discern to readers who measure creativity as a function of acute changes in the outward form of texts—acute changes such as those that characterized the development of European literature after the Renaissance. Thomas Bauer has described the latter as "catastrophic" change, which he juxtaposes with the "organic" change that defined Mamlūk literature during the Islamic middle period.[36] We can see an illustration of

32. M. M. Bakhtin, *The Dialogic Imagination: Four Essays*, trans. Caryl Emerson and Michael Holquist (Austin: University of Texas Press, 1981), 340.

33. See, for example, Jean Levi, "Quelques exemples de détournement subversif de la citation dans la littérature classique chinoise," *Extrême-Orient, Extrême-Occident* 17 (1995): 41–65.

34. Hallaq, *Authority, Continuity, and Change*, 215.

35. Derek Attridge, "Context, Idioculture, Invention," *New Literary History* 42 (2011): 681; Derek Attridge, *The Singularity of Literature* (Abingdon, UK: Routledge, 2004), 17–31. In a similar vein, within the context of Qur'ānic exegesis, Saleh writes, "Modifications and innovations could only succeed if they permitted a sense of continuity and harmony with the old way of doing exegesis." Saleh, *Formation of the Classical Tafsīr Tradition*, 101.

36. Bauer, "Mamluk Literature," 112ff. Similarly, in the context of Islamic law, Hallaq writes, "The modern notion of change (which tends to signify qualitative leaps and at times violent physical and epistemic ruptures from the past) was clearly absent from the conceptual world and discourse of the jurists." Hallaq, *Sharīʿa*, 183.

this organic change in the emergence and proliferation of the interwoven commentary, for example. Notwithstanding this development, however, Islamic commentary texts would demonstrate a remarkable stability over time in their outward form, and the mistake that many twentieth-century historians and reformers made was to equate this stability with intellectual stagnation.[37] Rather, the constraints of the commentarial form demanded even more intellectual creativity from Muslim commentators to overcome them,[38] while the opportunities afforded to them by the conventions of their craft allowed them to drag the anchors of the tradition in new and virtually infinite directions.

37. Bauer, "Mamluk Literature," 116; Robert Gleave, *Islam and Literalism* (Edinburgh: Edinburgh University Press, 2012), 28; Wisnovsky, "Arabic Philosophical Commentary," 151.

38. See Ahmed, "Post-Classical Philosophical Commentaries/Glosses," 344; Smith, *Imagining Religion*, 44.

Bibliography

Arabic-Language Sources

al-ʿAbbādī, Aḥmad b. Qāsim, and ʿAbd al-Ḥamīd al-Shirwānī. *Ḥawāshī ʿalā Tuḥfat al-muḥtāj bi-sharḥ al-Minhāj*. 10 vols. Cairo: al-Maktaba al-Tijāriyya al-Kubrā, 1938.

Abū Zayd, Ṭāhā Aḥmad. *Ismāʿīl al-Muqrī: Ḥayātuh wa-shiʿruh*. Ṣanʿāʾ, Yemen: Markaz al-Dirāsāt wa-l-Buḥūth al-Yamanī; Beirut: Dār al-Ādāb, 1986.

Aḥmad, ʿAbdallāh Nadhīr, ed. *Khizānat al-ʿulūm fī taṣnīf al-funūn al-islāmiyya wa-maṣādirihā*. Beirut: Dār al-Bashāʾir al-Islāmiyya, 1998.

al-ʿAjam, Rafīq. "*Al-Taʿrīfāt* li-Ibn ʿArabī." *Al-Abḥāth* 36 (1988): 3–50.

Āl Sulaymān, Mashhūr b. Ḥasan, and Aḥmad al-Shaqayrāt. *Muʾallafāt al-Sakhāwī*. Beirut: Dār Ibn Ḥazm, 1998.

Amīn, Muḥammad Muḥammad. *Al-Awqāf wa-l-ḥayāh al-ijtimāʿiyya fī Miṣr*. Cairo: Dār al-Nahḍa al-ʿArabiyya, 1980.

———. *Fihrist wathāʾiq al-Qāhira ḥattā nihāyat ʿaṣr salāṭīn al-mamālīk*. Cairo: al-Maʿhad al-ʿIlmī al-Faransī li-l-Āthār al-Sharqiyya, 1981.

Amīn, Muḥammad Muḥammad, and Laylā ʿAlī Ibrāhīm. *Al-Muṣṭalaḥāt al-miʿmāriyya fī l-wathāʾiq al-mamlūkiyya*. Cairo: American University in Cairo Press, 1990.

al-Āmulī, Shams al-Dīn Muḥammad. *Nafāʾis al-funūn fī ʿarāʾis al-ʿuyūn*. Edited by Mīrzā Abū l-Ḥasan Shaʿrānī. 3 vols. Tehran: Kitābfurūshī-i Islāmiyya, 1958–60.

al-Anṣārī, Zakariyyā b. Mūhammad. *Al-Aḍwāʾ al-bahija fī ibrāz daqāʾiq al-Munfarija*. MS al-Azhar 315938. Cairo.

———. *Asnā l-maṭālib: Sharḥ Rawḍ al-ṭālib*. Edited by Maḥmūd Maṭrajī. 6 vols. Beirut: Dār al-Fikr, 2008.

———. *Fatḥ al-ʿallām bi-sharḥ al-Iʿlām bi-aḥādīth al-aḥkām*. Beirut: Dār al-Kutub al-ʿIlmiyya, 1990.

———. *Fatḥ al-bāqī bi-sharḥ Alfiyyat al-ʿIrāqī*. Beirut: Dār Ibn Ḥazm, 1999.

———. *Fatḥ al-ilāh al-mājid bi-īḍāḥ Sharḥ al-ʿAqāʾid*. MS Laleli 2188 (fols. 1r–65r). Istanbul.

———. *Fatḥ al-raḥmān bi-sharḥ Luqṭat al-ʿajlān wa-billat al-ẓamʾān*. MS Laleli 297.3/03671-005. Istanbul.

———. *Fatḥ al-wahhāb bi-sharḥ Manhaj al-ṭullāb*. 2 vols. Cairo: ʿIsā al-Bābī al-Ḥalabī, 1925.

———. *Fatḥ al-wahhāb bi-sharḥ Tanqīḥ al-Lubāb*. MS Landberg MSS 465. Beinecke Library, Yale University, New Haven, CT.

———. *Al-Fatḥa al-unsiyya li-ghaliq al-Tuḥfa al-qudsiyya*. MS Laleli 297.4/01304-002. Istanbul.

———. *Ghāyat al-wuṣūl: Sharḥ Lubb al-uṣūl*. Cairo: Muṣṭafā al-Bābī al-Ḥalabī, 1941.

———. *Al-Ghurar al-bahiyya fī sharḥ al-Bahja al-Wardiyya*. 5 vols. Cairo: al-Maṭbaʿa al-Maymaniyya, n. d.

———. *Iḥkām al-dalāla ʿalā taḥrīr al-Risāla*. 4 vols. Cairo: Maktabat al-Īmān, 2007.

———. *Iḥkām al-dalāla ʿalā taḥrīr al-Risāla*. MS Arabic 3843. Chester Beatty Library, Dublin.

———. *Al-Iʿlām wa-l-ihtimām bi-jamʿ fatāwā shaykh al-islām*. Edited by Qāsim al-Rifāʿī. Damascus: Dār al-Taqwā, 2007.

———. *Al-Luʾluʾ al-naẓīm fī rawm al-taʿallum wa-l-taʿlīm*. Cairo: Maṭbaʿat al-Mawsūʿāt, 1901–2.

———. *Al-Luʾluʾ al-naẓīm fī rawm al-taʿallum wa-l-taʿlīm*. MS al-Maʿārif al-ʿĀmma 17621/3413. Al-Maktaba al-Azhariyya, Cairo.

———. *Risāla Fī Bayān al-alfāẓ al-latī yatadāwaluhā l-ṣūfiyya*. MS Taṣawwuf 83. Dār al-Kutub al-Miṣriyya, Cairo.

———. *Talkhīṣ al-Azhiyya fī aḥkām al-adʿiyya*. Beirut: Dār al-Bashāʾir al-Islāmiyya, 2005.

———. *Tuḥfat nujabāʾ al-ʿaṣr*. Edited by Muḥyī Hilāl al-Sarḥān. Baghdad: Baghdad University Press, 1986.

———. *Tuḥfat al-rāghibīn fī bayān amr al-ṭawāʿīn*. MS 56 Taṣawwuf Ḥalīm ʿArabī/443547. Dār al-Kutub al-Miṣriyya, Cairo.

———. *Tuḥfat al-ṭullāb bi-sharḥ Taḥrīr Tanqīḥ al-Lubāb*. Mecca: al-Maṭbaʿa al-Mīriyya, 1310 [1892/93].

al-Anṣārī, Zayn al-ʿĀbidīn. *Tuḥfat al-aḥbāb bi-faḍāʾil aḥad al-aqṭāb*. MS Zakiyya Arabic 573/454737. Dār al-Kutub al-Miṣriyya, Cairo.

al-ʿAsqalānī, Aḥmad Ibn Ḥajar. *Badhl al-māʿūn fī faḍl al-ṭāʿūn*. Riyad: Dār al-ʿĀṣima, 1991.

———. *Rafʿ al-iṣr ʿan quḍāt Miṣr*. Edited by Ḥāmid ʿAbd al-Majīd, Muḥammad al-Mahdī Abū Sunna, and Muḥammad Ismāʿīl al-Ṣāwī. 2 vols. Cairo: al-Maṭbaʿa al-Amīriyya, 1957–61.

al-ʿAydarūs, ʿAbd al-Qādir. *Al-Nūr al-sāfir ʿan akhbār al-qarn al-ʿāshir*. Edited by Aḥmad Ḥālū, Maḥmūd al-Arnāʾūṭ, and Akram al-Būshī. Beirut: Dār Ṣādir, 2001.

al-Aʿẓamī, Muḥammad Ḍiyāʾ al-Raḥmān. *Muʿjam muṣṭalaḥāt al-ḥadīth wa-laṭāʾif al-asānīd*. Riyadh: Maktabat Aḍwāʾ al-Salaf, 1999.

al-Baghdādī, Ismāʿīl Pāshā. *Hadiyyat al-ʿārifīn: Asmāʾ al-muʾallifīn wa-āthār al-muṣannifīn*. Edited by Rifat Bilge and İbnülemin Mahmut Kemal İnal. 2 vols. Istanbul: Milli Eğitim Basımevi, 1951.

———. *Īḍāḥ al-maknūn fī l-dhayl ʿalā Kashf al-ẓunūn ʿan asāmī l-kutub wa-l-funūn*. Edited by M. Şerefettin Yaltkaya and Rifat Bilge Kilisli. 2 vols. Istanbul: Milli Eğitim Basımevi, 1945.

Bāḥamīd al-Anṣārī, Khālid b. ʿAbdallāh. *Sharḥ Nukhbat al-Fikr*. Riyadh: Dār al-Iʿtiṣām, 2003–4.

al-Bujayrimī, Sulaymān b. Muḥammad. *Al-Tajrīd li-nafʿ al-ʿabīd* [*Ḥāshiyat al-Bujayrimī ʿalā Sharḥ Manhaj al-ṭullāb*]. 4 vols. Cairo: Muṣṭafā al-Bābī al-Ḥalabī, 1950.

al-Buṣrawī, ʿAlī b. Yūsuf. *Taʾrīkh al-Buṣrawī*. Beirut: Dār al-Maʾmūn li-l-Turāth, 1988.

Fihris al-kutub al-mawjūda bi-l-Maktaba al-Azhariyya. 6 vols. Cairo: Maṭbaʿat al-Azhar, 1962.

Fihris makhṭūṭāt Dār al-Kutub al-Ẓāhiriyya. 17 vols. Damascus: al-Majmaʿ al-ʿIlmī al-ʿArabī, 1947ff.

al-Ghamrī, Muḥammad. *Qawāʿid al-ṣūfiyya*. Cairo: Maktabat Madbūlī, 2003.

al-Ghazālī, Abū Ḥāmid Muḥammad b. Muḥammad. *Al-Wajīz fī l-fiqh al-imām al-Shāfiʿī*. Edited by ʿAlī Muʿawwaḍ and ʿĀdil ʿAbd al-Mawjūd. 2 vols. Beirut: Dār al-Arqam, 1997.

———. *Al-Wasīṭ fī l-madhhab*. Edited by Aḥmad Maḥmūd Ibrāhīm. 7 vols. Cairo: Dār al-Salām, 1997.

al-Ghazzī, Badr al-Dīn Muḥammad. *Al-Durr al-naḍīd fī adab al-mufīd wa-l-mustafīd*. Edited by Abū Yaʿqūb Nashʾat b. Kamāl al-Miṣrī. Giza: Maktabat al-Tawʿiyya al-Islamiyya, 2009.

al-Ghazzī, Najm al-Dīn. *Al-Kawākib al-sāʾira bi-aʿyān al-miʾa al-ʿāshira*. Edited by Jibrāʾīl Sulaymān Jabbūr. 3 vols. Beirut: Dār al-Āfāq al-Jadīda, 1979.

al-Ḥabashī, ʿAbdallāh Muḥammad. *Jāmiʿ al-shurūḥ wa-l-ḥawāshī: Muʿjam shāmil li-asmāʾ al-kutub al-mashrūḥa fī l-turāth al-islāmī wa-bayān shurūḥihā*. 3 vols. Abu Dhabi: al-Majmaʿ al-Thaqāfī, 2004.

Hādīzāda, Majīd, ed. *Majmūʿa-yi rasāʾil wa-muṣannafāt-i shaykh Kamāl al-Dīn ʿAbd al-Razzāq-i Kāshānī*. Tehran: Mīrās-i Maktūb, 2000.

Ḥājjī Khalīfa, Muṣṭafā b. ʿAbdallāh. *Kashf al-ẓunūn ʿan asāmī l-kutub wa-l-funūn*. 2 vols. Istanbul: Maarif Matbaası, 1941.

al-Ḥamawī, Yāqūt. *Muʿjam al-buldān*. 5 vols. Beirut: Dār Ṣādir, 1977.
al-Ḥaṣkafī, Aḥmad b. Muḥammad. *Mutʿat al-adhhān min al-Tamattuʿ bi-l-aqrān*. 2 vols. Beirut: Dār Ṣādir, 1999.
al-Haytamī, Aḥmad Ibn Ḥajar. *Al-Fatāwā al-ḥadīthiyya*. Beirut: Dār al-Maʿrifa, n. d.
———. *Al-Fatāwā al-kubrā al-fiqhiyya*. 4 vols. Beirut: Dār al-Fikr, 1983.
———. *Al-Īʿāb sharḥ al-ʿUbāb*. 2 vols. MS 5541: ف 1/1160. King Saud University, Riyadh.
———. *Tuḥfat al-muḥtāj bi-sharḥ al-Minhāj*. Printed in the margins of Aḥmad b. Qāsim al-ʿAbbādī and ʿAbd al-Ḥamīd al-Shirwānī's *Ḥawāshī ʿalā Tuḥfat al-muḥtāj bi-sharḥ al-Minhāj*. 10 vols. Cairo: al-Maktaba al-Tijāriyya al-Kubrā, 1938.
al-Ḥifnī, Yūsuf b. Sālim. *Ḥāshiyat al-shaykh al-Ḥifnī ʿalā Sharḥ Īsāghūjī*. Cairo: al-Maṭbaʿa al-ʿĀmira al-Sharafiyya, 1885.
Ḥuṣriyya, ʿIzzat. *Shurūḥ Risālat al-Shaykh Arslān*. Damascus: Maṭbaʿat al-ʿAlam, 1969.
Ibn al-Akfānī, Muḥammad b. Ibrāhīm. *Irshād al-qāṣid ilā asnā l-maqāṣid fī anwāʿ al-ʿulūm*. Edited by ʿAbd al-Munʿim Muḥammad ʿUmar. Cairo: Dār al-Fikr al-ʿArabī, 1990.
Ibn al-Ḥanbalī, Muḥammad b. Ibrāhīm. *Durr al-ḥabab fī taʾrīkh aʿyān Ḥalab*. Edited by Maḥmūd Muḥammad al-Fākhūrī and Yaḥyā Zakariyyā ʿIbāra. 2 vols. Damascus: Wizārat al-Thaqāfa, 1972ff.
Ibn Ḥazm, ʿAlī b. Aḥmad. *Rasāʾil Ibn Ḥazm al-Andalusī*. Edited by Iḥsān ʿAbbās. Cairo: Maktabat al-Khānjī; Baghdād: Maktabat al-Muthannā, 1954.
Ibn al-Ḥimṣī, Aḥmad b. Muḥammad. *Ḥawādith al-zamān wa-wafiyyāt al-shuyūkh wa-l-aqrān*. Edited by ʿAbd al-ʿAzīz Fayyāḍ Ḥarfūsh. Beirut: Dār al-Nafāʾis, 2000.
Ibn al-ʿImād, ʿAbd al-Ḥayy. *Shadharāt al-dhahab fī akhbār man dhahab*. 8 vols. Beirut: Dār al-Fikr, 1994.
Ibn Iyās, Muḥammad b. Aḥmad. *Badāʾiʿ al-zuhūr fī waqāʾiʿ al-duhūr*. Edited by Muḥammad Muṣṭafā. 7 vols. Wiesbaden, Germany: F. Steiner Verlag, 1931ff.
Ibn Jamāʿa al-Kinānī, Badr al-Dīn. *Tadhkirat al-sāmiʿ wa-l-mutakallim fī adab al-ʿālim wa-l-mutaʿallim*. Edited by Muḥammad Hāshim al-Nadawī. Al-Dammām, Saudi Arabia: Ramādī li-l-Nashr, 1994.
Ibn Khaldūn, ʿAbd al-Raḥmān. *The Muqaddimah: An Introduction to History*. Translated by Franz Rosenthal. 3 vols. Princeton, NJ: Princeton University Press, 1967.
———. *Shifāʾ al-sāʾil wa-tahdhīb al-masāʾil*. Edited by Muḥammad Muṭīʿ al-Ḥāfiẓ. Damascus: Dār al-Fikr, 1996.
Ibn Qāḍī Shubha, Abū Bakr b. Aḥmad. *Ṭabaqāt al-Shāfiʿiyya*. 4 vols. Hyderabad: Dāʾirat al-Maʿārif al-ʿUthmāniyya, 1978–80.

Ibn Shāhīn, ʿAbd al-Bāsiṭ. *Nayl al-amal fī dhayl al-Duwal*. Edited by ʿUmar ʿAbd al-Salām Tadmurī. 9 vols. Ṣaydā, Lebanon: al-Maktaba al-ʿAṣriyya, 2002.

Ibn al-Shammāʿ, ʿUmar b. Aḥmad. *Al-Qabas al-ḥāwī li-ghurar Ḍawʾ al-Sakhāwī*. Edited by Ḥasan Ismāʿīl Marwa and Khaldūn Ḥasan Marwa. 2 vols. Beirut: Dār Ṣādir, 1998.

Ibn Taghrībirdī, Yūsuf. *Al-Nujūm al-zāhira fī mulūk Miṣr wa-l-Qāhira*. 16 vols. Cairo: al-Muʾassasa al-Miṣriyya al-ʿĀmma, 1963ff.

Ibn Ṭūlūn, Shams al-Dīn. *Mufākahat al-khillān fī ḥawādith al-zamān*. 2 vols. Cairo: al-Muʾassasa al-Miṣriyya al-ʿĀmma, 1962ff.

al-Iṣfahānī, Abū Nuʿaym. *Ḥilyat al-awliyāʾ wa-ṭabaqāt al-aṣfiyāʾ*. 10 vols. Cairo: Maktabat al-Khānjī, 1932ff.

al-Isnawī, Jamāl al-Dīn ʿAbd al-Raḥīm. *Ṭabaqāt al-Shāfiʿiyya*. Edited by ʿAbdallāh al-Jubūrī. 2 vols. Baghdad: Iraqi Ministry of Awqāf, Maṭbaʿat al-Irshād, 1970–71.

al-Jabartī, ʿAbd al-Raḥmān. *ʿAjāʾib al-āthār fī l-tarājim wa-l-akhbār*. 4 vols. Cairo: Dār al-Ṭibāʿa, 1880.

Jābir, Ṭāriq Yūsuf Ḥasan. "Shaykh al-Islām Zakariyyā al-Anṣārī wa-atharuh fī l-fiqh al-Shāfiʿī." Master's thesis, University of Jordan, 2004.

al-Jamal, Sulaymān b. ʿUmar. *Ḥāshiyat al-Jamal ʿalā Sharḥ al-Manhaj*. 5 vols. Beirut: Dār Iḥyāʾ al-Turāth al-ʿArabī, 1970ff.

Jāmiʿ al-Zaytūna ʿammarahu Allāh: Barnāmaj al-Maktaba al-Ṣādiqiyya. 2 vols. Beirut: Markaz al-Khadamāt wa-l-Abḥāth al-Thaqāfiyya, 1980ff.

Jumʿa, ʿAlī. *Al-Madkhal ilā dirāsat al-madhāhib al-fiqhiyya*. Cairo: Dār al-Salām, 2004.

al-Jurjānī, al-Sayyid al-Sharīf. *Kitāb al-Taʿrīfāt*. Beirut: Maktabat Lubnān, 1985.

al-Juwaynī, ʿAbd al-Malik b. ʿAbdallāh. *Nihāyat al-maṭlab fī dirāyat al-madhhab*. Edited by ʿAbd al-ʿAẓīm Maḥmūd al-Dīb. 20 vols. Jeddah, Saudi Arabia: Dār al-Minhāj, 2007.

al-Kaḥḥāla, ʿUmar Riḍā. *Muʿjam al-muʾallifīn*. 15 vols. Beirut: Muʾassasat al-Risālat, 1993.

al-Kāshānī, ʿAbd al-Razzāq. *Muʿjam iṣṭilāḥāt al-ṣūfiyya*. Edited by ʿAbd al-ʿĀl Shāhīn. Cairo: Dār al-Manār, 1992.

al-Kattānī, ʿAbd al-Ḥayy. *Fihris al-fahāris wa-l-athbāt wa-muʿjam al-maʿājim wa-l-mashyakhāt wa-l-musalsalāt*. 3 vols. Beirut: Dār al-Gharb al-Islāmī, 1982ff.

al-Khʷārazmī, Muḥammad b. Aḥmad. *Mafātīḥ al-ʿulūm*. Cairo: ʿUthmān Khalīl, 1930.

al-Kurdī al-Madanī, Muḥammad b. Sulaymān. *Al-Fawāʾid al-Madaniyya fī-man yuftā bi-qawlih min aʾimmat al-Shāfiʿiyya*. Lebanon: Dār Nūr al-Ṣabāḥ & Dār al-Jaffān wa-l-Jābī, 2011.

al-Maḥāmilī, Aḥmad b. Muḥammad. *Al-Lubāb fī l-fiqh al-Shāfiʿī*. Edited by ʿAbd al-Karīm b. Ṣunaytān al-ʿAmrī. Medina: Dār al-Bukhārī, 1416 [1995–96].

al-Malījī al-Shaʿrānī, Muḥammad. *Manāqib al-quṭb al-rabbānī sayyidī ʿAbd al-Wahhāb al-Shaʿrānī*. Cairo: Dār al-Jūdiyya, 2005.

al-Mandaylī, ʿAbd al-Qādir b. ʿAbd al-Muṭṭalib. *Al-Khazāʾin al-saniyya min mashāhīr al-kutub al-fiqhiyya li-aʾimmatinā al-fuqahāʾ al-Shāfiʿiyya*. Beirut: Muʾassasat al-Risāla, 2004.

al-Maqrīzī, Aḥmad b. ʿAlī. *Al-Mawāʿẓ wa-l-iʿtibār bi-dhikr al-khiṭaṭ wa-l-āthār*. 2 vols. Cairo: Maktabat al-Thaqāfa al-Dīniyya, n. d.

———. *Al-Sulūk li-maʿrifat duwal al-mulūk*. Edited by Muḥammad Muṣṭafā Ziyāda. 4 vols. in 12 bound sections. Cairo: Maṭbaʿat Dār al-Kutub wa-l-Wathāʾiq al-Qawmiyya bi-l-Qāhira, 2006–7.

Al-Mawsūʿa al-fiqhiyya. 45 vols. Kuwait: Kuwaiti Ministry of Awqāf and Islamic Affairs, 1997.

Mubārak, ʿAlī Pāshā. *Al-Khiṭaṭ al-tawfīqiyya al-jadīda*. 20 vols. Cairo: Maṭbaʿat Dār al-Kutub wa-l-Wathāʾiq al-Qawmiyya bi-l-Qāhira, 2005ff.

al-Muḥibbī, Muḥammad Amīn. *Khulāṣat al-athar fī aʿyān al-qarn al-ḥādī ʿashar*. 4 vols. Beirut: Maktabat al-Khayyāṭ, 1966.

al-Munāwī, ʿAbd al-Raʾūf. *Al-Kawākib al-durriyya fī tarājim al-sāda al-ṣūfiyya*. Edited by Muḥammad Adīb al-Jādir. 5 vols. Beirut: Dār Ṣādir, 1999.

al-Muzanī, Ibrāhīm b. Yaḥyā. *Mukhtaṣar al-Muzanī*. Printed in the margins of Muḥammad b. Idrīs al-Shāfiʿī. *Kitāb al-Umm*. 7 vols. Cairo: Dār al-Shaʿb, 1968.

al-Nawawī, Yaḥyā b. Sharaf. *Rawḍat al-ṭālibīn wa-ʿumdat al-muftiyīn*. Edited by ʿAlī Muʿawwaḍ and ʿĀdil ʿAbd al-Mawjūd. 8 vols. Beirut: Dār al-Kutub al-ʿIlmiyya, 2000.

al-Qabbāb, Aḥmad b. Qāsim. *Fatwā l-Qabbāb fī sulūk ṭarīq al-ṣūfiyya*. Appended to ʿAbd al-Raḥmān Ibn Khaldūn. *Shifāʾ al-sāʾil wa-tahdhīb al-masāʾil*. Edited by Muḥammad Muṭīʿ al-Ḥāfiẓ. Damascus: Dār al-Fikr, 1996.

al-Qārī, Mullā ʿAlī. *Mirqāt al-mafātīḥ sharḥ Mishkāt al-maṣābīḥ*. 9 vols. Beirut: Dār al-Fikr, 2002.

al-Rāfiʿī, ʿAbd al-Karīm b. Muḥammad. *Al-ʿAzīz: Sharḥ al-Wajīz*. Edited by ʿAlī Muʿawwaḍ and ʿĀdil ʿAbd al-Mawjūd. 14 vols. Beirut: Dār al-Kutub al-ʿIlmiyya, 1997.

al-Ramlī, Shihāb al-Dīn Aḥmad b. Ḥamza. *Fatāwā al-Ramlī*. Printed in the margins of Aḥmad Ibn Ḥajar al-Haytamī. *Al-Fatāwā al-kubrā al-fiqhiyya*. 4 vols. Beirut: Dār al-Fikr, 1983.

———. *Ḥāshiyat al-Ramlī ʿalā Asnā l-maṭālib*. Printed in the margins of Zakariyyā al-Anṣārī. *Asnā l-maṭālib: Sharḥ Rawḍ al-ṭālib*. Edited by Maḥmūd Maṭrajī. 6 vols. Beirut: Dār al-Fikr, 2008.

al-Rāzī, Fakhr al-Dīn. *Jamiʿ al-ʿulūm (sittīnī)*. Edited by Sayyid ʿAlī Āl Dāwūd. Tehran: Bunyād-i Mawqūfāt-i Duktar Maḥmūd Afshār, 2003.

al-Saffārīnī, Muḥammad b. Aḥmad. *Ghidhāʾ al-albāb fi sharḥ Manẓūmat al-Ādāb*. 2 vols. Beirut: Dār al-Kutub al-ʿIlmiyya, 1996.

al-Ṣaʿīdī, ʿAbd al-Mutaʿāl. *Al-Mujaddidūn fī l-Islām min al-qarn al-awwal ilā l-rābiʿ ʿashar*. Cairo: Maktabat al-Ādāb, 1950.

al-Sakhāwī, Muḥammad b. ʿAbd al-Raḥmān. *Al-Ḍawʾ al-lāmiʿ li-ahl al-qarn al-tāsiʿ*. 12 vols. Beirut: Dār al-Jīl, 1992.

———. *Al-Dhayl ʿalā Rafʿ al-iṣr (Bughyat al-ʿulamāʾ wa-l-ruwāh)*. Edited by Jūda Hilāl and Muḥammad Maḥmūd Ṣubḥ. Cairo: al-Hayʾa al-Miṣriyya al-ʿĀmma li-l-Kitāb, 2000.

Salīm, Maḥmūd Rizq. *ʿAṣr salāṭīn al-mamālīk wa-natājuh al-ʿilmī wa-l-adabī*. 8 vols. Cairo: Maktabat al-Ādāb, 1947ff.

al-Saqqāf, Alawī b. Aḥmad. *Mukhtaṣar al-Fawāʾid al-Makkiyya fī-mā yaḥtājuh ṭalabat al-Shāfiʿiyya*. Edited by Yūsuf b. ʿAbd al-Raḥmān al-Marʿashlī. Beirut: Dār al-Bashāʾir al-Islāmiyya, 2004.

Sarkīs, Yūsuf. *Muʿjam al-maṭbūʿāt al-ʿarabiyya wa-l-muʿarraba*. 2 vols. Cairo: Maktabat al-Thaqāfa al-Dīniyya, n. d.

al-Sarrāj, Abū Naṣr. *Kitāb al-Lumaʿ fī l-taṣawwuf*. Edited by Reynold A. Nicholson. Leiden: Brill, 1914.

al-Ṣayrafī, ʿAlī b. Dāwūd. *Inbāʾ al-haṣr bi-abnāʾ al-ʿaṣr*. Cairo: Dār al-Fikr al-ʿArabī, 1970.

Shāfiʿī, Lamyāʾ Aḥmad ʿAbdallāh. *Ibn Ḥajar al-Haytamī al-Makkī wa-juhūduh fī l-kitāba al-taʾrīkhiyya*. Giza: Maktabat al-Ghadd, 1998.

al-Shāfiʿī, Muḥammad b. Idrīs. *Kitāb al-Umm*. 7 vols. Cairo: Dār al-Shaʿb, 1968.

Shahīd al-Thānī, Zayn al-Dīn. *Al-Fikr al-tarbawī ʿind Zayn al-Dīn b. Aḥmad (Munyat al-murīd fī ādāb al-mufīd wa-l-mustafīd)*. Edited by ʿAbd al-Amīr Shams al-Dīn. Beirut: al-Sharika al-ʿĀlimiyya li-l-Kitāb, 1990.

al-Shaʿrānī, ʿAbd al-Wahhāb. *Al-Anwār al-qudsiyya fī maʿrifat ādāb al-ʿubūdiyya*. Edited by Ramaḍān Basṭāwīsī Muḥammad. Cairo: al-Hayʾa al-Miṣriyya al-ʿĀmma li-l-Kitāb, 2007.

———. *Al-Anwār al-qudsiyya fī maʿrifat qawāʿid al-ṣūfiyya*. Edited by Ṭāhā ʿAbd al-Bāqī Surūr and Muḥammad ʿĪd al-Shāfiʿī. 2 vols. Cairo: al-Maktaba al-ʿIlmiyya, 1962.

———. *Laṭāʾif al-minan wa-l-akhlāq fī wujūb al-taḥadduth bi-niʿmat Allāh ʿalā l-iṭlāq*. Edited by Aḥmad ʿIzzū ʿInāya. Damascus: Dār al-Taqwā, 2004.

———. *Lawāqiḥ al-anwār fī ṭabaqāt al-akhyār (al-Ṭabaqāt al-kubrā)*. 2 vols. Cairo: Maktabat al-Ādāb, 1993ff.

———. *Al-Mīzān al-kubrā*. Edited by ʿAbd al-Raḥmān ʿUmayra. 3 vols. Beirut: ʿĀlam al-Kutub, 1989.

———. *Al-Ṭabaqāt al-ṣughrā*. Edited by ʿAbd al-Qādir Aḥmad ʿAṭāʾ. Cairo: Maktabat al-Qāhira, 1970.

———. *Al-Yawāqīt wa-l-jawāhir fī bayān ʿaqāʾid al-akābir*. 2 vols. Beirut: Dār al-Maʿrifa, 1974.

al-Shirbīnī, (al-Khaṭīb) Muḥammad b. Aḥmad. *Mughnī l-muḥtāj ilā maʿrifat maʿānī alfāẓ al-Minhāj*. 4 vols. Beirut: Dār al-Maʿrifa, 1997.

al-Subkī, Tāj al-Dīn. *Ṭabaqāt al-Shāfiʿiyya al-kubrā*. Edited by Maḥmūd Muḥammad al-Ṭanāḥī and ʿAbd al-Fattāḥ Muḥammad al-Ḥilw. 10 vols. Cairo: ʿĪsā al-Bābī al-Ḥalabī, 1964ff.

al-Suhrawardī, Abū Ḥafs ʿUmar. *ʿAwārif al-maʿārif*. Reprinted in Abū Ḥāmid Muḥammad al-Ghazālī. *Mulḥaq Iḥyāʾ ʿulūm al-dīn*. Egypt: al-Maktaba al-Tijāriyya al-Kubrā, n. d.

al-Sulamī, Abū ʿAbd al-Raḥmān. *Sufi Treatises of Abū ʿAbd al-Raḥmān al-Sulamī*. Edited by Gerhard Böwering and Bilal Orfali. Beirut: Dār el-Machreq, 2009.

al-Suyūṭī, Jalāl al-Dīn. *Al-Ḥāwī li-l-fatāwī*. 2 vols. Beirut: Dār al-Kutub al-ʿIlmiyya, 1988.

———. *Itmām al-dirāya li-qurrāʾ al-Nuqāya*. Beirut: Dār al-Kutub al-ʿIlmiyya, 1985.

———. *Mā rawāh al-wāʿūn fī akhbār al-ṭāʿūn*. Damascus: Dār al-Qalam, 1997.

———. *Taʾyīd al-ḥaqīqa al-ʿaliyya wa-tashyīd al-ṭarīqa al-Shādhiliyya*. Cairo: al-Maṭbaʿa al-Islāmiyya, 1934.

al-Zarkashī, Badr al-Dīn. *Luqṭat al-ʿajlān*. Edited by Muḥammad Jamāl al-Qāsimī al-Dimashqī. Cairo: Maṭbaʿat Madrasat Wālidat ʿAbbās al-Awwal, 1908.

al-Zarqāʾ, Muṣṭafā. *Al-Madkhal al-fiqhī al-ʿāmm*. 2 vols. Damascus: Dār al-Qalam, 2004.

al-Ziriklī, Khayr al-Dīn. *Al-Aʿlām*. 8 vols. Beirut: Dār al-ʿIlm li-l-Malāyīn, 1992.

European-Language Sources

Agrama, Hussein Ali. "Ethics, Tradition, Authority: Towards an Anthropology of the Fatwa." *American Ethnologist* 37, no. 1 (2010): 2–18.

Ahmed, Asad Q. "Post-Classical Philosophical Commentaries/Glosses: Innovation in the Margins." *Oriens* 41 (2013): 317–48.

Arberry, Arthur J. *The Chester Beatty Library: A Handlist of the Arabic Manuscripts*. 8 vols. Dublin: Hodges Figgis, 1956.

Ashtor, Eliyahu. *A Social and Economic History of the Near East in the Middle Ages*. Berkeley: University of California Press, 1976.

Attridge, Derek. "Context, Idioculture, Invention." *New Literary History* 42 (2011): 681–99.

———. *The Singularity of Literature*. Abingdon, UK: Routledge, 2004.

Al-Azem, Talal. "Precedent, Commentary, and Legal Rules in the Madhhab-Law Tradition: Ibn Quṭlūbughā's (d. 879/1474) *al-Taṣḥīḥ wa-al-tarjīḥ*." PhD diss., University of Oxford, 2011.

Azra, Azyumardi. *The Origins of Islamic Reformism in Southeast Asia*. Honolulu: University of Hawai'i Press, 2004.

Bakar, Osman. *Classification of Knowledge in Islam*. Cambridge: Islamic Texts Society, 1998.

Bakhtin, M. M. *The Dialogic Imagination: Four Essays*. Translated by Caryl Emerson and Michael Holquist. Austin: University of Texas Press, 1981.

Barthes, Roland. "The Discourse of History." Translated by Stephen Bann. *Comparative Criticism* 3 (1981): 3–20.

———. *S/Z: An Essay*. Translated by Richard Miller. New York: Hill and Wang, 1974.

Bauer, Thomas. "Literarische Anthologien der Mamlukenzeit." In *Die Mamluken: Studien zu ihrer Geschichte und Kultur: Zum Gedenken an Ulrich Haarmann (1942–1999)*, edited by Stephan Conermann and Anja Pistor-Hatam, 71–122. Hamburg, Germany: EB-Verlag, 2003.

———. "Mamluk Literature: Misunderstandings and New Approaches." *Mamluk Studies Review* 9, no. 2 (2005): 105–32.

Berkey, Jonathan P. *The Transmission of Knowledge in Medieval Cairo: A Social History of Islamic Education*. Princeton, NJ: Princeton University Press, 1992.

Blecher, Joel. "In the Shade of the *Ṣaḥīḥ*: Politics, Culture and Innovation in an Islamic Commentary Tradition." PhD diss., Princeton University, 2013.

Borsch, Stuart J. *The Black Death in Egypt and England: A Comparative Study*. Cairo: American University in Cairo Press, 2005.

Bosworth, C. E. "A Pioneer Arabic Encyclopedia of the Sciences: Al-Khawārizmī's Keys of the Sciences." *Isis* 54, no. 1 (1963): 97–111.

Böwering, Gerhard. *The Mystical Vision of Existence in Classical Islam: The Qur'ānic Hermeneutics of the Sufi Sahl al-Tustarī (d. 283/896)*. Berlin: Walter de Gruyter, 1980.

Brockelmann, Carl. *Geschichte der arabischen Litteratur*. 5 vols. Leiden: Brill, 1932–49.

Brown, Jonathan A. C. *The Canonization of Bukhārī and Muslim: The Formation and Function of the Sunnī Ḥadīth Canon*. Leiden: Brill, 2007.

———. "Even If It's Not True, It's True: Using Unreliable Ḥadīths in Sunni Islam." *Islamic Law and Society* 18 (2011): 1–52.

———. *Hadith: Muhammad's Legacy in the Medieval and Modern World*. Oxford: Oneworld, 2009.

Bruns, Gerald L. "Canon and Power in the Hebrew Scriptures." *Critical Inquiry* 10, no. 3 (1984): 462–80.

Clooney, Francis X. "Nammāḻvār's Glorious *Tiruvallavāḻ*: An Exploration in the Methods and Goals of Śrīvaiṣṇava Commentary." *Journal of the American Oriental Society* 111, no. 2 (1991): 260–76.

Collins, Randall. *The Sociology of Philosophies: A Global Theory of Intellectual Change*. Cambridge, MA: Harvard University Press, 1998.

Cornell, Vincent. *Realm of the Saint: Power and Authority in Moroccan Sufism*. Austin: University of Texas Press, 1998.

Crecelius, Daniel, and ʿAbd al-Wahhāb Bakr, trans. *Al-Damurdashi's Chronicle of Egypt*. Leiden: Brill, 1991.

Cureton, W. "An Account of the Autograph MS. of the First Volume of Ibn Khallikān's Biographical Dictionary." *Journal of the Royal Asiatic Society* 6, no. 2 (1841): 223–38.

Cutler, Norman. "Interpreting *Tirukkuṟaḷ*: The Role of Commentary in the Creation of a Text." *Journal of the American Oriental Society* 112, no. 4 (1992): 549–66.

de Callataÿ, Godefroid. "The Classification of the Sciences according to the *Rasaʾil Ikhwan al-Safaʾ*." *Institute of Ismaili Studies* (2003): 1–13.

de Jong, F. *Ṭuruq and Ṭuruq-Linked Institutions in Nineteenth-Century Egypt*. Leiden: Brill, 1978.

de Jong, Irene I. J. F. "A Narratological Commentary on the *Odyssey*: Principles and Problems." In *The Classical Commentary: Histories, Practices, Theory*, edited by Christina S. Kraus and Roy K. Gibson, 49–66. Leiden: Brill, 2002.

Dozy, Reinhart. *Supplément aux dictionnaires arabes*. 2 vols. Beirut: Librairie Liban, 1968.

Drewes, G. W. J. *Directions for Travellers on the Mystic Path*. The Hague: Martinus Nijhoff, 1977.

El-Rouayheb, Khaled. *Islamic Intellectual History in the Seventeenth Century: Scholarly Currents in the Ottoman Empire and the Maghreb*. New York: Cambridge University Press, 2015.

El Shamsy, Ahmed. *The Canonization of Islamic Law: A Social and Intellectual History*. New York: Cambridge University Press, 2013.

———. "The *Ḥāshiya* in Islamic Law: A Sketch of the Shāfiʿī Literature." *Oriens* 41 (2013): 289–315.

———. "Al-Shāfiʿī's Written Corpus: A Source-Critical Study." *Journal of the American Oriental Society* 132, no. 2 (2012): 199–220.

The Encyclopaedia of Islam. Edited by H. A. R. Gibb et al. 2nd ed. Leiden: Brill, 1954ff.

The Encyclopedia of Religion. Edited by Lindsay Jones. 15 vols. 2nd ed. New York: Macmillan, 2005.

Ephrat, Daphna. *A Learned Society in a Period of Transition: The Sunni ʿUlamāʾ of Eleventh-Century Baghdad*. Albany, NY: State University of New York Press, 2000.

Escovitz, Joseph H. "A Lost Arabic Source for the History of Ottoman Egypt." *Journal of the American Oriental Society* 97 (1977): 513–18.

———. *The Office of Qāḍī al-Quḍāt in Cairo under the Baḥrī Mamlūks*. Berlin: Klaus Schwarz Verlag, 1984.

Fernandes, Leonor. "Between Qadis and Muftis: To Whom Does the Mamluk Sultan Listen?" *Mamluk Studies Review* 6 (2002): 95–108.

———. *The Evolution of a Sufi Institution in Mamluk Egypt: The Khanqah*. Berlin: Klaus Schwarz Verlag, 1988.

Fish, Stanley. "Literature in the Reader: Affective Stylistics." *New Literary History* 2, no. 1 (1970): 123–62.

Frank, Richard M. "Two Short Dogmatic Works of Abū l-Qāsim al-Qushayrī." *Mélanges de l'Institut Dominicain d'Etudes Orientales du Caire* 15 (1982): 59–75.

Frenkel, Yehoshuʾa. "Political and Social Aspects of Islamic Religious Endowments (*Awqāf*): Saladin in Cairo (1169–73) and Jerusalem (1187–93)." *Bulletin of the School of Oriental and African Studies* 62, no. 1 (1999): 1–20.

Fuchs, Stephan. *Against Essentialism: A Theory of Culture and Society*. Cambridge, MA: Harvard University Press, 2001.

Gacek, Adam. *Arabic Manuscripts: A Vademecum for Readers*. Leiden: Brill, 2009.

Garcin, Jean-Claude. "Index des *Ṭabaqāt* de Shaʿrānī (pour la fin du IXᵉ et le début du Xᵉ S.H.)." *Annales Islamologiques* 6 (1966): 31–94.

Geoffroy, Éric. *Le soufisme en Égypte et en Syrie sous les derniers Mamelouks et les premiers Ottomans: Orientations spirituelles et enjeux culturels*. Damascus: Institut français de Damas, 1995.

Gerber, Haim. *Islamic Law and Culture, 1600–1840*. Leiden: Brill, 1999.

Gibson, Roy K. " 'Cf. e.g.': A Typology of 'Parallels' and the Function of Commentary on Latin Poetry." In *Classical Commentary: Histories, Practices, Theory*, edited by Christina S. Kraus and Roy K. Gibson, 331–57. Leiden: Brill, 2002.

Gleave, Robert. *Islam and Literalism*. Edinburgh: Edinburgh University Press, 2012.

Gramlich, Richard. *Das Sendschreiben al-Qušayrīs über das Sufitum*. Wiesbaden, Germany: Franz Steiner Verlag, 1989.

Gumbrecht, Hans Ulricht. *The Powers of Philology: Dynamics of Textual Scholarship*. Urbana: University of Illinois Press, 2003.

Hallaq, Wael B. *Authority, Continuity, and Change in Islamic Law*. Cambridge: Cambridge University Press, 2004.

———. "From Fatwās to *Furūʿ*: Growth and Change in Islamic Substantive Law." *Islamic Law and Society* 1 (1994): 29–65.

———. "On the Origins of the Controversy about the Existence of *Mujtahids* and the Gate of *Ijtihad*." *Studia Islamica* 63 (1986): 129–41.

———. *The Origins and Evolution of Islamic Law*. Cambridge: Cambridge University Press, 2005.

———. *Sharīʿa: Theory, Practice, Transformations*. Cambridge: Cambridge University Press, 2009.

Harley, A. H. "A Manual of Sufism." *Journal of the Asiatic Society of Bengal* 20 (1924): 123–42.

Henderson, John B. *Scripture, Canon, and Commentary: A Comparison of Confucian and Western Exegesis*. Princeton, NJ: Princeton University Press, 1991.

Hirschler, Konrad. *The Written Word in the Medieval Arabic Lands: A Social and Cultural History of Reading Practices*. Edinburgh: Edinburgh University Press, 2012.

Hoffmann, Philippe. "What Was Commentary in Late Antiquity? The Example of the Neoplatonic Commentators." In *A Companion to Ancient Philosophy*, edited by Mary Louise Gill and Pierre Pellegrin, 597–622. West Sussex, UK: Wiley-Blackwell, 2009.

Holland, Muhtar, trans. *Concerning the Affirmation of Divine Oneness*. Hollywood, FL: Al-Baz, 1997.

Homerin, Th. Emil. *From Arab Poet to Muslim Saint: Ibn al-Fāriḍ, His Verse, and His Shrine*. Cairo: American University in Cairo Press, 2001.

Hughes, Aaron. "Presenting the Past: The Genre of Commentary in Theoretical Perspective." *Method and Theory in the Study of Religion* 15 (2003): 148–68.

Ibrahim, Ahmed Fekry. "Al-Shaʿrānī's Response to Legal Purism: A Theory of Legal Pluralism." *Islamic Law and Society* 20, no. 1/2 (2013): 110–40.

al-Ibrashy, M. "Cairo's Qarafa as Described in the *Ziyara* Literature." In *Le développement du soufisme en Egypte à l'époque mamelouke*, edited by Richard McGregor and Adam Sabra, 269–79. Cairo: Institut français d'archéologie orientale, 2006.

Ingalls, Matthew B. "Between Center and Periphery: The Development of the Sufi Fatwa in Late-Medieval Egypt." In *Sufism and Society: Arrangements of the Mystical in the Muslim World, 1200–1800*, edited by John J. Curry and Erik S. Ohlander, 145–63. London: Routledge, 2011.

———. "Reading the Sufis as Scripture through the *Sharḥ Mamzūj*: Reflections on a Late-Medieval Sufi Commentary." *Oriens* 41 (2013): 457–76.

———. "Subtle Innovation within Networks of Convention: The Life, Thought, and Intellectual Legacy of Zakariyyā al-Anṣārī (d. 926/1520)." PhD diss., Yale University, 2011.

———. "Zakariyyā al-Anṣārī and the Study of Muslim Commentaries from the Later Islamic Middle Period." *Religion Compass* 10, no. 5 (2016): 118–30.

Jackson, Sherman A. "Literalism, Empiricism, and Induction: Apprehending and Concretizing Islamic Law's *Maqāṣid al-Sharīʿah* in the Modern World." *Michigan State Law Review* (2006): 1469–86.

Jwaideh, Wadie. *The Introductory Chapters of Yāqūt's Muʿjam al-Buldān*. Leiden: Brill, 1959.

Karamustafa, Ahmet T. *Sufism: The Formative Period*. Edinburgh: Edinburgh University Press, 2007.

Katz, Marion Holmes. "The 'Corruption of the Times' and the Mutability of the *Sharīʿa*." *Cardozo Law Review* 28, no. 1 (2006): 171–85.

Kermode, Frank. *The Genesis of Secrecy: On the Interpretation of Narrative*. Cambridge, MA: Harvard University Press, 1979.

———. *Pleasure and Change: The Aesthetics of Canon*. Oxford University Press, 2004.

Knysh, Alexander. *Al-Qushayrī's Epistle on Sufism*. Reading, UK: Garnet, 2007.

———. *Ibn ʿArabī in the Later Islamic Tradition: The Making of a Polemical Image in Medieval Islam*. Albany, NY: State University of New York Press, 1999.

———. *Islamic Mysticism: A Short History*. Leiden: Brill, 2000.

Kraus, Christina S. "Introduction: Reading Commentaries/Commentaries as Reading." In *Classical Commentary: Histories, Practices, Theory*, edited by Christina S. Kraus and Roy K. Gibson, 1–27. Leiden: Brill, 2002.

Landau-Tasseron, Ella. "The 'Cyclical Reform': A Study of the *Mujaddid* Tradition." *Studia Islamica* 70 (1989): 79–117.

Landberg, Carlo. *Kurzes Verzeichniss der Sammlung arabischer Handschriften des Grafen C. von Landberg*. 6 vols. MS Landberg MSS 0. Beinecke Library, New Haven, CT.

Lane, E. W. *An Arabic-English Lexicon*. 8 vols. Beirut: Librairie du Liban, 1968.

Lapidus, Ira M. *Muslim Cities in the Later Middle Ages*. Cambridge, MA: Harvard University Press, 1967.

Levi, Jean. "Quelques exemples de détournement subversif de la citation dans la littérature classique chinoise." *Extrême-Orient, Extrême-Occident* 17 (1995): 41–65.

Madsen, Carsten. "The Rhetoric of Commentary." *Glossator: Practice and Theory of Commentary* 3 (2010): 19–30.

Makdisi, George. *The Rise of Colleges: Institutions of Learning in Islam and the West*. Edinburgh: Edinburgh University Press, 1981.

Meier, Fritz. "Khurāsān and the End of Classical Sufism." In *Essays on Islamic Piety and Mysticism*, translated by John O'Kane, edited by Fritz Meier, 189–219. Leiden: Brill, 1999.

Melchert, Christopher. "The Transition from Asceticism to Mysticism at the Middle of the Ninth Century C.E." *Studia Islamica* 83 (1996): 51–70.

Melvin-Koushki, Matthew S. "The Quest for a Universal Science: The Occult Philosophy of Ṣāʾin al-Dīn Turka Iṣfahānī (1369–1432) and Intellectual Millenarianism in Early Timurid Iran." PhD diss., Yale University, 2012.

Messick, Brinkley. *The Calligraphic State: Textual Domination and History in a Muslim Society*. Berkeley: University of California Press, 1993.

Mitchell, Timothy. *Colonising Egypt*. Berkeley: University of California Press, 1991.

Mojaddedi, Jawid Ahmad. *The Biographical Tradition in Sufism: The Ṭabaqāt Genre from al-Sulamī to Jāmī*. Richmond: Curzon Press, 2001.

Most, Glenn W. "Preface." In *Commentaries—Kommentare*, edited by Glenn W. Most, vii–xv. Göttingen, Germany: Vandenhoeck and Ruprecht, 1999.

Muhanna, Elias. "Encyclopaedism in the Mamluk Period: The Composition of Shihāb al-Dīn al-Nuwayrī's (d. 1333) *Nihāyat al-arab fī funūn al-adab*." PhD diss., Harvard University, 2012.

———. *The World in a Book: Al-Nuwayri and the Islamic Encyclopedic Tradition*. Princeton, NJ: Princeton University Press, 2017.

Musharraf, Muhammad Nabeel. *A Roadmap for Studying Fiqh: An Introduction to the Key Texts of the Four Madhhabs*. Perth: Australian Islamic Library, 2017.

Nasr, Seyyed Hossein. *Islamic Science: An Illustrated Study*. London: World of Islam Festival, 1976.

Nemoy, Leon. "Arabic Manuscripts in the Yale University Library." *Transactions of the Connecticut Academy of Arts and Sciences* 40 (1956): 1–273.

Pagani, Samuela. "The Meaning of *Ikhtilāf al-Madhāhib* in ʿAbd al-Wahhāb al-Shaʿrānī's *al-Mīzān al-Kubrā*." *Islamic Law and Society* 11, no. 2 (2004): 177–212.

Parry, William T., and Edward A. Hacker. *Aristotelian Logic*. Albany, NY: State University of New York Press, 1991.

Pedersen, Johannes. *The Arabic Book*. Translated by Geoffrey French. Edited by Robert Hillenbrand. Princeton, NJ: Princeton University Press, 1984.

Pelikan, Jaroslav. *The Christian Tradition: A History of the Development of Doctrine*. Vol. 2, *The Spirit of Eastern Christendom, 600–1700*. Chicago: University of Chicago Press, 1977.

Petry, Carl F. "From Slaves to Benefactors: The Habashis of Mamluk Cairo." *Sudanic Africa* 5 (1994): 59–68.

———. *Protectors or Praetorians? The Last Mamlūk Sultans and Egypt's Waning as a Great Power*. Albany, NY: State University of New York Press, 1994.

———. "Some Observations on the Position of the Librarian in the Scholarly Establishment of Cairo during the Later Middle Ages." *MELA Notes* 2 (1974): 17–22.

Rapoport, Yossef. "Women and Gender in Mamluk Society: An Overview." *Mamluk Studies Review* 11, no. 2 (2007): 1–47.

Reber, Rolf, and Norbert Schwarz. "Effects of Perceptual Fluency on Judgments of Truth." *Consciousness and Cognition* 8 (1999): 338–42.

Reber, Rolf, Norbert Schwarz, and Piotr Winkielman. "Processing Fluency and Aesthetic Pleasure: Is Beauty in the Perceiver's Processing Experience?" *Personality and Social Psychology Review* 8, no. 4 (2004): 364–82.

Reuf, Martin. "Strong Ties, Weak Ties and Islands: Structural and Organizational Predictors of Organizational Innovation." *Industrial and Corporate Change* 11, no. 3 (2002): 427–49.

Rosenthal, Franz. *The Classical Heritage in Islam.* Translated by Emile and Jenny Marmorstein. London: Routledge and Kegan Paul, 1975.

———. *The Technique and Approach of Muslim Scholarship.* Rome: Pontificium Institutum Biblicum, 1947.

Sabra, Adam. *Poverty and Charity in Medieval Islam.* Cambridge: Cambridge University Press, 2000.

Said, Edward W. *Humanism and Democratic Criticism.* New York: Columbia University Press, 2004.

Saleh, Walid A. *The Formation of the Classical Tafsīr Tradition: The Qurʾānic Commentary of al-Thaʿlabī (d. 427/1035).* Leiden: Brill, 2004.

Sanders, James A. *Canon and Community: A Guide to Canonical Criticism.* Philadelphia, PA: Fortress Press, 1984.

Sartain, E. M. *Jalāl al-Dīn al-Suyūṭī.* Cambridge: Cambridge University Press, 1975.

Schoeler, Gregor. *The Genesis of Literature in Islam: From the Aural to the Read.* Translated by Shawkat M. Toorawa. Edinburgh: Edinburgh University Press, 2011.

Smith, Jonathan Z. *Imagining Religion: From Babylon to Jonestown.* Chicago: University of Chicago Press, 1982.

Sternberg, Robert J. "A Propulsion Model of Types of Creative Contributions." *Review of General Psychology* 3, no. 2 (1999): 83–100.

Sternberg, Robert J., James C. Kaufman, and Jean Pretz, "The Propulsion Model of Creative Contributions Applied to the Arts and Letters." *Journal of Creative Behavior* 35, no. 2 (2001): 75–101.

Stetkevych, Jaroslav. "Arabic Hermeneutical Terminology: Paradox and the Production of Meaning." *Journal of Near Eastern Studies* 48, no. 2 (1989): 81–96.

Stewart, Devin J. "Notes on Zayn al-Dīn al-ʿĀmilī's *Munyat al-murīd fī ādāb al-mufīd wa-l-mustafīd.*" *Journal of Islamic Studies* 21, no. 2 (2010): 235–70.

Storey, C. A. *Persian Literature: A Bio-Bibliographical Survey.* 5 vols. London: Luzacs, 1927ff.

Taylor, Mark C. *After God.* Chicago: University of Chicago Press, 2009.

Tracy, David. "Writing." In *Critical Terms for Religious Studies*, edited by Mark C. Taylor, 383–94. Chicago: University of Chicago Press, 1998.

Tyan, Émil. "Judicial Organization." In *Law in the Middle East*, edited by M. Khadduri and H. Liebesny, 236–78. Washington, DC: Middle East Institute, 1955.

Vallance, John T. "Galen, Proclus and the Non-Submissive Commentary." In *Commentaries—Kommentare*, edited by Glenn W. Most, 223–44. Göttingen, Germany: Vandenhoeck and Ruprecht, 1999.

Vollers, Karl. *Katalog der islamischen, christlich-orientalischen, jüdischen, und samaritanischen Handschriften der Universitäts-Bibliothek zu Leipzig*. Leipzig: O. Harrassowitz, 1906.

de Vries, Marieke, Rob W. Holland, Troy Chenier, Mark J. Starr, and Piotr Winkielman. "Happiness Cools the Warm Glow of Familiarity: Psychophysiological Evidence That Mood Modulates the Familiarity-Affect Link." *Psychological Sciences* 21, no. 3 (2010): 321–28.

Watt, W. M. *Free Will and Predestination in Early Islam*. London: Luzac, 1948.

Weiss, Bernard. "Medieval Islamic Legal Education as Reflected in the Works of Sayf al-Dīn al-Āmidī." In *Law and Education in Medieval Islam: Studies in Memory of Professor George Makdisi*, edited by Joseph E. Lowry, Devin J. Stewart, and Shawkat M. Toorawa, 110–27. Cambridge: E. J. W. Gibb Memorial Trust, 2004.

Wheeler, Brannon M. "Identity in the Margins: Unpublished Ḥanafī Commentaries on the *Mukhtaṣar* of Aḥmad b. Muḥammad al-Qudūrī." *Islamic Law and Society* 10, no. 2 (2003): 182–209.

White, Hayden. *Tropics of Discourse: Essays in Cultural Criticism*. Baltimore, MD: Johns Hopkins Press, 1978.

Wiederhold, Lutz. "Legal Doctrines in Conflict: The Relevance of *Madhhab* Boundaries to Legal Reasoning in the Light of an Unpublished Treatise on *Taqlīd* and *Ijtihād*." *Islamic Law and Society* 3, no. 2 (1996): 234–304.

Winkielman, Piotr, David E. Huber, Liam Kavanagh, and Norbert Schwarz. "Fluency of Consistency: When Thoughts Fit Nicely and Flow Smoothly." In *Cognitive Consistency: A Fundamental Principle in Social Cognition*, edited by Bertram Gawronski and Fritz Strack, 89–111. New York: Guilford Press, 2012.

Winter, Michael. *Society and Religion in Early Ottoman Egypt: Studies in the Writings of ʿAbd al-Wahhāb al-Shaʿrānī*. New Brunswick, NJ: Transaction Books, 1982.

Wisnovsky, Robert. "The Nature and Scope of Arabic Philosophical Commentary in Post-Classical (ca. 1100–1900 AD) Islamic Intellectual History: Some Preliminary Observations." In *Philosophy, Science and Exegesis in Greek, Arabic, and Latin Commentaries*, vol. 2, edited by Peter Adamson, Han Baltussen, and Martin William Francis Stone, 149–91. London: Institute of Classical Studies, University of London Press, 2004.

Index

ʿAbbāsid Caliphate of Cairo, 72
abridgment (*ikhtiṣār/mukhtaṣar*), 4, 15–16, 86n202, 100–7 passim, 155, 156, 159, 161, 163, 164, 166, 181, 182, 184, 187, 189, 190, 191, 192, 193, 194, 195, 196, 204, 223; and commentarial control, 169–70, 173–74, 176–77, 189–90, 190–91; operations particular to, 193–94. *See also* prompt lemma
Abshīhī, Shihāb al-Dīn al- (d. 892/1487), 61
Abū Ḥafṣ al-Ḥaddād (d. ca. 265/878–79), 150–51
al-ʿĀdil Ṭūmānbāy (Mamlūk sultan) (r. 906/1501), 76–77, 99
Aḥmad al-Zāhid (d. 819/1416), 45, 80
ʿAlāʾī al-Ḥanafī, Badr al-Dīn Muḥammad b. Qurqmās al- (d. 942/1535), 34, 38, 42, 58, 60, 61n94, 79, 82–83, 89; as a source for al-Anṣārī's biography, 34–35
amīn al-ḥukm (court trustee), 61, 67, 74
Āmulī, Shams al-Dīn Muḥammad b. Maḥmūd al- (d. 753/1352), 210, 213; his *Nafāʾis al-funūn*, 210, 217n71
anonymity. *See* rhetoric of anonymity
Anṣārī, ʿAbd al-ʿAẓīm b. Yaḥyā Sharaf al-Dīn al- (d. 1136/1723–24), 201
Anṣārī, ʿAbd al-Qādir Muḥyī l-Dīn b. Aḥmad Walī l-Dīn al- (d. 1043/1634), 200, 201–2
Anṣārī, Aḥmad Walī l-Dīn b. Yūsuf Jamāl al-Dīn al- (d. after 1008/1600), 199–200, 202
Anṣārī, Muḥammad b. Aḥmad b. Zakariyyā al- (d. ca. 841/1437–38), 37, 38, 40, 97, 98
Anṣārī, Muḥammad b. Zakariyyā al- (d. 904/1499), 48, 57–58, 59, 70, 73–74, 76, 86n200, 97, 98, 99
Anṣārī, Yaḥyā Muḥyī al-Dīn al- (d. 897/1492), 70, 71, 86, 98, 198–99
Anṣārī, Yaḥyā Sharaf al-Dīn b. Zayn al-ʿĀbidīn Yūsuf al- (d. 1092/1681), 201
Anṣārī, Yūsuf Jamāl al-Dīn al- (d. 987/1579–80), 85, 98, 199, 200, 201, 202
Anṣārī, Zakariyyā al- (d. 926/1520), 3; at al-Azhar, 39–42; birth and early childhood, 37–38; blending of Sufism and Islamic law through commentary, 137–44, 198, 216,

Anṣārī, Zakariyyā al- *(continued)* 222–24, 225, 226–27, 230–31, 235–36, 238; career advancement, 57–60; and the chief Shāfiʿī justiceship, 33, 45, 50–51, 59–60, 61, 63, 69, 74–75, 76, 77–78, 84n193, 86, 88, 92, 97, 98, 99, 178, 179, 180n52, 190, 225; charitable giving, 92–93; children and descendants, 48, 57–58, 59, 70, 73–74, 85–86, 198–202; death, 94–96, 99; difficulties with Mamlūk sultans, 62, 66–69, 71, 73, 75–76, 77–78, 79–80, 86–88; early career, 46–48, 49; education in Sufism, 40–45; eyesight problems and blindness, 62, 74, 75, 77–78, 80, 82, 85, 87, 92, 99; fatwas of, 46, 54–56, 87, 204, 219, 221–22, 224, 225, 226, 230, 235; first writings, 49; following retirement from chief justiceship, 82–85, 88–94; Friday sermons of, 68–69, 73, 74, 78–79; and the Ibn al-Fāriḍ controversy, 53–57, 89, 91, 97, 221–22, 238; and the later Shāfiʿī *madhhab*, 202–6; miraculous powers and visions, 41–42, 43–44, 52–53, 87–88, 95, 202; mother, 37, 38; as *mujaddid* (renewer), 197–98, 202; sources used for his biography, 33–35; stylistics of his writings, 69–70, 83, 126–27, 156–58; as a Sufi scholar, 53, 83, 91–92, 226–27, 238; Sufi training under al-Ghamrī, 43–45, 80; teachers, 37, 42–43, 46, 110–23; teaching persona, 49–50, 73, 81–82, 88–92; time in Mecca, 45–46; waqf difficulties, 51, 58–59, 61–62, 62–67, 69, 98; wife and in-laws (Nashīlī family), 48–49; writing process, 26n55, 82–85, 89

Anṣārī, Zakariyyā b. Yaḥyā b. Zakariyyā (d. 959/1552), 86, 198–99

Anṣārī, Zayn al-ʿĀbidīn Yūsuf al- (d. 1068/1657), 33, 200–1; his biography of Zakariyyā al-Anṣārī, 33–34, 43n25, 200, 201–2, 204

Arabic grammar, 8, 19, 40, 100, 101, 104, 121, 122, 123

ʿArūsī, Muṣṭafā al- (d. 1876), 127, 233–34; his *Natāʾij al-afkār* supercommentary, 127, 233

Ashʿarism, 141–42

al-Ashraf Jān Bulāṭ (Mamlūk sultan) (r. 905–6/1500–1), 75, 76, 99

Asnā l-maṭālib, 25n52, 67n115, 84n193, 89n217, 98, 100, 149, 162, 164, 165, 178–80, 181, 182, 183, 185, 187–88, 189–90, 192, 194, 195, 196n79, 222–24, 226, 227, 230, 231, 235, 236, 238

ʿAydarūs, ʿAbd al-Qādir al- (d. 1037/1628), 197–98

al-Azhar (seminary), 38, 39, 40, 41, 48, 55, 73, 80, 95, 96, 97, 201, 233, 234

al-Bahja al-Wardiyya, 49, 83n190, 84, 85, 164, 166, 167, 191n73, 204; al-Anṣārī's commentary on, 26n55, 49, 84–85, 89n217, 103, 164, 166, 167, 204, 205

Barsbāy (Mamlūk sultan) (r. 825–41/1422–38), 36

base text (*matn*), 4, 5, 11, 13, 14–18, 26–31, 133, 147, 149, 150, 151,

156–96 passim, 224, 229, 231, 233, 234; appearance within various commentarial forms, 16–18; commentarial tone of deference towards, 11–12, 26, 29, 30, 128–29, 151–53, 156–57; al-Qushayrī's *Risāla* functioning as, 126–36
Baybars (Malūk sultan) (r. 658–75/1260–77), 62–63
Baybarsiyya Khānaqāh, 76
Biqāʿī, Burhān al-Dīn al- (d. 885/1480), 47, 53, 54, 55, 56, 238
Bulbīs (Bilbeis), 37
Buṣrawī, ʿAlī b. Yūsuf al- (d. 905/1500), 64

Cairo, 37, 38, 41, 53, 55, 64, 68, 70, 72, 74, 76, 80, 85, 88, 89, 97
caliph/caliphate. *See* ʿAbbāsid Caliphate of Cairo
canon and canonization, 5, 10, 27, 28, 29, 30, 139n44, 140, 151–52, 194, 196, 232–33; and accidents of history, 232–33; as applied to al-Anṣārī's texts, 5, 158, 204–5, 233, 234; through commentary, 5, 170, 222–24, 226–27, 230–32
chief justiceship and chief justices (*qāḍī l-quḍāʾ*), 47n40, 50–51, 57n80, 59–60, 62, 63, 66, 67, 68, 71, 72, 73n144, 74, 75, 76, 77–78, 79, 82, 86, 87, 92, 97, 178, 179, 180, 190. *See also* Anṣārī, Zakariyyā al- (d. 926/1520), and the chief Shāfiʿī justiceship
chronicles (Mamlūk), 77; as a source for al-Anṣārī biography, 33, 35
Citadel (Mamlūk), 51, 60, 62, 75, 76n158, 78, 88, 96
coffee, 94
commentary: Islamic forms of, 7, 13, 16–19; method of analysis, 2, 229; Muslim justifications for, 7, 10–13; publication of, 24–26, 82–85; and redistribution of authority, 231, 239–40; relationship to canon, 5, 151–53, 204–5, 222–24, 226–27, 230–32, 233. See also *sharḥ*; *ḥāshiya*
commentary writing, 3, 4; al-Anṣārī's method of, 82–85; etiquettes of, 11–12, 18; Muslim motives for, 8, 10–13; and pedagogy, 7, 20–26; posthumous, 26. See also *ḥalaqa*
creativity, 1, 5, 12–13, 17, 30, 31, 146, 206, 230, 235, 236, 240–41; in al-Anṣārī's texts, 132, 145, 153, 231, 232, 234, 235–36, 238, 239; propulsion model of, 235. *See also* subtle innovation

Damascus, 55, 64, 67, 71n136, 78n162, 79n170, 96, 99
Darb Qarājā, 48
decline narrative, 1, 2, 196; commentaries as symbols of, 2, 5, 27, 31, 230, 240–41; internalized through the *fasād al-zamān* metanarrative, 152–53
Dhū l-Nūn al-Miṣrī (d. 243/857), 132
dictation (*imlāʾ*), 22, 24
didactic verse (*naẓm*), 16, 49, 69, 164, 166, 167
draft manuscript (*musawwada*), 24, 25, 82; of the *Iḥkām al-dalāla*, 127

education: connection to depravation during Islamic middle period, 40; popularization of learning activities,

education *(continued)*
9; role of waqf institutions in, 9–10; as seen in types of *ijāza*, 108–9. See also *ḥalaqa*
encyclopedic and anthological texts, 1, 10, 28, 208, 209, 210

fair copy manuscript (*mubayyaḍa*), 25
Fatḥ al-wahhāb, 102, 156, 158, 159–60, 204, 205
Fatḥ al-wahhāb (al-Anṣārī's direct commentary on the *Tanqīḥ*), 58n85, 102, 161–62, 163, 168
fiqh (practical jurisprudence), 42, 100, 101, 102, 103, 104, 106, 107, 110, 119, 120, 121, 122, 143, 202n17, 210, 220, 222. *See also* Islamic substantive law (*furūʿ al-fiqh*)
functional hermeneutics, 133

Ghamrī, Muḥammad al- (d. 849/1445), 43–45, 80, 97, 100. *See also* Mosque of al-Ghamrī
Ghazālī, Abū Ḥāmid al- (d. 505/1111), 37, 116, 183–86, 187, 188–89; his *Basīṭ fī l-madhhab*, 165, 184, 188, 189; his *Wajīz fī l-madhhab*, 160, 165, 184, 185, 186, 188; his *Wasīṭ fī l-madhhab*, 165, 184–85, 186, 187, 188; writings in *taṣnīf al-ʿulūm*, 208, 211
Ghazzī, Badr al-Dīn al- (d. 984/1577), 12, 13, 84n191, 90
Ghazzī, Najm al-Dīn al- (d. 1061/1651), 34–35, 38, 43, 60n90, 83, 87–88, 89, 90; as a source for al-Anṣārī's biography, 35
al-Ghurar al-bahiyya, 49n50, 103, 162, 166n26, 167. See also *al-Bahja al-Wardiyya*, al-Anṣārī's commentary on

God's friends (*awliyāʾ*), 39, 53, 54, 91, 129–30, 145

hadith criticism (*muṣṭalaḥ al-ḥadīth*), 69, 81, 84, 112, 115, 116, 198
hagiography: as source for al-Anṣārī's biography, 33–34; supernatural stories within, 35–36
Ḥājj. *See* Mecca, pilgrimage to
Ḥājjī Khalīfa, Muṣṭafā b. ʿAbdallāh (d. 1068/1657), 11, 12, 18
ḥalaqa (study circle), 7, 20–23, 24–25, 88, 89, 134; etiquettes and conventions of, 21–22
Ḥallāj, al-Ḥusayn b. Manṣūr al- (d. 309/922), 220–21
Ḥanafī, ʿAlāʾ al-Dīn al-Maḥallī al- (d. 897/1492), 61, 67
Ḥanafī *madhhab*, 30; al-Anṣārī's study of, 120, 121
Ḥaramayn (Two Holy Sanctuaries in Mecca and Medina), 63, 96, 199; wafs of, 63, 65, 66n111, 74. *See also* Mecca
al-Ḥasan al-Baṣrī (d. 110/728), 138–39, 143
ḥāshiya, 13–14, 17–18, 82n183, 127, 166, 167, 169, 191n73, 192, 193n75, 194, 195, 200, 233; liabilities of, 14–15
Haytamī, Ibn Ḥajar al- (d. 974/1567), 90–92, 197, 202n17, 203–4, 225–27, 230, 231–32, 235
Ḥijāz, 58n83, 63, 70, 74, 88, 90, 97, 203
hyponēma (private draft text), 24

Ibn Abī Sharīf, Burhān al-Dīn (d. 923/1517), 64, 78, 79n170, 80, 87–88, 92, 94, 199, 225

Ibn al-Akfānī (d. 749/1348), 209; his *Irshād al-qāṣid*, 209, 213
Ibn ʿArabī (d. 638/1240), 46n36, 53, 56n75, 63n100, 91, 215, 222–23, 224, 225, 226, 230, 235
Ibn al-Fāriḍ, ʿUmar (d. 632/1235), 53, 54, 55, 56, 57, 89, 91, 97, 220, 221, 222, 224, 225–26, 230, 238. *See also* Anṣārī, Zakariyyā al-, and the Ibn al-Fāriḍ controversy
Ibn Ḥajar al-ʿAsqalānī (d. 852/1449), 34, 42, 46, 47, 97, 110–23 passim, 206
Ibn Ḥanbal, Aḥmad (d. 241/855), 150
Ibn Ḥazm, ʿAlī b. Aḥmad (d. 456/1064), 208
Ibn Jamāʿa (d. 733/1332), 232–33
Ibn Khaldūn, ʿAbd al-Raḥmān (d. 808/1406), 210nn47–48, 211, 219, 220; his *Muqaddima*, 211, 218–19
Ibn al-Muqrī (d. 837/1434), 81, 156n2, 164, 165, 178, 180, 181, 182, 187, 189, 190, 192, 222, 231; his *Rawḍ al-ṭālib*, 67n115, 81, 162, 164, 165, 178, 179, 180, 183, 187–88, 189, 190, 192, 193–94, 195, 222–23, 224, 230, 231. See also *Asnā l-maṭālib*
Ibn al-Naqīb (d. 922/1516), 75–76, 78n162
Ibn al-Shammāʿ, ʿUmar (d. 936/1529), 54n69, 89, 99
Ibn al-Wardī (d. 749/1349), 49, 84, 120, 164, 166, 167, 204. See also *al-Bahja al-Wardiyya*
ʿĪd (Eid), 62, 71, 74, 75n150
Iḥkām al-dalāla, 4, 69, 98, 103, 233; in comparison to al-Anṣārī's other Sufi texts, 125; intended student audience, 126–27, 133, 134, 136; legal language of, 126, 131, 134, 135–36, 137–39, 216; manuscripts and printed editions of, 127–28, 233–34; reading the Sufis as scripture in, 137–45, 149, 153; recasting the *Risāla* through, 126, 129–37; and the *sharḥ mamzūj* commentarial form, 145–51
ijāza (license, certification), 4, 9, 25, 108–9, 202n15; al-Anṣārī's collection of, 4, 33, 42, 45, 46n36, 108–23; given by al-Anṣārī, 81, 89, 90, 91, 199, 206
Ikhwān al-Ṣafāʾ, 207
incarnationism (*al-ḥulūl*), 53, 56, 223
intellectual decline. *See* decline narrative
interwoven commentary. See *sharḥ mamzūj*
ʿIrāqī, ʿAbd al-Raḥīm al- (d. 806/1404), 69, 101
ʿIrāqī, Abū Zurʿa al- (d. 826/1423), 120, 161, 163, 166, 167, 168, 170, 171, 172, 174, 176, 177; his *Tanqīḥ al-Lubāb*, 161, 162, 163, 168, 170–71, 172–73, 174–76, 177, 193, 194, 195
ishāra (mystical allusion), 214, 215
Islamic middle period, 1, 3, 7, 8, 11, 12, 27, 40, 64, 137, 229, 233, 240; nature of commentary texts and commentary writing during, 13–26, 145–46; integration of legal, theological, and mystical realms during, 126, 137, 141–45, 198; Islamic law during, 4, 155, 195; routinization of Sufism during, 210–13, 214, 217–27; textualization trends during, 8–10
Islamic substantive law (*furūʿ al-fiqh*), 37, 81, 134, 144, 166, 168, 169,

Islamic substantive law *(continued)* 172, 178, 184; al-Anṣārī's writings in, 4, 5, 31, 98, 155–56, 158–66, 204–5, 222–224, 230, 235
isnād (chain of transmission), 27, 44, 45, 81, 91, 109, 125n1, 140, 141, 199n8, 206
Iṣṭanbūlī, Muḥammad al- (d. 878/1474), 55–56, 238
iṣṭilāḥ/iṣṭilāḥāt. *See* technical terminology

Jabartī, ʿAbd al-Raḥmān al- (d. 1237/1825), 201
Jamāliyya School, 94
judgeship: Islamic legal discussions of, 178–90. *See also* chief justiceship and chief justices (*qāḍī l-quḍā*ʾ)
al-Junayd (d. 297/910), 132, 142
Jurjānī, al-Sayyid al-Sharīf al- (d. 816/1413), 218
Juwaynī, ʿAbd al-Malik b. ʿAbdallāh al- (d. 478/1085), 115, 123, 165, 182–83; his *Nihāyat al-maṭlab*, 165, 182, 183, 184, 187, 188

Kāshānī, ʿAbd al-Razzāq al- (d. 736/1335), 217; his *Iṣṭilāḥāt al-ṣūfiyya*, 217–18
kashf (mystical unveiling), 82, 208, 225
Kattānī, ʿAbd al-Ḥayy al- (d. 1962), 199, 206
Khāʾir Bey (d. 928/1522), 96
al-Khaṭīb al-Shirbīnī (d. 977/1569), 89n217, 166n26, 203, 224
Khiḍr, 52
khirqa (initiatory frock), 43, 44, 80, 81n175, 99, 110
Khʷārazmī, Muḥammad b. Aḥmad al- (d. 387/997), 207; his *Mafātīḥ al-ʿulūm*, 207

legal compendiums (*mabsūṭāt*), 15–16, 23
librarian (*khāzin al-kutub*), 47, 97
al-Luʾluʾ al-naẓīm fī rawm al-taʿallum wa-l-taʿlīm, 104, 212–13

magistrates (*nawwāb*), 61, 63, 72, 75, 76, 79
al-Maḥalla al-Kubrā, 43, 97
Maḥāmilī, Abū l-Ḥasan Aḥmad b. Muḥammad al- (d. 415/1024), 163, 166, 168, 169, 172, 174; his *Lubāb fī l-fiqh al-Shāfiʿī*, 163, 166, 168, 169, 170, 171, 172, 173, 174, 176, 193, 195
Maḥmūdiyya collection, 47, 97
Mālik b. Anas (d. 179/796), 112, 138
Mamlūk literature, 28, 240
Mamlūk Sultanate, 36–37, 60; Ottoman conquest of, 92; periods of instability in, 72–73, 76–77, 78, 88. See also *specific sultans*
Manhaj al-ṭullāb, 104, 159, 160, 164, 204, 205
manuscripts (Islamic): developments to during the middle period, 9–10
maʿrifa (experiential knowledge of God), 130, 136, 141–42, 151, 213
Marj Dābiq, 88
Marwarrūdhī, al-Qāḍī al-Ḥusayn b. Muḥammad (d. 462/1069), 183
Matbūlī, Ibrāhīm al- (d. 877/1473), 52–53
matn. *See* base text

Mecca, 91, 96, 97, 99, 125n1, 149; pious residency in (*mujāwara*), 45; pilgrimage to (Ḥajj), 45–46, 58, 70, 97, 98, 199
menopause, 172–74, 193
monism (*al-ittiḥād*), 53, 56, 221, 222, 223
Mosque of al-ʿAlam b. al-Jīʿān, 47, 48n44, 57, 97
Mosque of al-Ghamrī, 43, 48, 80
Mosque of al-Ṭawāshī ʿAlam Dār, 47, 48n44
Mosque of al-Ẓāhir, 47
al-Muʾayyad Shaykh al-Maḥmūdī (Mamlūk sultan) (r. 815–24/1412–21), 36
muʿīd (teaching assistant), 22, 25, 47
mujaddid (renewer), 4–5, 36, 92, 197–98, 202, 236
mukhtaṣar. *See* abridgment
Muʾminī Fountain, 96
mustamlī (transcriber), 22, 25
al-Mutawakkil ʿAbd al-ʿAzīz b. Yaʿqūb (ʿAbbāsid caliph) (r. 884–903/1479–97), 72, 98
Muʿtazilism, 136
Muzanī, Ismāʿīl b. Yaḥyā al- (d. 264/877–78), 120, 158–59, 165, 182; al-Anṣārī's commentary on his *Mukhtaṣar*, 106, 159n9; his *Mukhtaṣar*, 158, 165, 181–82, 188

Nabatītī, ʿAlī al- (d. 917/1512), 49, 52
Najjār, Bahāʾ al-Dīn al- (d. ca. 575/1180), 208; his *Yawāqīt al-ʿulūm*, 208–9
naqīb al-ashrāf (marshal of the affairs of the Prophet's descendants), 61, 67, 75n150
Naqshwānī, Abū l-Hudā al- (d. 934/1528), 79
al-Nāṣir Muḥammad (Mamlūk sultan) (r. 901–3/1496–89). 71–72, 72–73, 98
Nawawī, Yaḥyā b. Sharaf al- (d. 676/1277), 81, 96, 114, 116, 118, 119, 157, 160, 164, 165, 171, 172, 173, 176, 184n62, 187, 195, 202; his *Majmūʿ*, 171, 176; his *Minhāj al-ṭālibīn*, 81, 119, 156, 159–60; his *Rawḍat al-ṭālibīn*, 81, 164, 165, 175, 187, 188–89, 192, 193–94, 223

Ottomans, 68, 96; conquest of Egypt, 92, 99; Ottoman period, 14, 227

parallel text citations (parallels), 27–28, 31; as a form of creative production, 239–40
plague (bubonic), 37, 70, 72, 86n202, 98, 198
private secretary (*kātib al-sirr*), 55, 57, 71, 72
processing fluency, 126, 146–49; and perceptions of familiarity, 147–48; and perceptions of truth, 148; and stimulations of positive affect, 147, 148. See also *sharḥ mamzūj*, rhetorical impact of
processions: celebratory, 58, 60, 75, 76; funeral, 60n93, 95, 96
prompt lemma, 169–70, 171, 173, 174, 176, 180–81, 191, 193, 194, 195, 196
purity law (*ṭahāra*), 166, 168–69, 170–71, 172–73, 174–76, 177

Qabbāb, Aḥmad b. Qāsim al- (d. 778/1377), 218
Qadariyya, 136
Qānṣawh al-Ghawrī (Mamlūk sultan) (r. 906–22/1501–16), 77–78, 79, 88, 99; criminal tribunals held by, 79–80, 86–88
Qarāfā (cemeteries), 54, 96; waqfs, 59, 67, 98
Qasṭallānī, Aḥmad al- (d. 923/1517), 83–84
Qasṭallānī, Quṭb al-Dīn al- (d. 686/1287), 215–17
Qāyātī, Muḥammad al- (d. 850/1446), 42, 46, 110, 111, 113, 115, 116, 120, 121
Qāytbāy, al-Ashraf (Mamlūk sultan) (r. 872–901/1468–95), 51–52, 55, 56, 57–60, 62, 65, 66–69, 71, 76n158, 77, 97, 98
Qur'ān, 8, 29, 37, 42, 90, 129, 130, 133, 138, 139, 139, 142, 144, 182, 208; al-Anṣārī's memorization of, 37; recitation of (*tajwīd*), 100, 103, 105, 106, 107, 111, 119, 138, 200
Qur'ānic exegesis. See *tafsīr*
Qurayshī, ʿAbd al-Karīm, al- (d. 465/1072), 4, 69, 80, 98, 125, 126, 128, 129, 130, 131, 132, 133, 135, 136, 137, 138, 143, 150, 151, 215, 216. See also *Risāla* (*Epistle*)
quṭb (axial saint), 91

Rabīʿ b. ʿAbdallāh, 38, 40
Rāfiʿī, ʿAbd al-Karīm al- (d. 623/1226), 157, 160, 165, 167, 173, 175, 176, 186, 187, 195, 202; his *ʿAzīz*, 165, 167, 186–87, 188–89
Ramlī, Shams al-Dīn al- (d. 1004/1595), 84, 89–90, 94, 203–4, 224n89
Ramlī, Shihāb al-Dīn al- (d. 957/1550), 89–90, 94, 180n52; his *Ḥāshiya*, 192, 193n75, 194, 195, 203, 204, 224–25, 226, 227, 230, 231, 235
Rāzī, Fakhr al-Dīn al- (d. 606/1210), 209
rhetoric of anonymity, 3, 5, 8, 26–31, 234, 239–41; Muslim reasons for, 28–29; as seen in parallel text citations, 27–28
Risāla (*Epistle*), 18, 69, 80, 85n199, 98, 116, 125, 126, 127–28, 129, 130, 131, 132, 133, 134, 135, 136, 137, 138, 139, 140, 141, 144, 145, 150, 153, 216, 233, 235. See also *Iḥkām al-dalāla*, recasting the *Risāla* through
rukhṣa (legal dispensation), 135, 168, 170n32

Sābiqiyya School, 51–52, 60n93, 95, 97
Ṣaḥīḥ al-Bukhārī, 37, 111; al-Anṣārī's commentary on, 24n51, 82n183, 83–84, 94, 105
Saʿīd al-Suʿadā' Khānaqāh, 73n146, 81–82
Sakhāwī, Muḥammad b. ʿAbd al-Raḥmān al- (d. 902/1497), 25n52, 34, 37, 38, 40, 43, 46, 47, 48, 55, 57, 58, 59, 60, 63, 70, 98, 178; assessments of al-Anṣārī, 45, 50, 53, 61, 62, 64, 65–66, 67, 69–70, 79, 84–85, 88–89, 93; as a source for al-Anṣārī's biography, 34, 46

Ṣāliḥī, Abū l-Barakāt al- (d. 896/1491), 65–66
Ṣāliḥiyya School, 58, 59, 60, 98, 199, 200, 202
Ṣānī, Jamāl al-Dīn al- (d. 931/1525), 61, 67, 74n148, 95, 225–26
Saqaṭī, Sarī al- (d. 251/865), 137
Sarrāj, Abū Naṣr al- (d. 378/988), 208n38, 215, 219n76
scripture, 126, 131, 139–40, 196. *See also* Sufis, lives of as a form of scripture
shadow puppet shows, 37
Shāfiʿī *madhhab*, 42, 90, 156, 157, 164, 173, 177, 184, 188, 225; al-Anṣārī's position within, 5, 202–6, 231; the *muʿtamad* position within, 157, 159, 161, 198
Shāfiʿī, Muḥammad b. Idrīs al- (d. 204/820), 87, 95, 112, 164, 165, 168, 170, 171, 175, 176; his *Kitāb al-Umm*, 164, 165, 173, 178, 181, 182, 188; mausoleum of, 58, 96
Shaʿrānī, ʿAbd al-Wahhāb al- (d. 973/1565), 29, 30, 39, 40, 41, 42, 43, 49, 50, 51, 52, 53, 55, 68, 83, 84, 85, 86, 94–95, 199, 206, 236n20; al-Anṣārī's *khirqa*-vesting of, 44, 80, 81n175, 99; as a source for al-Anṣārī's biography, 33, 35; studies under al-Anṣārī, 80–82, 92–93
sharḥ, 4, 13–15, 16, 155, 166, 182, 186, 192; etymology of, 13, relationship to *taʿlīqa*, 23–24; and commentarial control, 173–74, 174–76, 189–90, 191; operations particular to, 194–96. *See also* commentary; commentary writing
sharḥ mamzūj, 4, 17–19, 179–80, 181, 187–88, 189, 190, 222–23, 241; al-Anṣārī's reliance on, 19, 85, 126, 145, 149, 161, 191; and commentarial control, 126, 149–51, 173–74, 174–76, 189–90, 191, 231; examples of *ḥāshiya*s written as, 17n29; rhetorical impact of, 145–51, 153. *See also* processing fluency
shaykh, 36, 39, 43, 44, 45, 46, 52, 55, 88, 91, 95, 135, 137, 138, 223; Grand Shaykh of al-Azhar, 233; role in *ḥalaqa*, 21–22, 26; "of *taṣawwuf*," 47–48, 57, 97
al-Shiblī (d. 334/946), 144
Shirāzī, Quṭb al-Dīn al- (d. 710/1311), 209
social networks, 236–38; connections to creativity and innovation, 237–38
subtle innovation, 30–31, 147–48, 152–53, 196; in the *Iḥkām al-dalāla*, 128–37
Sufi Path, 110, 127, 130, 131, 132, 144
Sufis, 4, 40, 41, 42, 48, 53, 55, 56, 74, 76, 83, 91, 130; *dhikr* gatherings of, 40; lives of as a form of scripture, 126, 137–45, 149, 151, 153, 196, 235
Sufism: al-Anṣārī's early training in, 40–45; cross-fertilization with Islamic law during the middle period, 5, 198, 219–27, 235–36, 238; formalization trends within, 5, 198, 208–13; hierarchy of saints, 91–92; as practiced in waqf institutions, 43–45, 76–77, 80, 81–82

Suhrawardī, Shihāb al-Dīn Yaḥyā al- (d. 587/1191), 209
Suhrawardī, ʿUmar al- (d. 632/1234), 45, 116; Suhrawardī Sufi order, 45n33
Sunayka (village), 37, 38, 97
Sunquriyya School, 70n132, 73, 76
Supercommentary. See *ḥāshiya*
Suyūṭī, Jalāl al-Dīn al- (d. 911/1505), 69n127, 76–77, 89, 99, 197n3; his ascription of a technical terminology to the Sufis, 215, 219–22, 225, 227; his *Itmām al-dirāya* in *taṣnīf al-ʿulūm*, 211–12, 213
syngramma (book draft intended for publication), 24

tafsīr (Qurʾānic exegesis), 8, 81, 82n183, 100, 101, 104, 117, 123, 130, 131, 133, 139, 148n73, 198, 208, 213, 215, 240n25
taḥqīq (collating and editing of a manuscript), 25; al-Anṣārī engaging in, 84, 128
Taḥrīr Tanqīḥ al-Lubāb, 106, 161, 162, 163, 164, 171, 174, 193, 194, 195, 204
taʿlīqa (notes; lecture notes), 18n29, 23–24
tarsīm (writ of sequestration), 67, 69, 98
taṣḥīḥ (rule-review), 169, 171, 176, 191, 192, 193, 194, 195
taṣnīf al-ʿulūm (classification of the intellectual sciences), 206, 207–13, 214, 217n71; al-Anṣārī's contributions to, 212–13; appearance of Sufism within, 208–9, 210–12
taʾwīl, 131
technical terminology, 214–15; for Sufism, 56, 214–15, 217–23, 226–27, 235
thabat: See *ijāza*, al-Anṣārī's collection of
Tuḥfat al-ṭullāb, 107, 156, 158, 161–62, 163, 173, 174, 176, 204
Tustarī, Sahl al- (d. 283/896), 135

waqf, 9, 46, 48, 51, 58–59, 61–62, 64, 67, 68, 69, 74, 81, 94, 98, 199, 201; al-Anṣārī's restructuring of, 63–66, 98. *See also* Anṣārī, Zakariyyā al- (d. 926/1520), waqf difficulties
wuḍūʾ (ritual ablution). *See* purity law (*ṭahāra*)

al-Ẓāhir Khushqadam (Mamlūk sultan) (r. 865–72/1461–7), 50–51, 97
al-Ẓāhir Qānṣawh (Mamlūk sultan) (r. 903–5/1498–1500), 73, 74, 75
Zawāwī, al-Shihāb al- (d. 852/1448), 46, 47n39
Zayniyya-Ustādāriyya School, 46, 47, 97
zuhd (self-denial), 150, 220

www.ingramcontent.com/pod-product-compliance
Ingram Content Group UK Ltd.
Pitfield, Milton Keynes, MK11 3LW, UK
UKHW041002010525
458084UK00002B/31

9 781438 485188